The Cambridge Companion to
Modern Chinese Culture

At the start of the twenty-first century, China is poised to
become a major global power. Understanding its culture is
more important than ever before for Western audiences, but for
many, China remains a mysterious and exotic country. This *Companion*
explains key aspects of modern Chinese culture without assuming
prior knowledge of China or the Chinese language. The volume
acknowledges the interconnected nature of the different cultural forms,
from 'high culture' such as literature, religion and philosophy to more
popular issues such as sport, cinema, performance and the Internet.
Each chapter is written by a world expert in the field. Invaluable for
students of Chinese studies, this book includes a list of key terms, a
chronology and a guide to further reading. For the interested reader
or traveller, it reveals a dynamic, diverse and fascinating culture, many
aspects of which are now elucidated in English for the first time.

KAM LOUIE is Dean of the Arts Faculty at the University of Hong
Kong. He has taught at universities including Auckland, Nanjing,
Queensland and Australian National University. He has published more
than ten books on modern Chinese culture.

Cambridge Companions to Culture

The Cambridge Companion to Modern American Culture
Edited by CHRISTOPHER BIGSBY

The Cambridge Companion to Modern Irish Culture
Edited by JOE CLEARY *and* CLAIRE CONNOLLY

The Cambridge Companion to Modern Latin American Culture
Edited by JOHN KING

The Cambridge Companion to Modern French Culture
Edited by NICHOLAS HEWITT

The Cambridge Companion to Modern Italian Culture
Edited by ZYGMUNT G. BARAŃSKI *and* REBECCA J. WEST

The Cambridge Companion to Modern German Culture
Edited by EVA KOLINSKY *and* WILFRIED VAN DER WILL

The Cambridge Companion to Modern Russian Culture
Edited by NICHOLAS RZHEVSKY

The Cambridge Companion to Modern Spanish Culture
Edited by DAVID T. GIES

The Cambridge Companion to
Modern Chinese Culture

edited by
KAM LOUIE

CAMBRIDGE
UNIVERSITY PRESS

CAMBRIDGE UNIVERSITY PRESS
Cambridge, New York, Melbourne, Madrid, Cape Town, Singapore, São Paulo, Delhi

Cambridge University Press
The Edinburgh Building, Cambridge, CB2 8RU, UK

Published in the United States of America by
Cambridge University Press, New York

www.cambridge.org
Information on this title: www.cambridge.org/9780521681902

© Cambridge University Press 2008

First published 2008

Printed in the United Kingdom at the University Press, Cambridge

A catalogue record for this publication is available from the British Library

Library of Congress Cataloging-in-Publication Data

The Cambridge companion to modern Chinese culture / edited by Kam Louie.
    p.   cm. – (Cambridge companions to culture)
Includes index.
ISBN 978-0-521-86322-3 (hardback) – ISBN 978-0-521-68190-2 (pbk.)
1. China – Civilization – 1912–1949. 2. China – Civilization – 1949–   I. Louie, Kam.
II. Title. III. Series.

DS775.2.C452424   2008
951.05 – dc22   2008005089

ISBN 978-0-521-86322-3 hardback
ISBN 978-0-521-68190-2 paperback

Contents

List of illustrations   ix
Notes on contributors   x
Chronology of major events   xiii
List of abbreviations   xxi

1 Defining modern Chinese culture   1
   KAM LOUIE

2 Social and political developments: the making of the
   twentieth-century Chinese state   20
   PETER ZARROW

3 Historical consciousness and national identity   46
   PRASENJIT DUARA

4 Gender in modern Chinese culture   68
   HARRIET EVANS

5 Ethnicity and Chinese identity: ethnographic
   insight and political positioning   91
   WILLIAM JANKOWIAK

6 Flag, flame and embers: diaspora cultures   115
   WANG GUNGWU

7 Modernizing Confucianism and 'new Confucianism'   135
   SOR-HOON TAN

8 Socialism in China: a historical overview   155
   ARIF DIRLIK

9 Chinese religious traditions from 1900–2005: an overview   173
DANIEL L. OVERMYER

10 Languages in a modernizing China   198
PING CHEN

11 The revolutionary tradition in modern Chinese literature   218
CHARLES LAUGHLIN

12 The involutionary tradition in modern Chinese literature   235
MICHEL HOCKX

13 Music and performing arts: tradition, reform and
political and social relevance   253
COLIN MACKERRAS

14 Revolutions in vision: Chinese art and the
experience of modernity   272
DAVID CLARKE

15 Cinema: from foreign import to global brand   297
CHRIS BERRY

16 Media boom and cyber culture: television
and the Internet in China   318
LIU KANG

17 Physical culture, sports and the Olympics   339
SUSAN BROWNELL

Appendix   361
Index   377

Illustrations

Figures

1. Xu Beihong, 'Tian Heng and his 500 Retainers', 1928–30, oil on linen, collection Xu Beihong Memorial Museum, Beijing.   277
2. Gao Jianfu, 'Flying in the Rain', 1932, ink on paper, collection Art Museum, The Chinese University of Hong Kong.   278
3. Lin Fengmian, 'Exercise', c. 1934, exact medium unknown, presumed lost.   281
4. Shi Lu 'Fighting in Northern Shaanxi', 1959, ink and colour on paper, collection National Museum of China.   286
5. Fu Baoshi, 'Heavy Rain Falls on Youyan', 1961, ink and colour on paper, collection Nanjing Museum.   287
6. Zhu Ming, 'Taichi Single Whip', 1985, bronze, collection Hong Kong Land (installed on the podium, Exchange Square, Hong Kong).   290
7. Xu Bing, 'Book from the Sky' (detail), 1988, hand-printed book.   291
8. Fang Lijun, 'Series II, No. 2', 1992, oil on canvas, collection Ludwig Museum, Cologne.   292
9. Zhang Hongtu, 'Fan Kuan–Van Gogh', 1998, oil on canvas, private collection.   294
10. Still from *The Goddess*.   305
11. Still from *The Killer*.   311

Tables

1. Distribution of the Chinese language in China.   199
2. Distribution of non-Chinese languages in China.   201

Contributors

CHRIS BERRY is Professor of Film and Television Studies in the
Department of Media and Communication at Goldsmiths College.
His publications include (with Mary Farquhar) *Cinema and the
National: China on Screen* (2006); *Postsocialist Cinema in Post-Mao China:
The Cultural Revolution after the Cultural Revolution* (2004); and (editor)
Chinese Films in Focus: 25 New Takes (2003). He is currently co-editing
an anthology on Chinese television, and another on Chinese
documentary film.

SUSAN BROWNELL is Chair of the Department of Anthropology at the
University of Missouri–St. Louis. She is the author of a number of
books, including *Training the Body for China: Sports in the Moral Order of
the People's Republic* (1995) and *Beijing's Games: What the Olympics Mean to
China* (2008). She is also editor of *The 1904 Anthropology Days and Olympic
Games: Sport, Race, and American Imperialism* (forthcoming). Since 2000
she has been a member of the Research Council (now the Selection
Committee) of the Olympic Studies Centre of the IOC.

PING CHEN is Reader in Chinese and Linguistics in the School of
Languages and Comparative Cultural Studies at the University of
Queensland. His main research interests are in the areas of functional
syntax, discourse analysis, sociolinguistics and historical linguistics.
His publications include *Modern Chinese: History and Sociolinguistics*
(Cambridge University Press, 1999).

DAVID CLARKE is Professor in the Department of Fine Arts of the
University of Hong Kong. He is the author of a number of books on
Chinese art and culture, including *Modern Chinese Art* (2000) and *Hong
Kong Art: Culture and Decolonization* (2001).

ARIF DIRLIK is Professor of Chinese Studies at the Chinese University
of Hong Kong, and Distinguished Visiting Fellow, The Peter Wall
Institute for Advanced Studies, University of British Columbia. His

most recent publications include *Pedagogies of the Global: Knowledge in the Human Interest* (2005) and *Global Modernity: Modernity in the Age of Global Capitalism* (2007).

PRASENJIT DUARA is Professor of History and East Asian Languages and Civilizations at the University of Chicago. He is the author of *Culture, Power and the State: Rural North China, 1900–1942* (1988), which won both the Fairbank Prize of the AHA and the Levenson Prize of the AAS. He is also the author of *Rescuing History from the Nation: Questioning Narratives of Modern China* (1995) and *Sovereignty and Authenticity: Manchukuo and the East Asian Modern* (2003).

HARRIET EVANS teaches Contemporary Chinese Cultural Studies at Westminster University. Her publications include *Women and Sexuality in China: Dominant Discourses of Female Sexuality and Gender since 1949* (1997) and the co-edited *Picturing Power in the People's Republic of China: Posters of the Cultural Revolution* (1999).

MICHEL HOCKX is Professor of Chinese at the School of Oriental and African Studies, University of London. His research is on modern Chinese literature, literary media and literary scenes, most recently on Internet literature. His main recent publications are *Questions of Style: Literary Societies and Literary Journals in Modern China, 1911–1937* (2003) and (co-edited with Julia Strauss) *Culture in the Contemporary PRC* (Cambridge University Press, 2006).

WILLIAM JANKOWIAK is Professor of Anthropology at the University of Nevada, Las Vegas. He is author of over 100 articles and book chapters and six books. His most recent book (edited) is *Intimacies: Between Love and Sex Around the World* (2008). Currently he is working on a book that explores social change in a northern Chinese city.

CHARLES A. LAUGHLIN is currently Resident Director of the Inter-University Programme for Chinese Language Studies at Tsinghua University in Beijing. He taught modern Chinese literature at Yale University for ten years. He is the author of *Chinese Reportage: The Aesthetics of Historical Experience* (2002) and *The Literature of Leisure and Chinese Modernity* (2008), and editor of *Contested Modernities in Chinese Literature* (2005).

LIU KANG is Professor of Chinese Cultural Studies and Director of the Programme in Chinese Media and Communication Studies, Duke University. He is the author of eight books, including *Aesthetics and Marxism* (2000), and *Globalization and Cultural Trend in China* (2003).

KAM LOUIE is Dean of the Arts Faculty at the University of Hong Kong. He is the author of a number of books including *Inheriting Tradition: Interpretations of the Classical Philosophers in Communist China 1949–1966*

(1986) and *Theorising Chinese Masculinity: Society and Gender in China* (Cambridge University Press, 2002).

COLIN MACKERRAS AO is Professor Emeritus in the Department of International Business and Asian Studies, Griffith University. He has written widely on China, especially its theatre and ethnic minorities. Among his main recent publications are *China's Ethnic Minorities and Globalisation* (2003) and *The New Cambridge Handbook of Contemporary China* (Cambridge University Press, 2001).

DANIEL L. OVERMYER is Professor Emeritus, Department of Asian Studies and the Centre for Chinese Research, University of British Columbia, Honorary Visiting Professor at Shanghai Normal University and a Fellow of the Royal Society of Canada. He has published several books and a number of articles, including *Folk Buddhist Religion: Dissenting Sects in Late Traditional China* (1976) and *Precious Volumes: An Introduction to Chinese Sectarian Scriptures in the Sixteenth and Seventeenth Centuries* (1999).

SOR-HOON TAN is Head of the Philosophy Department at the National University of Singapore. She is author of *Confucian Democracy: A Deweyan Reconstruction* (2003) and editor of *Challenging Citizenship: Group Membership and Cultural Identity in a Global Age* (2005); and co-editor of *The Moral Circle and the Self: Chinese and Western Approaches* (2003), *Filial Piety in Chinese Thought and History* (2004), and *Democracy as Culture: Deweyan Pragmatism in a Globalizing World* (forthcoming).

WANG GUNGWU is the author of *The Chinese Overseas: From Earthbound China to the Quest for Autonomy* (2000). His recent essays are in *Diasporic Chinese Ventures: The Life and Work of Wang Gungwu,* edited by Gregor Benton and Liu Hong (2004). He was Vice-Chancellor of The University of Hong Kong, 1986–95, Emeritus Professor at the Australian National University since 1988 and Director of the East Asian Institute, 1997–2007, National University of Singapore (NUS). He is at present a Professor at NUS.

PETER ZARROW is a Research Fellow at the Institute of Modern History, Academia Sinica, Taipei. His primary research focuses on intellectual and political developments of the early twentieth century. He has recently authored *China in War and Revolution, 1895–1949* (2005) and edited *Creating Chinese Modernity: Knowledge and Everyday Life, 1900–1940* (2006).

Chronology

1895	China defeated in the Sino-Japanese War. Taiwan ceded to Japan, Japanese presence grows in Korea and Manchuria. Calls for more thorough reforms among Chinese elites.
1898	'100 days reform' led by Kang Youwei and Liang Qichao failed. Yan Fu's translation of T. H. Huxley's *Evolution and Ethics* published. He follows this with translations of J. S. Mill, Herbert Spencer, Adam Smith, and other Western writers.
1899	Liang Qichao advocates 'revolution in literature'.
1900	Anti-foreign Boxer Uprising swiftly put down. Beijing plundered by Allied troops.
1901	Boxer Protocol signed, imposing harsh conditions.
1902	Liang Qichao starts journal *New Fiction*, and advocates link between literature and politics.
1905	Traditional civil service examinations abolished. *Dingjun Mountain*, the first film to be produced in China, completed.
1907	Sun Yat-sen leads unsuccessful uprisings to overthrow Qing government in south China.
1908	Guangxu Emperor and Empress Dowager die. Pu Yi, still a child, becomes the 'last emperor of China'.
1910	Jiang Kanghu establishes the Chinese Socialist Party.
1911	October 10 uprising in Wuchang leads to general revolution in central and southern China, and to the end of Manchu rule.

1912	Republic of China (ROC) proclaimed; the Qing throne abdicates on February 12; Sun Yat-sen becomes provisional president in Nanjing, but relinquishes presidency to Yuan Shikai in Beijing. The Guomindang (GMD, Chinese Nationalist Party) is established by Song Jiaoren.
1913	Song Jiaoren is assassinated by Yuan's lackeys and the GMD banned; Sun Yat-sen returns to exile.
1915	'New Culture' movement begins. Chen Duxiu establishes the journal *New Youth* and promotes Western values in the names of 'Mr Democracy' and 'Mr Science'.
1916	Opposition forces Yuan Shikai to abandon plans for monarchy; Yuan dies and is succeeded as president by Li Yuanhong, while central rule weakens.
1917	Sun Yat-sen establishes a military government in Guangzhou. Chen Duxiu and Hu Shi proclaim a 'literary revolution'.
1918	Ibsen's *A Doll's House* performed in Beijing. Lu Xun's 'Diary of a Madman' appears in *New Youth*. First scheme of phonetic writing announced by Ministry of Education.
1919	Student protests against decisions of the Versailles Peace Conference that handed German concessions in Shandong over to Japan. This turns into the May Fourth Movement, which supported New Culture's attacks on Confucianism and other traditional 'evils', as well as attacking imperialism and warlordism.
1920	Socialist and anarchist groups formed in several major cities.
1921	First Congress of the Chinese Communist Party (CCP).
1922	Liang Shuming's *Eastern and Western Philosophies and Their Cultures* published. Debates about merits of Chinese culture compared to other cultures continue.
1924	The first national congress of the GMD pledges to cooperate with the CCP and seek aid and advice from the Soviet Union on the reunification of China.
1925	Sun Yat-sen dies.

1926	Chiang Kai-shek takes over the GMD and launches the Northern Expedition against various warlords in order to unify China.
1927	The revolutionary camp splits: Chiang Kai-shek crushes the CCP in Shanghai and other areas under his control. The Communists are driven into the countryside.
1928	Completion of the Northern Expedition and founding of the Nationalist government in Nanjing.
1929	National Art Exhibition held in Shanghai.
1930	Communist forces seize but then lose Changsha, capital of Hunan; Nationalist armies begin 'Extermination Campaigns' against the Communists. League of Leftwing Writers formed in Shanghai.
1931	Mao Zedong establishes the Jiangxi Soviet in the remote hill country of central China. Japan seizes Manchuria following the 'Mukden (Shenyang) Incident'.
1932	Japan creates Manchukuo with Pu Yi as head of the puppet state. China sends its first team to the Los Angeles Olympics.
1933	Communist Party's Central Committee moves from Shanghai to Ruijin, Jiangxi.
1934	The GMD's Fifth Extermination Campaign against the Jiangxi Soviet forces the Communists on the retreat that is later called the Long March; Chiang Kai-shek launches 'New Life Movement'.
1935	Mao Zedong gains control of the CCP at the Zunyi Conference in Guizhou; Communist forces arrive in Yan'an to end the Long March. Students in Beijing and elsewhere protest against government inaction in the face of Japanese aggression.
1936	Chiang Kai-shek is kidnapped in the Xi'an Incident, which ends government military campaigns against Communists and leads to a United Front between the GMD and the CCP against Japan.
1937	Sino-Japanese War begins; government loses control of Yangtze Delta; Rape of Nanjing; Communist forces reorganized under government control.

1942   Ding Ling publishes 'Thoughts on March 8' criticizing
CCP's failure to liberate women. Mao Zedong's 'Talks
in Yan'an'. These 'Talks' become CCP policy on cultural
matters for the next few decades. 'Rectification
campaign' against some intellectuals launched.

1945   Japan surrenders; end of Second World War. China
recovers Taiwan. The opera *The White-Haired Girl* pre-
mieres.

1946   American mediation attempts fail to prevent full-scale
civil war between CCP and GMD forces.

1947   Early Nationalist victories in the civil war melt away
as Communists go on the offensive; soaring inflation
and GMD corruption feed urban protest; government
suspends constitutional freedoms.

1948   Communist military victories in northeast, north and
central China pave the way for Nationalist collapse.
First colour film, the opera *Remorse at Death*, starring Mei
Lanfang, produced.

1949   People's Republic of China (PRC) founded in Beijing.
Nationalist government flees to Taiwan.

1950   Korean War; United States Seventh Fleet in Taiwan
Straits; China enters war. China signs Treaty of
Friendship with Soviet Union. Marriage and agrarian
laws passed. The Three Selfs Movement requires Chinese
Christians to cut ties with foreigners.

1951   Campaign against 'Counter-revolutionaries'.

1952   'Three Antis Movement' (against corruption, waste
and bureaucracy) ends; 'Five Antis Movement' (against
bribery, tax evasion, theft of state property, shoddy work
and theft of economic information) begins.

1953   Korean War ends. First Five-Year Plan begins.

1954   Purge of regional party leaders Gao Gang and Rao
Shushi. Chinese Script Reform Commission established.

1955   Agricultural cooperatives set up. Campaign to criticize
Hu Feng, writer who questioned CCP control over culture.

1956   Let a Hundred Flowers Bloom Movement encourages
intellectuals to speak their minds. The Chinese National

Symphony Orchestra formed in Beijing. First scheme of simplified Chinese characters promulgated.

1957   Feng Youlan proposes 'abstract inheritance' method in January for salvaging aspects of traditional philosophy. Controversies immediately follow. 'Anti-Rightist campaign' in which opposition voices suppressed.

1958   Second Five-Year Plan. Great Leap Forward. Beijing Television starts first television programmes in China. 'Manifesto for a Reappraisal of Sinology and Reconstruction of Chinese Culture' by New Confucianists published in Taipei.

1959   Peng Dehuai attacked for his outspoken criticism of Great Leap Forward policies and dismissed; rise of Lin Biao. Soviet experts begin to withdraw.

1960   Famine and millions of deaths caused by Great Leap Forward. Sino-Soviet split becomes public.

1961   Sino-Soviet polemics intensify. Wu Han's play *Hai Rui Dismissed from Office*, which indirectly criticizes Mao's handling of Peng Dehuai, staged.

1962   Border war with India. Mainland refugees pour into Hong Kong; ethnic minorities flee northwestern areas for the Soviet Union. Socialist Education Movement launched to emphasize class struggle in cultural matters.

1963   Jiang Qing, Mao's wife, criticizes cultural establishment. Calls for ban on traditional drama. The first of the 'revolutionary operas', *The Red Lantern*, staged.

1964   PRC explodes atomic device. *The East is Red*, an extravagant operatic celebration of CCP history and Mao's role in it, is staged. Two more revolutionary operas *Shajiabang* and *Taking Tiger Mountain by Strategy* performed.

1965   Battle lines drawn in struggle between 'revisionist' and 'proletarian' culture. Mao goes to Shanghai and encourages Yao Wenyuan to attack Wu Han's play as 'anti-Party poisonous weed'.

1966   Lin Biao enlists Jiang Qing to develop cultural policies for the military. The Great Proletarian Cultural Revolution officially begins; Red Guard rallies; Liu

Shaoqi, Deng Xiaoping and many cultural leaders
purged; riot in Macau. Universities and schools close.

1967   Revolutionary 'seizures of power'; armed clashes
in many parts of the country; Shanghai's People's
Commune established; burning of Britain's mission in
Beijing; riots in Hong Kong.

1968   Armed clashes between factions continue. Urban
'educated youth' sent to countryside to learn from the
peasants.

1969   Mao calls an end to the Cultural Revolution (though
he later speaks of it as continuing). Some universities
reopen.

1971   PRC replaces the ROC as China's representative in the
United Nations. In April, US table tennis team is invited
to China ('ping-pong diplomacy'). Henry Kissinger visits
China secretly. Lin Biao dies in a plane crash. Screenings
of model revolutionary dramas *The Red Lantern* and *The
Red Detachment of Women*.

1972   President Nixon of the United States visits Beijing; Japan
recognizes PRC, severs ties with Taiwan.

1973   Deng Xiaoping reappears in public. The Vienna
Philharmonic Orchestra and the Philadelphia Orchestra
visit China.

1974   Attempts to attack Deng in the thinly veiled 'Criticize
Lin Biao and Confucius' campaign.

1975   Chiang Kai-shek dies; his son Chiang Ching-kuo succeeds him as chairman of the GMD and ruler of Taiwan.

1976   Mao Zedong, Zhou Enlai, Zhu De die; Hua Guofeng
succeeds Mao. Deng Xiaoping purged again. Arrest of
'Gang of Four', one of whom was Jiang Qing, who played
key role in cultural matters in the Cultural Revolution.

1977   Denunciation of the 'Gang of Four'; Deng Xiaoping
returns to power.

1978   Deng Xiaoping launches economic reforms and open
door policy. 'Democracy Wall' activities begin. CCP issues
'Document 19', stating policy of protecting and respecting religious freedom, and also guaranteeing freedom
not to believe.

1979	The US gives PRC diplomatic recognition; US Congress passes the Taiwan Relations Act governing unofficial ties with Taipei. Students and scholars begin to travel abroad. Communes disbanded.
1980	Hu Yaobang appointed general secretary of the CCP; Zhao Ziyang appointed premier. Trial of 'Gang of Four'. Special Economic Zones launched.
1981	CCP formally denounces Cultural Revolution and reappraises Mao Zedong.
1982	UK and China agree to open talks on future of Hong Kong.
1983	Antispiritual pollution campaign to resist the effects of Western influence. Sino-British talks begin on the future of Hong Kong. China launches its first telecommunications satellite.
1984	Arthur Miller's *Death of a Salesman*, directed by the playwright, opens in Beijing. Margaret Thatcher and Zhao Ziyang sign Sino-British Joint Declaration on Hong Kong.
1985	The Bolshoi Ballet performs in Beijing. CCP orders modernization in education. *Yellow Earth* screened in Hong Kong International Film Festival.
1986	Students protest against corruption and for democracy. Shanghai Stock Market reopens after nearly forty years.
1987	Martial law lifted in Taiwan; Taiwanese allowed to visit relatives on Mainland. Communist party says China in 'initial stage' of socialism and calls for faster reforms.
1988	Hainan Island designated a province and Special Economic Zone. Chiang Ching-kuo dies; Lee Teng-hui, a native of Taiwan, succeeds him as president and chairman of the GMD.
1989	Exhibition of avant-garde work at the China Art Gallery in Beijing. Tiananmen Democracy movement; Gorbachev visits China; Zhao Ziyang replaced as leader of the CCP by Jiang Zemin. Tiananmen Incident when military evicts demonstrators, killing many. Mass protests in Hong Kong and Taiwan against military suppression in Beijing.
1990	Basic law, Hong Kong's post-1997 Constitution, promulgated.

1991	Collapse of Soviet Union alarms China's Communist leaders. First McDonald's Restaurant opens in Beijing.
1992	Deng Xiaoping calls for faster economic growth; CCP champions the 'socialist market economy'. Major Yangtze River and border cities open to foreign investment.
1994	Direct elections in Taiwan for the mayors of Taipei and Kaohsiung.
1995	Legislative elections in Hong Kong. Beijing hosts United Nations Women's Conference.
1996	Lee Teng-hui wins Taiwan's first presidential election. Tung Chee-hwa selected first chief executive of Hong Kong.
1997	Deng Xiaoping dies. Hong Kong reverts to Chinese control, becomes a Special Administrative Region.
1998	Asian financial crisis slows growth on Mainland, Hong Kong and Taiwan. China wins world respect for economic role in Asian crisis. Bill Clinton visits China.
1999	China recovers sovereignty over Macau. Falungong, a religious sect, outlawed.
2000	Chen Shui-bian, leader of the Democratic Progressive Party, elected president of Taiwan.
2001	China admitted to the World Trade Organization.
2002	Hu Jintao replaces Jiang Zemin as head of CCP and president.
2003	Severe Acute Respiratory Syndrome (SARS) outbreak. Half a million demonstrators march in Hong Kong against the anti-subversion Article 23.
2005	Chartered aircraft makes first direct flight between China and Taiwan since 1949. Tung Chee-hwa resigns, succeeded by Donald Tsang.
2006	African heads of state gather for China–African summit in Beijing, promising closer ties between the two regions.
2007	US worry over balance of trade deficits with China intensifies. Head of food and drug agency executed after scandals about safety of Chinese exports.
2008	Beijing Olympics.

Abbreviations

BBS	*Luntan*, bulletin board service
BFA	Beijing Film Academy
BOCOG	Beijing Organizing Committee for the Olympic Games
CANet	China Academic Network
CCP	Chinese Communist Party
CCTV	China Central Television
CPA	Catholic Patriotic Association
CR	Cultural Revolution
DTV	digital television
GANEFO	Games of the New Emerging Forces
GLF	Great Leap Forward
GMD	*Guomindang*, the Chinese Nationalist Party
IHEP	Institute of High Energy Physics
IMAR	Inner Mongolian Autonomous Region
IOC	International Olympic Committee
IPTV	Internet television
ITTF	International Table Tennis Federation
MRFT	Ministry of Radio, Film and Television
PLA	People's Liberation Army
PRC	People's Republic of China
ROC	Republic of China
SARFT	State Administration of Radio, Film and Television
SARS	Severe Acute Respiratory Syndrome
SMG	Shanghai Media Group, Shanghai Television
TAR	Tibetan Autonomous Region

1

Defining modern Chinese culture

By the start of the twenty-first century, China's status as a major international economic and political power was beyond dispute. China now manufactures everything from microchips to motor vehicles, and the 'Made in China' label is found in all corners of the world. Along with this economic influence, China's role in global political and cultural affairs is becoming both more significant and increasingly visible. China's hosting of the 2008 Olympics is just one of the more obvious manifestations of this impact. Chinese cultural products, ideas, customs and habits are steadily spreading around the world in the wake of China's economic and political reach. The chapters in this book explore the key domains in Chinese culture and reveal the dynamism produced by a formidable culture's interaction with both its own ancient, albeit never static, traditions and the flood of new global cultural influences. The connection between global economic and political weight and the changes in China's cultural realm are complex and profound. To understand contemporary China – an absolute necessity if one is to understand the world today – it is vital to appreciate the evolution of modern Chinese culture.

Interest in Chinese literature, philosophy, cinema, *qigong* and other cultural artefacts around the world is stronger now than ever before. There has been a plethora of books about Chinese culture published in anglophone countries and a steady increase in students enrolling in courses on Chinese language and civilization. This trend is set to continue. According to the Chinese Ministry of Education, by the beginning of 2007 the number of foreign students studying Chinese had reached 30 million, and is set to rise to 100 million before 2010. The Chinese government is investing considerable financial and human resources in its promotion of Chinese language and culture, best seen in the expansion of the government-sponsored Confucius Institutes, which since the in-auguration of the scheme in 2004 had grown to 145 by April 2007.[1]

Not surprisingly, in tandem with this upsurge of interest in 'things Chinese', there has also been an assertion of traditional elements, so that Chinese culture is projected as a unifying and largely static phenom-enon with contemporary culture reproducing and modernizing relics of China's historical past. The choice of the title 'Confucius Institute' is indicative of this homogenizing and backward-looking trend. The name itself implies a certain kind of Chinese culture that is to be promoted. Confucius' teaching has for some two thousand years been synonymous with the orthodox aspects of Chinese culture, and in that time it has been a philosophy that gave the appearance of a unitary way of life in the hugely diverse regions of China. Chinese governments have long tend-ed to lean more towards unity than diversity in their pronouncements about China and Chinese culture. Certainly, the current Communist Party (CCP) leaders are investing considerable resources in spreading this particular take on Chinese culture.

While most governments and education systems produce narratives of fixed 'national cultures', in fact cultures are in a perpetual state of change; and in the last hundred years the culture of China has changed more fundamentally and rapidly than at any other time in its long past. This is what makes modern Chinese culture such a fascinating subject. Certainly the contributors to this volume regard Chinese culture as dy-namic and diverse, and they demonstrate that dynamism and variety in their chapters. They show the continued evolution of Chinese culture in vastly different directions, driven by internal forces that are in constant interaction with influences from outside China's borders. Indeed, the notion of 'Chinese culture' is so unstable that when I began the project of editing this volume, my central problem was to decide precisely what constituted modern Chinese culture. I was presented with the par-adox of trying to pinpoint a phenomenon that was in a constant state of flux.

For large parts of the twentieth century, Western thinking on China was dominated by a fascination with her past glories such as Confucian philosophy and Tang poetry, or with Orientalist horrors such as images of Fu Manchu and bound feet. However, in the last few decades, with greater ease of travel in and out of Mainland China, such stereotypes have been largely dismantled and China's civilization has been increasingly demystified. Current interest focuses upon contemporary trends and is one of the keys to futurology, as China's vast potential economic power is translated into the reshaping of the world's global political order. Furthermore, academic research on Chinese culture covers topics that span the whole spectrum of society, ranging from the uses of museums of local folk exhibits to major historical ruins such as Yuanmingyuan, the Old Summer Palace which was burned down by British and French troops in 1860. Given the huge variety of manifestations of Chinese culture, the number of potential cultural sites for examination is endless. The sixteen chapters that follow are therefore not exhaustive, but are grouped around significant issues that together aim to give a holistic picture of Chinese culture today. Rather than attempting to be comprehensive, we have worked on the notion of change, so that all contributors show to varying degrees how their subject matter has changed since the beginning of the twentieth century. Why the focus on the twentieth century? To answer this question, it is perhaps best to outline our understanding of each of the concepts 'modern', 'Chinese' and 'culture'.

Modern

At first glance, the concept 'modern' should not present many problems since it should really be a matter of definition only. In English, the word 'modern' stems from the Latin '*modo*', which means 'recently' or 'of late'. In the study of European history, however, the 'recent' goes a bit further back. The start of the modern era is generally fixed with reference to the French Revolution of 1789 and/or the Industrial Revolution of the early nineteenth century. 'Modern culture' therefore describes a way of life that is still practised now, but is distinctly different from that before the Industrial Revolution.

In Chinese historical studies, especially in the periodization favoured by the CCP, the term '*jindai*' (literally the near-generation) is often used for 'modern'. However, this is taken to refer to the period between the Sino–British Opium War of 1840–1842, after which relations between China and the West became irrevocably enmeshed, and the May Fourth Movement of 1919, in which new ideas from Japan and the West were imported and re-evaluated against traditional values. In daily speech, the term *xiandai*, which translates as 'the period that has just been revealed', is the most common term for 'modern'. For example, modernization translates as '*xiandaihua*' in Chinese. In historical studies, however, *xiandai* often refers more specifically to the decades between 1919 and 1949, when the People's Republic of China (PRC) was established. And 1949 is then taken to mark the beginning of the contemporary '*dangdai*' (the current-generation) era.[2]

These three historical junctures each have their merits as the point of the start of 'modern China', but each implies a political position that does not necessarily reflect the actual cultural situation in China. If we are to take a periodization that is defined by cultural factors, none of the above is suitable – a different schema is required. I argue that it is most appropriate to place modern Chinese culture as beginning around 1900. While the Opium Wars of the mid-nineteenth century saw the increasing military presence of Western powers in China, culturally, the nation remained largely unchanged. I will not go into detail here, since in the next chapter Peter Zarrow performs an admirable task of providing the historical background to the closing years of the nineteenth century. However, even when the Europeans were dictating the terms of trade after each victorious military encounter with the Chinese, the material and mental landscapes of ordinary people remained largely untouched. The imperial and other mechanisms of governance, such as the civil service examination system, were still in place, and the voices of those advocating system-wide political and social change only became audible towards the end of that century.

Similarly, while the 'May Fourth Movement' around 1919 produced an unprecedented enthusiasm for new ideas, the groundwork had been established in the two preceding decades. While the May Fourth Movement gave rise to extremely important intellectual and political trends in China, including the birth of the Communist Party, the figures who had the most influence on the young at this time were without doubt late nineteenth-century reformists such as Kang Youwei and Liang Qichao, whose writings had converted not only the young emperor of the time, but also the revolutionaries. In fact, Mao Zedong called himself 'Kang Liang' for a time to demonstrate his debt to these late Qing thinkers.

Likewise, the third point often cited as the start of the 'contemporary' era – the establishment of the PRC in 1949 – does not adequately mark the turning point in terms of China's culture. Chinese society had fundamentally changed before 1949, and the CCP's success was a manifestation of this 'modern' transformation rather than the commencement of it. Even though the Communist regime claimed to be making a complete break with traditional thought, its history shows clear continuities with the immediate and distant past. Moreover, even if we assume that 'modern' equates to a readiness to engage openly with the world, under CCP rule China has only really actively joined the 'modern' world with the advent of Deng Xiaoping's open-door policy in the early 1980s.

There are compelling reasons for taking 1900 as the starting point of modern Chinese culture. As stated above, at the end of the nineteenth century late Qing reformers such as Kang Youwei and Liang Qichao were already calling for new ways of thinking and government, and this was also a time when major thought currents such as Social Darwinism were translated into Chinese by figures such as Yan Fu. While they advocated the introduction of Western thought into China, these men were solidly grounded in traditional Chinese learning. This was thus a time when the interaction between Chinese and Western ideas fired the imagination of a whole generation. When the May Fourth radicals vigorously promoted the twin Western saviours – 'Mr Science' and 'Mr Democracy' – as idols to be emulated by the young, this was done as a deliberate elevation of the Western cultural norms that were to replace Chinese standards and values. Likewise, the CCP also intended to wipe out all vestiges of feudal China, which were to be replaced by Marxism, another Western import. Nonetheless, whatever time frame we adopt to limit the scope of 'modern Chinese culture', the term still implies something that is based on something 'Chinese'. Indeed, whatever system is adopted, China continued to be 'Chinese', and despite the increasing modernization in the twentieth century, many core traditions continued to characterize the landscape. Indeed, had Kang Youwei succeeded in 1898 in his bid to introduce his form of 'original' Confucianism nationally, the new millennium might have seen a Great Commonwealth founded on a Confucian renaissance, similar to the modernization programme of the Meiji Restoration in Japan. Even though the so-called 100 Days Reform of 1898 did not succeed, it did mark the beginnings of 'modern' (with hints of Western) modes of both thinking and behaving while remaining Chinese.

In addition, in the years immediately before and after 1900, there was also a deliberate attempt to evaluate Chinese civilization holistically and from a perspective that many intellectuals of the time explicitly considered 'modern'. In the last few years of the nineteenth century, reformers such as Kang Youwei and Liang Qichao took a comprehensive and radical look at Chinese culture in the hope that it could be integrated productively into the world. At the same time, it was only at the start of the twentieth century that thinkers began to be concerned about defining a national identity. As Prasenjit Duara deftly shows in Chapter 3, ideas of nation and Chinese identity were ferociously advocated and debated throughout the century.

While I have stressed the importance of Chinese–Western interaction as one aspect of the advent of the modern period in China, Westernization does not automatically produce modernity. In many ways, the modern age became more 'Chinese', in the sense that people living in Chinese communities became more nationalistic and at times more inward looking. Thus, ironically, the 'internationalism' of the twentieth century created a self-conscious and sometimes fiercely expressed nationalism in China – from the xenophobic Boxers of 1900 right up to the pathologically Sinocentric radicals of the Cultural Revolution in the early 1970s and the 'China Can Say "No"' crowd of the late 1990s. There were times when the Centre could barely hold, such as the warlord period of the 1920s, and times when central control was strictly enforced, as seen in the early Communist period.

In this volume I have resisted the commonplace custom of dividing the twentieth century into 'modern' (Republican) and 'contemporary' (Communist). While the Nationalist–Communist divide can serve as a convenient means of viewing the major political juncture of the twentieth century, in cultural terms the complexities of both eras contain elements that are more than just Imperial, Nationalist or Communist. Indeed, these descriptors are often confusing or downright misleading. Modern Chinese culture, as I have argued above, included elements from the imperial era. Similarly, some of the most interesting ideas and practices of the Communist experiment came from the 1930s and 1940s. And the PRC has seen so many changes and diverse practices that it too cannot be easily slotted into one homogeneous 'culture'. As Arif Dirlik demonstrates in Chapter 8, the theorizing of, and commentaries upon, socialism in China have undergone tremendous changes in the twentieth century, and not always because of utilitarian imperatives of nation-building.

Taking the twentieth century and beyond as the modern frame has other interesting implications. The extraordinary developments in the Chinese world – indeed in the world in general – over the last few decades have meant that the new millennium has already witnessed a Chinese culture that was unimaginable only a few generations ago. The speed with which even the physical landscape is changing is equalled only by the psychological transformations that many have had to undergo. This is especially true of the last decade. Liu Kang's chapter on the phenomenal developments in television and the Internet illustrates the degree to which cyber culture has penetrated and transformed the lives of ordinary Chinese, particularly the urban young. The frequent claims of a spiritual vacuum by political leaders and public intellectuals are a reminder that there is indeed a crisis of recognition. The unrelenting and drastic transformations, both physical and mental, have left many reeling from a state of future shock.

Not only has Mainland China changed; its peripheries such as Taiwan, Hong Kong and Macau are becoming even more varied. Voices advocating an independent identity are heard from the former, while the latter have become more integrated and interdependent with the Mainland. The diasporic communities have also transformed beyond recognition. What were mainly groups from coastal regions of Guangdong and Fujian are now joined by people from the interior, speaking dialects that the old communities would not have understood. More importantly, the 'cultural level' – to be defined more precisely in the section on 'culture' – of the new diaspora is very different from that of the old. But of course there are many things happening now that are still 'traditional' and 'modern', and this book in capturing the twentieth century as modern does occasionally hark back to 'traditional' times, as well as what is happening in the twenty-first century, to explain 'modern' China.

Chinese

While defining the term 'modern' presents problems, the concept of 'Chinese' is even more difficult to pin down. In English, the word 'China' seems to have derived from the Qin (pronounced 'chin') Dynasty (221–206 BC), the first Chinese dynasty in which the various states that had previously existed were unified as one Chinese empire. This was also the period during which indirect contacts were made between the Chinese and Roman empires by way of the silk route. In Chinese, 'China' (Zhongguo) literally means the Middle Kingdom (or centring nation, if the idea of the emperor or capital city being a magnetic centre is accepted), giving rise to Sino-centric sentiments among many Chinese. Of course, over the centuries, the 'centre' of the country shifted, most often along the Yellow River in the north or the Yangtze River in the south. Nevertheless, for millennia, the Chinese empire referred to the geographical area covering regions around these two rivers. Within this area, myriad and dissimilar groups of peoples, languages and ways of life existed and continue to exist. Yet these groups all describe themselves as Chinese, in the same way that the large variety of peoples and entities in Europe call themselves European. To make matters even more complicated, just as 'European' can describe cultures that are outside Europe, so too is 'Chinese' an adjective that can travel the globe. Nonetheless, its origins stem from the Chinese empire.

The contributors to this volume are cognizant of the fact that 'Chinese' contains remnants of imperial times when 'China' was not only the centre of the world, but also 'all under heaven' (*tianxia*), a term that indicated the traditional Chinese view of the world: that the Chinese civilization was all there was in the universe. However, we are more concerned here with analysing current perceptions and realities. Mostly, we describe people and things in the People's Republic of China (PRC). We are also keenly aware that as well as qualifying people and things in China, the term 'Chinese' can also describe people of the 'national minorities' and the Chinese diaspora, scattered around the world, and ideas and things that may or may not have come out of China. The 'national minorities' aside, the diversity of Chinese ethnicities sets the scene for discarding the notion of an essential and fixed Chineseness. Debates about what it means to be Chinese have raged for decades. They continue right into the present time, and will no doubt intensify as the PRC and Taiwanese leaderships believe that it is more advantageous to govern a people with a more unified identity. However, as William Jankowiak shows in Chapter 5, while the Chinese state would like its people to be more culturally centric and converge towards some Confucian norm, in reality, even the Han Chinese are composed of people with variant languages and habits. The notion of ethnic, and therefore 'minority', identity is a fluid and contested one. Thus, again, 'change' provides the key to our discussions.

Often, people's self-perceptions are transformed by social forces beyond their control. However, there are times when they actively want to adopt a different persona, for example by assuming the customs and appearances of foreign cultures. A recent article from the *Washington Post* about new housing developments in China entitled 'Developers Build Ersatz European, American Communities for the New Middle Class' articulates this phenomenon graphically:

> The ding-dong from the neo-Gothic church next door signals
> to Wu Yuqing that it's time to wake up. On her way to the grocery
> store each day, she walks past the Cob Gate Fish & Chip shop and
> bronze statues of Winston Churchill, Florence Nightingale and

William Shakespeare. Tall men decked out in the red uniforms of the Queen's Guard nod hello.

The place looks a lot like a small town on the Thames River, but Wu's new home is actually in a suburb of Shanghai…

Shanghai's plan is … [to build] … a ring of satellite developments modeled after different parts of Europe, including German, Czech, Spanish and Scandinavian districts, in addition to the one that looks like London, known as Thames Town.[3]

The writer of this article calls these new townships 'ersatz', casting doubt on the authenticity not only of the buildings, but by implication of the cultural affectations of the residents. The article makes quite plain that the residents of these townships do not know anything about the European cultures that they aspire towards. Nevertheless, it is legitimate to ask: are these townships Chinese or European? Clearly, the article suggests they are Chinese, or fake Western as best. The word ersatz implies that. Suppose these townships were full of pale Englishmen, blonde Germans etc, living as they did in the old foreign concessions in Shanghai? Would they be considered European or still Chinese? That is to say, would these townships then be part of European or Chinese culture? What we are asking here is: does it matter if a place that is situated in China looks European or American and wants to imitate those lifestyles? Are they then Western? Or do they need white people living in them to be Western?

All the above questions can be asked with different referents. When is Chinese culture Chinese? In Mainland China? What about Hong Kong or Taiwan? Or, if we take the question even further, what about Chinatowns in the West? There, we have had for nearly a hundred years many districts that are called Chinatowns. These so-called Chinatowns are usually populated by Chinese shops, restaurants, and more importantly ethnic Chinese.

It is true that many older Chinese living in foreign countries believe that even though they live in the West – some having done so for generations – they are more knowledgeable about Chinese culture than those back in China. Of course, as Wang Gungwu shows in Chapter 6, there is a great variety of self-identities among the diasporic Chinese communities, and these identities also change over time, sometimes because of the environment in the host country, but more often because of the changing political situation in China itself. In addition, the claim by diasporic communities that they preserve the authentic home culture while those back in the homeland have lost it is common not just among Chinese, but also among other migrant communities. For example, many young migrant women experience considerable conflict with older generations in their families who complain that the young have lost the moral codes of their home countries. In immigrant countries such as Australia, this migrant syndrome was once quite common among Greeks and Italians, until the older generation realized that their homelands had changed and had left them behind.

The idea of Chinatown has always said more about an imagined Chinese culture of the non-Chinese in the host countries than about the actual cultures in the Chinatowns. For example, Barrio Chino in Barcelona is an area in the inner city that was once the red light district, and was seen to be an area of sex, drugs and crime. They called it Barrio Chino because presumably the Chinese were thought to indulge in sex, drugs and crime. Such an Orientalist use of Chinese culture was also highly evident in Polanski's movie *Chinatown*, starring Jack Nicholson and Faye Dunaway. As in Barcelona's Barrio Chino, the Chinese are almost invisible in the movie *Chinatown*: the title only makes sense if we agree that anything associated with even the name Chinese must be imbued with immorality, homicide and inscrutability.

Of course, not all imagined Chinese cultures are evil and corrupt. The Chinatown in the Australian aboriginal township of Cherbourg is also an imagined space, and no Chinese person has ever lived there, but it seems that those who lay claim to it do so because one of the women in generations past might have married a Chinese, and one influential female elder in particular decided that they would define themselves against the other inhabitants by holding on to this Chinese heritage, whether it was real or not. This was one way to counter the oppressive white domination that these communities suffered.[4] It can be argued that this Chinatown has as much to do with Chinese culture as that in Polanski's film *Chinatown*, but can we therefore erase the 'Chinese' qualifier in the term? Obviously, we can only answer in the affirmative if we are perfectly clear what 'Chinese' means and deny all others the right to claim some idea or thing as Chinese. Failing this, 'Chinese' becomes just about anything that we want to make it.

Nonetheless, some of the best minds in China in the last hundred years or so have been trying to devise ways of distilling what they consider to be the essence of 'Chinese culture' so that its good bits can be inherited and its rotten bits discarded. In the early twentieth century, for example, thinkers like Zhang Binglin, Liu Shipei and those of the 'National Essence' School tried hard to recover the best of Chinese culture. Even in the most radical phases of Communist rule, some of the most intense controversies among intellectuals have been concerned with ways of defining the essence of Chinese culture, and when that is done, preserving it. The most notable method devised for salvaging Chinese culture was proposed by Feng Youlan, whose 'abstract inheritance method' basically stated that, despite the fact that the 'feudal dross' of Confucianism should be repudiated and trashed, the essential goodness of Confucian humanism should be inherited in an abstract way so that the transition to a new Socialist society would not be too abrupt and the fine values of Chinese culture would not be forgotten.[5] Thus, it is not only in relation to popular culture such as cooking and dating behaviour that arguments are put forward to ensure that 'Chinese culture' is continued. Similar claims have been made even in the most abstract realms.

Outside the Mainland, these debates have been revived with a vengeance since China became more open to the outside world in the 1980s, with the revival of the so-called 'New Confucian' school of thought. This 'school' was begun by philosophers such as Liang Shuming and Xiong Shili who even before 1949 had argued for the revival of Confucianism in China. Their versions of Confucianism were heavily diluted by Buddhist elements, so much so that Liang has been described as 'the last Buddhist' as well as the 'last Confucian'.[6] While Liang and Xiong are now said to be the fathers of the New Confucianism school, their conservative ideas simply had no way of gaining acceptance in the Mainland after 1949. Their message that Confucianism or Chinese tradition held the key to a correct way to live in the modern world continued to be advocated by those who left China and lived in Hong Kong and Taiwan in particular. In Chapter 7, Sor-hoon Tan describes the ways in which the 'new' Confucian thought developed during the twentieth century.

On the Mainland itself, the so-called New Confucians were mostly ignored for some thirty years after China became Communist. It was only after the 'Asian Economic Miracle' and the opening up of China's economy after the 1980s that Confucianism came back into vogue. A relatively obscure document titled 'Declaration on Behalf of Chinese Culture Respectfully Announced to the People of the World', which had been published in 1958, was resuscitated as the beginnings of the formation of a new school of thought. The 1958 document was penned by four of the most vocal writers outside China known for their regular 'defence' of what they perceived to be the 'glories of traditional Chinese culture': Mou Zongsan, Xu Fuguan, Zhang Junmai and Tang Junyi. In fact, this document is not a systematic outline of any one philosophy as such; rather, it is an attempt by those who felt strongly about traditional Chinese philosophy to integrate it with a perceived modern and world culture.

As scholars who had fled China, the authors of the Declaration considered that China under Communism had lost its cultural heritage. Naturally, these writers were all but ignored in China. However, in the last twenty or so years, the Mainland's attitude towards traditional Chinese culture has changed dramatically. 'New Confucianism' gained popularity there and renowned philosophers who were considered New Confucianists were invited to lecture at Peking University and other prestigious institutions. One of these visiting scholars was Tu Wei-ming, a professor from Harvard University. Tu Wei-ming's most influential thesis concerning Chinese culture is succinctly summed up in his seminal essay: 'Cultural China: The Periphery as the Center'.[7] It is clear that the question of who has possession of Chinese culture has become of great interest to the tens of millions of ethnic Chinese who live outside China today. There is something incongruous about the claim that the practitioners of 'real' Chinese culture live not inside China, but abroad, especially at the apex of American thinking, Harvard. Nonetheless, the point has been made and made quite persuasively.

In refusing to recognize the changes in China that were taking place around them, the New Confucians before 1949 could be said to have been in a state of denial. The New Culture Movement in the early decades of the twentieth century had all but made Confucianism the antithesis of modernity. The Communist regime continued on the anti-Confucian path throughout the 1950s and 1960s, so that by the Cultural Revolution decade all 'old things' were vehemently attacked. Most interestingly, the Gang of Four during the anti-Confucius campaign of 1974 wanted to revive Legalism to replace Confucianism. Instead of wanting to be 'modern', they salvaged what they claimed to be indigenous Chinese in the philosophy of ancient thinkers such as the Legalists Xunzi and Hanfei. These classical philosophers were, as the Gang of Four rightly pointed out, at least indigenous Chinese. What the radicals did not emphasize was that Legalism was in fact an offshoot of Confucianism, and that the utilitarian Mozi and his followers were much more hostile to the Confucians, making Moism an indigenous system that was philosophically

much more an antithesis to Confucianism than Legalism could claim to
be. Nonetheless, casting aside the politics of the interpretations, and the
harshness of some aspects of Legalism, surely Legalism or the pragmatic
Moism would be a better route to an amalgam of Chinese and Western
essences than the deceptive notions of 'benevolent' Confucian management techniques that are being propagated now? This is deceptive because Confucius and past Confucian orthodoxy denigrated commerce,
but the New Confucians seem quite happy to accommodate the 'modern' Confucius as a business consultant. Even more heretically, the self-
proclaimed hedonist Yu Dan interprets the Confucian *Analects* as a text
on how to live a good life in the modern world. The populace, hungry for
spiritual sustenance that is both 'Chinese' and hip, eagerly buy into this
rendition, thereby making Yu Dan a new-style academic celebrity.[8]

Perhaps, in parallel to the term 'postmodern' that is now bandied
about in parts of the world, we have a post-Chinese Chinese culture. It
would be a political nonsense to talk about post-China. But in terms of
culture, using post-Chinese as a possessive adjective makes good sense.
This postmodern post-Chinese idea is often expressed as trans-national
Chineseness. In fact, in discussions of arthouse Chinese films, the transnational usage is standard. There have been few films since the Fifth
Generation movie directors that could be truly said to be purely Chinese,
since most are global productions. And the competition is also for international prizes. Chris Berry in Chapter 15 traces the film industry from
its beginnings as a Western import early last century to its emergence
as a global phenomenon; interestingly, he also demonstrates that with
the emergence of the Sixth Generation directors, the industry has
fragmented within China itself. As with every other aspect of Chinese
culture, the filmic form is in a state of flux. The same is true for other
art forms such as music and painting. Colin Mackerras in Chapter 13 and
David Clarke in Chapter 14 show how the performing and visual arts
have undergone dramatic changes due to the interplay of native traditions and traditions from without, including European and Soviet theories and practices. The result of all this intermingling tells much about
the globalization of culture, and these chapters on sight and sound are
excellent demonstrations of this process.

In China at present, classical European music is probably as popular
and performed as frequently as it is in any country in Europe. The degree
to which artistic pursuits that are considered 'modern' (and often Western) are nurtured ensures that whatever is produced or admired there

are fusions of many different styles, often with elements from ethnic Chinese artists working abroad as well. In the same way, Chinese literature in the twentieth century went through so many transformations due to influences from the outside world that to talk about a Chinese literature needs many qualifications. Thus, the history of modern Chinese literature that I co-authored is awkwardly titled *The Literature of China in the Twentieth Century* rather than simply 'Modern Chinese Literature' to delimit it temporally and spatially and distinguish it from all other literatures that are written in the Chinese language or are Chinese in content.[9] Of course, Chinese literature, even when it refers to that written in Mainland China, has numerous strands, and here again, change is the defining feature, as Charles Laughlin and Michel Hockx show in their chapters (Chapters 11 and 12) on the complexities of the noisy revolutionary and inward-looking involutionary literary traditions. If we consider the literature by Chinese diasporic writers about life in foreign lands in non-Chinese languages as part of the Chinese literary scene, the notion of post-Chinese is even more irresistible.

Culture

The word 'culture' is, in different ways, as complicated as 'Chinese'. In Chinese, the term 'culture' (*wenhua*) literally implies a process of transformation by *wen*, or writing. Thus 'culture' invokes writing. *Wen* originally came from the scratches made on ancient divination objects such as bones and tortoise shells, and was therefore a human attempt to reveal thought patterns in concrete form. It was also the precursor to writing, with its function of communicating and categorizing the universe. Certainly, it captures the idea of people in the priestly or writing classes making sense of the world. Traditionally, as Zong-qi Cai observes, *wen* denotes many things, including 'royal posthumous titles, ritual objects, rites and music, norms and statutes; dignified deportment, the polite arts, graphic cosmic symbols, eloquent speech, writing, rhymed writing, and belles-lettres'.[10] In short, *wen* denotes lofty symbols and writing. It still has these connotations today. Colloquially, to say that somebody has culture (*you wenhua*) means that they have an education and can write. The verbalizing particle *hua* in *wenhua* thus indicates the transformative effect of culture. Through cultivation, *wenhua* in theory can be achieved by all who aspire to it so that, through it, a cultured person is changed.

While change is implicit in the notion of *wenhua*, the change, or improvement, that it engenders has always been intimately linked to that which is mostly transcribed, including language, literature, religion and philosophy. In Chinese, more than in most other languages, the writing system was the site of intense struggles throughout the twentieth century. This is not surprising, since having writing skills is the prerequisite to having culture in the ordinary understanding of the word 'culture', since '*wen*', or writing, is literally part of the meaning of culture. As Ping Chen shows in Chapter 10, the struggle waged around the writing system is not just linguistic, but highly political. Difficulty in mastering language leads to debates about simplifying it, so that it is made more available to more people. Coupled with simplification, the more radical proposal argues for the advantages of Romanization and Pinyin, so that the memorization of thousands of characters is rendered unnecessary. While computers and the Internet have to a certain extent democratized the written language, 'culture' in Chinese retains its connotations of 'high culture'.

In the anglophone world, the notion of a 'high culture' is perhaps best expressed by Matthew Arnold (1822–88), who claimed that to have culture is to 'know the best that has been said and thought in the world'.[11] This elitist position is concise, but not very precise. To start with, what is best is not fixed and is thus highly contentious. More importantly, it was promoted at a time of empire, when Britannia ruled the waves. So, presumably, the best came out of Britain, and Arnold did not hesitate to proclaim this belief. By contrast, China in the nineteenth century was experiencing some of the worst moments in its history. Chinese culture then would not have been something that many people would have considered to be the best. More likely, in England, in the pursuit of truth and beauty, most would have chosen the Keatsian fancies of classical Greece.

While the colonial age in the nineteenth century gave the impression that European culture represented the most advanced form of civilization, the two World Wars shook the complacency of many Europeans. Those wars in concert with the anti-colonialist movements that followed helped lead to changes in attitudes towards culture. In the second half of the century, academia in the West began to argue for less lofty ideas and manifestations of human society, best exemplified by Raymond Williams' 1958 essay 'Culture is Ordinary'.[12] Such sentiments had a counterpart in China. The Maoist emphasis on creating a popular/peasant culture that 'served the people' was to have a lasting impact on how *wenhua* is understood. In both the West and China, the closing decades of the twentieth century were a time when 'Cultural Studies' began to take hold in universities, and, as well as 'subaltern' cultural items, non-written everyday objects such as cinema, television, kungfu and sex became prime areas of research into 'culture'. Thus, despite the fact that academics were getting involved in this new understanding of culture, *'wenhua'* was becoming less refined and elevated and more mass-based. More importantly, *wenhua* no longer needed to be based on *wen*, or the written.

But while this conception of culture is more democratic, it is also more anarchic. What is not culture? How individualistic can one go? When do I know that 'my culture' is the same as 'our culture'? This question is especially important for migrant societies such as Australia. In an age of globalization, it has also become increasingly important for other countries, including China. Thus, in the late twentieth century, the decline of the canons also brought consequences of uncertainty in literary and artistic fields. For rapidly developing countries such as China in particular, 'culture' is often appropriated by politicians and educationalists, who advocate maintaining and perpetuating culture as a social cohesive, and using it to stabilize societies through a process of mutual recognition of shared values.

Treating culture as synonymous with sets of meanings that distinguish groups from each other helps to create in-groups and out-groups. As such, it was effectively harnessed throughout twentieth-century China to further nationalist goals. Chinese culture has drifted away from its original meaning of *wenhua* as an elevated text-based phenomenon based in China, to one which can be used by people who reside not just on the Chinese Mainland but throughout the world. Even so, the claim to some sort of superior essence is still quite pronounced, so that my culture is somehow *wenhua* while your (referring to anyone who is not 'Chinese') culture can be seen as barbaric.

Wen refers not just to literary or cultural accomplishments. The fundamental utility of *'wen'* rests on its reference to power. Having *wen* in the past referred to those who had passed the civil service examinations. Thus, the *wenren*, or the scholar-gentry, which in China has reproduced itself through the civil service examination system for centuries, was clearly the controlling class. Even now, *'you wenhua'* generally refers to those who have finished a certain amount of formal education, normally senior secondary school. They usually have steady jobs and a regular income, such as teachers or bureaucrats who perpetuate social norms. These social norms, of course, were the traditionally Confucian 'culture' that in the twentieth century were becoming much more unstable and in flux. Traditionally, the *wenren* could only be men, since men were the only people allowed to sit for the civil service examinations that enabled them to become 'cultured'. However, in the twentieth century, gender boundaries were progressively being transformed, and Harriet Evans' discussion in Chapter 4 details the many intricacies associated with the breaking down of such boundaries.

In fact, the twentieth century, in our terms the period of modern Chinese culture, shows that this culture has become the site of intense struggle, with everyone claiming ownership of it, and in the process changing its meaning and content. Of course, there has been widespread agreement that Chinese culture has certain essential general ingredients, and both Feng Youlan's 'abstract inheritance method' effort and those of the New Confucians were attempts to salvage the 'abstract' and 'general' elements of this culture. Unfortunately, when they say 'Chinese culture', these theoreticians often imply more 'elevated' and conservative values. The argument for some essential Chineseness that rests on Chinese culture parallels the 'Asian values' debate that was fashionable in the 1980s and 1990s. Ultimately this was about eulogizing conventional practices such as treasuring family ties, respecting the old, valuing formal education and honouring hard work – practices that are found in most societies. Thus, no matter how we interpret modern Chinese culture, the only safe statement we can make about it is that it is vague and forever changing. Furthermore, the globalization process as a catalyst for change has not slowed down in the new millennium, but has become more intense than ever before. This will mean that Chinese culture will transform even more quickly as time progresses, and trying to stabilize its 'essence' for preservation will become more difficult. Its 'essence' has in fact become an ingredient for new fusions of different cultures.

This is not to say that local communities and cultures do not define individuals. Indeed, Daniel Overmyer in Chapter 9 emphasizes the overriding importance of local traditions of ritual and belief as the major form of Chinese religion. In many respects, these local cultures have long been the foundation of what it means to be Chinese for the majority of the population. When asked where they are from, people generally respond by naming their ancestral community, and, by implication, all the traditions it represents. Notwithstanding this important qualification, Overmyer does provide an overview of the beliefs and rituals of the major religions such as Daoism, Buddhism, Christianity and Islam in China, showing how they have been interacting and influencing life in China for millennia, and that in the twentieth century these interactions have become even more intense. The move towards globalization means that Chinese culture is something that is evolving almost in the way that was aptly summarized by Tan Sitong, who in 1896 attempted to integrate Confucianism, Christianity and Buddhism. Tan Sitong was executed two years later for his political activism in the promotion of heterodoxy, but when he proclaimed that 'the founders of the three religions [Christianity, Confucianism and Buddhism] are all one. When I worship one, I worship them all',[13] he was already one step ahead of those such as the New Confucianist Liang Shuming and the Communist radical Chen Duxiu who fiercely argued about the merits of Eastern and Western cultures a couple of decades later.

Ultimately, Chinese culture should describe how the Chinese people live and play as well as how they think. *Wenhua* is more than *wen*. In their play, the Chinese have also been keen to be part of the world community, and not just part of, but to lead in this arena as well. The time and effort invested in hosting the Olympic Games is but the most conspicuous example of this. As Susan Brownell shows in Chapter 17, this event is the culmination of decades of China's endeavours to be recognized as a world leader by other countries. The wish to achieve leadership status is not confined to the sporting arena, though it is of paramount importance in terms of China's international relations. Other aspects of Chinese physical culture such as martial arts are also gaining popularity abroad. Meanwhile, within China, Western forms of physical activity such as ballroom dancing are promoted as a means to physical and mental health.

Of course, sport is but one dimension of Chinese culture that has changed and is changing. Every other aspect of Chinese culture is also undergoing dramatic transformations. Furthermore, every other aspect of Chinese culture is becoming globalized. By taking the end of the nineteenth century as the beginning of modern culture and the whole of the twentieth century as the time frame that we have defined as modern China in terms of culture, therefore, the book should neatly bring the end back to the beginning, when the biggest concern was how to be both Chinese and a citizen of the world. In fact, now the case for taking all thoughts and practices as 'Chinese cultures' is even more pertinent, as we have truly multi-cultural cultural forms such as films and the Internet that bind the world even more closely together. For these forms are literally created trans-culturally, producing outcomes that are recognizably Chinese but also global.

Notes

1. Xinhua News Agency, *China Daily*, 10 April 2007, www.china.org.cn/english/photo/206586.htm

2. I should note here that while defining and thinking about one's relationship to 'modernity' has emerged as a topic of debate in both the West and China, my concern in this chapter is on periodization, and issues of modernity will be taken up in later chapters where relevant. Furthermore, in the West, much attention was focused on the question of postmodernity in the 1980s – and this proved to be of intense interest to Chinese intellectuals in the 1990s. While it is tempting to categorize China in the new millennium as postmodern, these concepts are far too complex to coherently incorporate into this short chapter.

3. Ariana Eunjung Cha, 'West Rises in China's Back Yard: Developers Build Ersatz European, American Communities for New Middle Class', *Washington Post*, 11 April 2007.

4. See discussion in Guy Ramsay, 'Cherbourg's Chinatown: Creating an Identity of Place on an Australian Aboriginal Settlement', *Journal of Historical Geography* 29, no. 1, 2003, pp. 109–22.

5. See discussion in Kam Louie, *Inheriting Tradition: Critiques of the Classical Philosophers in Communist China 1949–1966*, Hong Kong, Oxford University Press, 1986.

6. John J. Hanafin, 'The "Last Buddhist": The Philosophy of Liang Shuming', in John Makeham (ed.), *New Confucianism: A Critical Examination*, New York, Palgrave MacMillan, 2003, pp. 187–218. Guy S. Alitto, *The Last Confucian: Liang Shu-ming and the Chinese Dilemma of Modernity*, Berkeley, University of California Press, 1979.

7. Tu Wei-ming, 'Cultural China: The Periphery as the Center', *Daedalus: Journal of the American Academy of Arts and Sciences* 120, no. 2, 1991, pp. 1–32.

8. See report in Ting Shi, 'Making History Hip', *South China Morning Post*, 10 August 2007, p. A14.

9. Bonnie S. McDougall and Kam Louie, *The Literature of China in the Twentieth Century*, New York, Columbia University Press, 1997.

10. Zong-qi Cai, 'Wen and the Construction of a Critical System in "Wensin Diaolong"', *Chinese Literature: Essays, Articles, Reviews (CLEAR)* 22, 2000, p. 1.

11. Matthew Arnold, *Literature & Dogma: An Essay towards a Better Apprehension of the Bible*, Cambridge, Chadwyck-Healey, 1999, p. xxxiii.

12. Raymond Williams, 'Culture is Ordinary', in John Higgins (ed.), *The Raymond Williams Reader*, Oxford, Blackwell, 2001, pp. 11–24.

13. Cited in Kam Louie, *Critiques of Confucius in Contemporary China*, Hong Kong, Chinese University Press, 1980, p. 3.

2

Social and political developments: the making of the twentieth-century Chinese state

Over the course of China's twentieth century, the dynastic system crumbled; the traditional literati-gentry elite disappeared; state–society relations were transformed several times; three revolutions – of 1911, 1928 and 1949 – created new systems of governance; and a modernizing nation-state emerged. By the beginning of the twenty-first century, an economically dynamic China looked very different from the vast agrarian empire that had survived into the twentieth century. In many ways, the reforms that were under way by the early 1980s could be considered a fourth revolution: China opened up markets, welcomed foreign investment, and developed business opportunities – resulting in double-digit annual growth that released millions from poverty and turned China into a major trading nation. Nonetheless, in both its successes and failures, contemporary China still shows many legacies of the past. Above all, the political drive to make China into a world power has its roots in the sociopolitical transformations of the late nineteenth century, when Chinese elites first resolved to follow the path of 'wealth and power'.

A brief chapter on such a large subject can only present an outline of key developments. This chapter focuses on attempts to build a new nation by extending the 'rights and duties' of citizenship to previously disenfranchised groups over the first half of the twentieth century. It then briefly discusses the changes of the Maoist (1949–76) and reformist (1978–) eras. During the twentieth century, membership in the nation came to count as a – if not *the* – primary marker of identity, along with family, class and locality. This was partly a top-down process, as significant elements of the national elite appealed to subaltern groups for support and pursued an ideal of the 'nation' that entailed the active participation of all its members. It was also a bottom-up process, as specific groups, from intellectuals, businessmen and professionals, to workers, women, students and finally peasants, claimed membership in the nation, partly to pursue their own interests. Efforts to forge a modern China inevitably involved not only political questions such as the distribution of power and wealth, but also cultural questions. Indeed, ever more radical calls for political change also led to blanket condemnations of 'tradition' and 'the old culture'. Radicals regarded key Confucian values such as filiality and loyalism (loyalty to the emperor) as obstacles to the march of progress. The hierarchical assumptions of a settled agrarian civilization seemed incompatible with industrial modernity, or the values of equality and patriotism.

Nevertheless, attitudes toward family, state and society; ways of relating to other people and perceiving the world; and forms of artistic expression are never completely remade by mere revolution. The fact that today, in spite of China's mega-cities, the vast majority of people remain in the countryside – 800 million, though by no means are all of them full-time farmers – suggests that neither Communist nor post-Communist modernization schemes have completely remade society. That a distant bureaucracy is trying to impose its will on thousands of local societies even suggests a certain continuity with the ancient imperial political structure, although today's party-state is nothing like the ancient court. This chapter thus begins with a look at premodern social and political structures, not to suggest that they never changed but to show how they influenced the dramatic changes of the twentieth century, which in turn continue to influence China today.

Sociopolitical structures of the Qing

In 1644 a Manchu-led coalition of forces from the northeast, outside the Great Wall, led an invasion of China that created the Qing dynasty, the latest dynasty in a line of 'orthodox succession' that traditional historiographers have traced back (somewhat mythically) 4,000 years. The Qing outdid all its predecessors in building a vast empire that included much of Mongolia, Central Asia and Tibet, though these regions were largely left to their own devices. In China proper (south of the Great Wall and east of the Central Asian deserts and plateaus) the Qing simply laid a new level of administrators – trusted Manchus and Chinese alike – on top of the existing social structure. As under the earlier Ming dynasty (1368–1644), a gentry (*shi*) class of landowning families (and wealthy merchants – there was no strict division between landed and commercial wealth) supplied most of the candidates for the civil service exams to staff the bureaucracy. The examinations tested knowledge of the Confucian classics and their commentaries. The *shi* thus saw themselves as men of culture. That is, they were cultivated men who had not only memorized the classics and understood their various commentaries, but were also broadly trained in what we might call a humanistic tradition: able to appreciate and write poetry, produce good calligraphy, understand art, and generally pursue a lifestyle of refinement. They also emphasized the importance of moral education and in their own view, at least, represented a moral elite as much as a social and cultural elite.

By the Qing, if not long before, it is possible to speak of common cultural practices across China, in spite of linguistic differences and regional variations. Popular opera, travelling story-tellers and published fiction recounted familiar historical and mythological material; the spread of schools functioned to create a shared repertoire of beliefs and customs. Male literacy, defined as knowledge of at least a few hundred characters, may have been as high as 40 per cent, a proportion comparable to eighteenth-century Britain and Japan. Common religious practices, Buddhist beliefs, and Confucian ethical and philosophical norms were all widespread. The family formed the root of social and economic activities. Clans or lineages defined themselves through written genealogies, although most property was essentially owned by individual households – that is, nuclear or slightly extended families living in the same house.

Social strains were becoming evident by the end of the eighteenth century. Although the overall economy had seen considerable growth, many areas were now suffering from overpopulation, as farm sizes shrank. Even among the gentry, the exams were producing more graduates than there were official posts for them. The systemic problems the Qing faced were becoming evident: above all, fiscal strains, an inability to finance local government, and the consequent rise of what was in effect tax farming by local gentry. The fundamental causes of the massive Taiping Rebellion of the mid-nineteenth century, which lasted fourteen years and resulted in the deaths of 20 million people, lay in peasant anger with taxes and rents, as well as the reservoirs of popular anti-Manchuism that had been dormant for two centuries in southern China. But the specific events that prompted the rebellion also had much to do with foreign pressures. British frigates and troops had handily defeated incompetent Qing resistance in the Opium War of the early 1840s, leading to a series of foreign assaults and demands on China that persisted through the first half of the twentieth century.

Over the following decades, while the Qing remained formally sovereign, the foreign powers demanded indemnities; built 'concessions' or mini-colonies, of which Shanghai was the most important; created 'zones of influence' over much wider territories; constructed military bases; and sent over soldiers, merchants and missionaries. The foreign powers set *and collected* China's import tariffs, in addition to managing loans to the fiscally strapped government. China was never wholly colonized, but neither was it truly independent. The revolutionary leader Sun Yat-sen (1866–1925) later claimed the situation was worse than colonialism because China was under the control of many foreign powers instead of just one. Chinese Marxists (and others) termed these conditions 'semi-colonial'. At the same time, the British-led consensus of the Western powers sought cooperation with the Qing, if only because outright colonialism would have led to unnecessary expenses and rivalries. By the 1860s, for its part, the Qing was ready to support modest reform efforts, particularly in the area of military modernization. Some officials also supported educational reform to include up-to-date sciences and foreign subjects, but as long as the examination system remained in place educational reforms were limited.

In retrospect, the late Qing reforms can be seen as the beginning of a century of efforts to thoroughly remake the Chinese polity, society and even culture. But the twin disasters of imperialist onslaught and domestic rebellion, if survivable in the short run, furthered troublesome trends. Increased localism was one such trend, as gentry took more responsibility for their own districts, first in resisting the Taipings and then to restore order in the wake of the rebellion. Yet another trend was the urbanization of the gentry. Facing the onslaught of angry Taipings, the gentry naturally fled their country properties and moved to towns and cities that were better protected. And reform-minded gentry began to discuss political questions. This was not unprecedented, but the Qing had allowed only top officials to discuss policy and only when the emperor asked them to – 'factions' were strictly prohibited. Now, however, members of the gentry were writing books about what made the Western countries successful, about 'public opinion' and parliaments, about reforming the examination system, about the need to Westernize the school curriculum, and so forth. Urban merchants and gentry were beginning to build a public sphere where they could literally talk to one another (in teahouses and brothels, for example); by the end of the century, newspapers and opinion journals were also widespread.

Political storms and social change in the early twentieth century

In many ways, the Qing system seemed to be functioning well enough by the early 1890s. Under official sponsorship, military modernization and a degree of economic modernization were taking place. But a sharp awakening came with the disastrous war with Japan over influence in Korea in 1894–5. China's military technology should have been a match for Japan's, but divided command, corruption and sheer incompetence doomed its war efforts. Taiwan was ceded to Japan outright, and Japan's victory set off a more naked 'scramble for concessions' as the powers established de facto sovereignty over large regions that included rights to natural resources and railroad construction. China's defeat at the hands of the upstart Japanese shocked the political elite and quickly fuelled cries for more radical reforms. Under these circumstances, a group of younger gentry who had connections with powerful statesmen was suddenly able to set the political agenda. They are best called radical Confucians, Kang Youwei (1858–1927) preaching that Confucius himself had been a reformer and a visionary who foresaw the unfolding of time toward a utopian future. Using this evolutionary framework, Kang preached that China was ready for institutional reforms that would lead to a constitutional monarchy and eventually to full democracy. With the support of the court faction surrounding the Guangxu emperor, Kang and his disciples were able to launch the '100 days of reform' in the summer of 1898. A blizzard of edicts appeared in the emperor's name, shaking up the bureaucracy, the military and the educational system.

These edicts, modest as they appear in retrospect, threatened the political status quo in two ways. First, the bureaucracy was being told that it must abide by new standards, and thousands of students were being told that the Confucian classics they had laboured over for so long were no longer the route to an official career. And second, the Manchu court feared that Han Chinese would take over the highest levels of the Qing government. And so the Empress Dowager Cixi, in control of the court since the 1870s, moved to suppress the movement, execute its leaders and imprison Guangxu (her nephew – Cixi's power was based on previous years of serving as regent). The defeat of the reforms in September

1898 led directly to the Boxer Uprising, which Cixi decided not to suppress. The Boxers, north Chinese peasants, had their own pressing concerns, which had nothing to do with court politics or gentry intellectuals. North China was experiencing a prolonged drought. Thousands of peasants joined armies of men and women who attacked local missionaries and Chinese Christians and unsteadily made their way to Beijing. At the root of the movement was a social panic exacerbated by the drought. Prayers to the traditional gods were going unheeded, it was said, because of the pollution of the Christians. Beyond that, rumours spoke of Christians poisoning village wells; missionaries were said to be devils who practised incest, raped at random, and tore out the organs of Chinese for their evil magic – in other words, the embodiment of all that people feared.

Cixi and her conservative court supporters thought the Boxers represented popular support. In fact, the Qing had lost control of the situation in much of north China, although conditions in the south were unaffected. Finally, a well-publicized military expedition by the foreign powers, including Japan, put an end to the Boxers and issued new demands on the Qing. Cixi was allowed to return to Beijing, while China was assessed another 450 million silver taels in indemnities – nearly US$334 million at the time (equivalent to roughly 8,000 million dollars today). This was far more than the Qing treasury held; China was to pay it on an instalment plan, over 39 years at 4 per cent interest, bringing the total to nearly 1,000 million taels. (In the end, China never paid the entire sum, and the powers returned some of what was paid to China in the form of educational aid.) The point here is that after the Boxers, a broken, and very broke, Qing court finally resolved on serious reforms. While continuing to consider any criticism a matter of treason, the Qing's 'New Policy' reforms ironically revived the proposals of 1898. In 1905 the court even promised a constitution (some day); and in an even greater break with the past it abolished the examination system. New officials were to be recruited from the graduates of modern schools. But with Cixi's death in 1908, obscurantist and incompetent Manchus came to control the court, and the reforms – already under attack as too little too late – lost whatever steam they had.

Modern intellectuals emerged out of radical Confucianism's effort to strengthen the state in the 1890s. They began to think about how to mobilize the people, weighing the advantages of various new social, political and institutional arrangements. Ultimately, late Qing intellectuals questioned the entire cosmological order of traditional thought. Preeminent among this generation was Liang Qichao (1873–1929), Kang Youwei's foremost disciple. After the disaster of 1898, Liang fled to Japan and began putting some distance between himself and Kang. Liang dropped his explicit devotion to Confucianism. 'Truth' mattered more, he told Kang, though in fact he continued to follow many Confucian ideas. Between 1898 and the 1911 Revolution, Liang proffered discussions of the latest political thinking in Europe and Japan that influenced both officials and the growing number of revolutionaries. Liang's advocacy of reform scared the court, while it did not go far enough for the revolutionaries, but his voice was, above all, the voice of nationalism. Reformers wanted schools, popular literacy campaigns, novels, even poetry to be devoted to patriotism.

Reformers wanted to abandon the traditional cosmology that linked the emperor and Heaven and Humanity. Liang taught that the age was best explained by the relentless dictum of social Darwinism: progress or perish, or survival of the fittest. Historically, he explained Britain's rise as a new kind of 'national imperialism': not expansionism by military leaders but of the whole nation. Only if China could respond in kind would its resistance be successful. Liang thus advocated the creation of the 'new citizen', who would be active, courageous and loyal. Every individual should be a full member of the political community, recognizing both their rights and their duties. Nonetheless, Liang also feared excessive individualism, and here his lingering Confucianism proved useful in emphasizing an ethics of unselfishness. He feared that revolution would bring chaos and chaos would leave China completely prostrate before the imperialist powers.

For their part, the revolutionaries, who sought to overthrow the Qing, agreed with Liang about the basic need for nationalism, but defined it differently. They believed that the majority Chinese Han 'race' needed to throw out the Manchu overlords in order to install a republican government. Revolutionary students and intellectuals adopted the language of race and national self-determination that had become global by the end of the nineteenth century. Yet the concept of nation-state, after all, if carried to its logical extreme, would postulate that Manchus, Tibetans, Uyghurs and other groups should each have their own homeland like the Han. Few revolutionaries could countenance this; once the revolution was successful, the partitioning of China was not on the agenda. After the 1911 Revolution, the former revolutionaries turned to a vision of a multi-ethnic China, but they had already taught the vast majority in China proper to think of themselves as 'Han'.

The revolutionaries also paid great attention to what they called the 'national essence', a term adopted from the Japanese. Some of the leading anti-Manchu intellectuals such as Zhang Binglin (1868–1937) devoted their scholarship to the history of the Han race and its culture. They thus defined Chineseness in terms of cultural traditions – the high culture of literature, history and philosophy – and enlarged the traditional canon to include the other ancient schools of thought and Buddhism. How China could remain 'Chinese' in cultural terms even as it modernized is a question that has preoccupied intellectuals since the late Qing. One answer, as we have seen, was to reformulate Confucianism. Yet many intellectuals rejected Confucianism as a belief system, some turning instead to Buddhism, others rooting their identity as Chinese in history itself.

Finally, the revolutionaries were also republicans and something like socialists. China's crisis forced intellectuals to re-examine their assumptions about the nature of society. Aside from getting rid of the Manchus, what was revolution for? Did democratic ideals refer only to political participation or did they imply a deeper equality? More practically, how exactly would 'the people' run the new government? In the course of revolutionary praxis, several attempts were made to reach across class barriers. The populist stand of revolutionaries such as Sun Yat-sen was reflected in their appeal to secret societies, though most intellectuals and students shared little more than anti-Manchuism with the peasants and petty traders who sought protection in secret societies. Chinese anarchists called for 'social revolution' in the name of the workers and peasants, and envisioned a future in which boundaries of nation, class and gender had all been abolished and decision-making was in the hands of the 'whole people'.

The decade before the 1911 Revolution thus saw the rise of a new social group composed of students and intellectuals. This was a loose category encompassing both men and women who were able to express themselves in the public realm. They differed from the old gentry in their self-image as modern, in rejecting the verities of classical learning, and in their reliance on new institutions – the education system, the publishing industry, journalism, and political and other civic associations. They inherited both public respect from the old Confucian regard for education, and a reciprocal sense of responsibility for public service. Not coincidently, the decade before the 1911 Revolution saw an explosion in fiction-writing. Story-telling was an ancient art, but to traditional Confucians fiction had long been slightly suspect. Poetry, history, belles-lettres and above all philosophical commentary were proper forms of self-expression. However, short stories and novels began to proliferate around the turn of the twentieth century in newspaper literary supplements, student journals and bookstores. Fiction seemed the ideal way to explore the new world of confusing social change and the dilemmas facing youth. Women used fiction to highlight the horrors perpetuated by the patriarchy. Translations were also popular and perhaps helped introduce Western ideas. At the same time, romances, chivalry and science fiction also served as popular forms of imaginative escape. Late Qing fiction was a precursor to the even more self-consciously modern literature of the 1920s and 1930s.

As well as intellectuals, new social forces taking shape in the late Qing included capitalists and workers. Small when compared to China's overall population, these groups dominated urban areas, particularly treaty-ports. If Western capitalists had the advantage in raising funds, access to technology, and dealing with the government, the Chinese bourgeoisie had a certain advantage in low-tech industries, knowledge of local conditions and marketing. Politically, the bourgeoisie feared disorder but was sympathetic to patriotic appeals, and found it necessary to work with the warlords and foreign powers who had the final word on taxes, infrastructure, and even market conditions. Still, the bourgeoisie saw itself as progressive, for through industry China would be saved.

Workers in the Qing were generally craftsmen and transport labourers, but the construction of modern factories created a modern proletariat. By the 1910s, over 1.5 million workers worked in large-scale factories, railroads and shipping. As in other countries, women and children were recruited into factories as a more pliable labour force wherever possible. And as in other countries, hours were long and conditions dangerous. Early labour actions depended on native-place and ethnic ties. Nonetheless, in time workers came to identify less with their original village and more with their new residence – cities such as Shanghai, Tianjin, Wuhan and Guangzhou – and with their fellow workers. Proletarianization gave rise to a rhetoric of class conflict. The role of intellectuals and political organizers was indispensable in this, but workers were active agents in their own cause.

Women also represented a new social group. For they emerged into the public sphere with radicals' criticisms of Confucian social norms.

While gentry families – in some cases – had long educated their daughters, women's education did not begin to become widely accepted until the end of the Qing. The abolition of footbinding was another critical cause. Liang Qichao and others argued that China needed healthy, educated women to raise proper citizens. There was also concern that women should be able to earn a living, both to contribute to the national economy and for their own sakes. The nationalist cause thus justified the women's movement without necessarily promising full equality. A small number of radical women emphasized that their duties to the nation were not to be confined to serving the nation passively (as workers and mothers) but necessarily included personal empowerment. Yet in the wake of the 1911 Revolution, women were denied suffrage. Urban women did take jobs in business and the professions, divorce became easier, and the notion of free marriage spread rapidly, but in the countryside women's lives changed little.

Another new group whose role was to prove momentous was the military. The traditional armies were composed of either Manchu bannermen born into the profession or Chinese recruited from the lowest elements of society. Neither had proved competent in the nineteenth century, but efforts to build a modern, disciplined, well-equipped and proud force were unremitting. The new schools also featured physical education classes and games, signifying a new attitude towards the body that was rooted in militaristic desire. Young men of good families now decided to devote their careers to military service in another break with Confucian tradition. Only with the rise of warlordism in 1910 did militarism begin to be regarded as a curse, and even then the image of the good soldier truly committed to the nation remained powerfully appealing. The Communists brought the glorification of militaristic self-sacrifice to its apogee, and the figure of the soldier continues to play a major part in Chinese culture even today.

The 1911 Revolution ended the dynastic system, but it led to dictatorship, warlordism and further revolution. It was the final blow for the *shi*, those gentry who had studied the classics for years, taken the exams, and identified with the monarchy. The revolution did change some aspects of everyday life, at least in the cities: Chinese were soon seeing a new calendar, new hair styles as men cut off their Manchu-style queues, and new rituals of citizenship, such as making sacrifices to revolutionary martyrs, celebrating the new National Day, and displaying the national flag and singing national songs.[1] Perhaps most importantly, the 1911 Revolution further mobilized the new social groups: students and intellectuals, workers, women, the bourgeoisie and certainly the military, all of whom were to shape China's twentieth century.

Revolution renewed: the Nationalist and Communist movements

Politically, the early Republic first became a dictatorship under Yuan Shikai (1859–1916), a Qing (Han Chinese) general who promptly tried to found a new dynasty, and then slid into warlordism upon Yuan's death. Culturally, the early Republic was a period of tumultuous and cacophonous change. For intellectuals, the evils of imperialism and bad government were combined. But with the Manchus off the scene, there were no convenient scapegoats. Stunned by the debacle of Yuan Shikai's presidency and disillusioned with the revolution, in 1915 a number of leading intellectuals called for a moratorium on political activities. Their goal was to build a 'New Culture' for China first. 'The revolution of earlier years [1911] was a revolution in forms; now the revolution must be one of spirit,' wrote the Japanese-educated political scientist Gao Yihan (1884–1968). 'Our people already know full well how to carry out a revolution in political institutions; they do not yet know how to carry out a revolution in political spirit and educational principles.'[2] Chen Duxiu (1879–1942), dean at Beijing University, condemned Confucianism for poisoning the people's minds with superstitious respect for fathers and rulers that left them unable to appreciate democratic and egalitarian ideals. Chen promoted Western values in the names of 'Mr Democracy' and 'Mr Science' but also criticized Western nationalism and elitist social systems. Social Darwinism remained a key worldview, and the most idealistic of intellectuals was aware that China had to survive in a cutthroat world. But Darwinism also seemed to support the notion of humanitarian progress: that the world was moving in a more democratic and egalitarian direction.

In 1917 Hu Shi (1891–1962), a student of John Dewey, published a careful proposal for writing in the vernacular rather than the difficult and allusive classical language. He argued (in classical Chinese) that the vernacular offered not simply a way to reach the people, but a way for writers themselves to think more clearly by using a more direct style. The 'vernacular movement' grew to form the core of a new Chinese culture, replacing classical Chinese in the way the national languages of the European Renaissance replaced Latin as living embodiments of literature, philosophy and social concerns. Over the next few decades, the spare and allusive classical grammar disappeared from most publications, beginning with school books. The 1920s also saw an explosion of vernacular prose fiction and journalism. The short stories of masters such as Lu Xun expressed the New Culture's critique of tradition, while capturing much of the reality of urban life; escapist romances were also popular with the growing middle class.

The May Fourth Movement of 1919 reinvigorated political activism. Students in Beijing on that date protested the decision of the Paris (Versailles) Peace Conference that turned the German concession in Shandong over to the Japanese at the close of World War I. They were also protesting their own Beijing government's consent to the treaty and were aware of Tokyo's ties to leading Chinese politicians. The movement soon spread to Shanghai, where merchants and workers boycotted Japanese goods and factories. Culturally, 'May Fourth' ratified New Culture's attacks on Confucianism and the 'evils' of the family while simultaneously shaping a new kind of citizen's politics. It brought the power of student street demonstrations into touch with bourgeois and worker nationalism.

Chinese businessmen resented low tariffs and White racism, but their sharpest competitors were often Japanese. Boycotts of Japanese goods thus made economic sense to some Chinese businessmen – though not to those who worked for Japanese companies or imported Japanese goods. Similarly, for workers it made little difference materially if they worked in a Chinese company or a foreign company. Yet the appeals of nationalism undoubtedly had their own force, and the willingness of students to make sacrifices influenced other groups as well. Students started schools for workers and helped them manage strike funds. At the same time, while urban residents shared Nationalist sentiments and even warlords proclaimed their patriotic goals, people also had to make pragmatic choices about how they were to survive.

After a few months, the boycotts and strikes petered out, but in this fervid atmosphere of disgust with the imperialist powers and warlordism, revolutionary forces took new shape. Over the course of the early 1920s both the Nationalist Party (Guomindang, GMD) and the Chinese Communist Party (CCP) emerged as tightly structured, ideologically committed organizations. Both parties sought mass support, particularly among urban workers. Sun Yat-sen's GMD, based in Guangzhou, was a minor warlord player in its own right, dreaming of a 'Northern Expedition' that would reunite China. What made this dream even remotely possible was Russian aid. In the wake of the Russian Revolution, Lenin sought ways to keep the world revolution on track. By striking the capitalist powers where it hurt – their colonial enterprises that provided raw materials, cheap labour and markets – colonized peoples (including colonial bourgeoisie) would be allying themselves with the industrial proletariats. Representatives of the Communist International (Comintern) snuck into China in 1920 and worked with radical intellectuals to begin to form the CCP. And the Comintern found a willing 'bourgeois' ally in the GMD, at least after the Western powers and Japan rejected Sun Yat-sen's overtures. From 1924 to 1927 the Comintern gave the GMD financial aid, arms and, perhaps most importantly, over 100 advisors familiar with the nitty-gritty work of political organizing. The GMD built up its own army, staffed by Japanese-trained officers such as Chiang Kai-shek (1887–1975). Officers and soldiers alike were subject to strict ideological training.

In return, Sun had to accept Communists into the much larger GMD. Thus began the First United Front between the GMD and the CCP, which lasted from 1924 to 1927. Sun denied that Marxist Communism was suitable for China, a position that the CCP was forced to accept – for the time being. What Sun taught was the 'Three People's Principles' – these were updated from the version propagated in the 1911 Revolution. In particular, *nationalism* now referred to anti-imperialism (not anti-Manchuism). *Democracy* was largely envisioned as parliamentary politics with a strong executive, while Sun suggested that a period of 'tutelage' or military dictatorship would bridge the parlous gap between revolutionary victory and eventual democracy. *People's livelihood* remained a vague sort of state socialism that emphasized the development of infrastructure and heavy industry. For Sun, China's poverty stemmed from a lack of production, not inequality; others in the GMD as well as the CCP emphasized the importance of increasing both production and equality.

But before victory it would be necessary to harness revolutionary energies wherever they could be found. Students were one source; workers another. Both Nationalists and Communists reached out to Shanghai's hundreds of thousands of labourers. Tensions were already high in 1925 when a Japanese factory foreman killed a worker in a scuffle; at street demonstrations on 30 May, British police fired into the crowd, killing thirteen people and injuring many more. A general strike – especially successful in Shanghai and Guangzhou – and demonstrations followed in what became known as the 'May Thirtieth Movement'. Workers were even supported by the Chinese Chamber of Commerce, at least through the summer. The strike was finally called off in September.

The May Thirtieth Movement could not claim many concrete successes but it was as important as the earlier May Fourth Movement. It fuelled the rapid growth of both the GMD and the CCP. By the end of 1925 the GMD could put over 60,000 trained troops in the field. Sun Yat-sen died in March 1925, paving the way for Chiang Kai-shek to dominate the party as the Northern Expedition finally got under way. Meanwhile, the movement of gentry to the cities had left behind a kind of power vacuum in the countryside. In a pattern dating back to the late Qing, village leaders were caught in a dilemma: protect the village or accede to outside demands.[3] The state might increase revenues, but it crushed village autonomy. In turn, the state's legitimacy was weakened as its intrusive demands decimated the traditional rural elites that were its natural supporters. New village leaders ran things by force: this is the structural origin of the 'local bullies' cited endlessly in the political rhetoric of the day.

CCP-organized peasant groups were one element in the early success of the Northern Expedition, which fought its way up to the Yangzi. Then, in early 1927 CCP-led workers overthrew the warlord regime of Chinese Shanghai. Chiang, however, broke with the Communists in April; Communists were then hunted down and executed. In addition, Chiang had essentially staged a coup against significant elements of the GMD itself. He had made a fundamental choice about how radical the nationalist revolution was going to be – not very. Once in power, moving the national capital to Nanjing, Chiang sought to govern on a corporatist model, infiltrating and controlling civic organizations from unions to chambers of commerce. The GMD's success during the 'Nanjing Decade' (1928–37) was less than complete – many regional authorities were in fact old warlords only nominally answering to Nanjing. Still, Nanjing could claim the land taxes of five or six central provinces. Chiang thus had a basis on which he could build stronger state institutions. However, the GMD remained a quasi-Leninist party dedicated to ideological indoctrination, discipline and revolutionary mobilization on the one hand, and a lumbering bureaucracy that overlapped with purely state institutions on the other. The result was a combination of coercion and 'party-fication' (*danghua*) whereby institutions such as schools were to be ideologically remoulded. Unfortunately for the Nationalists, the Japanese invasion of Manchuria in September 1931, followed by six years of further incursions into northern China, deprived the GMD party-state of much of its legitimacy. Patriotic anger was resistant to party-fication.

Intellectuals, too, were to be party-fied, but the GMD had a difficult time enforcing the Three People's Principles. Liberals resisted on the grounds that their criticisms would help the government in the long run. And a surprising number of leftists, some secret CCP members and some outside the Party, managed to publish stories and poems, make films and produce art critical of the status quo. Intellectuals and artists alike portrayed the decadence of the cities and the human ruin of the countryside. Indeed, the 1930s saw a kind of discovery of the countryside by educated Chinese. Whether depicting proletarians or peasants, many artists sought to 'go to the masses'.

The CCP was nearly exterminated, but a few Communists did manage to create rural base areas somewhat protected from Nationalist pressures. In the early 1930s the Jiangxi Soviet was built up under the leadership of Mao Zedong (1893–1976). It was Mao – with no help from superiors in the CCP or from the Comintern – who broke with Marxist orthodoxy by forging a small Red Army out of bandits and former GMD troops, and who foresaw that it might be possible to recruit and indoctrinate peasant volunteers. Mao realized that the Jiangxi Soviet had to become a functioning government. Peasants tied to the land would not support the Communists if they thought the Red Army would move away and abandon them. The CCP also faced the daunting task of turning remote hill country into a stable economy capable of supporting itself. Thus radical land reform – confiscating all land and turning it over to 'poor peasants' – was self-defeating. Rather, *moderate* land reform was key to maintaining the productive energies of 'middle peasants' (without disaffecting 'rich peasants' too much).

These categories of rural class were invented in an ad hoc manner and did not necessarily fit complex local conditions. Still, essentially, landlords were defined as owners of land who rented it out but did not labour themselves. The Communists expropriated their land and distributed it to those who did not have enough. Rich peasants had a little more land than they could farm themselves; their excess land was expropriated but they were allowed to keep what they actually farmed. Middle peasants, who farmed their own land, were left alone. Poor peasants were defined as families who had to rent all or most of the land they farmed – and were to be given expropriated land. Mao frankly stated that peasants wanted land and the revolution would give it to them, and in return they would support the revolution. For peasants, land reform was not a passive process whereby they waited for outside Communists to give them land – how would outsiders even know who owned what land? Rather, the Communists found activists among the peasants who would lead their fellow villagers to denounce landlords and rich peasants, and in a series of village meetings determine who should get what. Land reform, carried out with violence or the threat of violence, was thus key to peasant mobilization.

When Chiang Kai-shek finally turned the full force of GMD armies on the Jiangxi Soviet in 1934, the Communists were forced on the 'Long March', which eventually brought them to the even more remote country of Yan'an, in Shanxi Province to the northwest. Here, Mao emerged as the leader of the CCP, resumed contact with the Soviet Union, built up the base area, and prepared for war with Japan. The CCP's popular anti-Japanese stance brought it student volunteers from across China, not unlike the situation of the GMD in the early 1920s. Chiang resisted calls for war with Japan, stating that it was necessary to defeat the Communists first. But when he was kidnapped by an anti-Japanese general (one of the GMD's imperfectly assimilated warlords) in December 1936, the Second United Front took shape. Japan invaded China proper in the summer of 1937. After about a year of intense fighting, the Nationalist government was pushed deep into the interior of China. By 1939, the rich heartlands and industrialized sectors of eastern China were under Japanese occupation; the poorer southwest Yangzi highlands under GMD control; and the even poorer northwest loess lands under the CCP. Twelve years of war and revolution followed the Japanese invasion. Thousands of battles and arguably thousands of revolutions – village by village – slowly strengthened the CCP, while the GMD decayed.

The war years allowed the CCP to build up a number of base areas both beyond Japanese lines and inside them. The Japanese, in spite of vastly superior troops and munitions, became bogged down in China. The CCP swelled to 1.2 million members, and the Communist armies grew to almost a million soldiers. The Communists were able to appeal both to nationalist sentiments and to the economic interests of poor peasants. Students, intellectuals and the urban populace in general were already anti-Japanese. Peasants, however, did not necessarily care to whom they paid taxes – what difference did it make to farmers' lives? Peasants were concerned with community grievances against the state, whatever that state was. In some cases, Japanese atrocities created anti-Japanese sentiment in the countryside, but harsh measures – such as burning down entire villages – also produced resentful acquiescence.

Perhaps the single most important ingredient in the Communist Revolution was the CCP's ability to provide responsible government in the northern Chinese countryside. What the CCP offered peasants during the war was not, strictly speaking, revolution. Instead of redistributing land, the Communists were forced to build functioning economic systems that provided what many peasants wanted most – security – while they gradually redistributed wealth in ways that seemed reasonable even to many of the rich. Communist policy was to reduce rents to 37.5 per cent of harvests, down from the usual 50 per cent or more; equally significant, interest rates on loans were reduced to 1.5 per cent a month. Progressive taxation and village elections profoundly changed village power structures. Wealth and power shifted from a few top families to a broader spectrum of middle and poor peasants in the course of a few years. This was a process that mobilized peasant activists village by village, and created a vast reservoir of support for the Communists across the northern countryside.

Soon after the war with Japan ended in 1945, the civil war began, and CCP policies turned more radical, mobilizing peasants to attack 'landlords' (including collaborators) and confiscate all their property. Peasants thus had to continue fighting for their gains: if the GMD returned, they might be killed. In the final analysis, the GMD, squandering its advantages of wealth and numbers, probably did more to lose the civil war than the CCP did to win it. The Nationalists returned to the cities as conquerors more than liberators, rampant inflation destroyed livelihoods, and Chiang Kai-shek's incompetent generalship left GMD troops overextended.

Still, the far-sighted leadership of the CCP was critical. Even in the middle of the anti-Japanese war, Mao Zedong paid attention to cultural matters. The 'rectification campaign' of 1942 was partly about suppressing dissent and partly about instilling a new 'style' of leadership in the future ruling elite, the Communist cadres. Gone would be the arrogance and smugness of the old literati; gone would be pedantry and physical laziness; gone, above all, would be the selfishness and clannishness that marked the old gentry. Given the growth of the CCP, which had attracted idealistic but overly critical students on the one hand, and practical but potentially corrupt peasants on the other, it was deemed necessary to indoctrinate members through small-group study and 'self-criticism'. Self-criticism had its roots in the Confucian desire to achieve sagehood, but now became a public, even state matter. Artists and writers were a particular target of rectification; they were not only to portray workers and peasants in their work: they were to 'serve the masses' and 'be at one with the masses'. The CCP was preparing to rule China. Literature and the arts were never neutral: they were always an 'ideological weapon'.

Epilogue: Maoist and post-Maoist China

The revolutionary energies of the CCP were by no means exhausted with victory – or 'liberation' – in 1949. After the horrors of war – at least 20 million dead, some 95 million refugees, and untold property damage – millions of people committed themselves to remaking China, to a 'new China'. In some respects, revolutionary forces were not played out until Mao's death in 1976. Under Mao, these forces contributed to consolidating state powers, and to penetrating and disciplining society. By the mid-1950s the government had nationalized industry and collectivized farms. While 'bad classes' such as landlords and capitalists were excluded from the body politic, the Chinese as a whole were promised that they would become rich after a period of hard work.

Rural cadres brought the new party-state into villages in a way the old gentry never could. As a result, the state was able to extract agricultural resources (essentially, taxes paid in kind) for investment in urban industry. The extent of the party-state's ability to penetrate society can be seen in the Great Leap Forward (1958–60), which led to the starvation of perhaps 30 million people. The GLF began as a massive production drive – double-cropping, planting wastelands, digging wells, building pig iron factories – promising the utopian dream of a world of plenty. In the event, overcrowded crops died, the wells dried up, and the brittle iron was useless – but Mao, his reputation at stake, refused to stop the GLF until it was too late to avoid a disaster that took years to recover from.

The Communists froze society. Peasants were not allowed to leave their communes; urban workers became a somewhat privileged class with better access to housing, health care, schools, pensions and urban entertainment. Outside the party-state/society division and the urban/rural division, Maoist China was relatively egalitarian. The fundamental institutions of the new China were the commune in the countryside and the 'work unit' (*danwei*) in the cities. A commune was as large as the old counties with up to 200,000 residents, but most peasants continued to farm village lands (as 'workteams') and live in nuclear families. A work unit was not merely a place of employment but usually provided housing, food and even education for its members. Another piece of the institutional framework was a permanent class-label system: police dossiers kept track of one's class background. And both criminals and dissidents were incarcerated in work camps where, in addition to providing unpaid labour, they were subject to 're-education'. The Maoist years saw periodic mass campaigns whereby the 'masses' were mobilized to criticize named targets ('rightists') or achieve production targets. The most remarkable mass campaigns were the GLF and the Cultural Revolution (1966–9), but campaigns were a nearly constant feature of life.

Mass campaigns also functioned to destroy many vestiges of traditional culture, or at least to force a range of practices, from popular religion to classical poetry, underground. The regime deliberately destroyed much of what was left of the old society. The family survived – and the nuclear family, at least, was even strengthened in some ways, as its members were often the only ones individuals could trust not to betray them during criticism campaigns. But the old lineage associations and temple societies that had controlled so much of rural China were swept away in the rising waters of collective farms and communes. Above all, the old marketing systems that had supported much of rural life during the Qing were abolished. The institutions of everyday life separated people into villages or communes and work units like independent 'cells' that were coordinated by higher authorities, although mass campaigns brought people together, at least at times.[4] Aside from cadres and urban workers, those who could claim the class labels of *poor* or *lower-middle* peasants benefited. Their chances of achieving cadre status in the commune were improved, and they were somewhat protected from criticism during mass campaigns. They constituted the 'masses' and in effect claimed full citizenship.

Like the 'bad classes', intellectuals were often hounded by the new state. They were subject to extensive re-education and underwent many rounds of self-criticism. But unlike, say, landlords, they remained essential to the new China's educational system, its propaganda system and its economic system. In the humanities and social sciences, the scope for independent research was reduced to almost nil. Artists faced persecution ranging from public humiliation to years of labour camp for the merest implication of criticism. Some 300,000 persons were labelled 'rightists' in the anti-rightist campaign of 1957, for example, and imprisoned. The lack of a Soviet-style tradition of *samizdat* resistance in Maoist China is sometimes attributed to the Chinese Confucian tradition of identification with the state, and it is true that many modern intellectuals continued to believe in the revolution even when they were persecuted by it. But even then at times voices of cautious dissent could be heard in literature, art and even academic disciplines such as history. One example is a 1959 historical study (later turned into a play) about the despotic Ming Taizu (r. 1368–98: read Mao) and his honest but critical minister Hai Rui (read loyal party cadres). This was not exactly a stirring call for popular resistance or even a critique of the Communist system, but it was enough to call forth Mao's ire. This play was one of the factors that prompted Mao to call for a 'Cultural Revolution', which, among other things, was an attack on his opponents in the Party.

Virtually all survivors of the Maoist era were both victims and collaborators. This is clearly seen in the Cultural Revolution (CR), which began as yet another ritualized mass campaign. Yet it was soon deritualized, leading to near-chaos in the cities and many rural areas, and at least indirectly delegitimating the Maoist regime. This time, to sum it up in a simple formula, accused rightists fought back, accusing their accusers of rightism. At first, only children of good class backgrounds became Red Guards, and they attacked not cadres but the usual intellectuals (teachers were an early target) and capitalists. But a second phase of the CR, clearly encouraged by Mao to help him in his power struggle with other leaders, emerged when new Red Guards began to attack the original Red Guards. These new 'rebel Red Guards' often did not come from 'red' backgrounds and had faced systematic discrimination even though they, too, believed in the virtues of the new Maoist society. They attacked as un-Communist the privileges granted to cadres (and cadres' children). This line also had great appeal for workers and workers' children, who felt oppressed by the work-unit system and threatened by the power of officials. As early as mid-1967, Red Guard factionalism had spread to factories, government work units and even the countryside. Actual street fighting was threatening to get out of control. So-called 'ultra-leftist anarchism' was too much for Mao to accept, and he brought in the Army to restore order, a project completed by 1969. Anywhere from 500,000 to more than a million people died during the course of the CR: many were beaten to death by Red Guards and many committed suicide, but most were killed by the Army. Millions of urban youths were 'sent down' to the countryside, where they faced unimagined privations that contradicted everything they had believed about the accomplishments of the revolution.

If today's leaders of China have their way, the Cultural Revolution will prove to be the last of a series of traumas besetting the Chinese since the nineteenth century. The CR, though a political struggle, was so named in deliberate emulation of the attack on tradition of the New Culture movement in the 1910s. Since the CR disproportionately victimized intellectuals, cadres and ultimately urban youth, it actually created the very counter-revolutionary sentiment, albeit still not made explicit, that it had been designed to forestall. Ultimately, people learned to think more critically, even while the CR left widespread disillusionment with any kind of revolution.

At the same time, it was becoming clear that although China's GDP was growing, average incomes were not. The Maoist economy had made real strides, partly thanks to mass mobilization: general if rudimentary improvements in education, infrastructure and health care served as the basis for steady if slow growth in agricultural output and stronger growth in industry. But by the 1970s, due to the inefficiencies of central planning, more and more capital was required just to maintain production levels. Worker discontent over stagnant wages was rising. Workers and especially peasants lacked incentives. The countryside suffered from structural problems: due to the decision to try to make each region economically autarchic, planting crops unsuitable to local conditions was endemic, and above all, the government's taxes (i.e. compulsory purchases of grain) were too high. Villagers were left with only enough for subsistence.

With the death of Mao in 1976, China was ready for the reforms of Deng Xiaoping (1904–97). Within just a few years, the new CCP leadership had destroyed the Maoist system and given China an economically dynamic market economy. Though still a poor country, China's GDP has grown by 9 to 12 per cent a year since 1978, the fastest rate in the world. However, while China steadily replaced central planning with markets in the 1980s and 1990s, the state retains a major role in building infrastructure, directing investment and as final landowner; the Chinese economy has become more or less capitalist but is hardly neo-liberal. Official ideology proclaims that China is not capitalist but following 'socialism with Chinese characteristics' and 'market socialism' that will eventually lead to true socialism. As a description of contemporary China this is nonsense, but it does justify the party-state's political control.

The post-Maoist state abandoned efforts to police every aspect of society, hoping to police critical aspects all the more successfully – critical aspects such as limits on dissent and the one-child policy. Political elites deliberately reduced intrusive institutions such as mass campaigns, criticism and self-criticism rituals, ideological controls and the thought police, and even class dossiers. But controls were not eliminated entirely. Household registration, for example, was relaxed to allow rural people to move to cities; however, migrants still find it difficult to get housing, send their children to public schools, or receive medical or unemployment benefits.

Two decades of reform resulted in the 're-emergence' of society as a vibrant sphere of more or less autonomous action. China today appears to have many features in common with the society of the early twentieth century, or perhaps the Nanjing Decade. China again sees migrants streaming in from the countryside for any kind of job (100 million by the beginning of the twenty-first century); cruel exploitation in factories; a major role in world trade, stemming from its cheap manufactures; and armies of beggars and prostitutes. Many people live on the edge, with no guarantees of schooling, health care or pensions. Professionals, however, have also returned to China's urban mix, produced by both China's own universities and foreign universities. Of course, there are also major differences from the past. China's elites are in a much stronger position, and government at every level is stronger than it was in the warlord era, or even the Nanjing Decade. And China's position in the world is much stronger too. It is true that by the beginning of the twenty-first century the government faced numerous protests, demonstrations, and even riots, but such incidents are kept local; any attempts to organize on a national scale are suppressed. It is possible that protests, generally aimed at specific local issues such as land grabs or environmental degradation, act to let off steam; it is certain that the rise of consumer culture deflects attention from political questions.

The first great reform of the Dengist era, in place by the early 1980s, amounted to a return to family farming. In no small part, farmers took things into their own hands, decollectivizing the communes and daring the government to intervene. Dengist policy systematized decollectivization and the revival of rural markets. Peasants do not 'own' the lands they farm but lease them from the state and, after paying their taxes, can sell their produce. Reforms of industry came more slowly – if most peasants were glad to see decollectivization, workers feared losing their privileges.

After a brief slowing of the pace of reform in the wake of the violent suppression of the Tiananmen Square democracy demonstrations in 1989, the reforms resumed in the 1990s with ever greater encouragement of foreign investment and domestic entrepreneurship. Eventually, 'capitalists' (still an official category) were even welcomed into the Communist Party itself. Thus China's remarkable economic growth since the 1980s rested on a sharp break with Maoist institutions but also on the basis of the Maoist infrastructure.

With the Dengist reforms, people began to travel and find work on their own: the old cellular walls crumbled. One reason that marketization proceeded smoothly was that Maoist institutions had barely lasted a generation: people had not forgotten all the complex informal institutional arrangements necessary for trade. Yet while millions have moved out of poverty during the reform era, economic reforms have created losers as well as winners. Inequality has increased enormously over the past generation. Roughly speaking, those who have benefited most clearly from the reforms include successful entrepreneurs, state administrators, managers in the business sector and professionals. The clearest losers are unemployed or underemployed workers and peasants. Most peasants are better off in absolute terms than they were, say, in 1976, but rural incomes have been stagnant since 1985. Workers, too, benefit from a growing industrial sector. However, the suppression of independent unions means that wages are barely above subsistence, and that working conditions remain hard and dangerous. Similarly, the position of women has changed in complex ways: some have clearly benefited, while others have been forced into arranged marriages and prostitution. Migrant workers and ethnic minorities are particularly disenfranchised.

Another major externality of the reforms has been systemic pollution of air and water; the countryside has been no less vulnerable than the cities. Pollution has led to widespread cases of cancers and birth defects. Government leaders are well aware of these problems but the logic of pursuing GDP growth impedes efforts to find solutions. Their hope is that China can grow out of these problems economically while 'patriotism' fills the spiritual vacuum left by the death of Maoism.

For intellectuals and artists, the turn of the reform era has meant greater freedoms, within limits, as well as greater pressures to produce for the market. In effect, Dengist China privatized cultural production ranging from cosmopolitan high art and design to 'true crime' comics. An important symbolic move in the late 1970s was to clear the names of virtually all the 'rightists' who had been purged during the Maoist years. This was also the period when 'scar literature' emerged, exploring some of the traumas of the Cultural Revolution. Writers used fiction to examine the pain caused to individual families, although systematic exploration of the Party's role in the CR was not allowed. A space emerged where intellectuals and students could assume a cautiously critical stance. Talk of 'democracy' has never died out since the late Qing; in the latter phases of the Cultural Revolution, some Red Guards were thinking about how the law might regularize the unruly democratic potential of mass movements, and their ideas fuelled the short-lived democracy movements of the Dengist years. Today, academic journals are freer than newspapers, and newspapers are freer than films or pop music; the Internet is said to be policed by 40,000 monitors, not to mention software that automatically sniffs out suspicious sites (those dealing with Taiwan, Tibet, pornography, human rights, religion and political dissent). Essentially, the government today cares little about what people say, especially in private, although organized activities are an object of suspicion. Clubs for ballroom dancing, chess, English language and a thousand other innocuous activities are only loosely monitored; religious groups and non-governmental organizations (NGOs) for women's rights, poverty alleviation, organic farming and the like are more closely watched but tolerated; while outright political activity subjects its participants to instant arrest. Associational forms suppressed during the Maoist era, particularly lineages and local temples, have revived since the 1980s, but there are no independent political parties or labour unions. The government especially watches for any alliances between intellectuals and workers. These conditions also suit China's numerous foreign investors.

The violent suppression of the pro-democracy movement demonstrations at Tiananmen Square in 1989 was a shock to many intellectuals, but while many would like to see the government subject to a legal system, many also fear a rush to democratization. The party-state is transforming itself into a more technocratic and modernizing elite that eschews revolutionary utopianism. That said, proponents of capitalist growth have made rapturous promises that the Chinese will become a wealthy people. The old utopian dream thus continues in new, consumerist guise. In actuality, early twenty-first century China remains a poor country: GDP *per capita* was only around US$1,500–1,700 in 2005, even though *overall* GDP, according to official figures, surpassed Italy's, making China's economy the fourth largest in the world. Over the last century and a half, efforts to turn China into a cohesive nation and a powerful state have led down many twisting paths. Whether consumerist patriotism can serve as a binding ideology, and how ordinary people are to claim rights as citizens, are not, of course, questions that only Chinese face today. Chinese culture will continue to reflect these tensions in this new age of globalization.

Notes

1. Henrietta Harrison, *The Making of the Republican Citizen: Political Ceremonies and Symbols in China, 1911–1929*, New York, Oxford University Press, 1999.
2. Cited in Jerome B. Grieder, *Intellectuals and the State in Modern China*, New York, Free Press, 1981, pp. 225–6.
3. Prasenjit Duara, *Culture, Power, and the State: Rural North China, 1900–1942*, Stanford, Stanford University Press, 1988.
4. Vivienne Shue, *The Reach of the State: Sketches of the Chinese Body Politic*, Stanford, Stanford University Press, 1988.

Guide to further reading

Chang, Hao, *Liang Ch'i-ch'ao and Intellectual Transition in China*, Cambridge, MA, Harvard University Press, 1971.

Chen, Yung-fa, *Making Revolution: The Communist Movement in Eastern and Central China, 1937–1945*, Berkeley, University of California Press, 1986.

Chow, Tse-tsung, *The May Fourth Movement: Intellectual Revolution in Modern China*, Stanford, Stanford University Press, 1967.

Ci, Jiwei, *Dialectic of the Chinese Revolution: From Utopianism to Hedonism*, Stanford, Stanford University Press, 1994.

Friedman, Edward, Paul G. Pickowicz and Mark Selden, *Chinese Village, Socialist State*, New Haven, Yale University Press, 1991.

Goldman, Merle, *China's Intellectuals: Advice and Dissent*, Cambridge, MA, Harvard University Press, 1981.

Goodman, David S. G., *Social and Political Change in Revolutionary China: The Taihang Base Area in the War of Resistance to Japan, 1937–1945*, Lanham, MD, Rowman & Littlefield, 2000.

Hart-Landsberg, Martin and Paul Burkett, *China and Socialism: Market Reforms and Class Struggle*, New York, Monthly Review Press, 2005.

Isaacs, Harold R., *The Tragedy of the Chinese Revolution*, Stanford, Stanford University Press, 1961.

Kuhn, Philip A. *Origins of the Modern Chinese State*, Stanford, Stanford University Press, 2002.

MacFarquhar, Roderick and Michael Schoenhals, *Mao's Last Revolution*, Cambridge, MA, Belknap Press, 2006.

Perry, Elizabeth J., *Shanghai on Strike: The Politics of Chinese Labor*, Stanford, Stanford University Press, 1993.

Perry, Elizabeth J. and Mark Selden (eds.), *Chinese Society: Change, Conflict and Resistance*, London, Routledge, 2000.

Selden, Mark, *China in Revolution: The Yenan Way Revisited*, Armonk, NY, M. E. Sharpe, 1995.

Siu, Helen F., *Agents and Victims in South China: Accomplices in Rural Revolution*, New Haven, Yale University Press, 1989.

Solinger, Dorothy J., *Contesting Citizenship in Urban China: Peasant Migrants, the State, and the Logic of the Market*, Berkeley, University of California Press, 1999.

Strauss, Julia C., *Strong Institutions in Weak Polities: State Building in Republican China, 1927–1940*, New York, Oxford University Press, 1998.

Yeh, Wen-hsin, *Provincial Passages: Culture, Space, and the Origins of Chinese Communism*, Berkeley, University of California Press, 1996.

3

Historical consciousness and national identity

Most Chinese are extremely proud of their long and continuous historical civilization, which some claim extends for five thousand years. But for much of the twentieth century, Chinese revolutionaries had a very ambivalent and mostly negative view of these millennia, believing that they produced a slavish and feudal mentality. The vicissitudes of modern historical consciousness in China closely reflect the kind of nation and society that regimes and intellectuals battled over in their search for a new China and an identity for the Chinese people. In other words, if we want to understand how Chinese leaders and people see their society and their role in the world, we need to consider their changing views of history.

For much of the last hundred years, one of the central historical questions that has preoccupied scholars and statesmen seeking to make sense of China's present relates to the transition from a Confucian, imperial society to a modern nation-state. In contrast to many other non-Western societies, imperial China possessed several characteristics that would facilitate this transition – as well as several that would hinder it. The former included the existence of a unified bureaucratic state, a politicized gentry elite with a sense of societal responsibility, a relatively open society largely free of ascriptive roles, and a highly developed pre-industrial economy and entrepreneurial expertise.

On the other hand, the obstacles included China's exploitative encounters with imperialist powers from the second half of the nineteenth century, which left the government severely incapacitated. Moreover, the bureaucracy and gentry elites represented a thin layer at the top of society that was incapable of – and often resistant to – the efficient mobilization of resources and population required for a competitive capitalist world. Sun Yat-sen, the father of modern Chinese nationalism, frequently complained that the people were like a 'loose sheet of sand' with limited capacity to hold together for the common purpose of the nation. The statesmen of the early twentieth century, such as Liang Qichao, also noted that without a forward-looking, progressive sense of history, China could not begin to think of itself as a nation with a future.

Indeed, modern historical writing was born, along with the nation-state, some time in the late eighteenth century in Europe, and emerged in the non-Western world in around the late nineteenth and early twentieth centuries. Such writing frequently served to plant a concept of the nation, instil a love for it – and hatred for its enemies – and create citizens who would serve the nation in this new world. In this new conception of history, the nation – its people and culture, not the dynasties and aristocracies – was the collective agent or subject of history. The linear, evolutionary movement of the nation itself had a propulsive effect since the goal of much historical writing at the time was to recover the very idea of a common, or potentially unified, people who could realize their modern destiny. This effect was catalyzed by the contemporary social Darwinist vision of the world in which a country was doomed to eternal colonization and extinction if it did not become a strong nation-state (with colonies of its own).

To be sure, Chinese civilization had a sophisticated and rich tradition of historical writing. For instance, the history written by the great Han dynasty (206 BC–AD 220) historian, Sima Qian, was characterized by a quite modern conception of time in which he urged the creation of new institutions for a new generation. But this linear temporality remained a distinctly minor key in the historiography. Much historiography during the late imperial period (from around AD 1000 until 1911) sought to return to the ancient ideals of the sage-kings (the legendary Yao and Shun whom Confucius emulated) and to 'slight the present in order to favour the past'. Moreover, dynastic chroniclers also tended to record events as the expression of cyclical cosmological patterns in which human and supernatural agencies were intertwined. Thus natural catastrophes such as floods and popular rebellions that brought down dynasties were understood as expressions of Heaven's displeasure with the monarch and bureaucrats whose moral laxity had caused the dynasty to lose Heaven's mandate to rule.[1]

Imperial Chinese historiography therefore did not think of time in an evolutionary or progressive sense in which the future could always be made anew by humans; or, in other words, in which future developments were an integral part of the entity known as history. Reinhart Koselleck has summed up the modern conception of historical time as one in which there was a break between 'experience' and 'expectation', whereby instead of expecting to live the lives their ancestors experienced, people began to expect a different future for themselves.[2] The past was linearly linked to the future, but the latter would not be the same as the past. Although in the everyday view of history this is not an issue, how one could remain the same or deeply continuous with the past and yet free to progress into something different presents quite a vexed problem for historians and nationalist thinkers all over the world.

At the very end of the nineteenth century in China, when the Confucian literati and other publicly minded people became convinced that Japanese and Western imperialists were about to divide up the Qing empire (founded by the Manchus in 1644) and that China as a cultural and political entity would cease to exist, they began to look around the world not only for new military technologies but also for political, economic and cultural institutions that would enable China to survive in the modern world. As they debated each other for solutions, they began to absorb the new conception of time and history as the most basic assumption about the new world. The linear, progressive and human conception of history became the precondition for understanding their society, their past and the future.

Liang Qichao and new history

By the early twentieth century, Chinese history came to be written in the Enlightenment mode of liberation from medieval, autocratic domination. The historian Liang Qichao, who was perhaps the first to write the history of China under the sign of progress, made it clear that a people could not become a nation without a linear history. The world history that he wrote in 1902, *New Historiography* [*Xinshixue*], was not only written as an account of the European conquest of the world, but was also written from the European perspective of bringing enlightenment to the world. Whereas his one-time mentor Kang Youwei had adapted the idea of progress into the categories of Confucian historiography, Liang's narrative represents a total repudiation of traditional Chinese historiography as unable to give meaning to the Chinese national experience.[3]

During these early years, this European model came to China via Japan where Meiji (1869–1912) historians had been developing the new history of the Japanese people and culture as a whole. They utilized such techniques as periodization and archaeology to establish the origins and continuous history of Japan. In response to the European historical narrative of conquest as a 'civilizing mission', the Japanese historians sought, in addition to their national history, to develop the history of civilization in East Asia that tracked its uncertain spiritual progress (its *zeitgeist*) in the region. In later decades, this East Asian civilizational history (*toyoshi*) would be used by some of these historians to justify Japan's domination over China and the rest of Asia as the progressive leader of an ancient civilization.

In China, Liang's *History* tried to create an emancipatory yet continuous history by utilizing the division of periods into ancient, medieval and modern. He criticized traditional Chinese historiography for dividing history into monarchical reigns and ignoring the history of the people-nation (*guomin*). In Liang's periodization, ancient Chinese history extended from the sage emperors to the Qin unification (221 BC): 'This was a China of China. This was the period when the Chinese people(s) developed themselves, competed among themselves, and organized among themselves. They were victorious over the barbarian races.' The medieval period was the history of a China of Asia that would extend to the Qianlong era (1796). This was a time when China had interactions with other Asian peoples and developed its centralized autocracy. While the Han people were often physically overwhelmed by central Asian races, spiritually, the Han managed to overcome them, and by the end of the period the races of Asia (I believe he means the Han and China's Central Asian neighbours) came together to form a great race that could face the outsiders. The modern period was one of China in the world in which the Chinese would, together with other Asian peoples, rid themselves of autocracy and compete with Western nations. Indeed, so closely was his conception of history linked to the nation-state that Liang explained the division of periods in linear history using the metaphor of a treaty between nation-states marking their respective jurisdictions.[4]

In this model, we see an antiquity that saw the birth of the true China – a China of China. The ancient age is the age of the creation of a people and culture, pure and original. The medieval age is one of decay – inner ills, outer barbarians and autocracy vitiate the purity of the people, and efforts to renew the spirit work only temporarily. The modern period is one of renewal – often through struggle – and change, change towards progress. The modern period may or may not come with a renaissance; certainly the idea of a renaissance dramatizes the general disposition of the modern era to recover a lost past – the problem of reconnecting with the past even as one sheds the accretions of a middle age, whether this be Confucianism, barbarian rule or superstition – as one forges ahead in a new world. The entire apparatus then works to recover the continuity of culture and people even while it allows the historian to reject that against which one will fashion the future.

Subsequent periodizations of Chinese history often elaborated upon Liang's basic scheme. But within this scheme there was considerable debate in which dissenting positions were frequently shaped by the political perspectives of the advocates. A major debate, and a problem that endures to this day, concerned exactly who constituted the Chinese people. Was China the nation of the Han, the dominant ethnic group or nationality that comprised over 90 per cent of the population? Should China include what we now call the 'minority nationalities' such as the Manchus, the Mongols, the Muslims and the many smaller groups in the peripheral regions of empire? Although the numbers of the latter were small, the area they occupied historically covered around two thirds of the Manchu, Qing empire. Should these peoples and their territories be excluded from the new Republic? Could the Han be seen as the dominant and superior group within this empire made over into a nation, or should the new nation be a republic of different nationalities? In other words, who was to constitute the nation and what kind of relationship would prevail between its constituents – the question of identity – was a major problem.

History and the Republic (1912–1949)

In this way, claims to nationality and concomitant claims to rights and duties came to be justified on historical grounds. The birth of the nation from the empire was accompanied from the start by fierce battles over the identity of the nation. From around 1900 until 1911 when the Manchus fell, the reformists who wanted to transform China into a constitutional monarchy debated and fought the Republican revolutionaries. Liang Qichao represented the reformist faction during the early years, and his careful delineation of the middle period in which 'the races of Asia came together to form a great race facing the outsiders' was a coded way of saying that the Manchu emperors of China and their empire peopled – perhaps sparsely, but over large parts – by non-Han peoples should be seen as part of the new Chinese nation. The revolutionaries, on the other hand, wanted to expel the Manchus because they were considered despotic and foreign, and to occupy a lower order of civilization (like the other non-Han peoples in the empire).

The most passionate statement from the revolutionary point of view was made, not by Sun Yat-sen, who was a moderate in this regard, but by Zou Rong and his mentor, Zhang Binglin. In *Revolutionary Army*, Zou wrote,

> When men love their race, solidarity will arise internally, and what is outside will be repelled. Hence, to begin with, clans were united and other clans repelled; next tribes were united and other tribes repelled, finally the people of a country became united and people of other countries were repelled. This is the general principle of the races of the world, and also a major reason why races engender history... China is the China of the Chinese. Countrymen, you must all recognize the China of the Chinese of the Han race.

Zhang, who was also greatly influenced by social Darwinism, used the Han lineage or clan system to construct a Han nation from a putative ancestral link to the mythical Yellow Emperor, and called on the Han to struggle against the inferior Manchu race with their alien surnames.[5]

After the Republic was established in 1912 and Han dominance asserted, the revolutionaries agreed to a Republic of Five Nationalities and settled on the appellation *zhonghua minzu* (the Chinese nationality) for the nation. Although the loyalty of the different peoples to the Republic was never fully settled – with the Mongols establishing their republic in Outer Mongolia and Tibetans and Muslims seeking independence – the Chinese nation-state has more or less retained the borders of the Manchu empire. Nonetheless, the relationship between the Han and the other nationalities continued to be a changing and troubled one and this is reflected in the historical writing.

With the onset of the Japanese invasion of China (1932–45), even the finest and most critical Chinese historians such as Gu Jiegang began to make deep historical claims upon the peoples of these vast borderlands, because these zones were contested by the Japanese and other imperialist powers. While the Japanese dominated the northeast (or erstwhile Manchuria) and colonized Taiwan from 1895, the Russians often supported groups in the northwest, the British in Tibet, and the French in the southwest. In a 1938 text entitled *A History of the Changes in China's Frontier Regions*, Gu, who had done more than any other historian to explode nationalist myths and give the minorities an important role in the making of the nation, began to deploy the stereotypes of traditional Chinese history. He revealed that his purpose in compiling such a work was not only to demonstrate without a doubt to the Japanese imperialists ('our covetous, powerful neighbors'), but also to enlighten the Chinese people, that the Han peoples had spread to Manchuria, Mongolia and even into Korea during the Tang and earlier dynasties and thus had historical claims there.[6]

Soon after the fully fledged outbreak of the Sino-Japanese war in 1937, Chiang Kai-shek, the president of the Republic in China from 1927–49 and leader of the GMD party, reversed the Republic's formal commitment to the autonomy of the 'five nationalities'. In 1939, a GMD ordinance asserted that 'in our country, the racial, cultural and blood fusion (*hunhe*) among different groups has long been completed and should not be arbitrarily analysed'.[7] In 1943, Chiang Kai-shek declared in *China's Destiny* that 'the Chunghua nation ... has grown by gradual amalgamation of various stocks into a harmonious and organic whole'.[8] By the 1947 edition, the idea that these various stocks were 'originally of one race and lineage' and that 'the distinction between the five stocks is territorial as well as religious, but not ethnological' had been added.[9]

Chiang himself was acutely aware of the teaching of 'Chinese history' and 'Chinese geography' as a means of producing 'a citizen who loves his country more than his own life'.[10] Towards this end, not only were historians and other scholars urged to demonstrate the bases of Chinese historical claims to the peripheries in their research, but history and geography textbooks at every level of the school system were required to contain material about the problems of the border regions in order to cultivate a proprietary feeling for these regions that had not existed in the old empire. The popular media, including films and slide shows about the regions and customs of the peripheral people, were also mobilized to further this identification among the common people.

Thus, even though the Republic was a politically unsettled period, not only was history utilized to make nationality claims, but historical pedagogy was an important institutional means of disseminating this historical knowledge and cultivating national identity. The identity-building function of historical education was not limited simply to the problem of territorial claims. Historical knowledge and education became deeply involved in creating an understanding of the past that could shape the people's self-image in the best interests of the nation, whether in its struggle for survival against imperialist powers or to succeed in a globally competitive environment.

The May Fourth Movement, which spanned the years 1917 to 1921, is justly regarded as China's Enlightenment because students and professors at Beijing University and in other provincial cities not only protested imperialist machinations, but also revolted against centuries of Confucian orthodoxy and patriarchy. Their slogan was 'Down with Confucius and Sons, Long Live Messrs Science and Democracy.' The movement ushered in a new era of modern egalitarian and nationalist values founded upon a radical vision of history that in some ways went beyond anything Liang or Sun had proposed. Whereas Liang repudiated the nature of imperial historiography, he found much in Chinese history that could be utilized to foster a new identity and loyalty to the nation. Others of the earlier generation, such as Zhang Binglin who had denounced the Manchus, were critical of Confucianism (in particular because it promoted universal values unsuited to nationalism) but sought to fashion a modern China from the vast reservoir of alternative historical traditions (*zhuzixue*) that had been suppressed by Confucianism, including Legalism, Moism and Daoism as well as Buddhism.

Dr Hu Shi, an educationist and philosopher who studied with John Dewey at Columbia University, represented an interesting bridge between the two approaches. Although he wrote for the radical, flagship May Fourth journal *New Youth*, Hu by no means sought to negate the past. Rather he promoted the vernacular Chinese literature (*baihua* or plain speech) that had flourished in popular society since late imperial times as the alternative to classical Chinese language, the language of the literati that few others could comprehend and which continued to dominate serious writing in his time. This vernacular tradition had produced great and much-loved novels such as *Dream of the Red Chamber*, *Journey to the West* and *All Men are Brothers* (also known as *Water Margin*) and, much in the way that vernacular European cultures overcame the domination of Latin, Hu Shi sought to produce a new historical consciousness that the roots of the Chinese nation lay with the people and their language. Indeed, the *baihua* movement emerged as one of the most powerful and enduring consequences of the May Fourth era; it remains the foundation of the Chinese national language.[11]

Hu Shi not only produced a history of China that was parallel to the history of vernacularization and popular sovereignty in Europe. He was surely aware of Liang Qichao's earlier essay 'On the Relationship between Fiction and the Government of the People' in which Liang had observed the power of fiction to produce transformations in the individual's sense of self and ability to produce the 'new citizen' loyal to the nation and the government. It is worth mentioning in passing that Liang anticipated Benedict Anderson's famous concept of the 'imagined community' in which he argued that popular, printed fiction played the principal role in the creation of the nation in people's imagination. Although he distanced himself from political activism until the anti-Japanese war, Hu Shi like Liang recognized the importance of the older fiction in generating a renovated identity. In his words, it was time for Chinese 'to reorganize the national past and recreate [its] civilization'.

But the writers of the May Fourth generation, particularly its most celebrated hero, Lu Xun, placed little value on the role of traditional fiction, vernacular or literati. For them, without a total, in fact an iconoclastic, attack on Chinese tradition and history, the Chinese people could never be transformed and the new nation would be still-born. Lu Xun was, of course, an enormously complex and self-doubting revolutionary writer. But the Chinese Communist Party, which was born out of the effervescence of the May Fourth Movement in 1921 and developed a powerful revolutionary agenda of transformation, could not afford the luxury of self-doubt. Communist historians, who subscribed to a unilinear teleological history of the world, found themselves following European theory in characterizing the history of China as representing the transition from slavery to feudalism, and found little value in the depths and achievements of Chinese history. The identity they sought to create was that of people who struggled against their own feudal elites and the foreign imperialists who stood in the way of their true destiny. In large part, historical research became the search for the seeds of revolutionary forces among the peasant uprisings that crowded the Chinese historical record. The Taiping Rebellion of the mid-nineteenth century, with its combination of Christian and radical levelling tendencies, was a major source of historical inspiration for the Communists.

But just as liberal historians such as Gu Jiegang became more nationalist in their historical investigations, the Japanese invasion also led to the search for national roots among the Communists. Much of this was conducted at the level of popular culture – or what the Maoists would call National Culture – looking for folk traditions that could serve as the basis of identity but also transformed so that they could be made revolutionary and support the goals of mass mobilization and self-renovation. Thus the old-style drama and popular operas loved by the masses (and once considered the pillars of feudal literature) had to be preserved, but revised with a scientific interpretation. Similarly, traditional Chinese medicine came to be institutionalized as the 'people's science'. The Confucian classic *The Book of Songs* was now seen as the repository of 'people's literature': where Confucians saw noble selflessness and ritual piety, Communists found protests against feudal rites and oppression of women. The historian Joseph Levenson commented, '[T]he Communists found that a complete disavowal of the old China was psychologically impossible even for them... The need for compensation implies an attachment to the old tradition, an attachment on the part of Communists which is not belied but evinced in their repudiation of that tradition.'[12]

The Mao era, 1949–1976

We might see what Levenson viewed as a psychological dependence on nationalism as a rift, an aporia that is common to all progressive national histories whether in China, France, Kenya or the United States. The predicament of national history lies in its task to bridge an unbridgeable gap: this history must create the conditions of a progressive future in which our expectations diverge from our experiences in the past, while at the same time it must establish the continuity of a people so that national claims to the land and culture can be firmly established. Ernest Renan summed it up in what to us may seem the impossible 'hymn of every *patrie*': 'We are what you were; we will be what you are'. Notwithstanding Levenson's claim, this aporia has been particularly difficult for the Communists in China to address.

Because of both their ideological predisposition to see the past as feudal and imperialist and their self-perception as inheritors of the May Fourth legacy, the Communists often displayed a ferocious hostility towards the past. They attacked the 'living past', not only among the elites but among the people. In particular, they conducted campaigns in which they dispossessed and eliminated popular religious communities, associations, properties, ceremonies and festivities that were often associated with temples and markets, especially during the 1950s. Although today there is a return to religious devotion and community activities among the populace, it is a circumspect revival and the authorities are alert to alternative ideas of community and moral authority such as those among the Falungong that became visible in the late 1990s. In the 1960s, the Cultural Revolution, which erupted as a farcical and tragic incarnation of May Fourth iconoclasm, brought new meaning to the assault on the 'living past'. The drive to vaporize every sign of the past entailed the dangerous eugenic idea of the 'bloodline theory' in which children and grandchildren of 'class enemies' were targeted for attack because of the stigma of their ancestors.

While there was a need for the Chinese regime, like all other nation-states in modern society, to link the past with the future, during the first thirty years of the PRC the attack on the past overwhelmed the attachment to it. Notably, it was during periods when the nation-state felt threatened by external competitors or invaders that aspects of the past were restored as fit for study and dissemination. During the anti-Japanese war, when the CCP forged a united front with the GMD and viewed society more inclusively in order to rally the largest possible numbers for the national cause, a number of radical intellectuals of the May Fourth persuasion such as He Bingsong and Feng Youlan turned to a more China-centred history, and Marxists became increasingly influential in historical circles. This was also the period during which the CCP sought to find the roots of the people in folklore and popular culture. The next period marked by a nationalist turn towards history occurred during the rift with the Soviet Union in the 1950s.

After the establishment of the People's Republic of China, the Soviet model became for the Chinese Communists both the most progressive and the best means for the Chinese people to stand tall in the world. Soviet advisors played a major role in establishing new institutions, and professional historians were also expected to follow their vision of materialist history. In the Soviet view, however, China represented a rather backward state in the evolution towards socialism. Thus it did not take long for differences to appear between PRC and Soviet historians over the right to interpret Chinese history. For instance, historians such as Fan Wenlan objected to the Soviet idea that the imperial Chinese state had merely effected a political unification and Chinese nationalism had developed only with the emergence of bourgeois capitalism in the twentieth century. Fan protested that *national* unification had begun with the Qin–Han unification in the third century BC, far earlier than it had elsewhere in the world.[13]

Chinese historians also objected to Soviet historians consigning China to the Asiatic mode of production. Derived from Marx's writings about Asian societies, this model posits a stagnant agricultural society without private property and ruled over, not by a class, but by a despotic state that extracted all its surplus and limited commerce. Within the progressive conception of historical materialism, this characterization rendered China even less advanced than ancient Greece and Rome, which had slave modes of production.[14] One can readily sympathize with the Chinese objections to such disparaging and hopelessly inaccurate historical characterizations, but also note how Marxist theory reproduced here the civilizational hierarchy of Enlightenment imperialism. This framework of linear, progressive history shared by two socialist states was accompanied by a competition over which was better equipped historically to attain the goals of socialism. Indeed, competitiveness tended to become a crucial, if not central, feature of the worldview, and shaped the relations between the two states for the next thirty years.

During these years, historians needed to tread a careful line between pursuing the revolutionary historical vision of a future radically different from the past, and undertaking a rearguard action, albeit in a minor key, against efforts to belittle China's historical honour. The goals of the socialist regime were to achieve egalitarianism and collectivism, and historical research that characterized modern Chinese history as 'semi-feudal and semi-colonial' focused on class struggle, popular uprisings, and the striving of different peoples or national minorities (*minzu*) for the same class and anti-imperialist national goals. The renowned historian Hu Sheng declared in 1954 that the Taiping Rebellion, the violent anti-foreign Boxer Uprising of 1900 and the anti-Manchu Revolution of 1911 were the 'three revolutionary climaxes' that would constitute the basic paradigm or narrative of modern Chinese history.[15]

Indeed, a new revolutionary identity was being created. As David Apter and Tony Saich have demonstrated, revolutionary history became intertwined with the manner in which Mao Zedong and the CCP narrated their claims to leadership over the GMD and Mao's rivals. During the Japanese invasion, the Communists had made their base in the remote and inaccessible Yan'an Soviet in northwest China. From this bleak environment they launched guerilla attacks on the Japanese occupiers and developed the disciplined and highly motivated body of cadres that would dominate the leadership of the People's Republic after 1949. These cadres honed their commitment and loyalty to Mao and revolution by internalizing the 'semi-feudal and semi-colonial' version of Chinese history through emotionally charged collective readings – a process Apter and Saich call 'exegetical bonding'.[16] These texts and techniques were subsequently disseminated to the wider population through schools and myriad other institutions. During the Cultural Revolution, an exaggerated form of exegetical bonding would occur through the personal and collective readings of the *Quotations of Chairman Mao* Red Book which embedded the revolutionary history.

The rearguard defence of the past took the form of showing that China historically had a highly developed material culture that included great scientific inventions such as the compass, the seismograph, gunpowder, paper money, printing techniques and much else. The revolutionary paradigm depicted the Chinese past as feudal rather than Asiatic. Compared to the latter, the former would show China as part of mainstream world history and not consigned to an exceptional and stagnant mode of production. The advancements in technology and organization in Chinese history made it much more comparable to other feudal societies in the world. Indeed, Chinese historians were able to find the 'sprouts of capitalism' in late imperial China, as well as forms of managerial capitalism that indicated a society pregnant with modernity. The question of national identity and pride would not go away.

The reform era and globalization

Since the opening of China in 1979, there has been considerable relaxation of state ideological and political controls in many areas of life and culture. But the writing of history has been slower to change than other academic disciplines. In part, this is testimony to the importance of history to the legitimacy of the nation-state that still calls itself a socialist, if not revolutionary, state.

But if professional historians were bound by state controls on academia, non-academic interpretations of history, especially in the new media, rose to the task of producing a new history for a new age. None was more daring and influential than *Heshang* [*River Elegy*], a six-part documentary series that was first broadcast on television in June 1988. It had a powerful impact on the intelligentsia and the urban viewing public, and may be seen as a crucial event in the chain that triggered the spring 1989 student protests in Tiananmen Square. This serial presented itself as a historical narrative, indeed a counter-narrative to the official revolutionary nationalist history. Its basic message was that Chinese culture and history are tyrannical and brutalizing; the Yellow River (the river of the title), along with the Great Wall, represented the stagnant Asiatic mode of production, and constituted the central metaphor of this misery. By contrast, Western civilization is seen as dynamic, and is symbolized by the openness of the blue ocean that transports science and democracy across the seas. A crucial event in this history was the closing of China to the outside world from the Ming dynasty: 'For humankind as a whole, the fifteenth century was an extremely critical century. The human race began to move its gaze from the continent to the seas. History gave a fair chance, both to Orient and to Occident, to make a choice.'[17] With China's turn inwards, it lost this opportunity.

Although the *Heshang* narrative adopted the iconoclastic spirit of the May Fourth Movement, by asserting that China was characterized by the Asiatic mode of production and by admiring Western imperialism, it violated the two core values of revolutionary nationalism. As its critics untiringly pointed out, it was highly selective in its presentation of the historical materials and passionate in its rhetoric. But it was also unprecedented in being perhaps the first mass media production in China that successfully reached out and moved vast numbers of people to question the official historical narrative. *Heshang* circulated in video form and hand-copied scripts even before the competition broke out in the publishing industry to acquire the script. It was enthusiastically received, particularly by high school students in both urban and rural areas. One of the co-authors of the script, Su Xiaokang, wrote that a million youths came to debate *Heshang* in Guangzhou.[18] *Heshang* represented a counter-history that radically altered and questioned historical perceptions of the self in order to move the future in a different direction. This direction, of course, was that of globalization, modernization and democratization. And just as surely, when the discussion turned political and the enthusiasts fell silent, its denunciation was national and civilizational: 'you have flogged our ancestors with impunity,' its detractors claimed. The rearguard took charge.

Since the crushing of the uprising in Tiananmen in 1989, the Communist regime has been much more favourably disposed to Nationalist history and alternatives to the revolutionary narrative. A 'reformist' narrative of history had been debated in academia in the 1980s, but emerged full blown in the 1990s. It substitutes three other events from the late nineteenth and early twentieth centuries for the 'three revolutionary climaxes': namely, the Self-Strengthening movement from the 1860s when reformist Confucian statesmen such as Zeng Guofan and Li Hong-zhang sought to adapt a few Western institutions such as the military into the fabric of Confucian society; the 100 days reform Movement of 1898 led by Kang Youwei and Liang Qichao, and the Bourgeois Revolution of 1911. Popular uprisings are noticeably missing from this narrative, and many of the villains of the revolutionary narrative such as Zeng Guofan and Confucian reformer Kang Youwei began to appear in an increasingly favourable light. Interestingly, in the 2003 TV series *Towards the Republic*, watched by hundreds of millions of viewers, this reformist narrative had become even more conservative and frankly statist. Thus the Empress Dowager Cixi and President Yuan Shikai, *de facto* heads of state between 1900 and 1916 and long regarded as bitter opponents of reform, are treated with great sympathy and shown to have been devoted to the greater interests of the nation-state. The revolutionary narrative has been overturned, but the power of the nation-state has been fortified in history.

In many respects, though, professional historians today find themselves relatively free from the interpretive straitjacket of class struggle, popular uprisings and the standard of a single narrative. Several innovative historians have adopted the 'history from below' approach that established its importance in the West with the appearance of E. P. Thompson's *The Making of the English Working Class* or Eric Hobsbawm's *Primitive Rebel*. This approach seeks to eschew strictly defined class or law-governed histories imposed from above in favour of a view of the people as agents of their own histories. Zhao Shiyu, for instance, has studied popular religion, temple life and carnivals in late imperial China. He shows that this religious life, while interlinked with official culture, could subvert and threaten it as well as provide a refuge for women typically confined to the domestic area. Sometimes the research reflects critically even on sacred events such as the May Fourth. In an essay on the movement in Shanghai, Feng Xiaocai noted that the intellectual perception of the May Fourth Movement as a popular nationalist movement was quite different from the scene on the ground. It was less the spirit of patriotism that motivated the popular movement than rumours that the Japanese were spreading poison in the food. As panic gripped the population, they began to riot and occasionally attacked Japanese residents in China and even other Chinese.[19]

Yet academic freedom continues to face limitations, sometimes from unexpected quarters. Most recently, in January 2006, there was a case in which the journal *Bingdian* [*Freezing Point*] was shut down after controversy generated by an essay written by a senior professor, Yuan Weishi from Guangzhou. The journal, which was known for its serious and provocative essays, was reorganized and subsequently relaunched in March. The thrust of Yuan's essay was to criticize Chinese school history textbooks for distorting the record, especially in regard to the imperialist role in the Second Opium War (1858–60) and the Boxer Rebellion (1900). According to Yuan, this kind of pedagogy can only inflame nationalistic passions and produce youth such as the violently chauvinistic Red Guards of the Cultural Revolution. Indeed, he finds Chinese historical consciousness quite comparable with that of the Japanese: 'the two have something in common: the mainstream culture in society lacks deep reflection on its contemporary history'. Yuan concludes with a plea for a more calm and rational historiography so that China can properly engage in its modernization project.[20]

There are two matters of interest in this episode. The first is that most of Yuan's criticism derived from a comparison with Hong Kong history textbooks, which according to Yuan present a 'more complete picture' of both events and do not demonize the foreigners alone. This alternative view, so close to home, is likely to continue to unsettle the field of knowledge within China. The second point is the vitriolic response to the essay in *Bingdian* from many sections of its readership. Some historians criticized the essay for 'seriously violating historical truth, delivering a mistaken judgment on history, and gravely misleading the youth'. Others claimed that Yuan had 'grievously hurt the feelings of the Chinese people'.[21] Although the decision to close down the journal and change its editorship was made by the government, the groundswell of nationalist opposition among the readership cannot be ignored.

We can also see this pattern in the realm of public history: relative freedom from state strictures accompanied by a zone of constraint emanating from a popular nationalism. While museums have often been the site of displays and formation of a national historical identity, in Shandong, perhaps one of the most historically rich regions of China, dwindling government support has led museums to look elsewhere for support. It is only museums in remote places and still dependent on government support that continue to follow the revolutionary or reformist narrative. In the major cities, museums have branched out in different directions – such as the history of alcohol, folk-culture or mining – and are often driven by market considerations. James Flath suggests that

since 1992, with the guarantee of the security of historical sites from attacks such as the Cultural Revolution, it has become acceptable even in
connection with historical subjects of national significance to display
such politically incorrect items as the many rooms of Kang Youwei's con-
cubines or the Catholic church as the first location of the provincial CCP
headquarters.[22]

This liberal approach may also be seen in the management of the historical monument Yuanmingyuan, the Qing emperors' summer palace
and gardens filled with architectural replicas from China and Europe.
Until recently, this site was remembered chiefly for its devastation and
national humiliation at the hands of Western imperialists during the
Second Opium War and the Boxer Rebellion. Haiyan Lee's analysis of the
various recent efforts to utilize and represent this site reveals the state to
be quite neutral about whether it should be kept as a site of ruins and thus
of national humiliation and vengeance, or restored as a glorious history of
imperial romance and cosmopolitanism. Indeed, she argues that the job
of the state today is to balance the two, as it must also balance the relationship between history as commercial pleasure and history as a reminder of
national humiliation. The nation-state's principal concern appears to be
to ensure that globalization – the desire for global goods and values – is
not overcome by the desire for national authenticity or vice-versa. Lee argues that Yuanmingyuan is 'an ideal schooling ground for the art of socialist neo-liberal citizenship: of being able to reconcile authoritarianism
and freewheeling capitalism, patriotic loyalty and transnational imagi-
nary, self-righteous rage and aesthetic and sensual enjoyment.'[23]

But while public displays now seem to be much less state-driven, they
do not necessarily exclude nationalism in their mode of presentation.
For instance, on Liugong Island in Shandong, once the headquarters of
the former Beiyang Navy, there is a new museum dedicated to the defeat
by the Japanese Navy in 1895. It houses enormous dioramas of Chinese
crushing the Japanese foes, but contains few reminders of the actual
Chinese defeat.[24] From the mid-1990s, regional museums became much
more interested in displaying and boosting regional rather than national
history. But these regional narratives are not incompatible with the national story; they generate a voluntary rather than a coercive integration
with the centre, spawning mass cultural patriotism from below. This
kind of cultural patriotism has generated a tense situation and a 'relics
warfare' across the China–Korea border over the problem of Koguryo,
an ancient Korean kingdom in present-day Chinese territory claimed

by the Chinese as Chinese.[25] This kind of popular nationalism expressed through history is a natural result of years of government textbook pedagogy and other historical education; but it is also a creation that takes on a life of its own.

A final way in which history and national consciousness are being transformed in China today relates to the subtle transformation of the territorial conception of nationhood discussed above in the context of the Republic of Five Nationalities. The People's Republic of China (*zhonghua minguo*) of 1949 was similarly founded upon goals of equal citizenship – indeed of affirmative action – for its fifty-six nationalities. Like other decolonizing nations, the PRC was committed to a civic, territorial model of nationality over one that stressed the dominant ethnic nationality of the Han. With the rapid advance of globalization over the last few decades, the territorial model has been coming increasingly under stress as overseas Chinese capital and connections have become more and more important for China's global competitiveness. The effort to integrate the overseas Han Chinese into the nation has led to a spatial reimagination of the nation from the territorial China to the ethnic one. This has been accompanied by an intensification of economic investment and activity in the coastal regions of China, away from the hinterland where we also find most of the minority populations. There has thus been a reorientation of national and historical identification.

Tu Wei-ming, a professor of Chinese philosophy at Harvard University and one of the most prominent overseas Chinese scholars, proposed a narrative through which one could identify Chineseness across the world. Tu identified concentric circles of 'cultural China', beginning with the first symbolic universe comprising Mainland China, Hong Kong, Taiwan and Singapore, to a second comprising the Chinese diaspora, and finally, in a Confucian gesture, to a third symbolic universe comprising all who empathize with Chinese culture, including many non-Chinese scholars of China. The recent publication of the *Encyclopedia of Chinese Overseas*, an excellent and authoritative history of the overseas Chinese edited by Lynn Pan, is in fact framed by these concentric circles of Chineseness. In its less academic form, this vision of nationality finds – or revives – an alternative ethnic or cultural integration (minus the empathetic foreigners) in the ideology of the children of the Yellow Emperor (*yanhuang zhizi*) and the new attention to Confucianism.[26]

According to Professor Tu, this concentricity may also be understood as two types of Chineseness – one political and the other ethnic. Tu's two types of Chineseness more or less match the two types of nations and nationalisms I have mentioned: the civic territorial conception of the People's Republic of China and the ethnic or ethno-cultural one. There have been historiographies associated with these two types of Chineseness, and James Liebold has recently written about the relationship between the racial and territorial notions among Republican historians as both contesting and intertwined. He finds such an ambivalent relationship resurgent even today among PRC historians.[27] The recent spread of the historical narrative of the ethnic nation linking Han Chinese to overseas Han Chinese in a kind of 'deterritorialized nationalism' has occurred at the expense of the territorial nation. Together with the imbalance in regional development in China, it has led, at the ethnic frontiers of the nation, to counter movements of irredentist or ethnic nationalism in Tibet, Mongolia and Xinjiang. The government's campaign to develop the west – *Xibu dakaifa* – is a response to this perceived imbalance. But the campaign itself is a double-edged sword that both increases investment in the interior and increases control over the region and floods it with Han people and culture.

Over the last century, historical consciousness in China has been chiefly used to enable the emergent nation to find its place in the world, to create a population that identifies with the nation-state, and to mobilize this population for the survival and success of the nation-state. At the same time, we have seen the contours of the nation – who was to be included and who excluded, to what extent and what aspects of the past were acceptable – change quite dramatically over the century. With every turn, we have seen demands on academic history and popular historical consciousness to adapt to these changes. History has also been central to understanding the dominant values of the changing present because it is a source of legitimacy for those engineering these changes.

But even as the configuration of the nation-state and nationalism has changed, the ideology of nationalism appears to have grown. Limiting ourselves just to China's relations with East Asian nations, despite the growth of economic ties with Japan, Korea and Taiwan and what is being referred to as the 'peaceful rise of China', political tensions have also been rising. Not surprisingly, they are being expressed in the realm of history; in the discourse of identity and the claims arising from it. History textbooks and claims to historical heritage and territories are at the centre of these tensions. They include the Japanese government's decision to publish textbooks without due acknowledgment of Japanese war atrocities in China and East Asia; the Korean protest over China's declaration of Koguryo as Chinese; the hundreds if not thousands of small and large islands contested by China, Korea, Japan and others; and most of all, the bitter contest between the PRC and Taiwanese nationalism over Taiwan. These issues have been a fundamental part of the historical pedagogy of nationalism not only in China but in each of the East Asian societies. They have become crucial to the individual's sense of self-worth, and are thus fuel for a sometimes runaway nationalism that can come to threaten the state itself. If the 'peaceful rise of China' is to continue, it may be necessary to pluralize historical education and its goals in this region.

Indeed, we may be seeing some pluralization in historical education taking place even as we speak. In 2006, Shanghai produced a new set of history textbooks. The high-school history books were notable for eliminating references to Mao Zedong and toning down the references to Japanese aggression, imperialism, class struggle and even nationalism. To be sure, these texts met with fierce condemnation across the nation on the grounds that they diluted national solidarity and identity. Yet they seem to have survived the assault and the very debate itself points in a hopeful direction.

Notes

1. See Michael Puett, *The Ambivalence of Creation: Debates Concerning Innovation and Artifice in Early China,* Stanford, Stanford University Press, 2001; and Achim Mittag, 'Historical Consciousness in China: Some Notes on Six Theses on Chinese Historiography and Historical Thought', in Paul Van Der Velde and Alex McKay (eds.), *New Developments in Asian Studies: An Introduction*, London, Kegan Paul, 1998, pp. 47–76.
2. Reinhart Koselleck, *Futures Past: On the Semantics of Historical Time* (trans. Keith Tribe), Cambridge, MIT Press, 1985, pp. 276–81.
3. Liang Qichao, 'Xinshixue' [New history], Yinbingshiwenji (ed. Lin Zhijun), 1970 reprint of 1932 edition, Taibei, Taiwan Zhonghua shuju, 1903, v. 4, 1–30.
4. Liang Qichao, 'Zhongguoshi xulun' [A systematic discussion of Chinese history], *Yinbingshiwenji* 1, 1902, v. 3, 10–12.
5. Zou Rong, translation in John Lust, *The Revolutionary Army: A Chinese Nationalist Tract of 1903*, Paris, Mouton, 1968. See also Kai-wing Chow, 'Imagining Boundaries of Blood: Zhang Binglin and the Invention of the Han "Race" in Modern China', in Frank Dikotter (ed.), *The Construction of Racial Identities in China and Japan*, University of Hawai'i Press, Honolulu, 1997, pp. 34–52.
6. Gu Jiegang, 'Zhongguo Jiangyu Yangeshi' [A history of the evolution of China's border regions], Changsha, Shangwu Yinshuguan, 1938, p. 4.
7. Quoted in Liu Xiaoyuan, 'The Chinese Communist Party and the "Nationality Question" 1921–1945', Unpublished paper, 1999, p. 38 n. 2.

8. Chiang Kai-shek, *China's Destiny* (trans. Wang Chung-hui), New York, Macmillan, 1947, p. 4.

9. *Ibid.*, p. 4, p. 12, p. 239 fn. 1.

10. In Richard Wilson, *Learning to be Chinese: The Political Socialization of Children in Taiwan*, Cambridge, MA, MIT Press, 1970, p. 276.

11. See Jerome B Grieder, *Hu Shih and the Chinese Renaissance: Liberalism in the Chinese Revolution, 1917–1937*, Cambridge, MA, Harvard University Press, 1970, pp. 80–5.

12. Joseph R. Levenson, *Confucian China and its Modern Fate: A Trilogy*, Berkeley and Los Angeles, University of California Press, 1965, p. 176, p. 190.

13. Q. Edward Wang, 'Between Marxism and Nationalism: Chinese Historiography and the Soviet Influence, 1949–1963', *Journal of Contemporary China* 9, no. 23 (2000), 95–111.

14. Timothy Brook (ed.), *The Asiatic Mode of Production in China*, London, M. E. Sharpe, 1999, pp. 14–15.

15. Hu Sheng, 'Zhongguo jindai lishide fenqi wenti' [The question of periodization in modern Chinese history], in *Lishi yanjiu*, 1959 n. 1, 5–15.

16. David E. Apter and Tony Saich, *Revolutionary Discourse in Mao's Republic*, Cambridge, MA, Harvard University Press, 1994.

17. Su Xiaokang and Wang Luxiang, *Deathsong of the River: A Reader's Guide to the Chinese TV Series* Heshang (trans. Richard W. Bodman and Pin P. Wang), Ithaca, NY, Cornell East Asian Series, 1991, p. 131.

18. *Ibid.*, pp. 290–1.

19. Zhao Shiyu, *Kuanghuan yu richang: Ming Qing yilaide miaohui yu minjian shehui* [Carnivals and everyday life: Temple fairs and popular society since the Ming and Qing], Beijing, Sanlian shudian, 2002; Feng Xiaocai, 'Shanghai xiaceng minzhong dui wusi yundongde fanying: yi "Riren zhidu" fengchao wei zhongxin' [The response of Shanghai's lower strata towards the May Fourth Movement: centring upon the Japanese poisoning agitation], *Shehui kexue yanjiu* 3, 2005, 136–45.

20. Yuan Weishi, 'Modernization and History Textbooks', *EastSouthWestNorth*: www.zonaeuropa.com/20060126_1.htm

21. See Zhang Haipeng's critique of Yuan's article, published in the resumed *Bingdian*: http://blog.chinesenewsnet.com/?p=8072&cp=1 Zhang Haipeng, 'Fandi fanfengjian shi jindai zhongguo lishide zhudi' [Anti-imperialism and anti-feudalism are the themes of modern Chinese history], Tuesday, 28 February 2006.

22. James A. Flath, 'Managing Historical Capital in Shandong: Museum, Monument and Memory in Provincial China', *The Public Historian* 24, no. 2, Spring 2002, 50–3.

23. Haiyan Lee, 'The Dialectics of Ruins in Yuanmingyuan', Paper prepared for MLA Convention, Washington, DC, 2005, 39–40.

24. James Flath, 'Managing Historical Capital', 55.

25. Yonsoon Ahn, 'Competing Nationalisms: The Mobilization of History and Archaeology in the Korea-China Wars over Koguryo/Gaogouli', *Japan Focus*, 9 February 2006.

26. Tu Wei-ming, 'Cultural China: The Periphery as the Center', in *Daedalus* 120, no. 2, Spring 1991, 22.

27. James Leibold, 'Competing Narratives of Racial Unity in Republican China', *Modern China* 32, no. 2, April 2006, 181–220.

Guide to further reading

Duara, Prasenjit, *Rescuing History from the Nation: Questioning Narratives of Modern China*, Chicago, University of Chicago Press, 1995.

Gu Jiegang, *An Autobiography of a Chinese Historian* (trans. Arthur W. Hummel), Taipei, Ch'eng-wen Publishing Co., 1966 reprint.

Harbsmeier, Cristoph, 'Some Notions of Time and of History in China and in the West, with a Digression on the Anthropology of Writing', in Chun-chieh Huang and Erik Zücher (eds.), *Time and Space in Chinese Culture*, Leiden, E. J. Brill, 1995.

Levenson, Joseph R., *Confucian China and its Modern Fate: A Trilogy*, Berkeley and Los Angeles, University of California Press, 1965.

Mittag, Achim, 'Historical Consciousness in China: Some Notes on Six Theses on Chinese Historiography and Historical Thought', in Paul Van Der Velde and Alex McKay (eds.), *New Developments in Asian Studies: An Introduction*, London, Kegan Paul, 1998, pp. 47–76.

Puett, Michael, *The Ambivalence of Creation: Debates Concerning Innovation and Artifice in Early China*, Stanford, Stanford University Press, 2001.

Wang, Q. Edward, *Inventing China through History: The May Fourth Approach to Historiography*, Albany, State University of New York, 2001.

'Between Marxism and Nationalism: Chinese Historiography and the Soviet Influence, 1949–1963', *Journal of Contemporary China* 9, no. 23, 2000, 95–111.

4

Gender in modern Chinese culture

'The saturation of cultural texts with metaphors of masculinity and femininity is nowhere more obvious than in the case of the modern, perhaps the most pervasive yet elusive of periodizing terms.'[1] These introductory words of Rita Felski's *The Gender of Modernity* could just as easily apply to the complexities of China's twentieth-century articulations of the modern as to the European texts of Felski's study. From the outset, they broadly suggest that both concepts – the modern and gender – have acquired meaning through reference to each other. At the same time, they hint at the difficulties in defining them. Neither the modern nor gender refers to fixed or stable entities of time, social practice or representation. Neither can be defined through a lens focused solely on the contours of European trajectories of modernity and gender. 'Alternative' modernities can be seen in the commercial developments of China in the late seventeenth and early eighteenth centuries, in the images of domestic spaces that featured in Shanghai's commercial print culture of the 1920s, or in the formation of the student as a political subject of anti-colonial struggle in the early part of the twentieth century.[2] The meanings and forms of femininity and masculinity that configure social relationships and cultural practices, bodies and spaces in China's modern history have similarly been the subject of extensive scholarly debate. What forms have femininity and masculinity taken in the constitution of Chinese modernity? How has China's modernity been envisaged through narratives of the feminine and the masculine? What are the historical and global parameters of meaning defining the gendered subject that contribute to contemporary Chinese discourses of femininity and masculinity? These are just some of the questions that recent scholarly research on gender in China explores.

From Shanghai's commercial advertisements of the 1920s to the revolutionary operas and ballets of the Cultural Revolution and the consumerism of contemporary urban spaces, gendered narratives – and here
I examine those that refer to Han women and men – have been powerful
metaphors of social and political change, depicting boundaries between
the modern and the traditional, the revolutionary and the revisionist,
the past and the future. They can also be read as normalizing statements
about the desires and practices of ordinary men and women. Changing
images of women across the twentieth century have encapsulated ideals
of and desires for the modern through new ideas about who women
were and what they could do. They have offered a range of new subject
positions for women to explore in the day-to-day spaces and imaginings
of their lives. Alongside women's increasing presence in the industrial
workforce, education and politics, they have been part of a radical transformation of social and cultural life, denying the gendered subject a
fixed ontology.

The general nature of the relationship between the 'modernity' of
the Eurocentric post-Enlightenment model and other colonial and
postcolonial modernities can be characterized as 'a belief in ideologies
of progress and improvement, although the meanings and objectives
signified by these terms may vary'.[3] Defined through conflict, struggle and cultural contestation with colonial power and its ownership of
'modernity', the modernity of the 'other' charts an erasure of the authentic 'native'.[4] Dressed in his Zhongshan suit, the authentically 'Chinese'
revolutionary of the early twentieth century betrays cues of both 'tradition' and the 'modern'. Is the cigarette-smoking Shanghai beauty,
with her bobbed hair and flapper attire, more Chinese or Western? The
narratives of femininity and masculinity through the different stages
of China's twentieth-century modernity similarly demonstrate the
unequal negotiation between competing ideas associated with the West,
the global and the Chinese. The history of gender in modern Chinese
culture is thus one of an uneven relationship with Western femininities
and masculinities. Never just the cultural translation of Western terms
and values, or simply the product of local understandings of gendered
difference, how does the gendered subject of China's modernity depart
from the terms of modern global discourse? As China stakes its future
on its successful integration with global capital, how do contemporary
versions of femininity and masculinity depart from the dominant model
in which 'modernity appears as a masculine phenomenon, in which the

male ideals of rationalist, competitive individualism, progress and order are promoted and contrasted with the feminine ideals of emotion, social bonds, continuity, and "tradition"'?[5]

Contemporary debates about gendered relationships and practices can, in China as elsewhere, be seen as an effect of women's increasing public agency, the global women's movement and international feminist thought. But whatever its focus, an analysis of gender and modern culture is not synonymous with an analysis of women's social and cultural practice. Gender may be understood as the changing, contingent and asymmetrical constructs of femininity and masculinity that are ascribed to bodies, social and cultural practices and relationships across time. Crucially, gender refers to changing articulations of knowledge and power associated with the embodied practices of men and women, and that operate as a major principle of social and cultural organization, defining, legitimating and reproducing differences, knowledge of these differences, and the hierarchies embedded in them.[6] Gender is thus constituted through historical and cultural practice. Cultural texts such as film, art and literature produce gender not through sociological or ethnographic analyses of women's and men's actions and relationships, but through descriptions and imaginings. Gender thus acquires meaning through cultural texts as well as social practices.

Dominant narratives of gender in contemporary China largely echo the standard temporalities of Chinese Communist Party (CCP) historiography, according to which the modern past, including the women's movement, is seen through three stages. According to this narrative, after a brief period of liberal and individualist approaches to women's emancipation between the May Fourth and Republic eras, Communist Party rule successfully laid the basis for women's liberation through facilitating women's participation in the social labour force. Following the standard Marxist approach, the CCP's approach to 'woman-work' was premised on the principle that economic independence through social employment was the condition for the attainment of gender equality. However, the Mao years imposed an artificial neutralization of gender difference, which though successful in increasing women's participation in social and political life also operated as a kind of masculinist straitjacket that denied women full agency and suppressed their essential femininity. The end of Mao's rule and the beginning of market reform facilitated the renewed expression of natural gender differences and the rearticulation of desires, aspirations and self-identifications that the harsh strictures of Mao's egalitarianism had denied. If liberating for many, the market 'deregulation' of gender also led to the resurgence of old inequalities suppressed during the socialist era and the production of new gender injustices as a spontaneous and inevitable consequence of the demands for economic efficiency and production. In accordance with the mainstream analyses of gender difference in China, as represented by China's official organization empowered to speak for and about women, the All China Women's Federation, gender inequality continues to refer to imbalances between men and women as the consequence of socio-economic structures of unequal distribution of wealth and power. Put simply, the attainment of gender equality is thus synonymous with the attainment of equal access to education, health and material prosperity for girls and women.[7]

Reflecting on these questions has political as well as academic significance. Modernity is a powerful term, embedded in the aspirations and desires of politicians, governments, and ordinary women and men. It derives its power by operating through marks of inclusion and exclusion between the colonized and the colonizer, the local and the global, distinguishing groups, sectors and classes through their differential access to social and material advantage. Narratives of gender similarly construct boundaries of acceptance and marginality, identifying practices and aspirations that confirm the desirability of the modern. While, as I discuss below, these narratives question established ideas about 'normal' social relationships, the dominant historiography of gender in China's twentieth century approaches gender difference and conflict either as an effect of socioeconomic forces, or as the expression of Maoist egalitarian imaginings. Dominant versions of China's gendered history ascribe an inevitability to the post-Mao market rejection of the gender egalitarianism of the Mao years; according to this, 'liberation' from the straitjacket of the Cultural Revolution allowed gendered subjectivities to seek their 'natural' expression in the commercialized opportunities and pleasures of the global market. Gender contradictions are thus explained as the inevitable effect of the deregulated market; the gendered subject appears as a socioeconomic entity, whose acquisition of the marks of femininity and masculinity is principally defined by her/his place in the commoditized economy. This 'official' approach to gender and gender equality exercises a profound influence on the ways that ordinary women and men understand their lives as gendered subjects in China. At the same time, it obscures the very different ways in which women may remember and identify their own histories; the three-way periodization of this dominant version of gender in modern China conceals many continuities across the different periods while hiding experiences and expectations of gender that challenge dominant and official themes.

To draw on the term gender as a category of analysis of narrative formulations of femininity and masculinity in past times is to trace the historical emergence of the gendered subject before the term 'gender' made its appearance in the Chinese lexicon. I do not use the term to retrospectively attribute a consciousness of 'gender' to individuals' subjective identification as women and men. Much less do I use it to imagine an historical and sociological category – the female subject – in China as identifying herself through the familiar sex stereotypes of the modern Western tradition. Rather, I use it as an analytical device to delineate the boundaries of normative expectations of what and who men and women were within dominant cultural discourses as they were framed through different moments.

May Fourth derivations

The gender origins that contemporary Chinese discourse draws on in explaining its own history begin with the multiple ideological and intellectual influences on women and women's emancipation circulating in China before and around the time of the 1919 May Fourth Movement. These were formulated largely by progressive male intellectuals in the pages of the new journals, newspapers and books that mushroomed during the period; many were also inspired by liberal Western ideas of individual rights – often translated from Japanese texts – that circulated at the time. Progressive debates about the 'woman question' saw the traditional patriarchal family and marriage system as the main barrier to women's emancipation in China. The solution to the 'woman question' was commonly conceptualized as emancipation of the individual from traditional social and familial constraints, in particular the patrilineal system of arranged marriage. Chen Duxiu, founding editor of the period's flagship new journal *New Youth* [*Xin qingnian*] and later to become the first general secretary of the fledgling Chinese Communist Party, saw in the 'West' an example of independence and freedom for women that the 'Confucian Way' had for centuries impeded. Famously, when Ibsen's *A Doll's House* was performed in Beijing in 1918, it sparked debate among the predominantly male intelligentsia, who saw in it 'the primacy of individual fulfilment over social restraints, [implying] a wide ranging rebellion against Confucian norms, and [suggesting] new possibilities for China's young, male and female'.[8] Prominent Western exponents of birth control and monogamous marriage such as Margaret Sanger and Ellen Key talked to eager audiences, and discussion groups and study associations formed to discuss women's education, free love and marriage, the nuclear family, women's political participation, and the ethics of women's rights and the law. Sexological, psychological and ethical treatises were translated and disseminated through the new publications. If liberal journals such as the *Chinese Ladies' Journal* or the *Ladies' Home Journal* had little sympathy for the radical leanings of many of the most outspoken exponents of women's rights, they still joined in the clamour for freedom to select marriage partners, for an end to parental interference in young people's choices, and about what to look for in a husband.

The female subject positioned by these debates was as unsettled as were her cultural derivations. The pioneering Marxist philosopher Li Da's 1919 discussion of '*nüzi jiefang*' referred to a kind of humanistic reintegration of women into the political demand for 'persons' rights' (*renquan*, also translated as 'human rights'). For Li, woman (*nüzi*) was a category whose liberation depended on recognition of her status as a person endowed with the same rights as all others. In 1923, a member of the Canton Peasant Movement Training Institute, Xiao Chu'nü, called for women's liberation to start with the 'self's essence' (*ziji de xing*), with the 'essential femaleness' (*nüxing*) of women. In an essay entitled 'The Basic Meaning of Women's Liberation', Xiao argued that women should not demand liberation from society in the expectation that society would grant it to them, but should 'take it' (*qu*) by liberating themselves from customary expectations and practices. Li Dazhao, one of the first Chinese intellectuals to openly declare his Marxist credentials and one of the founding members of the CCP, called for 'great unity throughout the world' (*shijie de da lianhe*) as the condition for women's full liberation. For him, woman was essentially a collective subject, whose agency rested on her participation in full social liberation.[9]

Socialist narratives

With the founding of the CCP came the formulation of ideas about women and women's liberation that later became the core of the CCP's official discourse of gender. The fledgling Party passed a series of resolutions committing itself to women's liberation and to women's economic, social and educational rights, all based on the principle that the women's movement had to be integrated with the anti-imperialist and anti-feudal struggles. The woman of these struggles was a collective political agent, whose emancipation demanded recognition of women as members of oppressed classes. By contrast, other articulations of woman, inscribed for example in the notion of *nüquanzhuyi* (generally translated as 'feminism') became identified in Party doctrine with a partial and implicitly divisive approach to the whole notion of people's/human rights. By 1926, articles appeared denigrating the gains of the previous stages of the women's movement. 'Women's activists' (*funüzhuyizhe*) came under attack on the grounds that they were too narrow-minded in their perspective on the 'struggle between the sexes' (*liangxing douzheng*).[10] Henceforth, renewed invocation of *nüquanzhuyi* ipso facto signalled a challenge to the Party's version of 'liberation'; contestation of the Party's position on women was specific, isolated and short lived. In accordance with the classical Marxist position, the subject of 'women's liberation' (*funü jiefang*) was the collective political subject whose liberation depended on liberation for all.

The dominant principles of the narrative depiction of women that ran through all cultural production in the early People's Republic were fixed in 1942 when the feminist writer Ding Ling published an essay entitled 'Thoughts on March 8' on the literary page of *The Liberation Daily* in Yan'an on 9 March. In the essay she criticized the Party's policy of gender unity, and drew attention to its failure to live up to its claims to liberate women. Women, she wrote, were still subject to contempt and misery, were overworked, were expected to play a double role, and were criticized if they failed in either. The Party attacked Ding for her 'narrow feminist standpoint' and for ignoring the difficulties in forging new social and economic roles for women. Later, Ding retracted her position and agreed that the first priority for women and men was to cooperate and work together for the revolution. Ding Ling's self-criticism was not only an individual response to sanctions used to silence her; it demonstrated the impossibility of following through a critique that inscribed an epistemological challenge to the Party's principles of 'woman-work'.

In an extraordinarily influential paper, Tani Barlow suggested some time ago that the terms for 'woman' – *funü, nüxing, nüren* – themselves denote epistemological differences in the conceptualization of gender.[11] *Funü* was the collectivist woman of Maoist ideology, in contrast to *nüxing*, the essential feminine woman evoked in the previously individualist discourse of the May Fourth discussants, and *nüren*, the subject of humanist principles. Ding Ling's challenge to the Party in 1942 indicated that the differences between the two terms indicated a fundamental incompatibility between two theories of knowledge about what woman – female, feminine, the possibilities of sex and gender – and therefore the requirements of women's 'liberation' – signified. The rectification movement in Yan'an was the key political moment that confirmed the future fate of challenges to Party ideology; Yan'an transformed the CCP from a political movement into an established discourse community which, by cementing loyalties to shared myths and ideals, maintained methods of discipline and subscribed to a common set of 'cultural, educational and moral forms of power'.[12] A similar argument can be used to refer to the CCP's discourse of woman and gender. Yan'an signified the dominance of the CCP's collectivist approach to the women's movement, and 'individualism' fast became a synonym for the selfish, morally suspect, and eventually the bourgeois and reactionary. The authorities' response to Ding Ling was to emphasize the 'unity' of women with men in the processes of women's liberation, confirming socialist 'woman' as a political and social subject participating in the liberation of the nation. With the CCP's consolidation of state power in 1949, the epistemological parameters of 'woman' were fixed by the classical Marxist formula. Women's liberation lay in women's equal entry into the public sphere of production and labour; transformation of gender relations of power depended on women's transformed place in the socioeconomic structure.

As components of the CCP's discursive controls, these early approaches to the 'woman question' have had a profound and determining influence on the cultural formation of gender difference in China since 1949. Publicly available cultural texts produced during the Mao years envisaged the female subject in much the same terms as the Women's Federation chairperson, Deng Yingchao, implied in a work report she delivered to the Second National Congress of Chinese Women in which she said that ten years of practice had proven that mobilizing the masses of women to participate in production was the basic key to improving equality between men and women and to achieving the thorough liberation of women. The woman of China's socialism was a wife, mother, mother-in-law and grandmother, and as such she carried out a series of naturalized as well as social obligations. However, she was principally defined through class and political considerations, rather than through bodily and potentially sexual interests that might suggest other axes of power and difference-producing social inequalities. As a social subject of socialist modernity, she was depicted through similar expectations of collective responsibility and political commitment as the man. The various revisions of the famous Communist play, opera and film, *The White Haired Girl*, illustrate how Communist narratives constructed gender difference through class.[13] Through successive revisions between its initial production in Yan'an and those of the 1950s and mid-1960s, the plot of *The White Haired Girl* moved from an initial story centred on a young peasant girl's rape by a local landlord, to one that portrayed her struggle against him as a class exploiter. The Cultural Revolution version of the play removed all references to the initial rape by describing Xi'er as a social and political subject defined by the dominant meanings of class and nation. An affirmative socialist femininity thus referred to expectations of social behaviour and attitude, including struggle and conflict, which made no reference to the domestic and sexual articulations of gender difference unless these could be explained through class. Even though different narratives of the time might frequently depict other versions of femininity, these functioned as negative metaphors for individualist and bourgeois behaviour; they suggested possibilities of a sexualized and even consumerist notion of femininity that could not be incorporated within CCP discourse. Under the rhetoric of 'what men could do, so could women do, men and women are the same', explicit expressions of gender difference were replaced by what some have called a gender neutrality, in which typically feminine representations of gender were disavowed as signs of a counter-revolutionary and bourgeois mentality.

Between the 1950s and the mid-1970s, the totalizing political controls of the Party ensured that public cultural representations of women conformed to the discursive principles fixed in Yan'an. Images of proletarian heroism produced in the 1960s and 1970s obscured romantic and sexualized narratives of femininity from public view. Posters featured images of women workers and farmers, robust reminders of the individual's proper commitment to the collective cause. As Rae Yang put it in her autobiographical account, 'As Red Guards we could not and would not wear skirts, blouses, T shirts, shorts and sandals. Anything that would make girls look like girls was bourgeois. We covered up our bodies so completely that I almost forgot that we were boys and girls. We were Red Guards, and that was it.'[14] The art, literature, films, operas and ballets produced during the Cultural Revolution featured women in strong roles, as militant fighters and political activists. 'Positive' images of women prevailed – images that by disrupting the conventional associations of dependent femininity positioned women in new roles and positions. Whether characterized as 'socialist androgyny' or 'gender neutrality', and whatever the political message they conveyed, these images defined a powerful ideal of socialist femininity, the characteristics of which remained fixed in place throughout the Mao era. Neither political nor academic debate about women permitted public spaces for alternative versions.

Market narratives

Almost as soon as the curtain fell on the Cultural Revolution, images of a sweet and gentle femininity eclipsed the 'androgyny' of the Cultural Revolution years. The Women's Federation journal, *Women of China*, recommenced publication with cover images of beautiful women dressed in diaphanous garments in pastel shades. If the Party's ideological controls were still heavily present in, for example, stories about the benefits of the single-child policy, and as the 1980s progressed in the mantra of 'to get rich is glorious', new women's magazines also appeared, with stories and images of romantic bliss and individual expression. A new tolerance in literature and the arts facilitated discussion of issues such as love and sexuality, marking a turning point in recuperating the individual voice from its obscurity in the collective realm. Collections of stories by 'women writers' were heralded as the expression of new voices free from ideological constraints. Femininity and sexuality rapidly became themes of vibrant public debate, with diverse opinions circulating through magazine editorials, feature articles, interviews and readers' letters about the attitudes and conduct appropriate to the modern woman. Public discussion on such topics seemed to relegate the orthodoxy of Maoist discourse to the annals of unwanted history. Although widely seen as a liberatory expression of a critique of the Maoist past, the 'explosion' of sex-related representations in public life also put sex into discourse as an explicit object of scrutiny.[15]

The female body represented in these new romantic images was invariably young, fashionably dressed, in good health and sexually desirable. She represented wealth, social mobility and success, and urban location, all features associated with the individualized opportunities and practices of the reform strategy. The metaphoric rewards held out to women for identifying with the images in women's magazines were the material and emotional emblems of commercial success – romantic engagement with wealthy young entrepreneurs, good looks, and exciting social and travel opportunities. The female subject of these images, however, was denied the agency given to the absent male spectator. As the homemaker, she consumed the commodities her husband created. As the beautiful and gentle companion, she awaited the guidance and protection of her husband. Her completion as a woman depended on the implied presence of the male. She affirmed Chinese masculinity as the creator of China's economic success. Furthermore, just as any presence invokes its absence, the beautiful woman also represented the exclusions and marginalizations reinforced by the same market processes that constructed her. Her eternal youth and urban identification denied the possibility of success to those women whose images were never seen in the same privileged places – the old women, the peasant women, the young female migrants working sixteen hours a day in the factories of Shenzhen – in other words, all those who had had the benefit of neither foreign travel nor education and whose socioeconomic and cultural position prevented their access to the fashionable urbanite's pleasures.

In many ways, the reformist imagining of gender difference suggested the masculinist mode of modernity that Hodgson summarized and to which I have referred above. Surveys about ideal marriage partners confirmed the binary of the active, successful and productive man, and the gentle, supportive and passive woman. While stories of the 'strong woman' (*nü qiangren*) – invariably the successful entrepreneur – extolled the benefits of the market, they took second place to the visual prominence of the young and yielding beauty. A respondent and dependent femininity was neatly mapped onto the female body, just as a strong and creative masculinity was mapped onto the male. More recent images, however, are beginning to complicate this simple dichotomy, with an increasing diversity of masculinities and femininities that reject, blur and diffuse the binary associations of heteronormativity. From the 'bad girl' image of the teenage rockstar, to the oiled muscularity of famous sportswomen, the androgynous appearance of male performance artists, and the public performances of 'traditional' *qigong* masters, contemporary images of gender are fluid and diverse. The female body-builder, for example – tall, strong and with well-developed muscles – confounds the fine, cute and gentle feminine image of mainstream male choice. Mainstream media articles and online discussions debate such issues as the changing 'look' of male icons over the past three decades, and the historical legacy of the feminine look of the *naiyou xiaosheng* ('cream man'). Lively debates about the boundaries of acceptable male behaviour took place when the '*Jiayou, hao nan'er*' ('Go, go good men', officially labelled 'My Hero') Pop Idol contest took place in China over the summer of 2006. Particular attention was given to one of the more androgynous contestants, Xiang Ding, who was vilified by some for his ultra-feminine looks at the same time that his soft looks attracted large numbers of votes from the young female audience.

The femininities and masculinities that are at the heart of contemporary consumer culture in China thus demonstrate a complex range of influences and meanings, reasserting hegemonic influences in the formation of gender at the same time as they contest them. Some read them as the local expression of the homogenization of culture under the forces of globalism; the image of the beautiful and fashionable young urbanite becomes a site where the hegemonic forces of global capital are integrated into local formation of gender identity. Her constitution becomes part of a global process that blurs clear distinctions between the 'Chinese' and the 'West'. It thus has little to distinguish it from renderings of global modernity. Others, in contrast, argue that space and positionality are crucial to the interpretation of these images. In different 'Chinese' locations, for example, the image of the modern 'Mainland sister' may be a metaphor for a range of nationalist and patriarchal suppositions, signifying threat, danger and provocation.[16] The globalization of cultural forms and images is never simply one of homogenization; repatriation of image and its re-presentation in local contexts produces diverse dialogues in local contexts that disturb the unitary force of the global.[17] Though driven by the partnership of the global market and the party-state, consumer culture thus opens up possibilities for individual agency that are not directly determined by either. The image of the fashionable female becomes much more than the emblem of consumer modernity. She offers a choice in the formation of new female subjectivities that potentially disrupts the stability of party-state and parental authority. She also becomes a visual reminder of the way in which the cultural formation of gender is negotiated between the local party-state and the global, in ways that replicate neither a simple accommodation of 'Western' nor 'patriarchal' controls.

Academic debates

Removed from the vivid publicity of commercial media images, gender
has received more sober but nonetheless significant attention in academic debate. In quantitative, theoretical and methodological terms, the
reform era has seen an effective 'great leap' in academic studies of gender
in China, with the publication of detailed analyses of gendered patterns
of employment, labour migration and education; birth control policy,
demographic change and reproductive health; marriage, family and
divorce; domestic violence, abduction of girls, prostitution and pornography; rates of HIV/AIDS infection and sexually transmitted diseases;
representations in the media and advertising; and so on.

The initial, critical impetus for this attention came from scholars
working outside or at the margins of the Women's Federation, who
pioneered the establishment of women's studies programmes in key
universities and colleges in the 1980s. The 1995 United Nations World
Conference on Women was a 'watershed' in these developments, and
subsequent years saw the establishment of many more centres and
courses. Through the work of such scholars as Li Xiaojiang, Li Yinhe,
Tan Shen and others, the elaboration of 'gender' as an analytical construct facilitated analyses of the social relationships between women
and men that did not attribute inequalities and injustices to imperfec-
tions in the socioeconomic system – in other words, to issues of class
and social differentiation – as did the All China Women's Federation.
Although scholars differed, sometimes greatly, over the interpretation
and value of gender as a category of analysis, as was – and continues to
be – commonplace in gender studies debates in Europe and America,
the articulation of women as social rather than biological beings influenced the establishment of large numbers of gender studies training
programmes, workshops, and women's NGOs whose energies went to
challenging the gendered hierarchies of social and cultural practice.

A key issue in the early days of its appearance in the critical vocabulary of Mainland scholars concerned the correct terminology (*xingbie,
shehui xingbie*) to use to distinguish the term 'gender' as a social and cultural construct from the normative connotations of binary sexual difference. In many ways this debate intersects with the critical revisions
of the concept in anglophone contexts. Both indicate the impossibility
of reading into it any fixed definition. Both also provide the evidence
that gender is what we want it to be; it becomes a mode of identification

of historical and contemporary subjectivities through the meanings we ascribe to it. However, although these debates have frequently focused on the analytical distinction between gender and sex, as has also been the case in Western discussions, these have not been a replication, much less a cultural translation, of Western terms and interpretations. A number of Chinese scholars, most notably the prominent feminist Li Xiaojiang, have argued that the sex/gender distinction that emerged in second-wave Western feminist thought is the product of post-Enlightenment European thought, and cannot be mapped onto China. Until the arrival of Western medical and sexological ideas in China in the early 1900s, social gender took precedence over anatomical sex in defining the male and the female. Li Xiaojiang thus argued that if Chinese conceptualizations of male and female referred to social practice, 'it would be redundant to introduce the notion of gender (*shehui xingbie*, literally social sex difference) to the Chinese language, since *nü* (woman/female) and *nan* (man/male) are already understood as social and not natural beings'.[18]

The Women's Federation has also been responsible for much of the recent research on women's inequality in Chinese society. Indeed, as the organization officially authorized to speak about and for women, it could not fail to address the issue. Many key individuals in the research, provincial and other sections of the organization have been active and tireless internal lobbyists for the acknowledgment of gender as a critical space of articulation in China. At a central policy level, however, the Women's Federation continues to put forward a socioeconomic rather than a gender analysis of gender inequalities. In line with CCP analysis in general, it approaches the current ever-widening gender polarities in economic and social life as the inevitable consequence of the greater complexity of Chinese society and culture under the impact of the global market. Through the Women's Federation, the Party's prerogative over defining the meanings and tasks of women's liberation has thus had a profound and limiting effect that has thwarted the critical possibilities of gender. In part, this can be explained with reference to the history of the Party's imposition of a fixed ideology of gender equality. Li Xiaojiang has argued that the shortcomings in achievements of gender equality in the first period were the necessary effect of an understanding of women's liberation as something to be bestowed or imposed by the Party authorities, and not as a process formulated in autonomous spaces defined by women themselves. While the Party consistently defined the principal aims and processes of the Women's Movement, and stressed the importance of women's agency in accordance with its strategic identification of the goals and processes of the revolution as a whole, its 'bestowal' of policies and practices oriented to furthering women's interests in their own liberation did not fundamentally construct women as agents of their own transformation. Indeed, the Party's conservative response when ordinary women did act as agents, in seeking divorce, for example, or in selecting a marriage partner, suggests that the expression of female agency outside officially sanctioned parameters disturbed women's capacity to function as effective vehicles of power. Furthermore, the discursive influence of the Party's definition of women's liberation has prevented the entry of gender into general academic debates. The field of gender and feminist theory is notable for its absence from the interdisciplinary and self-reflexive theoretical approaches of the social sciences in China. In contrast to the male intellectual's concern for women's liberation during the May Fourth period, contemporary male intellectuals approach gender equality as a matter of the past, resolved by the radical transformation in the social position of women over the past decades.[19] In a political and social environment in which the Women's Federation is still seen as the legitimate voice on women's issues, and in which debates about gender have largely been sustained in under-funded and vulnerable women's studies programmes, the critical possibilities of gender have effectively been thwarted. Mainstream academia's relegation of gender to low-status 'women's studies' scholars has confirmed its isolated position in critical discourse. The compartmentalization of 'women's issues' (funü wenti) by and within the party-state has therefore prevented a view of social issues as gendered, and has effectively prevented recognition of the relevance of 'gender' as a political and analytical category to those outside the circumscribed spheres of feminist and women's studies scholars. It is therefore not surprising that Chinese scholars have devoted minimal attention to masculinity. Li Yinhe and Wang Xiaobo's *Tamen de shijie* [*Their world*] broke new ground as the first serious study of male homosexuality in contemporary China.[20] Yi Zhongtian's 1998 publication of *Zhongguo de nanren he nüren* [*Chinese men and women*] was one of the first to reflect on the category of 'man' as well as 'woman' in Chinese literature and culture.[21] By and large, however, apart from these and a few notable English-language exceptions, the academic field of gender is still circumscribed by the limits of its appeal beyond small circles of largely feminist scholars and activists.

Narrative interventions

The idea that the 1978 'turning point' introducing 'open-door reform' to China signified a rupture with revolutionary gender practices, making way for the spontaneous and liberatory expression of essential gender differences, naturalizes the power of market forces to define the shape and meaning of gender practices and relations in line with stereotypically Western versions of modernization. Inscribed in dominant discourse, and institutionalized in the practices of the Women's Federation, this view also stultifies academic and media debate. While the 'before and after Mao' approach has a very general value for identifying the key macro socioeconomic and political shifts that mould the practices and relationships of day-to-day life, it also functions as a kind of epistemic block on alternative temporalities of gender. As a potent form of historical intervention, it constructs a past of gender that legitimizes the teleology of the present. However, scholars from different disciplines challenge its terms and the analytical straitjacket it imposes. Contradictory but coexisting concepts of womanhood emerge, challenging the binaries of the 'traditional' and the 'modern', the 'socialist/Chinese' and the 'market/Western/global'. Contemporary China can be described, for example, as 'a unique context where the survival of traditional culture, the legacy of radical socialism, and global capitalism, are competing with each other'.[22] Socialist and post-socialist modernities overlap unevenly in working women's narratives of their lives spanning the decades of the People's Republic of China.[23] Guo Yuhua, a Beijing-based anthropologist with lengthy experience of village life in China's northwest, suggests that women's understanding of key moments and movements such as 'revolution' and 'liberation' fundamentally departs from the temporalities of Party history. While men narrate their experiences of revolution through the dominant framework established by the party-state's main political campaigns, women chart their lives through a bodily temporality – 'body-time' – of childbirth, sickness and food.[24] The inventions and interventions of Party historiography become fixed as self-evident truths, repeatedly rehearsed in popular and official discourses. In the process, they obscure shifts and ambiguities within and across the 'periods' of gender and modernity established in mainstream narratives of Chinese modernity.

Guo's article vividly depicts local disruptions to the standard narratives of gender described in the sections above. It is a reminder of the creativity of memory in protecting spaces of experience from external and controlling interventions. However, these narratives also give their own internal evidence of formulations of femininity and masculinity that disturb the teleology of gender transformation of which they are a part, and that offer glimpses of subjectivities that the dominant historiography of gender has erased. Put simply, the figure of the 'new socialist woman' of the 1950s and the 'iron girl' of the Cultural Revolution tells only a partial – albeit powerful – history of gender.

Narratives and images of women during China's socialist modernity offered an unsettled fluctuation between women's social capacity to change – to do as men did – and women's fixed association with childcare and domestic work based on a biological and reproductive definition of femininity. Socialist discourse expected women to devote their energies to the collective and the state, but it also endowed women with natural responsibilities to the domestic sphere that the rhetoric of male–female equality did not shift. Women repeatedly appeared in the (official) women's and youth journals of the 1950s and early 1960s as more passive and dependent than men, and reproductively designed to make a greater contribution to childcare and family welfare than their husbands. Young women's naturalized interests in romantic and materialistic matters were repeated metaphors for the bourgeois and the individualist. At the same time, they could also serve to boost policy priorities when the need arose. During the mid-1950s, coinciding with rising pressures on the urban economy under the effects of large-scale migration to the cities, the slogan 'Let's be pretty' encouraged women to make the best of 'returning home'. A new legitimacy ascribed to permed hairstyles and floral printed skirts appeared as a reward for withdrawing from the urban labour market. Interior domestic spaces depicted in posters of the early 1970s were inhabited by women and children, and vary rarely men. The imaging of women as young mothers of bouncy colourfully clad babies reinforced the naturalized association between femininity and reproductive care. Ideals of revolutionary heroines might grant a 'manly spirit' to the female body, but ideological correctness could not always disguise the 'voluptuous appeal and ... beauty' of the feminine image, with 'handcuffed hands, whipped body, long and braided hair and torn red silk dress'.[25] The limits of the transformative possibilities of femininity were defined by women's 'natural' capacities, responsibilities and interests.

If these references unsettle the gender neutrality of representations of the socialist era, autobiographical narratives of the period reveal the freedom that distance from typically feminine associations offered young women in their self-identification as political and social subjects. 'Socialist woman' was neither the defeminized entity suggested by post-Mao narratives nor the docile subject of egalitarian revolutionary discipline. For Xiaomei Chen, 'the androgynous play between the manly woman and the womanly man' during the Cultural Revolution created an 'ambiguous space', giving her a sense of balance and freedom.[26] Rae Yang acknowledged a similar experience of freedom and autonomy in *Spider Eaters*, her account of growing up in Mao's China.[27] She describes how her simple 'uniform' of the Red Guards gave her a sense of self as a political subject that was undisturbed by concerns with gendered appearance. Far from being a constraint on a naturalized femininity, the grey and green colours and simple lines of her clothes gave her confidence in her status as an equal actor with other women and men of her age and outlook. These brief examples show that socialist discourse, visual as well as textual, was far from holding out a closed set of positions for women's self-identification.

Finally, the levelling out of the disjunctures of the recent past in dominant narratives is part of a discursive process shaping contemporary as well as past configurations of gender. The pretty femininity that celebrated the new era of reform was widely proclaimed as the expression of natural gender difference, free from the constraints of Mao puritanism. The 'modern woman' heralded China's path to a modernized future, and the female body became an emblem of a modernity that echoed the model of the West. Even the 'traditional Oriental beauty' of the catwalk contests appeared 'Western' insofar as she had large eyes and was taller than the 'Chinese beauty' of 'un-reinvented' tradition.[28] Her sweet form celebrated and bolstered a reinvigorated masculine creativity responsible for the advances of the consumer market. However, this version of contemporary femininity ignores others that interfere with the hierarchical implications of its image. The consumption of images and products manufactured by domestic and global economic interests that often seem to confirm familiar gender stereotypes is not synonymous with a simple acceptance of hierarchical gender relations. Not so long ago, the All China Women's Federation opposed beauty contests on the grounds that they 'misled' young women by exaggerating the importance of 'external beauty'. But while many women of the Cultural Revolution generation may hold the view that young women's fashions in urban China today signify a dependent femininity constructed by and for male expectations and pleasures, their daughters see something different. For them, the possibility of making choices between different shapes and colours of femininity signifies the freedom to express desires and values denied their mothers' generation. Hence, tinting hair a shade of red may signify a rebelliousness and self-assertiveness in response to conservative-minded parents. Experimenting with different poses and 'looks' in the private space of a photographer's studio may encourage the performative expression of fantasies that necessarily need to be contained in day-to-day life. It is in the context of such individual and local practices that the images of fashionable beauty acquire more particular meanings. And even though their presence in local magazines may be inspired by global capital in its regional and local forms, their readers interpret them in terms that do not simply sustain the dominant 'masculinist' model. The choices young women make in 'reading' these images do not indicate a simple attachment to the global/Western as a synonym for the modern, much less to a desire to 'look like' the quintessential 'Westerner'. Rather, they see the foreign/Western/global as one – for some, certainly, the most important – of various sites of inspiration, including Japan, Korea, Taiwan and Hong Kong, which contribute to the formation of local tastes and desires.

The images these magazines offer their readers thus represent a range of possible gender meanings. The global production and dissemination of images of fashionable modern femininity establish the general boundaries containing the choices of urban China's young women. However, within local cultural contexts, the specificities of young women's choices can be seen as an assertion of agency, and not simply as pandering to consumer trends, or returning to some conventional notion of femininity. Young women's interpretations of different 'looks' demonstrate that there is no single 'femininity' associated with the image of the beautiful woman. For these young women, consumer capacity grants the possibility of affirming desires that are linked more to their search for independence and autonomy within a patriarchal social and political environment than to conformity to the stereotypical gender images of global culture. Young women's responses to fashion images thus suggest an ambivalent negotiation of gender and social identities that by no means always correspond with the dominant narratives of the party and global capital. 'Femininity' emerges as a creative convergence of individual desires, local gender and sexual politics, and global consumer capitalism, all competing in a conflicted space. Making choices between different 'looks' is inseparable from the formation of new female subjectivities in which the inscriptions of the party-state and global capitalism tell only part of the story.

Epilogue

A discussion about the cultural narratives of gender in modern China is much more than an academic one, as I have already pointed out. It is through such narratives that gender comes to be understood as an axis and principle of social organization, differentiation and contestation – in other words, of practices and representations that function as markers of inclusion and exclusion, access and marginality. As we have seen, the view of gendered difference that emerges from the mainstream periodization of China's social and political transformation constructs femininities and masculinities in mainly socioeconomic terms, sustaining a view of Chinese modernity that operates according to the Western/global teleology of development and progress. Against this backdrop, the local fissures in modern narratives of gender in China have repeatedly demonstrated alternative possibilities of practice and self-identification that challenge the validity of this universalizing rendering of modernity. Some of these can be discerned in the plural readings of contemporary images and texts, which question the characterization of the essentially feminine woman naturally re-emerging from the constraints of Mao ideology. Others are seen in local knowledges and memories of gender as lived experience that diverge from the dominant temporalities of Party history. These fissures are the cultural spaces of difference in which ordinary social subjects demonstrate their distance from the terms of the party-state. It is these that indicate the contradictory, fractured and messy realities of gender that women, and men, live out in their relationships with family, locality and state. An analysis of gender narratives that incorporates acknowledgment of these fissures thus permits a disruption of dominant versions of gender. Even though alternative perspectives are obscured by the normalizing power of the party-state to erase different interpretations of its past and present, they are nonetheless a living reminder of the disruptive potential of local cultural narratives to challenge the subjectifying terms of dominant renderings of the modern.

Notes

1. Rita Felski, *The Gender of Modernity*, Cambridge, MA, Harvard University Press, 1995, p. 1.
2. Timothy Brook, *The Confusions of Pleasure: Commerce and Culture in Ming China*, Berkeley and Los Angeles, University of California Press, 1999; Leo Ou-fan Lee, 'The Cultural Construction of Modernity in Urban Shanghai: Some Preliminary Reflections', in Wen-hsin Yeh (ed.), *Becoming Chinese: Passages to Modernity and Beyond*, University of California Press, 2000, pp. 31–61; Fabio Lanza, 'Politics of the Unbound: "Students" and the *Everyday* of Beijing University', *Positions: East Asia Cultures Critique* (forthcoming).
3. Dorothy L. Hodgson (ed.), *Gendered Modernities: Ethnographic Perspectives*, New York, Palgrave, 2001, pp. 8–9.
4. Rey Chow, 'Where has the Native Gone', in *Writing Diaspora: Tactics of Intervention in Contemporary Cultural Studies*, Bloomington and Indianapolis, Indiana University Press, 1993, pp. 27–54.
5. Hodgson, *Gendered Modernities*, pp. 8–9.
6. Susan Brownell and Jeffrey Wasserstrom (eds.), *Chinese Femininities/Chinese Masculinities: A Reader*, Berkeley and Los Angeles, University of California Press, 2002, p. 1.
7. Naihua Zhang, 'Searching for Authentic NGOs: The NGO Discourse and Women's Organizations in China', in Ping-Chun Hsiung, Maria Jaschok and Cecilia Milwertz, with Rei Chan (eds.), *Chinese Women Organizing: Cadres, Feminists, Muslims, Queers*, Oxford and New York, Berg, 2001, p. 171. In line with its dominant Marxist definition of its work, the Women's Federation defines its key functions as '*tuanjie, dongyuan guangda funü canyu jingji jianshe he shehui fazhan, daibiao he weihu funü liyi, cujin nannü pingdeng* [to unite and mobilize the broad mass of women to participate in economic construction and social development, and to represent and protect women's interests to achieve male-female equality]'. From 'Zhonghua funü lianhe hui jianjie' [Brief Introduction to the Chinese Women's Federation]. See www.women.org.cn.
8. Carolyn T. Brown, 'Woman as Trope: Gender and Power in Lu Xun's "Soap"', in Tani E. Barlow (ed.), *Gender Politics in Modern China: Writings and Feminism*, Durham and London, Duke University Press, 1993, p. 74.
9. For the references in this paragraph, see Harriet Evans, 'The Language of Liberation: Gender and *jiefang* in early Chinese Communist Party Discourse', in Jeffrey N. Wasserstrom (ed.), *Twentieth Century China: New Approaches*, London and New York, Routledge, 2003, pp. 193–220.
10. 'Guangdong funü jiefang xiehui diyici daibiao dahui ji yijue an' [Decision of the First Congress of the Guangdong Women's Liberation Association], in *Zhongguo funü yundong lishi ziliao* 2, 672–5; Yang Zhihua, 'Zhongguo funü yundong zuiyan' [The Errors of China's Women's Movement], in *Zhongguo funü yundong lishi ziliao* 2, 555–61.
11. Tani E. Barlow, 'Theorizing Woman: Funü, Guojia, Jiating', in Angela Zito and Tani E. Barlow (eds.), *Body, Subject and Power in China*, Chicago, University of Chicago Press, 1994, pp. 253–89.
12. David Apter and Tony Saich, *Revolutionary Discourse in Mao's Republic*, Cambridge, MA, Harvard University Press, 1994, pp. 66–7.

13. Meng Yue, 'Female Images and National Myth', in Tani E. Barlow (ed.), *Gender Politics in Modern China*, Durham and London, Duke University Press, 1993, pp. 118–36.

14. Rae Yang, *Spider Eaters: A Memoir*, Berkeley, CA, University of California Press, 1997, p. 213.

15. Harriet Evans, *Women and Sexuality in China: Dominant Discourses of Female Sexuality and Gender since 1949*, Cambridge, Polity Press, 1997; Emily Honig and Gail Hershatter, *Personal Voices: Chinese Women in the 1980s*, Stanford, CA, Stanford University Press, 1988.

16. Shu-mei Shih, 'Gender and a New Geopolitics of Desire: The Seduction of Mainland Women in Taiwan and Hong Kong', *Signs* 23, no. 2, 1998, 287–319.

17. Arjun Appadurai, 'Disjuncture and Difference in the Global Cultural Economy', *Public Culture* 5, no. 3, 1990, 1–24.

18. Li Xiaojiang, 'With what Discourse do we Reflect on Chinese Women? Thoughts on Transnational Feminism in China', in Mayfair Mei-hui Yang (ed.), *Spaces of their Own: Women's Public Sphere in Transnational China*, Minneapolis, University of Minnesota Press, 1999, p. 262.

19. Zhong Xueping, *'Hou funü jiefang yu ziwo xiangxiang'* [Post-women's Liberation and Self-Reflections], in *Dushu* [Reading], November 2005, 13–20.

20. Li Yinhe and Wang Xiaobo, *Tamen de Shijie: Zhongguo nanxing tongxing lian quanluo toushi* [Their World: A Perspective on China's Male Homosexual Community], Taiyuan, Shanxi renmin chubanshe, 1992.

21. Yi Zhongtian, *Zhongguo de nanren he nüren* [Chinese Men and Women], 1998; Xueping Zhong, *Masculinity Besieged? Issues of Modernity and Male Subjectivity in Chinese Literature of the Late Twentieth Century*, Durham, Duke University Press, 2000; Kam Louie, *Theorising Chinese Masculinity: Society and Gender in China*, Cambridge, Cambridge University Press, 2002; Brownell and Wasserstrom (eds.), *Chinese Femininities*.

22. Yunxiang Yan, *Private Life under Socialism*, Stanford, CA, Stanford University Press, 2003, p. 233.

23. Lisa Rofel, *Other Modernities: Gender Yearnings in China after Socialism*, Berkeley, Los Angeles and London, University of California Press, 1999.

24. Guo Yuhua, 'Xinling de jitihua: Shaanbei Jicun nongye hezuohua de nüxing jiyi' [Psychological Collectivisation: Women's Memories and the Cooperativization of Agriculture in Jicun Village, Northern Shaanxi], *Social Sciences in China* 4 (2003), 48–61.

25. This is a reference to the erotic appeal of the famous painting of Wu Qinghua, the strong and shapely heroine of the revolutionary model ballet *The Red Detachment of Women*. Entitled *Full of Hatred [Manqiang chouhen]*, this oil painting was a copy of the stage photograph of the same image from the ballet performance. Xiaomei Chen, 'Growing Up with Posters in the Mao Era', in Harriet Evans and Stephanie Donald (eds.), *Picturing Power in the People's Republic of China: Posters of the Cultural Revolution*, Lanham, Rowman and Littlefield, 1999, pp. 101–22.

26. Chen, 'Growing Up with Posters', p. 110.

27. Rae Yang, *Spider Eaters*. See also Xueping Zhong, Wang Zheng and Bai Di (eds.), *Some of Us: Chinese Women Growing Up in the Mao Era*, New Brunswick, New Jersey and London, Rutgers University Press, 2001.

28. Susan Brownell, 'The Body and the Beautiful in Chinese Nationalism: Sportswomen and Fashion Models in the Reform Era', *China Information* 13, no. 2/3, Autumn/Winter 1998–99, 36–58.

Guide to further reading

Barlow, Tani E., 'Theorizing Woman: Funü, Guojia, Jiating', in Angela Zito and Tani E. Barlow (eds.), *Body, Subject and Power in China*, Chicago, University of Chicago Press, 1994, pp. 253–89.

Brownell, Susan, and Jeffrey Wasserstrom (eds.), *Chinese Femininities/Chinese Masculinities: A Reader*, Berkeley and Los Angeles, University of California Press, 2002.

Croll, Elisabeth J., *Feminism and Socialism in China*, London, Routledge and Kegan Paul, 1978.

Evans, Harriet, *Women and Sexuality in China: Dominant Discourses of Female Sexuality and Gender since 1949*, Cambridge, Polity Press, 1997.

Honig, Emily, and Gail Hershatter, *Personal Voices: Chinese Women in the 1980s*, Stanford, CA, Stanford University Press, 1988.

Li, Xiaojiang, 'With what Discourse do we Reflect on Chinese Women? Thoughts on Transnational Feminism in China', in Mayfair Mei-hui Yang (ed.), *Spaces of their Own: Women's Public Sphere in Transnational China*, Minneapolis, University of Minnesota Press, 1999, pp. 261–77.

Rofel, Lisa, *Other Modernities: Gendered Yearnings in China after Socialism*, Berkeley and Los Angeles, University of California Press, 1999.

Yan, Yunxiang, *Private Life under Socialism*, Stanford, CA, Stanford University Press, 2003.

Zhong, Xueping, Wang Zheng and Bai Di (eds.), *Some of Us: Chinese Women Growing Up in the Mao Era*, New Brunswick, N J and London, Rutgers University Press, 2001.

5

Ethnicity and Chinese identity: ethnographic insight and political positioning

Ethnic identity is never static; nor is it a consistent social category. This very fluidity accounts for the presence of competing postures within a community. The internal conflict between individuals as private selves and as members of groups can result in the expansion, however momentary, of group affiliation and consciousness. Left unchecked, the assertion of group identities, especially ethnic identities, can tear a nation-state apart. In contemporary China, the central government actively promotes the nation-state as the primary source of emotional transference and personal identification. In making the nation the paramount reality the state hopes to subsume alternative, potentially competing forms of identity under the umbrella of nationalism. The Chinese state has demonstrated a willingness to use severe negative sanctions on those who challenge its authority in an effort to buttress national unity at the expense of ethnic identity.

The origins, meanings and expressions of Chinese ethnicity are intertwined with the central government's ethnic policies that, in so many ways, are in conflict with ethnic identity. The dichotomy arises from pursuing cultural models that are anchored in the contradictory principles of multi-culturalism and mono-culturalism. These competing ideals are constantly demonstrated in the state's policies toward ethnic minorities in China. Striving to uphold these two ideals results in the promotion of certain policies that support an ethnic minority's interests while at the same time implementing policies that undermine minority cultural values. This chapter will examine each of these models in turn.

The multi-culturalist, or multi-ethnic, state model supports the efforts of ethnic minorities to retain their cultural heritage through the institution of affirmative action policies. For example, advocates of

multi-culturalism support the creation of autonomous regions and prefectures to preserve ethnic identities and traditions. Multi-culturalists
also support the extension of preferential treatment to minorities on the
college entrance exam and providing them with government employment opportunities. In contrast, the mono-culturalist model highlights
individual achievement over group entitlement. It favours a model
of social integration that seeks to incorporate individuals rather than
groups (i.e. ethnic nationalities) into mainstream society. From a mono-
culturalist perspective, China, much like America and France, strives to
coopt its minorities, especially members from the educated elite, into
perceiving and acting as if they are 'Chinese', thereby reducing potential
interest in participating in a resistance movement.

Implicit in Chinese culture is the presumption that there are fundamental axioms or ways of living in the world. In highlighting ethical
considerations over biological presumptions, Chinese society has become relatively open to interethnic marriage and thus cultural blending. Because Chinese culture, with a few notable exceptions, is not based
in a belief that people have different degrees of 'purity', it has tended to
devalue group identity over individual accomplishment. In this milieu,
'dynasties could come and go without undermining a people's ethical
sensibility, social solidarity, or cultural stability'.[1] In time, these ethical
principles provided a basis for the construction of a shared national cultural identity that was open to anyone who behaved properly.

Given these convictions, the Chinese state expects that in time everyone – including ethnic minorities and marginalized Han – will 'converge
toward an imagined center that historically has been coterminous with
the Confucian ethos'.[2] In this way, China is more culturally centric than
nationalistic. This culturalistic orientation has also contributed to the
rapid assimilation of China's diverse peoples.

The movement towards an imagined cultural centre is evident in the
shift in how peasants are seen. In the 1980s, Hohhotian urbanites (both
Han and the Mongol ethnic minority) perceived peasants as a marginalized occupational group that was in every way culturally 'inferior'. Many
admitted, however, that if the behaviour of peasants changed to fit within the prevailing urbanized cultural standard they would no longer be
stigmatized or perceived as inferior. By 2000, many urbanites from peasant backgrounds had transformed themselves in public manners into
typical urbanites. Consequently, they were perceived as less marginal
and thus almost as social equals. The qualification to extending them

greater respect arises from the state's residential classification system, which continues to assign social status based on the mother's birthplace. In doing so, the state maintains a dual citizenship between its rural and urban populations. Still, the cultural logic of 'appropriate cultural standards' has enabled China's peasant farmers to undercut the state's administrative distinction and gradually transform themselves into respectable citizens. A similar logic is at work within many of China's ethnic minority communities.

The majority of Han Chinese never abandoned their preference for mono-culturalism. For most, it remains a strong value-orientation that continues to shape the ethnic strategy of China's national leadership. This results in a series of paradoxes whereby the Communist Party acknowledges the importance of cultural diversity, while simultaneously seeking to introduce institutional changes that blur cultural differences between groups. The endeavour to implement two dichotomous cultural models results in polarization within many ethnic communities between those who want greater autonomy and those who prefer closer integration within Chinese society. It also accounts for the fact that many minorities hold onto a disjointed sense of personal identity. The tensions between these two cultural models – multi-cultural and mono-cultural – continue to be played out in shifting social policies involving the intersection of ethnic interests and national concerns that also shape the responses of China's minority and majority populations to issues of absorption and separation.

The government's oscillation between the competing models has also influenced its minority policies, which range from 'soft' to 'hard' measures designed to promote as well as undermine minority ethnic unity. The soft policies actively promote affirmative action incentives, and are designed to win favour among the minority population and facilitate acculturation into Chinese society.

The soft policies are remarkably consistent with de Tocqueville's philosophy that held that the best government is one that provides talented individuals from society's lower strata (or in this case, minority groups) with material incentives to support and not oppose the prevalent social convention. In contrast, the 'hard' policies use negative sanctions to arrest and imprison anyone who publicly argues against the state's official position. The post-Tiananmen years have seen the introduction of more draconian policies toward minority peoples in almost every autonomous region of the PRC. Hard measures are used to clamp down on elements believed to be fostering dissent, advocating independence, or carrying out terrorist attacks.[3]

Cultural diversity and the myth of Han Chinese homogenization

The Qing dynasty collapsed in 1911, but the new Republic of China remained fragmented. The largest minority populations (e.g. the Mongols, Uyghurs and Tibetans) failed to join the newly formed and highly ineffectual Chinese republic.[4] Most of China's ethnic minorities assumed they were not Chinese, but rather independent nations. However, the end of the empire tradition found ethnic minorities remarkably unprepared to advance their claims for independent statehood. The Manchu policy of 'divide and rule' undermined ethnic nationalistic sentiment by stressing kinship as the defining group allegiance. Ethnic group identification was weakly developed among most minority populations. Prior to the twentieth century, the steppe (or grasslands) was homeland to the Mongols, Uyghurs and Kazaks. As China and Russia-based empires enclosed and occupied this region, the ethnic nationalists faced limited options. Whether 'independent' under Russian or Japanese rule or 'autonomous' under China, the fate of these groups was dictated by larger geopolitical interests.[5] The efforts of some minority elites to seek fuller, more meaningful political independence were largely ineffective. Independence for the ethnic minorities was a position that neither the Soviet Union nor the new leadership of the Republic of China would accept. Much of the oscillation in contemporary China's minority policy is a reflection of philosophical idealism and pragmatic adaptations that have never lost sight of the ultimate goal; that is, the political unification of all peoples living in the People's Republic of China.

Both historic and contemporary China, like European societies in the seventeenth century, have a weak sense of national identity. The objectification of a Chinese national identity did not occur until the late nineteenth century, when Sun Yat-sen, the first provisional president of the Republic of China, actively promoted the notion of a unitary multi-ethnic nation-state over the ethnic nationalism ideal that would have made the nation-state coterminous with its largest ethnic group, the Han people.[6] Sun's reluctance to make China officially a mono-cultural nation-state was entirely pragmatic: Han ethnic identity was relatively undeveloped, having been formed largely in opposition to the Manchus, who had formed the Qing dynasty (1636–1911) that ruled China. Although the Han despised the Manchus, most people identified more with their locality than with the idea of 'Hanness'. For most, Han was a categorical term and not the basis for the establishment of an emotionally salient collective identity. Aware of these limitations, Sun promoted the idea that China was a multi-ethnic state respectful of cultural diversity.

In spite of China's enormous cultural and ethnic diversity, it is often portrayed for political purposes as basically a homogeneous nation-state, with a long history of cultural and social unity.[7] This official position hides the enormous cultural and linguistic diversity within the People's Republic of China (PRC) that includes 91 million people officially designated as belonging to minorities living throughout China. These minorities speak a wide variety of languages, including Sino-Tibetan (Mandarin, Tibetan, Kam-Tai, Miao-Yao), Turkic-Altaic (Kazakh, Uyghur, Mongolian, Manchu-Tungus, Korean), and Austro-Asiatic (Hmong, Vietnamese). Although ethnic minorities account for less than 9 per cent of China's total population, they occupy nearly three fifths of its total territory, including most of China's border regions. There are different kinds of minorities in China, ranging from deeply assimilated Hui to culturally distinct Kazaks. Most live in or near one of China's 156 minority autonomous areas (5 regions, 30 prefectures and 121 counties).[8] They also tend to have a lower standard of living, 'with 143 out of 311 poor counties (or 46 per cent) being in minority areas'.[9]

The official position is that China's largest ethnic group, the Han, are a culturally homogeneous majority, but this position is debatable. Although the Han Chinese share a common written language, there is enormous linguistic diversity among them. Linguists identify eight major spoken language groups that are mutually unintelligible. For example, speakers of Cantonese – spoken by around 60 million people in Guangdong Province and in Hong Kong and Macao – cannot understand native speakers from Beijing or Shanghai.[10] Cultural diversity among the Han Chinese is found by examining the history of the Hakka, who migrated more than 1,700 years ago from north into southern China (e.g. Guangdong, Jiangsu and Fujian). This group of people is officially registered as Han Chinese. However, they are aware of having different origins from neighbouring Han. For example, in the past, they lived in isolated and walled compounds, and during the imperial era Hakka women did not bind their feet. But despite a history of cultural distinctiveness, the Hakka have not sought to be, and nor are they, officially recognized as a distinct ethnic group. In effect, they remain nothing more than a social category.

Further evidence of the diversity in Han ethnic identity can be found in the way people develop a particular relationship with a specific geographical region or native place – an identification that can serve as the basis for the development of an individual's sociability network. Native place identities (usually developed without the government's formal recognition) are formed through tracing genealogical ties that link an individual with his or her parents' or grandparents' birthplace. Native place identities are anchored in the pragmatics of ordinary life and are based in the need for social support and personal affiliation. For instance, the Subei people who live in and around the Shanghai region hold strong convictions about their social distinctiveness, and consider themselves a viable, albeit officially unrecognized, ethnic group. Their sense of identity arises from the belief in a shared affiliation with a people from a specific geographical region (e.g. Jiangsu province).

Native place identities can also arise from the government's efforts to promote regional identification. In Shanxi in north China, the provincial government has successfully sought to promote economic development by highlighting the province's unique foods, cultural traits and economic accomplishments. This has enhanced the local people's pride in and identification with the region, and this has resulted in a more expansive form of native place identity: a provincial identity based on the perception that one is a Shanxi person.[11] In this way, a person's native place can promote a sense of fictive kinship that can serve as an unofficial ethnic identity.

For many Han Chinese, especially those living in border areas, a minority's autonomous region has become a new, significant source of personal identity. Two and three generations ago, the Han settlers in the autonomous regions included youth sent to the countryside in the wake of the Cultural Revolution, retired and demobilized servicemen, and political prisoners and criminals. These original Han migrants did not identify themselves as local, but continued to retain their identity from their place of origin. Now, however, their offspring consider themselves to be local residents. Like the British citizens banished to nineteenth-century Australia, these Han see themselves as 'Inner Mongolians' or 'Xinjiang people'. In every way, the birthplaces of these offspring have become their native places. They have positive feelings about the region's food habits and cultural traits that may also be associated with a particular minority group. For most, it is irrelevant that the autonomous region is associated with a particular minority. This generation has developed a strong sense of connectedness with the fate of the region. These are the new non-ethnic minorities of Inner Mongolia, Xinjiang and Tibet. But not every minority population is pleased with this shift and the appearance of this new source of regional identification. For example, many Mongols retain ambivalent feelings toward this new form of identification. They appreciate the Han's respect for their region and enjoyment of many of the local ethnic foods and cultural elements, but, on the other hand, they do not like the dilution of their ethnic heritage through an outsider's eagerness to engage in what many view as a form of cultural appropriation through their development of a broader, more inclusive, form of regional identity.

It is China's extensive cultural diversity as manifested in linguistic expression and local customary practices that has led Dru Gladney to suggest that China could easily lapse into social fragmentation.[12] Clearly, there are segmentational forces at work. This does not mean, however, that there are not equally powerful forces that pull individuals back toward strong identification with the nation-state. The average Chinese readily acknowledges, often with pride, the existence of enormous dialect/language distinctions, dietary differences, and wide-ranging local customs. But this recognition is seldom qualified by concern for China's political integrity. For most Han, as well as many ethnic minorities, China remains a unified nation-state, albeit one with intriguing cultural differences.[13] For most Chinese, it is national identity rather than ethnic identity that is the primary source of emotional identification.[14] Further evidence of strong nationalistic bonds is found in the nationwide reaction to the accidental 1999 Belgrade embassy bombing, the 2001 Hainan spy plane encounter and, with the exception of urban-based minorities (e.g. Mongols, Uyghurs and Tibetans), a unified position in favour of Taiwan's reunification with the Mainland. The strength of a person's nationalism derives from their emotional identification and thus connection with the nation-state. This does not mean that local identities are no longer significant. They remain so. It does mean, however, that in some contexts national identity can also quickly and readily become an equally powerful force in shaping an individual's emotional identification and political loyalty.

State politics, ethnic identification and ethnic assertion

Ethnic groups, in spite of their own assertions, are not immutable and pure, with roots in a timeless past. Rather, they are the by-product of the convergence of people of disparate backgrounds, whose struggles often produce a belief in a shared history that serves as a rallying point in the creation of a common identity. Ethnogenesis, or the origins of a culture's identity, is a complex process that examines the relationship between structural forces (e.g. demographic, economic, political, and so on) and formation of group membership or identity.

In cultures organized around interaction based on criteria other than a shared ethnicity, there is a dilution of interest in the politics of ethnic assertion. This is especially so in southwest China, the 'home of an astonishing array of minority ethnicities that has seldom posed a serious threat to the government'.[15] Shih also found political identity to be unmistakably weak among the Zhuang, Tujia and Miao (minorities inhabiting southwest China), who act as if the ethnic label is a categorical term 'imposed on them and thus [with] no clear meaning for them'.[16] Mary Rack also found this to be true for the Miao, who organized their associations and thus identity around residential bonds and seldom on the basis of the state-imposed ethnic label Miao.[17]

However, in many nation-states, where the central government serves as the final arbiter of ethnic claims, its policies can also serve as a source of increased interest in ethnic identification and thus ethnic competition. Consequently, the government's ethnic minority policies often serve as a powerful force in shaping or reducing ethnic consciousness. This pattern can be found among several minority populations in southwest China. Before the institutionalization of the state's ethnic minority policy, several ethnic groups thought it was unimportant to petition for official recognition. However, in light of the state's new ethnic classification system, some groups began to think of themselves as strikingly different from their neighbours and thus petitioned the state to be formally recognized as distinct ethnic groups. For example, prior to 1949, most Bai, a minority group in Yunnan (southwest China), saw no difference between themselves and the local Han population. They spoke a Tibetan–Burman language that had taken more than 60 per cent of its vocabulary from Mandarin Chinese and, significantly, most Bai considered themselves to be Han. All this changed when the Bai were officially recognized as a distinct ethnic group. Today, the majority of Bai perceive themselves as a viable minority with a history distinct from the people they once thought they were – the Han Chinese.[18] In this way, what had been categorical has become a new basis for group identification and allegiance.

The Chinese state's role in the creation of the Bai ethnic identity is not unusual. The shift in ethnic allegiance is often a typical response to changes in state ethnic policy. In the 1950s the central government established special commissions to investigate whether a given population was an ethnic minority. At first, more than 400 groups petitioned for official recognition. Most were dismissed, told to reapply (a polite form of dismissal), or ordered to wait (e.g. Sherpas, Kucong and Chinese Jews). Over time, however, the petitions of other groups were accepted. A comparison of the 1953 census with the 1990 census reveals the transformation in ethnic affiliations. For instance, in 1953 only 41 ethnic minorities were listed; whereas in the 1964 census, 53 ethnic minorities were listed, and the 1990 and 2000 censuses identified 56 ethnic minority groups.[19]

Besides being classified by the state as an official ethnic minority, some ethnic groups increased in population size when individuals received permission to change their official ethnic classification from Han to an ethnic minority. Individuals can request a change in ethnic status if they are at least one quarter minority (i.e. have a parent(s) or a grandparent(s) who were from an ethnic minority). This voluntary shift in ethnic classification accounts for some of the increase in China's minority population. For example, the Manchu increased their population from 4.2 million to 9.8 million; whereas the Tujia, in southern China, doubled their population from 2.8 to 5.8 million.[20] A shift in ethnic classification is also found in Inner Mongolia. During the Cultural Revolution (1966–76), many Mongols reclassified themselves as ethnic Han to avoid persecution. In the calmer 1980s, many petitioned the government to be reclassified as Mongols. Today, it is common knowledge that some Han Chinese paid bribes to have their child classified as Mongolian in order to receive special governmental considerations and benefits. In this sense, the overall increase in some of China's ethnic minority populations arises more from a shift in ethnic identification, real and fictive, than from an increase in reproduction.[21]

If the state's ethnic classification policy can awaken latent feelings of ethnic consciousness, it has a similar impact on the Han Chinese, especially those living in the various autonomous regions. Many Han are disgruntled with the government's affirmative action policies. They argue that such policies are unfair because they value group rights over individual achievement. The Han Chinese dialogue over 'fairness' has had an indirect impact in highlighting the Han's sense of ethnic distinctiveness. This increase in awareness is less pronounced among Han living outside an autonomous region where the question of minority rights, and thus the government's ethnic policy, is a non-issue.

Dru Gladney argues that the Han Chinese used China's minorities as an object of erotic projection. In doing so, the Han inferiorized minorities (as more indecent), while superiorizing themselves (as capable of social propriety and ethical decency).[22] Gladney argues that the 'erotic/exotic minority' dichotomy served to heighten the Han sense of moral superiority and thus ethnic distinctiveness. Bulag qualifies and extends Gladney's 'erotic/exotic minority' thesis by noting that it does not hold for all minorities, only those in southern China, while extending the thesis by pointing out that Han Chinese considered minority men in northern China to possess highly desirable masculine traits.[23] Clearly, fantasizing, desiring and yearning to use or possess a minority's presumed cultural traits served to highlight Han distinctiveness, and thereby increase awareness of being Han and thus being a non-minority. The increased sexual openness in Chinese society has made the erotic available to anyone. With the shift in public morality, the ethical distinction between the 'morally proper' Han and the 'sexually loose' minority has vanished from the Chinese landscape, and other social markers such as national standing have been substituted. Therefore, the nation, and not ethnicity, has become the primary unit of social comparison.

In the 1980s, whatever sense of cultural superiority an individual Han felt in comparison to a minority group quickly diminished whenever they compared China's economic development to that of more prosperous societies and geographical regions such as Hong Kong, Taiwan, Europe, the USA, Japan, South Korea and Australia. Most considered their country to be backward. Today, the nation-state's relative international standing has usurped its ethnic minority populations as the primary marker of social comparison. The substitution of the nation-state has contributed to forging a deeper attachment to the importance of a Chinese national identity. It has also resulted in a greater appreciation of China's ethnic minorities. This has led to some tinkering with the prevalent folk cultural evolutionary framework: minorities serve, on one hand, as a means of assessing social progress, while at the same time being perceived as unique communities who live different, albeit respectable, lives. Today, along with claims to ethnic superiority can also be found assertions of tolerance, respect and appreciation of China's cultural diversity. In effect, this is further evidence of the importance of the other side of Chinese ethnicity: national identification.

The impact of structural factors on ethnic minorities

The central government often introduces ethnic policies that are designed to enhance China's national development while also benefiting its minority communities. Minorities, as citizens of China, expect to obtain benefits from the state's new economic policies, while not diminishing the vitality of their cultural traditions. Although the government acknowledges this concern, it often disguises the intended impact of its economic policies on integrating its border regions more completely into Chinese society. The central government has tended to favour policies that range from forced population transfers, through encouraging internal migration, to the creation of urban zones of economic development.

The first problem minority communities faced was the social costs that came with the massive influx of Han Chinese into China's autonomous regions. Although the state established autonomous regions to protect the cultures of minorities, it did little to prevent the illegal influx as it regarded the effects as beneficial to China's long-term goal of integrating its autonomous regions into China proper. In the early 1950s, one way in which the state tacitly sought to achieve the goal of national integration was through massive population transfers that resulted in the 'filling up' of autonomous regions. The policy was expanded in the 1980s with the so-called 'self-drifting' Han, who entered autonomous regions without official government permission in search of economic opportunity. These Han immigrants settled in Tibet, Inner Mongolia, Yunnan and Xinjiang's newer industrial cities and transportation centres.

The impact of internal migrations in transforming Xinjiang's ethnic configuration is revealed in the national census. In the 1940s, the Han population was around 200,000, but by 2000 it had jumped to over 6 million. A similar pattern is found in Inner Mongolia, where Han migration and settlement resulted in a shift in the ratio of Han to Mongols from 4:1 in 1949 to 10:1 by 1960. Today the population of Inner Mongolia (c. 2002) is 11.2 per cent (or 2,681,000) Mongols and 81 per cent (or 20,914,000) Han. In Tibet there are 2.5 million Tibetans in the Tibetan Autonomous Region (TAR) and 2.9 million in adjacent Qinghai, Gansu,

Sichuan and Yunnan provinces. Due primarily to Tibet's harsh environment, Han settlers are not the region's largest ethnic group and tend to live more in towns and in the region's expanded urban centres.

The relentless internal Han migration into the autonomous regions both heightened and blurred ethnic unity. Today, most ethnic groups, albeit with some regret, are resigned to being a minority population in their own autonomous region. This resignation has not resulted, however, in a full-scale political absorption or cultural assimilation. For some, it sparked a re-evaluation of their commitment to the state's minority policies. For others, it resulted in a heightening of their commitment to ethnic resistance, and is linked with a desire to defend their ethnic group's cultural borders. Their resistance ranged from simply voicing disapproval among kin and friends to actively petitioning the local and national governments to re-evaluate their ethnic policies. In some instances, families actively encouraged their child(ren) to adopt more defiant opposition to the Han Chinese, while others advised moderation.

Xinjiang: the Uyghurs and Hui as case studies

Xinjiang is China's largest province and occupies a sixth of its land area. It remains among the most state-centred of all China's provinces. Its trade routes link it with several different continents, making it one of Asia's most complex zones of cultural interaction. Further complicating matters, Xinjiang is not a single territory, but two distinct areas bisected by the uninhabited Taklimankan Desert. This feature transforms Xinjiang into separate geographical zones. The southern zone is poorer than the northern areas, which are also more urbanized.[24] Numerous ethnic minorities live in Xinjiang, and the Uyghurs and the Hui are two of the largest ethnic minorities. The responses of the Uyghurs and Hui to the government's oscillating policies are typical of the problems, dilemmas and resolutions that confront most minority communities in China. While there are always local variations, and thus not every community responds in a similar fashion, their responses are remarkably representative of the issues that confront most Chinese ethnic minorities as they seek to live in a multi-ethnic nation-state that holds pronounced monoculturalist assumptions about how best to live in the world.

In Xinjiang, social groups are delineated more by the occupational categories of intellectual, peasant and merchant than by family organization and descent ideology. This has undermined efforts to form a pan-oasis

Uyghur identity. Discussions among the occupational groups yield distinct positions regarding what it means to be Uyghur. It is not unusual for the three primary social groups to have different conceptions of the significance of Uyghur ethnic identity, particularly in terms of the role played by religion. Many Uyghur intellectuals believe that peasants have withdrawn into Islamic traditionalism, while peasants see Islam as intrinsic to Uyghur ethnic identity. For their part, peasants view secular intellectuals who oppose Islam as out of touch with their own people. In contrast, the majority of intellectuals are anti-Islamic and believe that science and Western education are the only means of bringing progress to the Uyghurs, a view that finds resonance with official PRC doctrine.[25] While the positions of the intellectuals and peasants are the most polarized, the merchants tend to view religion and politics from a more pragmatic stance.

There are a multitude of geographical divisions among the Uyghurs that include the Dolans, Lopliks, Abdals, Keriyaliks, Kashgarliks, Eastern Uyghurs (Turpan and Hami), and the Kuldjaliks or Taranchi (Ili) and the Urumqiliks. The Taranchi, 'Tillers of the Soil', were oasis Turks who were considered a separate ethnic group until 1949, but are now considered Uyghurs. The Dolans live in the Merkit area near Kashgar. Because it is their custom to walk barefoot, outsiders, especially urbanites, view them as both poor and primitive, even though they are no poorer than many other oasis dwellers in the south of Xinjiang. The Lopliks live near Lop Nor in a fishing community. Today, some Uyghurs view the Dolans and Lopliks as separate ethnicities. The Abdals are a peripatetic group living in southern Xinjiang who are Alevi- or Shias influenced heterodox Muslims. They are often called on to perform circumcisions. Most Abdals are quite poor; and because they beg for alms, many Uyghurs commonly refer to all beggars as 'Abdals'.[26]

A new social group comprising educated urbanites living primarily in Urumqi, the capital of Xinjiang, is the Urumqilik. Their children tend to intermarry amongst themselves and identify more with the capital city than with their parents' native place or their parents' oasis. In addition to these long-time divisions, the expansion of market exchanges across national borders is resulting in the re-establishment of cross-border alliances that are based on economic rather than pan-ethnic solidarity. In this sense, Xinjiang remains an ethnically divided region.

This lack of unity can readily be found among the Uyghurs, who remain divided by internal religious differences. Uyghur Islam is a blend of various religious traditions that combine animistic elements with Sufi beliefs and Sunni doctrine to form a decentralized religion.[27] In addition, in place of an organized clergy, Uyghur Islam is intensely localized. Each village and city ward congregation has its own leadership, religious interpretation, and position toward the central government's minority policy.[28] This local orientation contributes to the production and maintenance of an intensely parochial worldview.

By the 1980s, the term 'Uyghur' had become more acceptable to the majority Turkic population of Xinjiang as it organized its identity in opposition to all groups that were not culturally and linguistically similar to it. For most indigenous inhabitants, the new ethnic label has become an emotionally salient identifier. Because identities have numerous components, 'precisely which aspect of identity comes to the immediate fore, and when, depends on the issue at hand and the social context'.[29] In this way, it is not Chinese policies but the legacy of social division imposed by Xinjiang's geography that remains the most critical factor in shaping local identities. For most Uyghurs, identity remains intertwined with family, clan and local oasis obligations.[30]

The emphasis on kinship affiliations is paramount in understanding how Uyghurs perceive the Hui, an ethnic minority that constitutes China's largest Muslim nationality, with 18 million adherents to be found throughout China. In Taiwan, the Hui are not officially recognized as an ethnic group, but rather are viewed as Han who practise Islam. On the Mainland, they live primarily in urban communities and practise cultural traditions organized around pork taboo, entrepreneurship, craft specializations, and a belief in Islam.[31] However, not all people who are classified as Hui follow these cultural practices. In southeast China there are Hui lineages that ignore dietary restrictions and typical religious observations. Instead, they emphasize their foreign ancestry, which happens to be Muslim, thereby making them Muslim too.[32]

In Xinjiang, the Hui (or in the regional parlance Tungans) are bilingual and occupy an intermediary or ambivalent position between the Han and the Uyghurs. Over time, this close association has resulted in Hui culture resembling more closely the local cultures in which they live. For example, Hui in Turpan and Hami more closely resemble the local Uyghurs than many other Hui in other parts of China. Moreover, almost all Turkic Muslims of Xinjiang view them as friends of the Han Chinese administration. Some Uyghurs even claim that the Hui are actually half Han and thus impure in their Muslim observance, as Han do not practise the Islamic faith. Uyghurs frequently have difficulty distinguishing Hui from Han.[33]

Although the Uyghurs and Hui are both Muslim, they do not participate in one another's religious practices. Hui pray in separate mosques and maintain separate Islamic schools. Furthermore, they revere different Islamic saints. Although the Han and Hui often speak the same language, some Han feel that Hui are dishonest and fear that because Hui are Muslim they might betray the Han. Uyghurs, on the other hand, express the same view in reverse: they fear that the Hui will side with the Han, with whom they share both language and a common cultural heritage. The Hui schoolteachers also serve as intermediaries for Uyghurs and Han in Mandarin language instruction at Uyghur schools. Their outlook serves to promote an ethos of cultural tolerance toward state policies.

In Uyghur schools, Hui teachers stress the importance of being loyal citizens to China, China's cultural heritage, and China's potential to become a great nation. The Hui outlook is consistent with the national government's effort to have ethnic minorities transfer their loyalty from the ethnic group to the all-encompassing nation-state.[34] The Hui's effort as well as their intermediate status in Han–Uyghur relations, while influencing mutual group perceptions, has not eliminated ethnic loyalties or ethnic tensions. In fact, some minorities define themselves more in opposition to the Hui than to the Han. For example, among the Hohhotian Mongolian community, whenever something goes wrong, Mongols and Han sarcastically remark that the municipal government is run by Hui. In this case, the Hui are regarded as less educated, and thus unenlightened compared to the Mongols and Han. The Hui in a number of different northern cities are becoming more adamant in their disapproval of certain Han economic behaviours, which they complain are culturally insensitive. In Hohhot, capital of Inner Mongolian Autonomous Region (IMAR), between 2005 and 2006, there was a series of violent incidents in which Hui groups demanded that restaurants near the historic Hui district cease serving alcohol or dishes that contained pork. If the owner refused, the restaurant was destroyed. The municipal government, for its part, appears to have been unable to marshal an effective response.

The government's lack of response to these complaints is not without its irony. Protests led by Mongolian students in 1981, 1995 and 2005 were met with immediate condemnation and arrests, while the actions of the Hui are met with indecision and a willingness to negotiate. The new-found Hui radicalism has benefited from the national government's desire to forge a closer relationship with oil-rich Arab states. Not wanting to offend the international Muslim community, the local and regional authorities have been instructed to deal with these incidents in a moderate manner.[35] The state's privileging of the Hui's interests over those of the Mongols and Han has contributed to the reification of Hohhot's ethnic borders. Although members of the different ethnic groups cannot be readily identified by dress, each group has maintained tacit, albeit strongly guarded, borders that have been effective in maintaining cultural distinction and thus ethnic memory. In this way, ethnic borders are forged and sustained through ethnic competition over issues of personal dignity, material gain and cultural standing.

Language and education and their implications for Chinese ethnicity

The contradictions that arise from the central government's commitment to a mono-culturalist policy while insisting it is a multi-ethnic state can be found in an examination of China's educational language policy. In spite of claims to the contrary, China's language policies tend to favour the mastery of Mandarin (*putonghua*).[36] Although the state allows minorities to attend native language instructional schools, it is generally understood that excellence in Mandarin is required to enter college. Children who attend native language schools are seen as being at a disadvantage. This is a pragmatic issue. The ability to speak Mandarin has great utility, not only for passing the university entrance exam but also in obtaining a coveted career in government service or more effectively participating in the national market economy. Further, studies of language acquisition consistently reveal that children often refuse to learn a language they perceive as inferior or useless in daily interaction. Given that Mongolian herders and farmers are frequently perceived by Han Chinese as 'culturally backward', as well as the fact that most urban children only speak Mandarin, it is not surprising that Han children refuse to learn a minority language while their minority playmates, yearning to be accepted by their more numerous Han playmates, lose interest in speaking their native language. In this way, a consequence of forced and tacit population transfers has been to make it extremely difficult for many minority communities to transmit their languages to their children. In response to the loss of language some urban minorities stress

the importance of their children becoming bilingual or even trilingual –
in their native language, Mandarin and English. Presently, this ideal remains one based more in hope. In this and so many other ways, China's
covert language policy is designed to form part of its larger 'civilizing
project' that will embrace a life-orientation necessary for the establishment of a unified nation-state.[37]

The increasing economic integration of minorities into China's national economy has engendered a shift in outlook: minority families
must decide whether to protect their children's cultural identity by
sending them to a minority language school, or forsake that cultural
border in favour of attending a Mandarin-speaking school that will give
them a better opportunity to compete and succeed in the larger society.[38]
Many Mongols, Uyghurs, urban Yi and urban Tibetans are torn between
motives of ethnic pride, which calls for the preservation of minority language, and their interest in their children getting ahead.[39] The dilemma
is especially acute among minority government officials who are torn between the conflicting expectations of social rank, ethnic identification
and national loyalty. As the beneficiaries of the government's entitlement programme, they have the most to lose in any conflict over the
programme. This reality affects the degree to which they will publicly
support or disagree with state policy.

These conflicting obligations have shaped their choice of educational
programmes as well as their views towards cultural isolation. Aware of
the full benefits of government employment, minority officials send
their children to Mandarin instructional schools. In Xinjiang, some
urban-based Uyghur families practise a kind of ethnic-economic compromise. They strive to protect their daughters, who represent the cultural embodiment and continuity of their ethnicity, by sending them
to Uyghur-language instructional schools, while pushing their sons
to learn Mandarin in order to more effectively compete in Xinjiang's
emerging market economy. By contrast, among Mongols, Tibetans and
urban Yi, minority families prefer to send children of both sexes to Mandarin instructional schools.

This orientation often leads to dual loyalties, to the nation-state and
then to one's ethnic group. For some, the dualism can result in a diminished commitment to 'things ethnic' as opposed to 'things national'.
However, this is not always clear-cut – many minorities appear to have
no difficulty in perceiving themselves as having a strong Chinese identity as well as an equally salient ethnic identity.

Identity is a multi-layered phenomenon. Therefore, it is possible to have a minority identity as well as a national identity.[40] Having two identity orientations does not necessarily entail developing an anti-majority sentiment. Bulag also found in Inner Mongolia a similar trend in which Mongols' identification as citizens of China resulted in a reduction in their interest in ethnic nationalism.[41] Colin Mackerras made a similar observation based on his multi-site Tibetan ethnic survey that found a remarkably high minority loyalty toward the Chinese state.[42] For most, having two sources of identification – ethnic identity and national identity – poses few problems. They form, as such, one of several possible references for the construction of a viable self-image in contemporary Chinese society.

Struggle over history, culture and identity

The active pursuit of a monoculturalist model has shaped China's official position on national and regional historiography. For the central government, there is only one kind of historical narrative; that is, stories that demonstrate people's allegiance to China. Because empires and nations depend upon history for their legitimacy, interpretative disagreements can quickly become contested terrain.[43] There is much at stake. Because people's identities tend to be intertwined with their attachment to a specific historical narrative, it is difficult to really accept a revisionist explanation. This is especially so in contemporary China where there are always conflicting historical interpretations concerning a minority's history and thus its place in Chinese society.

The official view holds that China's autonomous regions were always an inalienable part of China. This position constitutes the foundation stone for the formulation of China's unifying mythology that is organized around the themes of social solidarity and perpetual cultural continuity. Accordingly, Han Chinese have always lived in every region in China. This is a position that undercuts the ethnic nationalist's claim of prior ethnic exclusivity. The state's obsession with upholding a historiography that insists upon perpetual national unity can also be found in explanations of the origins of Taiwan's original inhabitants. Contrary to Western scholarship that traces Taiwanese origins from Malaysia, Chinese historians insist that Taiwan's aboriginal populations, who lived on its plains (*pingpu*) and in its mountains (*gaoshan*), came from Mainland China.

The exclusive concentration on events and people that promoted national unity can be found in Inner Mongolian high-school history textbooks that celebrate only those Mongols who, throughout the 1930s and 1940s, fought against the Japanese and the corrupt Guomindang government, demonstrating in the process a total commitment to establishing the People's Republic of China, and thus becoming admirable Chinese citizens. In contrast, the ethnic Nationalist interpretation, a view not taught in middle or high schools, champions those Mongols such as De Wang (Demcigdonrow in Mongolian), Amarsanaan, Togtokh and Gadameiren who struggled for Inner Mongolian political autonomy and independence.

For ethnic Nationalists the core question has always been: how much political autonomy? A few ethnic Nationalists insist on complete separation and independence from the PRC. Others take a more pragmatic position, and argue for an increase in political autonomy. In IMAR an indirect index of a Mongol's political allegiance is his or her reaction to Ulanfu, a Tumete Mongol who did not speak Mongolian but held a high rank in the national government. Most Mongols, especially those who do not speak Mongolian, regard him as doing the best with a bad situation, while others, especially those who speak Mongolian, believe he should have resisted the incorporation of Inner Mongolia into the People's Republic of China. In providing an alternative historical interpretation, minority intellectuals have become advocates for their ethnic groups. In offering an explanation contrary to the government's official position, they also expose themselves to possible negative sanctions. For some, it is a price they are willing to pay.

Competing notions of ethnic integrity in urban China

There is a lack of consensus in China's urban ethnic communities about the meaning of ethnic authenticity. Because of the different notions of what constitutes ethnic integrity, an intense rivalry often erupts within the minority communities over its meaning. The debates often centre on the degree to which ethnic interaction should be fluid or restrictive. Presently, there are four distinct postures, which can be described as ethnic Nationalist, multi-culturalist, traditionalist and assimilationalist. This typology is heuristic and not definitive. It also applies more to ethnic minorities situated in urban communities than to those in rural settings. As most researchers are less interested in probing intra-ethnic diversity, this is just an assumption. It is important to remember that it is not unusual for an individual, depending upon their age, social status, life experience and the importance of a particular public issue, to shift their position on the meaning and importance of ethnic loyalty and thus integrity.

The ethnic Nationalist view, held most strongly among urban intellectuals, is characterized by a tendency toward radical politics that may or may not favour ethnic separation, but always aims to promote minority interests that involve greater political autonomy and a sweeping re-evaluation of the official history of the region. Ethnic Nationalists prefer to see 'nationality as a political, territorial, linguistic group with tangible rights'.[44] The commitment to ethnic nationalism is restricted to a smaller segment of China's larger ethnic minority urban communities. However, for most Westerners, as well as for China's central government, it is the ethnic nationalistic posture that holds the greatest interest. The lack of strong support for separation, as opposed to increased political and economic autonomy, is never fully realized. This is due, in part, to it being curtailed by another value – cultural pluralism or multi-culturalism – which ideally insists upon mutual respect, understanding and harmony between individuals from different ethnic groups. In this way, the more strident ethnocentric tendencies are held in check, and some degree of balance is achieved.

The multi-culturalist view holds that everyone should preserve their culture, with different cultures interacting peacefully within one nation. It is often characterized by an emphasis on 'ethnic pride', which embraces highly individual strategies to promote ethnic honour, solidarity and personal interest. Most government minority officials tend to adopt a multi-culturalist perspective. Because they have the most to lose, their public voice is usually a qualified response. This does not mean that minority officials are not willing to defend minority interests, or that they have 'sold out' their ethnic group. On the contrary, most officials do defend, at least in the abstract, ethnic minority interests. However, their defence is conducted from within the political system. They do not want to leave it, as it continues to reward them. In this way, giving minority individuals a stake in the system, the government has sought to dampen enthusiasm for ethnic nationalism.

In contrast to the multi-culturalist perspective, the traditionalist view is characterized by a complete focus on one's birth locality or native place. Traditionalists may live in urban settings but their emotional orientation remains focused on their home towns. For example, the traditionalist repeatedly returns home to attend weddings and funerals. In every way, they are, to invoke a popular folk expression, 'in the city but not of the city'. More importantly, traditionalists retain a strong preference for only associating with other traditionalists. In contrast, the assimilationist view is characterized by a denial of being a minority, and is manifested in a total indifference to minority cultural heritage. Because of the government's affirmative action policy, there are tangible benefits in being officially classified as a minority, a factor that makes some minorities reluctant to abandon completely their ethnic affiliation.

Unsurprisingly, within most minority urban households, there is a range of conflicting opinions over the relevance of minority cultural heritage both for personal identity and for establishing a career. In large measure, these discussions centre on an individual's conception of ethnic integrity. This internal dialogue is often voiced most strongly when it comes to approving or disapproving of interethnic marriage. Intermarriage rates between minorities and the Han population vary by region. For Turkic Muslims, intermarriage between a Han (an unbeliever) and a Muslim is the fundamental cultural taboo. In Xinjiang intermarriage is so infrequent as to be virtually non-existent. Those few who do transgress are disowned, and their children are never accepted into the larger extended family.[45] Unlike Buddhism, which is more tolerant of intermarriage between believer and non-believer, the local interpretation of the Islamic religion is that marriage can only take place between believers, though in practice the Hui Muslims, especially their more prosperous members, have been more favourably predisposed to entering into an interfaith marriage. Given the Han reluctance to convert or in any way sensitize themselves to Uyghur cultural practices, the religious factor makes Islam an effective border for the development and maintenance of a salient ethnically charged consciousness. Intermarriage rates constitute a primary index that determines the degree of ethnic closure and thus the relative strength of cultural borders. This is less true for Mongols, Tibetans and Dai in Xishuangbanna, who have a higher frequency of intermarriage with Han Chinese.

Advocates of the multi-culturalist view hold that neither proficiency in linguistic expression nor a spouse's ethnicity is essential. It may be highly desirable, but it is not critical as an ethnic marker. In its place is an emphasis on a subjective conviction, a pride in all 'things ethnic'. Most minority members, excluding assimilationists, remain proud of their cultural heritage and enjoy the government's benefits. The entitlement policy, however, continues to provoke Han resentment, while discouraging minorities who are leaning toward an assimilationist orientation from publicly denying their cultural heritage. Because minorities, regardless of orientation, feel that they have something to gain, or believe that in the long run their children will benefit, they continue to favour government entitlements.

In sum, China's central government is not entirely convinced of the overall political loyalty of its minorities. As a result, its policies continue to oscillate between the use of hard and soft sanctions, which compel some minority communities to revisit what it means to be an ethnic minority as well as a national citizen in contemporary Chinese society. The strength of nationalistic sentiment among China's ethnic minorities remains the unexplored area in studies of Chinese ethnicity. The problem is compounded in part by Western researchers who focus more on ethnic Nationalist posture than they do on the enormous variation within an ethnic community. Further, few researchers have explored the degree to which Han and minority interaction mutually influence each other. Since I began field research in 1981 among China's ethnic minorities, I find understanding their nuances, cultural practices, and oscillating postures towards national and local identity continues to be a most intriguing intellectual soup. The exploration of the reasons behind an individual's adopting different public and private postures toward 'things ethnic', 'things national' and 'things personal' has just begun.

Notes

1. Stevan Harrell, *Ways of being Ethnic in Southwest China*, Seattle, University of Washington Press, 2001, p. 37.
2. Harrell, *Ways of Being Ethnic in Southwest China*, p. 37.
3. Justin Rudelsom and William Jankowiak, 'Acculturation and Resistance: Xinjiang Identities in Flux', in S. Frederick Starr (ed.), *Xinjiang: China's Muslim Borderland*, New York, M. E. Sharpe, 2004, p. 301.
4. Suisheng Zhao, *A Nation-State by Construction: Dynamics of Modern Chinese Nationalism*, Stanford, Stanford University Press, 2004, pp. 66–7.
5. James Millward and Nabijan Tursun, 'Political History and Strategies of Control, 1884–1978', in S. Frederick Starr (ed.), *Xinjiang: China's Muslim Borderland*, New York: M. E. Sharpe, 2004, p. 84.
6. Suisheng Zhao, *A Nation-State by Construction*, p. 22.
7. Dru Gladney, *Dislocating China: Muslims, Minorities and Other Subaltern Subjects*, Chicago, University of Chicago Press, 2004, p. 6.

8. Barry Sautman and June Dreyers (eds.), *Contemporary Tibet: Politics, Development and Society in a Disputed Region*, New York, M. E. Sharpe, 2006, p. 88.

9. Sautman and Dreyers, *Contemporary Tibet*, p. 88.

10. Gladney, *Dislocating China*, p. 6.

11. David Goodman, 'Reforming the Local, Constructing China: Place Identity in a North China Province', Morrison Lecture, Australian National University, November 2004.

12. Gladney, *Dislocating China*, pp. 37–47.

13. Colin Mackerras, *China's Minorities: Integration and Modernization in the Twentieth Century*, New York, Oxford University Press, 1995.

14. Mary Rack, *Ethnic Meanings, Local Meanings*, London, Pluto Press, 2005.

15. Morris Rossabi, 'Introduction', in M. Rossabi (ed.), *Governing China's Multiethnic Frontiers*, Seattle, University of Washington Press, 2004, p. 12.

16. Chi-Yu Shih, *Negotiating Ethnicity in China: Citizenship as a Response to the State*, New York, Routledge, 2002, p. 88.

17. Rack, *Ethnic Meanings*, p. 13.

18. David Wu, 'The Construction of Chinese and Non-Chinese Identities', in Tu Wei-ming (ed.), *The Living Tree: The Changing Meaning of being Chinese Today*, Stanford, Stanford University Press, 1994, p. 159.

19. Gladney, *Dislocating China*, p. 9.

20. *Ibid.*, p. 175.

21. *Ibid.*, p. 175.

22. *Ibid.*, pp. 2–3.

23. Uradyn Bulag, *Mongols at China's Edge*, New York, Rowman and Littlefield, 2002.

24. S. Fredrick Starr, 'Introduction', in Starr (ed.), *Xinjiang*, pp. 3–11.

25. Rudelsom and Jankowiak, 'Acculturation and Resistance', pp. 299–319.

26. *Ibid.*, p. 303.

27. Gladney, *Dislocating China*, p. 195.

28. Graham Fuller and Jonathan Lipman, 'Islam in Xinjiang', in Starr (ed.), *Xinjiang*, p. 332.

29. *Ibid.*, p. 338.

30. Justin Rudelsom, *Oasis Identities: Dissecting Uyghur Nationalism along China's Silk Road*, New York, Columbia University Press, 1997.

31. Gladney, *Dislocating China*, p. 167.

32. *Ibid.*, p. 187.

33. Rudelsom and Jankowiak, 'Acculturation and Resistance', p. 304.

34. Shih, *Negotiating Ethnicity in China*, p. 445.

35. Gladney, *Dislocating China*.

36. Arienne Dwyer, *The Xinjiang Conflict: Uyghur Identity, Language Policy and Political Discourse*, Washington, DC, East–West Center, 2005, p. 9.

37. Harrell, 'Introduction', in Harrell (ed.), *Cultural Encounters on China's Ethnic Frontier*.

38. Dwyer, *The Xinjiang Conflict*, p. 39.

39. William Safran, *Nationalism and Ethnoregional Identities in China*, London, Frank Cass, 1998, p. 5.

40. Dwyer, *The Xinjiang Conflict*.

41. Bulag, *Mongols at China's Edge*.

42. Colin Mackerras, 'China's Minorities and National Integration', in Leong Liew and Shaoguang Wang (eds.), *Nationalism, Democracy and National Integration in China*, London, RoutledgeCurzon, 2004.

43. Harrell, 'Introduction', p. 21.
44. Bulag, *Mongols at China's Edge*, p. 161.
45. Rudelsom and Jankowiak, 'Acculturation and Resistance'.

Guide to further reading

Brown, Melissa, *Is Taiwan Chinese? The Impact of Culture, Power and Migration on Changing Identities*, Berkeley, University of California Press, 2004.

Brown, Melissa (ed.), *Negotiating Ethnicities in China and Taiwan*, Berkeley, University of California Press, 1996.

Goldstein, Melvyn, *The Snow Lion and the Dragon: China, Tibet, and the Dalai Lama*, Berkeley, University of California Press, 1997.

Harrell, Stevan (ed.), *Perspectives on the Yi of Southwest China*, Berkeley, University of California Press, 2001.

Iredale, Robert, Naran Bilk and Fei Guo (eds.), *Chinese Minorities on the Move*, New York, M. E. Sharpe, 2003.

Lipman, Jonathan, *Familiar Strangers: A History of Muslims in Northwest China*, Seattle, University of Washington Press, 1998.

Mackerras, Colin, *China's Ethnic Minorities and Globalisation*, New York, RoutledgeCurzon Press, 2003.

6
_____

Flag, flame and embers: diaspora cultures

More than thirty million people of Chinese descent live in over one hundred different countries and territories as migrants, settlers and sojourners. Most would qualify to be part of the diaspora and, insofar as people identify themselves as Chinese or have that identity ascribed to them, it can be said that they are bearers of Chinese diaspora cultures. The assumption that they all have something in common stems from their origins, whether distant or recent, in China. But some of them left China only recently while others have ancestors who have lived outside China for generations, often in different countries and even on different continents. Thus it would be misleading to think of them as having much in common. Also, Chinese people settled in lands as far apart as Indonesia and Canada, Tahiti and the Netherlands. To suggest that the Chinese who have lived among such different host peoples share the same culture would be unwarranted. However hard some Chinese might have tried to stay the same wherever they went, evidence can be found that some of them have distinct cultures. Some are complex and interconnected cultures that have grown over centuries in different communities while others are peculiar to small clusters of families that still claim to be Chinese.

This chapter focuses on modern cultures and explores similarities and differences arising from variations in the age, size and location of each community. It also recognizes that cultures change when introduced to different elements of modernity and are, therefore, not equally modern. It does not attempt to account for each of the cultures, but uses examples from the three main regions of the world where the Chinese have settled. Southeast Asia is clearly the most significant because at least 75 per cent of the diaspora still live there. The numbers in each polity were not large before the nineteenth century and, as in Korea, Japan and other areas where the local peoples were more or less Mongoloid, Chinese have been able to assimilate over time and when necessary. Since the mid-nineteenth century, however, large-scale migrations have taken place and this has encouraged the Chinese to define their ethnicity more consistently. About that time, two other regions, North America and Australasia, received significant numbers of Chinese, and ethnic and cultural adjustments there created different problems. More recently, the numbers migrating to Europe have increased and it is possible that there will be a fourth region of significant communities before long. There are also notable communities in Central and South America as well as in parts of Southern Africa where numbers have risen or fallen, but these have remained small. This chapter will outline the main cultural experiences of the larger diaspora communities.[1]

Historical background

In a volume on modern Chinese culture, attention will be given to Chinese responses to modernity as sojourners and settlers, but their encounters with modernity began in Southeast Asia at least two centuries ago. This modernity refers to the European transformations that took off during the latter half of the eighteenth century. The Chinese engaged that culture directly when they traded with the modernizing Europeans in Asia. Initially, they were confident that their culture was strong, if not superior. Although most Chinese left China without any formal education, they could count on the protective cultures of coastal China where they originated to give them their sense of identity and support their values abroad. Those successful in business followed the examples of trading guilds in China, and that enabled merchant cultures to be replicated abroad. These were better prepared to deal with local authorities, whether native or European, and could adopt useful Western practices while being convinced that the high culture of China still represented a greater civilization. The more successful the Chinese were, the more they tried to bring the values extolled in imperial China to their new homes abroad and transmit these values to their progeny.

The sense of cultural security was not uniform. For example, it began to break down quite early in the face of a determined Catholic church in the Spanish Philippines that forced the Chinese to adopt Christianity. Elsewhere, Chinese lives were shaped by Dutch mercantilist policies that tightened control over their social organizations. After the middle of the nineteenth century, in the colonies in North America and Australasia, the Chinese had both negative and positive experiences with the Europeans they met, and were forced to be resourceful and adaptable in new ways. In the goldfields, the Chinese used their cultural resources to deal with some very rough justice; and in the fast-growing urban centres, they acquired new knowledge wherever they could, notably in modern schools open to their children. But confidence in Chinese culture was still strong in most parts of the European empires, especially in British territories such as the Straits Settlements and the Federated Malay States, where Chinese concentrations were significant in cities like Penang and Singapore, and mining towns like Kuala Lumpur and Ipoh.

It was not until the twentieth century that transformative changes accompanying political revolutions in China began to dominate the lives of Chinese everywhere. Living abroad, their ideas of culture were alternatively buffeted by pride and despair about developments in China, by the desire to learn about wealth, power and scientific progress from the West and, for those living in neighbouring lands in Asia, by the need for practical accommodations in order to deal with increasingly turbulent local and colonial realities. Far from home at the colonial frontiers, large numbers of Chinese confronted modernity in a great variety of ways, but most of them were ready to modify the cultures they brought with them in order to tackle rapidly changing political and business conditions.

Many kinds of migrant peoples in the world are now called diasporas. For the generations of Chinese who settled abroad, *huaqiao* (meaning sojourners and, in English, Overseas Chinese) was the term used. 'Diaspora' was applied to them only recently, largely in the context of globalization. The new definitions of 'diaspora' avoid reference to any specific type of dispersal or exile and try to generalize the word so that it may be used for every kind of migrant community everywhere. Nevertheless, the word reminds us that Chinese have been compared to 'exiled' Jews to whom the Old Testament word applied, not only in the West but also, however inappropriately, even in Asia. The comparisons highlight the differences and similarities in the two communities. On the surface, similarities in their entrepreneurial activities and the high price they often had to pay for their successes are striking. The differences, however, are much more important, most of all in the way the two peoples preserved or modified their respective displaced cultures; the Jews through their religion and their lack of a territorial home and the Chinese through their family ties and their pride in an imperial civilization.

Definitions vary, but 'diaspora' is used here merely as shorthand for the Chinese terms *huaqiao* and *huaren*, commonly translated as sojourners, Overseas Chinese, or ethnic Chinese. It does not include the people of Hong Kong–Macau and Taiwan. Although it is true that Chinese cultures abroad largely share the same origins in the southern Chinese provinces, they are the products of encounters between Chinese minority cultures and majority cultures in *foreign* territories. If that difference was blurred or ignored, it would be very difficult to understand the Chinese abroad and their cultures and impossible to talk of Chinese diaspora cultures. Thus the cultures that are clearly identified with Hong Kong–Macau and Taiwan are also excluded.

However, diaspora cultures did begin with southern provincial cultures that were also transplanted to Hong Kong–Macau and Taiwan and were similarly influenced from the end of the nineteenth century by the modern cultures of Shanghai and other treaty ports. From the point of view of many China writers, it is understandable that they consider all such manifestations of culture, whether far abroad or just off the coast of China, as hybrid variants of modern Chinese culture. But modern diaspora cultures contain many more ingredients and are not just variants because they are the products of living overseas and adapting to cultures that are non-Chinese. Diaspora cultures are not limited to preserving cultural artefacts diffused from a central core, such as language, art motifs and technical skills that respond to cultural changes, whether at home or abroad, but focus on the peoples who make the cultural choices. This chapter is concerned with the people who consider culture meaningful to their lives and also with their use of new modern factors to shape their culture. It also notes that, while the diasporas are in the front line of globalization, China today is becoming economically stronger and politically more influential and this may bring changes to future developments in diaspora cultures.

The plural word 'cultures' reminds us that the phenomenon of culture is manifold. Its constituent parts are so multifarious that volumes could be written about them. This chapter, therefore, concentrates on how the Chinese turned to their cultures in identity politics and trading networks, with special attention given to the adaptations made in response to modernization. 'Diaspora cultures' refers to those, strongly influenced by Chinese sojourning and migrating traditions, which have adapted to realities over which the diaspora have little control. Their survival depended on the size of their communities and the range of their activities. What made their cultures distinctive depended on how their communities remained connected to one another, and also to their homeland, by blood ties, religious practices and cultural pride. But diaspora cultures could not, and still cannot, depend solely on those links. Local conditions were very important. These varied from the nature and quality of the cultures they lived with to those conditions that permitted foreign peoples to retain their identity and allowed diaspora cultures to exist, and to those that actively encouraged the Chinese communities to embrace other religions, master new skills and even change their names and lifestyles. At their most attractive, such conditions could lead to total assimilation by their local hosts.[2]

Diaspora cultures have had little place in China studies. This is understandable because they are usually seen as variations of coastal China's provincial cultures. Scholars in China, in particular, have tended to note them briefly as extensions of Chinese civilization. When they occasionally encountered the local-born of part-Chinese ancestry – for example, the *peranakan* of the Malay archipelago – they were inclined first to regret how un-Chinese their culture had become and then wonder that these local-born people still regarded themselves as Chinese. The more attentive looked at what they saw as residuals of bygone popular traditions that have been modified or even distorted by localized adaptations. These were treated as objects of curiosity, artefacts that characterized a sub-ethnic group that would disappear when the local-born Chinese either studied Chinese language, history and culture and returned to the fold, or accepted assimilation by the new national cultures that now surrounded them.

Bearing this in mind, diaspora cultures may be distinguished by the decisions that the Overseas Chinese have made at various times: (a) those who have always wanted to *huigui* or return to their origins in China; (b) those who are willing to adapt to local life while preserving their ideas of Chinese culture as long as possible in order to protect their communities; (c) those who have agreed to sink roots in their adopted countries while evolving distinctive local cultures and becoming politically and socially integrated; and (d) those who accept that, if conditions allow, their future lies in their becoming assimilated with the local cultures. The results of these decisions are not discrete as they shade from one to the other. For this chapter, diaspora cultures will concentrate on the experiences of those in groups (b) and (c) because they are more concerned with how diaspora cultures might emerge and thrive.

I shall concentrate on twentieth-century cultures. Most Chinese brought with them the rudiments of local Fujian and Guangdong cultures. The bearers of the cultures were single males or males who left their families at home. Coming from the poorer classes, they were determined to make a living through thrift, hard work and risk-taking, and they sent money home whenever they could. Some of them had a variety of technical skills beyond that of farming and labouring, and they had better chances of success. On the whole, they were expected to be at least bold, industrious, versatile and adaptable, even calculating and opportunistic. In this self-selective way, these attributes characterized most Chinese who remained abroad and contributed to the diasporic cultures that emerged among them. Some of those who assimilated and joined the native elite classes are known to have added vigour to local cultures. Well-known examples are the families that produced, in modern times, several political leaders of Thailand and the Philippines.

The Chinese who had trading backgrounds would have been familiar with the extensive official, local place and lineage networks in imperial China that their families had developed. They knew how important these networks were and paid close attention to the culture associated with them. But for most Chinese, it was enough that the basic features of clan and place, sworn brotherhoods and specific bonds of the workplace enabled them to organize and defend themselves abroad and keep them in touch with their families at home. It would not occur to them to develop their own cultures through learning the skills and values of foreign peoples. Even during the twentieth century, they were slow to realize that their newly acquired modern skills could be valuable to China. Most of them would look to the authorities in China to encourage them to bring back capital and technologies to help China's economy. This attitude remained the norm among most sojourning communities.

Two other factors are also relevant. Chinese values and institutions had little appeal to the peoples of Southeast Asia. Hindu–Buddhist cultures were deeply rooted there, and, while tolerant of the Chinese, native peoples were not receptive to the cultures the Chinese brought with them. When the indigenous leaders on the Southeast Asian mainland lost faith in Hindu–Buddhist institutions, they adopted Theravada Buddhism. In the archipelagic Malay world when the ruling classes did the same, they turned to Islam. On the Chinese side, imperial rulers and functionaries were not interested in offering their values to those out-side their highly integrated political system. Therefore, Chinese influ-ences in the region were mainly material and technical. China was a market place for the region's wide range of commodities, and offered in return manufactures such as silk, ceramics, shipping materials and some agricultural practices. These influences were extensive, but Chinese re-ligious and moral values rarely commanded attention.[3]

The other concerns imperial policies pertaining to overseas trade. The earliest Chinese traded with Korea and Japan during the first millennium and many migrated there. Later, in the south, after the independence of Vietnam, the Chinese who traded and migrated there found cultures similar to their own. Most Chinese migrating to these countries accepted local ways and eventually became indistinguishable from the native peo-ples. But when they traded in the Hindu–Buddhist, and later Muslim, lands of Southeast Asia, the patterns were different. Merchants went in significant numbers from the Song (960–1276) and Yuan (1276–1368) dy-nasties and evolved forms of cultural support to help them to survive. After that, trade was greatly stimulated by the extraordinary expeditions of Admiral Zheng He early in the fifteenth century, and the pressure on coastal Chinese to extend that trade was intense. But neither of the two dynasties that followed, the Ming (1368–1644) or the Qing (1644–1911), was helpful. After the fifteenth century, heavy restrictions were applied to private trade with foreign countries. Thus, while merchant classes within China became stronger as the national market grew and gained respect-ability by embracing the culture of literati officials, they were greatly constrained from trading overseas. As a result, their practical and entre-preneurial values had little impact on official thinking. In comparison, Europeans brought their economic and scientific revolutions with them and these were backed by the armed naval power needed for long-distance trade. They were also supported by joint trading organizations with new mercantilist ideas and a measure of missionary zeal. Together with the industrial revolution and the rise of nation-states in Europe, Europeans established new kinds of world empires. That national imperialism en-sured that modern European cultures dominated the world.

Responses to modernity

Diaspora cultures may be divided into those that closely followed cul-tural change in China, and those variant adaptations that evolved first in Southeast Asia and later in America and Australasia through a combination of Chinese and other cultures. The former accepted modern ways and ideas taken up by Chinese in China, while the latter were the result of choices by Chinese living abroad who were very careful what they took from the Europeans they worked with. The settled Chinese who had sunk roots locally developed their diaspora cultures from mixing with indigenous peoples even before dealing with the modern West. First-generation arrivals in America and Australasia kept their own institutions, customs and values intact, and did so through regular references to cultures in China, using the latter as the standard against which deviations could be corrected. This was common practice in communities that were regularly enlarged by newcomers from China.

From the end of the nineteenth century onwards, improved transportation and the circulation of newspapers and books from China ensured that the impact of modern ideas and lifestyles on coastal Chinese was also obvious to those living abroad. The impact was even greater following the establishment of local Chinese schools staffed by teachers sent from China, and the arrival of journalists to edit local Chinese newspapers further updated and strengthened cultural connections with China. The rise of nationalism, especially in the context of the war with Japan, brought Chinese affairs closer to every Chinese living abroad. A modernizing Chinese culture became more real and showed the diaspora the paths that modernization could take. For the newcomers and their families, that culture was what really counted. If they had any idea of diaspora culture, they would have seen it as successful extensions of China's culture.

In addition, there are two extreme examples in which vestiges of Chinese cultures may be attached to people of Chinese descent who do not need that label. At one extreme, a submerged sense of being Chinese is found among scattered and isolated groups who want to continue doing business between indigenous peoples and other Chinese. They have some knowledge of the Chinese language but have no access to any kind of Chinese education. Being small in number, they are tolerated because they are no threat to the local populace. Some of them also nurse their inherited artefacts as private acts of defence and defiance. They thus hold on to a muted form of diaspora culture but are really people in transition whose children may either assimilate if they remain in isolation much longer or move towards marginal sub-cultures if there are opportunities to do so. Such examples may be found in remote highland regions of mainland Southeast Asia and some of the isolated islands of maritime Southeast Asia and Oceania.

The other variety is likely to become more widespread and is largely identified by factors outside of Chinese communities altogether. It is the product of modern education, including higher professional, artistic and technological education. For such people of Chinese descent, vestiges of Chinese culture are assumed to be present in their make-up, even as their personal identities are thoroughly integrated with elite cosmopolitan cultures that transcend national cultures. Their successes ensure that they are never lost to the diaspora even if they add nothing to diaspora cultures. The fact that their accomplishments have added lustre to images of the Chinese means that vestiges of what might be Chinese are a source of pride to all Chinese, native or diaspora.

But the differences between cultural extensions among Southeast Asian peoples mostly under European colonial rule, and those affirming Chinese culture among European colonial migrants in the Americas and Australasia became politically important. On the one hand, in proximate Southeast Asia where so many Chinese settled, any kind of extension from China, not to say an emotional anti-Japanese nationalism, indicated the potential for power projection and degrees of control over the local Chinese sojourners. Some saw this as a kind of China-centred diaspora culture, creating little Chinas in their midst even as native leaders were discovering their own respective nationalisms.

It is not necessary to dwell here on diaspora cultures that systematically adjusted to follow cultural developments in China. Suffice it to say that the variations among them are interesting. In various parts of Southeast Asia where local diaspora cultures had emerged, cultural pressures from China created tensions, and the social and political repercussions were often serious. Examples abound in the 1920s and 1930s, notably in Thailand and the Dutch East Indies, and the Anglo-Malay authorities in Malaya adopted severe measures to keep modern Chinese cultures under control. These cultures became even more threatening after the end of World War II, especially after the Chinese Communist Party's victory in 1949. The ideological Cold War that divided Southeast Asia triggered methodical efforts to eliminate this kind of extended Chinese culture, both the socialist and nationalist varieties, among local Chinese communities. For at least five decades, the pressure throughout the region to push settled Chinese towards domesticated varieties of diaspora cultures, if not total assimilation, was great.[4]

In the migrant states of North America and Australasia, Chinese immigrants encountered racial and cultural barriers in lands where the Europeans claimed priority and ownership. Unlike Chinese mandarins who served in Western capitals and wrote their impressions of Western achievements, and Chinese students who admired the West that they studied, very few Chinese in the migrant states saw the finer sides of Western culture. Instead, they were mainly exposed to resentful poor whites whose working-class cultures were no better than their own. Most of these Chinese who met with discrimination and injustice lived in isolated communities or lived ghetto lives in 'Chinatowns', and many were reluctant to learn directly from the Europeans they met. Thus Chinese sojourners preferred to keep their own cultures as best they could. But they were open to what was changing in China in response to the Western challenge. Steamships and the telegraph enabled modern newspapers from China to reach them and several sizable Chinese communities produced newspapers of their own. That way, they kept up with the modernizing culture in China and learned to appreciate how much the Chinese were learning from the West. There were a few who accepted opportunities to seek local professional education and were content to conform to their settler society lifestyles if they could preserve a few Chinese cultural artefacts.[5] Ironically, when the position of the Chinese improved in these societies, and many more Chinese were welcomed after the 1960s, these Chinese had the widest of cultural choices in their relatively liberal societies. On the one hand, the politics of Mainland China and Taiwan raised profound questions about modern Chinese cultures, including those in Hong Kong–Macau. On the other, the whole range of global and transnational cultures was open to the educated among them, including recent immigrants from Chinese territories and from other diaspora communities in Southeast Asia, Oceania, Central and South America and elsewhere. For them today, the most important factor affecting their cultural choices is the apparent disarray of modern Chinese cultures in Mainland China itself.

The idea of local variants and adaptations of diaspora culture was prominent in Southeast Asia where long-settled Chinese communities developed mixtures of local and Chinese traditions while adapting to European ideas of trade and governance. With the encouragement of native rulers and Western officials, many could seek autonomy for the cultures they had established, even though, until the twentieth century, most Chinese abroad were content to serve the colonial power structures.

The spirit of Chinese culture, including famous stories of loyalty and morality that local Chinese retold in languages such as Thai and Malay, remained important. There were other strong responses to Western civilization. For example, two men were remarkable by taking two opposite positions: Gu Hongming (1857–1928) from the Straits Settlements excoriated European religions and political systems and favoured a modernizing Qing mandarinate, while Lim Boon Keng (Lin Wenqing, 1869–1957), from another part of the same British colony, admired modern science, medicine and business methods but insisted on remaining faithful to Confucian values.[6]

These two men represented two sides of what has been called Baba or *peranakan* culture, a blend of Sino-Malay and Anglo-European cultural features that is found throughout the Malay archipelago, especially where the indigenous peoples have been converted to Islam. It can be compared to many other mixed cultures, most distinctly those of the Sino-Filipino (Christian mestizo) and Sino-Thai (Buddhist Lukchin), where they have become more or less part of mainstream Filipino and Thai urban cultures today. The Baba cultures, however, are not associated with the dominant Muslim cultures of Malaysia and Indonesia. They have in Singapore moved from being based on their 'Malay' mother tongue to become English-speaking and some of their descendants are now able to use Chinese (*huayu*, which is close to *putonghua* in China) and turn to new China connections.

All these cultures do not resemble the cultures of the Han Chinese in China. They could be regarded as remnants and fragments distinguished by the fact that some of their practitioners insist that they are Chinese while others stress that they are proud to be of Chinese descent. Among them, only Baba culture could be identified as a peripheral example of diaspora culture. On the other hand, significant numbers of Chinese people in the new nations of Southeast Asia still want to retain key elements of Chinese culture while confirming their loyalty to the local state.

Modern choices

By the 1930s, Chinese people everywhere, and especially outside China, began to understand the nature and importance of the modern cultures that gave the West its advantage over everybody else. Nevertheless, their response was ambiguous. It was one thing for the diaspora to master the new marvels of science and engineering, even to the point of acknowledging the underlying universal truths as a kind of 'scient-ism'. It was another thing to see China emulate the sovereign European nation-states and reject any interference by Westerners and the Japanese. Taken together with the resentments and grievances that the diaspora remembered, the Nationalists in the diaspora developed a strong desire to participate in anti-colonial and anti-imperialist movements. For two highly emotional decades, during the 1930s and 1940s, the diaspora was drawn into China politics to an extent totally unknown in the past, when all aspects of culture were turned to political ends. At this point, it would appear that events were pushing cultures among the Overseas Chinese towards being no more than an extension of Chinese culture. China was being invaded; war-torn China pulled at the emotional strings of Chinese everywhere and called on them to reidentify with China. The states and so-cieties among whom these Chinese lived were alarmed, seeing such iden-tification with Chinese nationalism as the beginnings of strong political influence in their territories. For the diaspora, especially the local-born who had settled abroad, this led them to a position of double jeopardy.

When World War II ended and China was among the victors, the Chinese everywhere were expected to choose Chinese nationalism and support the power to give them back their dignity and self-respect. The cultural demands of such an identity directed the local-born to catch up with developments in China. For a decade or so until the end of the 1950s, this was the difficult choice they had to face. Again, the pressures of political change were great. Three major challenges were to make cultural concerns irrelevant. Firstly, the civil war in China after 1946 re-sulted, to everyone's surprise, in Communist victory in 1949. Secondly, decolonization came swiftly with the end of the European empires and, wherever the Chinese presence was strong, local Nationalists clearly did not want politicized Chinese people in their midst. Thirdly, the trium-phant allies in World War II opened up an ideological contest for power that led to the Cold War, and this spread to every corner of the globe. For the Chinese with new-found pride in China's re-emergence among the Powers, Communist China's decision to side with the Soviet Union made the choices stark. On the whole, the Chinese abroad, with a show of re-sistance in some places, followed the political inclinations of the elites of their adopted countries. The alternative was to return to China or to join the rebels against newly independent governments. In the case of well-established nation-states, the decision to stay was understood to be a statement against taking the side of Beijing.

Where cultures were concerned, never had it been clearer to the Chinese abroad that issues of culture were directly linked with political transformations. Nation-states everywhere took the place of empires, and their concerted efforts to act together in international organizations were to ensure that empires did not return. In rejecting the national empires of the nineteenth and twentieth centuries, China's neighbours in particular looked warily at a resurgent China. Diaspora cultures were not an issue. If their countries of adoption sided with Beijing, socialist internationalism was the determinant factor. Beijing had little say in the cultural characteristics of fraternal countries. The diaspora in each of them either conformed to the local variant of socialist culture or totally embraced that of the Chinese motherland.

Elsewhere, those of Chinese descent who did not wish to return to China had to minimize links with the Chinese government and have nothing to do with the proletarian cultures that emerged there. Local choices, however, depended on national policies in each country and were often flexible. Apart from total acceptance of indigenous cultures where this was possible or officially encouraged, there was room for negotiation if Chinese communities were keen enough to seek their autonomous existence. Where they had the numbers, as in Singapore and Malaysia, the struggle was fierce not only with the respective national authorities but also among the Chinese themselves. For the rest, especially in countries where the numbers were very small (this applied to most of the nations where Chinese are found), identity politics was dominated more by racial stereotypes than by cultural manifestations. Where policies towards minorities became liberal, as in North America and Australasia after World War II, there was room to manoeuvre and legal systems and political groupings could be used to protect cultural retentions and even revivals. There was no simple formula for success. A great deal depended on Chinese community leaders in each country and the will of their supporters.

Comparisons between the diasporas in the new Asian nations close to China and in the liberal nations of North America and Australasia make this point clear. During the Cold War, political loyalty was the key and ideological disposition was an important factor in determining one's loyalty. In China's neighbourhood, the culture of the Chinese as a significant minority, especially one with considerable economic clout, was often treated as a political statement. Such communities had to go to great lengths to prove that the statement did not mean any kind of allegiance to the Chinese nation. In some environments, this was difficult because large sections of the diaspora displayed attitudes that did not equate their affirmation of political loyalty with adopting native cultures. Under these conditions, their cultural autonomy came at the expense of political participation and even minimized their chances of upward social mobility. But this was the price many Chinese were prepared to pay to uphold their pride and autonomy.

Where nation-states were more secure, it was easier to distinguish between loyalty and cultural preferences. This was especially so in successful migrant nations in North America and Australasia where liberal democratic traditions were used to change primordial attitudes towards race and ethnicity. After periods of discrimination, the local-born Chinese acquired full citizenship rights and this enabled them to participate together with all other minorities in every kind of activity. As a result, more choices were open. Most of them felt free to adopt local cultures and demonstrate their skills in cultures that they could now treat as potentially their own. Yet others went further to refresh their cultural roots either by mastering Chinese traditional learning or by turning to modern and contemporary China (including Taiwan, where traditional learning was for a while encouraged) for inspiration. Insofar as the developed nations of the West had influence on their Asian allies in the Cold War, they provided examples that enabled their diaspora Chinese to remain hopeful of cultural preservation.

In the end, wealth and power are key factors in determining the future of cultures, whether a culture flourishes, attracts and challenges other cultures or whether it is a diminishing heritage among very few people or a splendid museum display admired by many. Thus unified China since 1949 was a turning point for a failed ancient imperial civilization to return with a self-modernizing vision. In that context, the varieties of impact that China will now have on the diaspora is something everyone concerned notes with increasing care. How that will be manifested in diaspora cultures will be of growing importance. To what extent will the revived culture of China have strong political and ideological overtones for the diaspora?

Cultural variety

We can only speak of diaspora cultures when most sojourners have decided to become settlers. For most Chinese, that process began during the nineteenth century, but was culturally significant only during the twentieth century. By the second half of the twentieth century, those who did not return to China and those who were not totally assimilated were left to shape a variety of cultures that can be connected with the diaspora. These cultures are still works in progress and are fluid enough to intermesh with one another or disappear altogether in time to come. But it is possible to point to their varying degrees of viability and why they suggest that diaspora cultures may well find the place they deserve in modern Chinese culture.

The communities that might qualify as diasporas vary greatly in size, and each would have its own characteristics. The following three may all survive into the future.

1. *The faithful.* This group has projected Chinese culture abroad as the only authentic one that will always be meaningful because it is connected closely with developments in China. This articulate and vocal group was seriously weakened by the political turmoils of Soviet and Maoist ideologies in Mainland China, especially the excesses of the Cultural Revolution. More recently, it has been divided by the politics of reunification and the Taiwanese nationalism that has been aroused. This alternate political identity that the majority in Taiwan now claim may not affect diaspora cultures directly, but Taiwanese assertions of local identity over its Chinese origins which are also influenced by diasporic experiences may in the long run impact on the faithful in new and unpredictable ways.

   For most of the faithful, however, the economic successes of China have given them reason to hope that a corner has been turned and Chinese culture will be freshly defined and given new life in China itself. If that happens, there will no longer be the need to be defensive. The recent migration of large numbers to North America, Australasia and Europe, which is likely to continue for a while, represents the greatest movement of educated Chinese talent ever known. The new migrants from the Mainland have joined the intellectual ranks of the existing diaspora and are adding an authenticity to the cultures brought out by earlier emigrants from Taiwan, Hong Kong and Macau. While those from the Mainland may have rejected the Maoist ideology imbedded in their culture, they have also conveyed some fresh faith in the China connection. Given their educational backgrounds, should they actively participate in local diaspora cultures they are likely to embolden others to join them to redefine their faith in a rich and adaptive Chinese tradition. Certainly the examples set by Yang Chen Ning in the sciences, Tu Wei-ming and Yu Ying-shih in the humanities and Tan Dun in the performing arts will have reverberations for decades to come. In time, the augmentations could continue to draw inspiration from China and change the composition of other diaspora cultures in yet unknowable ways. But, for now, these diaspora cultures of the faithful will resemble one another wherever new Chinese migrants are numerous.

2. *The peripheral.* Beyond the faithful are many diaspora cultures that vary from place to place. They are the products of communities of earlier Chinese sojourners and the next three or four generations of descendants. These communities have become distinctive in various countries in Southeast Asia where they have been open to other cultures and acknowledge the benefits they have received from direct contacts with varieties of modern European cultures. They have added to what they inherited from earlier Chinese cultures but have consciously tried to keep the changes within the framework of a proud ancient heritage. They continue to strive for a modified authenticity that could win recognition not so much from their fellow nationals as from the Chinese of China. If the latter should appreciate their efforts and consider their cultures as part of a significant cultural periphery, these diaspora communities would see that as a major achievement. Much depends on their numbers and their connection with Chinese education. Not surprisingly, the communities in Malaysia and Singapore are prominent, and smaller groups in Indonesia, the Philippines and Thailand have regained confidence recently. Lee Kuan Yew and his local-born colleagues in Singapore who have access to political power are exceptional, but it suggests that political participation may be essential.[7]

Can such peripheral cultures be identified in North America and Australasia? In both regions, the pull towards powerful modern Western cultures is strong. At the same time, the influx of newcomers from Hong Kong, Taiwan and the Mainland supports close cultural relations with China, links that would encourage them to maintain interest in mastery of the Chinese language. If both pulls remain as strong as they are today, the possibility of diaspora cultures in each region becoming peripheral to both Chinese and host cultures, each in distinctive ways, is there. The communities on such peripheries would have opportunities to build bridges between their adopted countries and a rising China and minimize the anxieties that such a China could arouse. Who could inspire this? Could successful Chinese such as Y. M. Pei and David Ho in the professions and academia and Li Ang in cinema provide the core of future peripheral cultures? One condition for that to happen is that the study of the Chinese language should be easily available to every generation of diaspora Chinese. That would be an enormous challenge in the West, especially when there is no guarantee that modern Chinese culture will be universally admired and attractive to future generations.

3. *The marginal.* On the edges of the peripheral cultures are cultures that might be described as marginal and Chinese because the groups that support these cultures identify themselves as Chinese. Within larger Chinese communities in Southeast Asia, there are minorities descended from earlier settlers whose cultures are distinctive. This can only happen when the majority culture in the host country is not so dominant and attractive that the local-born would sooner or later assimilate totally. Yet they have moved away from their ancestral cultures far enough for them to be marginal to the peripheral cultures that still seek to emulate the cultures in China. Their educated members have combined older Chinese cultural artefacts with indigenous and modern Western cultures and moulded their own sub-cultures. These local-born Chinese have worked on the margins and sought their successes largely through their deep connections with local powers, and do not necessarily see themselves as part of the larger diaspora communities dominated by the faithful and the peripheral. They have been prominent in colonial Southeast Asia where they were able to flourish in the niche areas between native and European authority. Early examples are easier to identify because, cut off from contact with China, they gained influence by being bold and innovative. Oei Tiong Ham in the Netherlands East Indies, the family of Khaw Soo Cheang in southern Thailand and Penang, and Tan Cheng Lock in Malaysia are examples. Today, they are well integrated as loyal nationals and are harder to distinguish. Some may comfortably move in peripheral cultural circles while others may be seen as more or less assimilated. Under the circumstances, it is also more difficult for them to gain wider recognition in highly competitive areas of endeavour that require strong community support. Individual achievements, however, may still be respected by the diaspora.[8]

In Southeast Asia, the historical examples of *peranakan* culture in the Malay-Muslim world, that of the Sino-Thai in Thailand and that of the 'Tsinoy' in the Philippines suggest that, given the right constellation of circumstances, such marginal cultures could retain their respective places for a long time. But the pressures of national and global cultures are growing. Unless they increase their numbers, some will converge with their dominant local cultures or let their members break out altogether to adopt modern cultures elsewhere. On the other hand, the numbers on the margin could increase if there are rewarding incentives to work across community and national borders. Elsewhere in North America and Australasia, two scenarios are possible. At one end, global skills heighten further the advantages of being marginal.

There is little need for cultural labels here once the achievements of successful individuals are appreciated in themselves. At the other, a distinctive future 'modern Chinese' culture may emanate from an amalgam of Mainland, Taiwan and Hong Kong–Macau cultures. If this one day helps to set the standards for 'global modern' culture, the margins of the diaspora may seek to excel in that realm. This does not seem likely today but the resilience and inventiveness of Chinese cultures, whether central or peripheral, should not be underestimated. Looking ahead at the foreign local-born who now represent quite different cultural milieus, future examples of those such as Ma Yoyo in the performing arts, Maxine Hong Kingston and Amy Tan in literature, Adrienne Poy Clarkson in public affairs and David Henry Huang in the theatre may be the kind of people from whom distinct cultural niches might be carved out on the diasporic margins.

In the face of modern national cultures, the three kinds of diaspora cultures identified here are unlikely to remain distinctive for long. In one exceptional case, diaspora culture could remain at the core of Singapore culture. And this could help another retain its autonomy in Malaysia. For the rest, much will depend on the dominant majorities and the national policies they control. To some extent, the rise of China could also offer more choices for the future, but China's diplomatic relations in the world will not address their cultural concerns. What will be decisive is the quality of the modern culture that China projects to the outside world. If that is neither imperial nor heavily Confucianized but contains attractive universal attributes that invite admiration from a global audience, diaspora cultures could reinvent themselves regularly and never lose their claims to Chineseness.

Notes

1. Basic information about Chinese culture overseas may be found in Lynn Pan (ed.), *The Encyclopedia of the Chinese Overseas*, Second Edition, Singapore, Editions Didier Millet, 2006. While it does not have a separate section on cultures, it deals with many cultural features in the sections 'Institutions' and 'Relations'. A good introduction to the many flavours to be found is Josephine M. T. Khu (ed.), *Cultural Curiosity: Thirteen Stories about the Search for Chinese Roots*, Berkeley, University of California Press, 2002.
2. The essays in Linda Y. C. Lim and L. A. Peter Gosling (eds.), *The Chinese in Southeast Asia*, Singapore, Maruzen Asia, 1983 and in Jennifer W. Cushman and Wang Gungwu (eds.), *Changing Identities of the Southeast Asian Chinese since World War II*, Hong Kong, Hong Kong University Press, 1988, capture most of the major changes that impacted on the culture of the Chinese in Southeast Asia. For other parts of the world, see note 5 below.

3. Claudine Salmon explores an exceptional area in her edited book, *Literary Migrations: Traditional Chinese Fiction in Asia (17–20th Centuries)*, Beijing, International Culture Publishing Corporation, 1987.

4. Leo Suryadinata, *China and the ASEAN States: The Ethnic Chinese Dimension*, Singapore, Singapore University Press, 1985 is a good introduction to this complex subject.

5. For examples of cultural change during the first half of the twentieth century see Adam McKeown, *Chinese Migrant Networks and Cultural Change: Peru, Chicago, Hawaii, 1900–1936*, Chicago, University of Chicago Press, 2001; for other periods, see essays on North America and Australasia in Wang Ling-Chi and Wang Gungwu (eds.), *The Chinese Diaspora: Selected Essays*, 2 volumes, Singapore, Times Academic Press, 1998; also the issues of *Chinese America, History and Perspectives*, San Francisco, Chinese Historical Society of America, published annually since 1987; and Eric Rolls' two volumes on Australia, *Sojourners* (1992) and *Citizens* (1996), both published by University of Queensland Press in Brisbane.

6. The first parts of Gu's biography by Lo Hui-min were published in *Papers on Far Eastern History* no. 38 and *East Asian History* no. 6, December 1993 and no. 9, June 1995, Canberra, 'Ku Hung-ming: Schooling' and 'Homecoming, pts 1 and 2'. For Lim Boon Keng, the most thorough study is Lee Guan Kin (Li Yuanjin), *Lin Wenqing de sixiang* [The thoughts of Lim Boon Keng], Singapore, Yazhou yanjiu xuehui (Singapore Society of Asian Studies), 1991.

7. This approximates Group B in my *China Quarterly* study (1970) of Malayan politics, where I distinguish it from Group A that looks always to China and Group C that identifies with local polities. At the time, I argued that this was the largest group in each Southeast Asian country. Today it has become smaller. Wang Gungwu, 'Chinese Politics in Malaya', reprinted in *Community and Nation: Essays on Southeast Asia and the Chinese*, Singapore and Sydney, Heinemann and George Allen & Unwin, 1981, pp. 173–200. Recent writings on the Chinese in North America and Australasia suggest that this peripheral group is a growing group there, if only because of the large numbers of well-educated new migrants arriving from Hong Kong, Taiwan and the People's Republic of China.

8. The literature describing the cultures of marginal Chinese is largely in the languages of the various countries in which Chinese communities have developed. Japanese and European scholars have used some of these writings in the context of assimilation and acculturation research. For Southeast Asia, see Leo Suryadinata, *Ethnic Chinese as Southeast Asians*, Singapore, Institute of Southeast Asian Studies, 1997. In North America, the growth of a Chinese literary and performing arts community writing in English has underlined the many new uses of marginality that have encouraged younger generations of artistic Chinese everywhere.

Guide to further reading

Cushman, Jennifer W. and Wang Gungwu (eds.), *Changing Identities of the Southeast Asian Chinese since World War II*, Hong Kong, Hong Kong University Press, 1988.

Khoo Joo Ee, *The Straits Chinese: A Cultural History*, Amsterdam and Kuala Lumpur, The Pepin Press, 1996.

McKeown, Adam, *Chinese Migrant Networks and Cultural Change: Peru, Chicago, Hawaii, 1900–1936*, Chicago, University of Chicago Press, 2001.

Pan, Lynn (ed.), *The Encyclopedia of the Chinese Overseas*, Second Edition, Singapore, Editions Didier Millet, 2006.

Tan Chee Beng, *The Baba of Melaka: Culture and Identity of a Chinese Peranakan Community in Malaysia*, Petaling Jaya, Pelanduk Publications, 1988.

Wang Ling-Chi and Wang Gungwu (eds.), *The Chinese Diaspora: Selected Essays*, 2 volumes, Singapore, Times Academic Press, 1998.

Zhou Nanjing *et al.* (eds.), *Huaqiao huaren baike quanshu* [Encyclopedia of Overseas Chinese], 12 volumes, Beijing, Zhongguo huaqiao chubanshe, 1999–2001.

7

Modernizing Confucianism and 'new Confucianism'

For some people, Confucianism, a philosophy that looks to a mythical past as an ideal for inspiration, has become obsolete as societies historically under Confucian influence modernize. However, reports of the death of Confucianism are premature. While it has been eclipsed by Western thought and practice for significant periods, Confucianism has undergone a revival in many East Asian societies in the last few decades. Many people continue to identify Confucianism as the mainstream, even the definitive core, of Chinese culture. Confucianism has played many different, sometimes contradictory, roles in modernization, which is understood here as social progress through technological advancement, new modes of production, distribution and exchange for sustained economic growth, new social differentiation and rationalized organizations, increased social mobility, equality, and political participation in sovereign nation-states.

Modernizing Confucianism: nineteenth-century beginnings

Nineteenth-century reformists attempted to adapt Confucianism to Western modernity, first through the 'self-strengthening movement', which sought to combine Confucianism with Western technology. Western guns and ships that played such a crucial role in the defeat of the Chinese troops in the key battles of the nineteenth century convinced the Chinese that they needed to 'learn barbarian techniques to control the barbarians'. Qing officials, Lin Zexu, Zeng Guofan, Li Hongzhang, and Zuo Zongtang – all of whom were Confucians – saw the need for change to meet the challenges of a new era. Their insistence on learning from the

West was premised on the need to strengthen China, and they saw the latter's weakness as merely a matter of 'technique' and craft, which had traditionally been considered of low importance in Confucian thinking. They remained confident that in its ultimate values, in the things that really mattered, Confucianism was superior, and defined human civilization. China's humiliating defeat by Japan in 1895 clearly proved that the superficial and haphazard approach to learning Western techniques – by setting up a few factories to manufacture weapons and build ships, establishing foreign language schools, and sending a handful of officials and students to America to acquire and implement Western methods, narrowly defined and barely understood – had not worked.

One of the self-strengtheners, Zhang Zhidong, advocated Western learning that went beyond techniques of manufacturing guns and ships to include methods of administration.[1] He argued for reform of Chinese education according to the formula, 'Chinese learning for substance, Western learning for use' (*Zhongxue wei ti*, *xixue wei yong*), *zhongti xiyong* for brevity. He believed that Western learning was needed to 'maintain the state, preserve the doctrine of Confucius, and protect the Chinese race'. Wm. Theodore de Bary noted that the Chinese Communist Party's selective approach to Confucianism, which was demonstrated in Gu Mu's keynote speech during the 1994 conference to celebrate the 2545th birthday of Confucius, was a return to this conservative reformism 'that sought to adopt Western methods while still holding on to a Chinese "essence"'.[2] No doubt the CCP hopes that this formula will safeguard its authoritarian regime as much as Zhang Zhidong hoped that it would protect the Qing autocratic state legitimated by imperial Confucianism.

According to Joseph Levenson, the *zhongti xiyong* formula was a rationalization that was doomed to fail, since Chinese learning had been valued as *ti* because of its *yong*. To promote Western learning as *yong*, rather than protecting Chinese learning as *ti*, resulted in the supplanting of the latter.[3] Western techniques were more than useful mechanical methods that could be appropriated without more fundamental change; they challenged the entire Confucian way of life 'by encouraging a social alternative, the commercial–industrial way of life, which likewise made the Confucian learning seem increasingly irrelevant – and Confucian sanctions (such as the family system) increasingly impossible'.[4] Philosophically, the formula distorts the neo-Confucian notion of *tiyong*, which implies an intrinsic organic relation between the *ti* and *yong* of all things, into one of external relation involving no more than superficial juxtaposition of arbitrarily separated elements of different cultures. It obscures rather than clarifies the relationship between Western thought and practice representing modern cultures on the one hand, and Confucianism as an entire culture or way of life on the other, because it fails to appreciate that in any culture, substance and use are intrinsically and organically related. Modernizing Confucianism requires transformation of both substance and use.

Zhang staunchly defended a conservative Confucian morality that emphasized the 'three bonds' (*sangang*) subordinating minister to ruler, son to father, wife to husband, and insisted that without first building a strong foundation in Confucian morality, learning from the West would lead to disaster, with 'the strong becoming rebellious leaders and the weak, slaves'. In one respect, Zhang's conservative reformism may be said to have been anti-modern: he was fiercely opposed to 'people's rights'. Not only did he argue that the people were not ready to be given rights because of lack of education and property; he dismissed the claim that 'everybody has the right to be his own master' as a distortion by Chinese translators of what amounted to no more than everyone 'having intelligence and wisdom to do useful work', and viewed the checks and balances in Western parliamentary systems as meaning that 'nobody is his own master'. Zhang consciously resisted both the ultra-traditionalists who believed that modernization meant destruction of Confucianism and, despite many points of agreement with them, the more radical reformism of those led by Kang Youwei, who played such a key role in the short-lived '100 days reform' in 1898.

Kang rejected the imperial Confucianism defended by traditionalists and more conservative reformists as the product of false classics and distortions of Confucius' teachings. He believed that the classics that had formed the basis of orthodox Confucianism since the later Han, the 'Old Texts' including the *Zhou Li*, the *Yi Li*, the *Zuo Zhuan* and the *Mao Shi*, were forgeries. He followed the Next Text School in preferring the *Gongyang* commentary on the *Chun Qiu* (Spring and Autumn Annals), which he believed provided the best interpretation of Confucius' teachings. The *Gongyang* school believes that the authentic classics were not transmitted but authored by Confucius. Furthermore, even the authentic classics do not contain all of Confucius' teachings, the most important of which have been transmitted orally. Rather than treating the *Chun Qiu* as a historical record, *Gongyang* scholars treat the classic as a repository of enduring principles, containing Confucius' 'great meanings conveyed in subtle words', which should be interpreted in light of actual politics. These beliefs allowed Kang great latitude in interpreting the classics and understanding Confucius' teachings, from which he was able to draw significant social and political meanings useful to his reformism.

Kang presented Confucius as a reformer, the founder of a '*jiao*' (school of teaching), rather than as a transmitter of ancient learning. The classics written by Confucius were not historical records since there was no way to know China's remote past, and Confucius as a sage did not require sanction of the past to validate his teachings. Confucius was an 'uncrowned king' who designed institutions for good government. As a commoner undertaking a task perceived as belonging to kings, although the precedent had been set by Yao and Shun, Confucius needed to be subtle in his approach. To avoid trouble and persuade people to accept his reforms, he attributed these reforms to the ancients. Therefore, the 'three dynasties' (referring to institutions traditionally attributed to the legendary sage kings) in Confucius' teachings do not constitute a nostalgic account of a past Golden Age but Confucius' own creation, showing the way to a perfect society yet to be realized.

Kang purported to draw from Confucius' teachings, transmitted through the *Gongyang* school, a theory of historical evolution wherein the world progresses from the age of chaos (*shuailuan shi*), through the age of rising peace, (*shengping shi*) to the age of supreme peace (*taiping shi*). In Kang's later works, rising peace and supreme peace came to be identified with the *Liyun* (*Book of Rites* chapter: 'Evolution of Rites') notions of minor peace (*xiaokang*) and great unity (*datong*) respectively. Autocratic institutions suited the age of chaos, constitutional monarchy suited rising peace, and participative democracy suited supreme peace. According to Kang, China at the end of the nineteenth century needed to replace autocracy with constitutional monarchy, but was not yet ready for participative democracy. China's problem resulted from clinging to obsolete autocratic institutions appropriate only for the age of chaos; China had therefore been weakened and prevented from making progress. After the failure of the reforms drove him into exile, Kang wrote commentaries on the *Analects* and other Confucian texts that interpreted them in line with his reformism. He also developed the notion of 'great unity' into a radical philosophy that advocated, among other things, gender equality and the abolition of the family.

While too radical even for other contemporary reformists, apart from a small band of loyal followers, and utterly repugnant to traditionalists,

Kang's modernization of Confucianism did not go far enough for the even more radical modernizers, who turned completely against traditional Chinese culture, especially Confucianism. Commentators have laid part of the blame for later iconoclasm at Kang's door, since questioning Old Text classics opened the door to questioning all classics and doubting the authority of antiquity, which grounded traditional Confucianism, facilitating a sweeping rejection of Confucianism that saw no point in distinguishing between the true teachings of Confucius and the historical practice. Kang's post-1898 activities, especially his attempts to establish Confucianism as a religion in conjunction with monarchical restoration, also seem anti-modernization. These were not reversals in his philosophical and political positions. His view of historical evolution places China at a point suited to a constitutional monarchy rather than a democratic republic, even though his utopian vision – captured in the posthumously published *Datong Shu* [*Book of Great Unity*] – remains one of a world held in common by all for all, without private property, social hierarchy, racial or gender discrimination.

Kang's petitions to the Qing court and the Republican government to establish Confucianism as a state religion may be seen as anti-modern because they go against the secularization trend that has been identified with modernization, and resort to state power, which undermined the separation of church and state and religious pluralism associated with modern polities. Confucians also resisted Kang's move to transform Confucianism into a religion modelled on the Christian Church. The debate about whether Confucianism is a religion, which dates back to the Jesuits' arrival in China and continues to resurface today, has no conclusive outcome as the answer depends on one's definition of religion and Confucianism. Kang himself adopted what appears to be an oxymoronic definition of religion when he judged Confucianism to be superior to Christianity because it did away with 'divine authority'.[5] One could turn this against the 'anti-modern' charge by seeing it as advocating something similar to a non-theistic 'civil religion', a modernized form of religion.

Not surprisingly, Kang's radical reinterpretations of Confucianism draw accusations that he was using the name of Confucius to destroy Confucianism, and charges that he was not a Confucian at all. Today's modernizers of Confucianism are similarly at risk of being accused of apostasy. Hsiao Kung-ch'uan argues persuasively that Kang remains a Confucian even though he sometimes used the classics to express his own views, and went far beyond other Confucian revisionists in rejecting family relations in his utopian vision. If one understands Confucianism as a broad stream of thought to which numerous individuals have contributed by studying the writings associated with the tradition, thinking about Confucius' teachings in relation to important problems, and using them as a guide in life, then Kang was as much a Confucian as many others who have been influenced by non-Confucian teachings, such as Daoism and Buddhism, and have added their distinctive interpretations and thinking to Confucianism. Even when unpersuasive and questionable in methodology, Kang's radical interpretations are still arguably extensions rather than perversions of Confucius' and Mencius' teachings. Recent scholarship has employed more sophisticated methods and more persuasive argumentation to reach conclusions that are basically similar to Kang's, interpretations that render Confucianism compatible with modernity. The emphasis on equality in Kang's *Datong Shu* has become an important feature of modern New Confucianism.[6] Later modernizers of Confucianism should appreciate Kang's example of radical reinterpretations of Confucian texts that open the door to transforming the substance of Confucianism with the aid of Western learning, while maintaining the continuity of the Confucian tradition.

Even though some maintain that Chinese culture is Confucian, the dominance of Confucianism in Chinese culture cannot be taken for granted after the nineteenth century. Confucianism now plays a very different role in Chinese society and politics. Most prominent nineteenth-century Confucians were scholar-officials, men of action and influence who could practise their philosophy in government; in the twentieth century, the most prominent Confucians taught in universities. While some politicians continued to enlist Confucianism in the service of authoritarianism, and others argued for Confucian democracy, more people considered it irrelevant. The main problem in earlier years was how to convince Confucians to accept modernization; the current problem is how to convince modern Chinese to retain or revive Confucianism. The strongest enemies of nineteenth-century Confucian modernizers were traditionalists who refused modernization; the strongest enemies of today's Confucians are those who see no need for Confucianism in modern life. However, in the latter half of the twentieth century, the rapid economic rise of East Asia prompted a re-evaluation of the relationship between Confucianism and modernization, reversing previous views about their incompatibility. Recently, as scholars have questioned the value and content of concepts of modernization and modernity, even accusing them of being ethnocentric and the intellectual accompaniment to Western/American imperialism, some Confucians have begun to explore the possibility of improving on Western modernity or contributing to an alternative Chinese modernity with modernized Confucianism.

New Confucianism: a Chinese culturalist response to the challenge of Western modernity

The most prominent developments in Confucianism since the early twentieth century have been associated with thinkers who described themselves or are described as *Xin Rujia*, which can be translated as Neo-Confucians or New Confucians. The former translation is usually qualified as 'Contemporary Neo-Confucians', 'Modern Neo-Confucians' or 'New Neo-Confucians' to distinguish these thinkers from Song and Ming dynasty Confucians, who have also been referred to as 'Neo-Confucians' since Feng Youlan used the term *xin rujia* to refer to the philosophy of the Cheng brothers and Zhu Xi in his *History of Chinese Philosophy*. Using the expression 'New Confucianism' is one way to avoid confusion, but 'contemporary Neo-Confucianism' has the advantage of registering the philosophical continuity between the two groups. Although some scholars use the terms contemporary Neo-Confucianism and New Confucianism interchangeably, for Liu Shuxian, contemporary Neo-Confucianism refers to the philosophical movement initiated by Xiong Shili and further developed by his students Mou Zongsan, Tang Junyi and Xu Fuguan, with only Liu himself and Tu Wei-ming as third generation; New Confucianism translates *xin ruxue*, a term used by PRC scholars since the 1980s to refer to a larger group, including Xiong Shili, Liang Shuming, Ma Yifu and Zhang Junmai (Carsun Chang), Feng Youlan, He Lin, Qian Mu and Fang Dongmei (Thomé H. Fang) in the first generation, Mou Zongsan, Tang Junyi and Xu Fuguan in the second generation, and Cheng Chung-ying and Yu Ying-shih in the third generation.[7]

There is little consensus about who are the New Confucians. For some, New Confucianism is synonymous with modernized Confucianism, and Kang Youwei, even Zeng Guofan and Zhang Zhidong, qualify as members. At its most exclusive, the description could be restricted to only Xiong Shili, Mou Zongsan and Liu Shuxian. I define New Confucianism by its commitment to promoting Confucianism based on a belief in the perennial relevance and value of Confucianism, and its strategy of achieving this goal through creative transformations of the philosophy transmitted by past Confucian thinkers with the aid of non-Confucian ideas, especially modern Western ideas. This would include thinkers loosely linked by 'family resemblance' rather than designate any kind of highly integrated homogeneous movement. While commentators usually see New Confucianism as a philosophical movement, most agree that cultural concerns are important to New Confucians either as motivation or extension of their metaphysical preoccupations.

New Confucianism differs from earlier Confucianism in having to respond to Western modernity. Its response is culturalist in asserting the primacy of culture in both diagnosis and explanation of the problems posed by Western modernity to China, and in the solution it advocates. It differs from other forms of contemporary scholarship on Confucianism in its self-conscious cultural commitment. Many scholars point to the 1958 'Manifesto for a Reappraisal of Sinology and Reconstruction of Chinese Culture', signed by Carsun Chang, Mou Zongsan, Tang Junyi and Xu Fuguan, as a landmark for New Confucianism. The document asserts that the problem of China, which has become a world problem, can be solved only 'with genuine understanding of her culture in both its actualities and its potentialities'. Moreover, 'the problems of Chinese culture have their universal significance', and the West has something to learn from 'oriental thought'. It criticizes sinology – dominated by missionaries interested in converting China, those interested in relics of dead civilizations, or those with the *realpolitik* concern of dealing with present-day China – for being driven by motives that undermine genuine understanding of China and Chinese culture. It appeals for studies that focus on the 'true nature of Chinese culture' and its 'natural development'. It objects to positivistic approaches devoid of respect and sympathy, which ignore the difference between culture and natural science. The authors call for affirmation that 'Chinese culture is vibrantly alive'. They identify the study of heart–mind and human nature (*xinxing zhi xue*), which had been neglected by sinologues, as central to Chinese culture, viewed as 'the objective expression' of Chinese spiritual life. This central interest in *xinxing* can be traced back to Confucius, and was the central preoccupation of the Song Ming Neo-Confucians; it also became the central theme in New Confucian works.

The manifesto also objects to misleading comparisons of Song Ming philosophy to Western rationalism, naturalism or materialism, which contribute to misunderstandings of Chinese culture as being limited to external social control, with neither spiritual nor metaphysical interests. It also acknowledges that Chinese thought has shortcomings and needs to be expanded by taking into consideration ideas of other cultures, such as democracy and science; this should be done not by measurement against external standards but by nurturing the seeds of democracy and scientific tendencies within Chinese culture itself. As a harbinger of the increasingly international orientation of New Confucianism, the Manifesto addresses not merely the Chinese community but 'the world', and anticipates that, while China needs 'to be consummate in fulfillment of the propensity of her culture, her work of democratic, scientific and industrial reconstruction', the West needs 'self examination as the leader of the world, in the spirit of "reviving the perished and restoring the broken", of various cultures'.[8]

The New Confucian response to iconoclastic modernizers

It is no coincidence that this Manifesto has been singled out as the founding document of the New Confucian movement. Three of its signatories constitute the second generation of New Confucians; Mou and Tang especially are central figures, whose membership in the movement is almost never questioned. And its fourth signatory, Carsun Chang, sparked one of the most important intellectual debates of Republican China over 'Science and Philosophy of Life'. Chang's 1923 lecture at Qinghua University argues that, for all its usefulness, science has limitations and cannot provide a philosophy of life that is subjective rather than objective, intuitive rather than logical, synthetic rather than analytic, and assumes free will rather than causal determination and uniqueness of individuality rather than uniformity of nature. The debate was part of the struggle between those who believed that a new culture of science and democracy must completely replace traditional Chinese culture, and those who believed that traditional Chinese culture, including Confucianism, had perennial value.

Guy Alitto suggests that it was Liang Shuming's earlier lectures, published in 1922 as *Eastern and Western Cultures and their Philosophies*, that prepared the ground for the public reaction to Chang's lecture. The iconoclasm of the New Culture movement and the disillusion with Westernization following World War I were the catalysts for Liang Shuming's reflections on culture. Even though Liang may be more Buddhist than Confucian in some respects, his defence of Chinese culture and of Confucianism as a philosophy that has meaning and value not only for the Chinese but for the world secures him a place as a founder of New Confucianism.[9] Liang was not conservative in the sense of defending the prevailing culture of the Chinese people throughout the ages. This 'habitual culture' distorts Confucius' teachings. Among past Confucians, he singled out Wang Yangming and his student Wang Gen (Taizhou school) as coming close to Confucius' philosophy of life. Liang's understanding of Confucius emphasizes spontaneity, which means that the ethical life does not lie in rigid principles or external goals. This leads to a rejection of the oppressive sociopolitical system that has been attributed to Confucianism. Liang insisted that a true Confucian must live life to the full, by valuing every present moment rather than being enslaved by external regulations and goals. Liang was no simple traditionalist. In his eyes, traditionalists did a poor job of defending traditional culture and were wrong to oppose Western democracy and science. At the same time, he was opposed to the iconoclasts and those who advocated some kind of eclectic East–West cultural blending, who shared the traditionalists' lack of clarity about the nature of Chinese culture and its differences from other cultures.

Liang defined culture as a people's way of life – spiritual, social and material. According to Liang, the value of a culture lies in its distinctive differences from others. These differences must be sought in the 'ultimate root' of culture, which is found in the characteristic 'will', which takes different directions according to which problems (obstacles presented by the environment) and approaches to their solution dominate a culture. Western culture, Chinese culture, and Indian culture represent three ideal types of culture, although a society may have a combination of their characteristics. In Liang's view, Western culture focuses on problems of material life and approaches them by changing the natural and social environment to satisfy desires. Social problems are analogous to problems of physical nature in that one confronts other people and authority as one confronts external objects, and mechanisms/institutions are invented to solve social problems. The characteristic will is 'forward seeking', overcoming the other to satisfy oneself. Science and democracy are its greatest achievements. Eastern cultures, divided into Chinese and Indian, may seem backward when measured by these Western achievements, but have actually followed different paths. The greatest achievement of Chinese culture is Confucius' philosophy of life based on a metaphysics of change and the central notion of harmony. Problems of 'other heart–minds' dominate Chinese culture. People are harder to change to one's satisfaction than inanimate objects; they also have desires and wills of their own. The Chinese approach to problems emphasizes self-harmonizing and the self-moderating of desires. Rather than changing the environment, the Chinese adapt themselves and value contentment and endurance; the will steps aside. Indian culture, whose greatest achievement is found in the religion of Buddhism, focuses on existential problems that cannot be solved. Its approach is to remove the problems by eliminating desires and transcending this world; the will turns back on itself.

According to Liang, no culture is inherently superior to others; each is suited to particular circumstances. Cultures cannot be blended but one may need to give way to another as circumstances change. Liang saw a natural progression that would take human beings from a focus on material problems to social problems and eventually spiritual problems, moving from the path of Western culture, to the Chinese, and then to the Indian. Liang attributed both Chinese and Indian cultural achievements to the genius of Confucius and the Buddha. Unfortunately, Chinese and Indian societies were not ready for them and neglect of the first path simply led to failures of the majority in prematurely attempting the second and third paths. Given its unsuccessful attempt to follow the second path shown by Confucius, a revival of Buddhism would be disastrous for China since its world-transcendence attitude would further impede the solution of China's most pressing problems, which were those of the first path. Hence, Liang supported complete acceptance of not just the mechanisms but also the spirit of Western science and democracy. The ancient Greeks had been on the first path, but because the path was not self-consciously pursued, Western society took a detour onto the third path of religious transcendence before returning to the first. The pursuit of the first path, which resulted in Western modernity, would have to exhaust itself before the West would turn to a different path, which would be the second path represented by the Chinese ideal type. According to Liang, the various problems of Western modernity, summarized in terms of reducing life to a series of means of pursuing external goals, resulting in feelings of emptiness and meaninglessness, alienation and spiritual crisis, showed that the West was rapidly reaching that point. Liang identified, not very persuasively, signs that Western thinkers, such as Henri Bergson, Bertrand Russell, Rudolf Euken and Kropotkin, were turning to the 'Chinese' path.

As problems of modernity were already evident in the West, Liang argued that China's 'complete acceptance of Western culture' must fundamentally correct the latter's attitude, and critically readopt China's original attitude. Liang's position is contradictory: given his rejection of cultural blending, and his belief that the fundamental attitude of a culture, evident in the direction of its will, holistically gives rise to all its characteristic thinking, practices and products, how is it possible to Westernize completely while retaining or reviving the fundamental attitude of Chinese culture? It would have been more consistent for Liang to claim that while the West moves towards a 'Chinese' path, the Chinese, having abandoned their original path, would not be ready to return to it until China, like the West, had exhausted the first path. Other New Confucians are less averse to cultural blending, while being mindful of Liang's objection to superficial and piecemeal borrowings and imitations that ignore the organic relations between the spirit and the manifestations of each culture. Liang was highly critical of those who saw no contradiction at all between Confucianism and Western modernity. He scathingly rejected as anti-Confucian Kang Youwei's attempt to modernize Confucianism by rendering it compatible with Western utilitarian, acquisitive and competitive attitudes. His critique of Western modernity, which accompanied his admission that China needed to learn from the West, for all its tension, has become an important theme in New Confucianism. His conviction that Confucianism understood correctly offers solutions to the problems of Western modernity and has an important part to play in some future world culture is shared by other New Confucians. However, he did not go as far as some New Confucians in taking Chinese culture and Confucianism as 'ultimate commitment'. The second path of Confucius is not the 'end of history'. Liang believed that after solving the problems of the first and second paths, a society would move on to the third path found in Buddhism, although he seemed to think that, even then, enlightenment would be reserved for the select few.

Liang's views stimulated debates that lasted for two decades, and *Eastern and Western Cultures* continued to be published in the early years of the PRC. The relationship of socialism to Chinese culture was a concern to many Chinese Communists, and some argued for 'critical inheritance' of Chinese culture as part of 'socialist cultural reconstruction'. Although Liang was criticized in 1955 for his too enthusiastic praise of Chinese tradition, both positive and negative assessments of Confucianism continued through the 1950s and 1960s as scholars in Communist

China debated the class status of Confucius, whether he was a material-ist or an idealist, whether Confucian ethics were reactionary or progres-sive, and the nature and relevance of Confucius' influence on education. Opinions about Confucius were almost universally positive at the start of the 1960s, but discussions of Confucianism became increasingly po-liticized, and by the beginning of the 1970s, the verdict on Confucianism was unanimously negative.

Although Confucius was seldom the explicit target during the Cul-tural Revolution, Confucianism was implicated in the 'four olds' that were attacked – old culture, old ideology, old customs and old habits. Positive evaluations of Confucius were condemned as politically moti-vated attempts to undermine the dictatorship of the proletariat. These criticisms were repeated in the anti-Confucius campaign in the 1970s, which produced mass denunciations of Confucius and his ideas, and served the political purposes of arguing for continuing Cultural Revol-ution policies and attacking Zhou Enlai. Confucian discourse in Mao's China was severely limited by the use of Marxist Maoist ideology as the criterion for assessment, and discredited by being constantly entangled with the CCP's political struggles. First-generation New Confucians who stayed in the PRC suffered harsh treatment during the various purges. New Confucianism could not flourish in that stifling environment, and for the next three decades, Chinese scholars residing outside the PRC be-came the torch-bearers for the Confucian tradition.

New Confucianism overseas

In Mou Zongsan's own view, his philosophical career was spent mostly in reflecting on the problems of human reason set out by Immanuel Kant. The issues are Kantian in form, but the content is Chinese culture. Sec-ond-generation New Confucians believe that China's problems in the modern age relate primarily to its culture. They too seek a course between resisting cultural change and a change that would mean the total loss of Chinese culture. For Mou, Confucianism is the mainstream of Chinese culture, the dynamic force that determines the direction and form of Chi-nese life. Chinese culture will flourish and develop without losing itself only if the primacy of Confucianism is maintained. Mou was vehemently against any cultural transformation of Chinese societies that would mar-ginalize Confucianism. The Chinese have a special responsibility to Chi-nese culture. A person's life flows from the history and culture of his or her people. The Chinese cannot Westernize completely because they lack that primordial link and response to American culture that only Americans have, or to English culture that only the English have. Attempting to replace one's culture with that of another only results in self-defeat. Others can conquer one's territories, but they cannot conquer one's culture; only we ourselves can defeat our own culture by losing confidence in it, by abandoning our own cultural responsibility. Chinese Westernizers risk losing their souls; they end up neither Chinese nor Western, alienated from themselves and from the very source of their being.

Mou understood culture as the manifestation of spiritual life. The study of culture is not about cultural artefacts; it must discern the forms in which human individuality and spirit are manifested among a people. Every nation, every people, creates particular forms of manifesting their humanity, which is itself universal. The source of culture, identified in Confucian terms of *xin* ('heart–mind') and *li* ('cosmic pattern' or 'principle'), is moral creativity, the source of human goodness; it is universal. The presence of the universal, though constrained by the inevitable limits of any particular form that manifests it, makes every particular culture a world culture at the same time. That there is something universal to all human beings ensures the possibility of communication across different cultures and peace among them. That this universal source can only be manifested in particular forms gives significance and value to cultural diversity, and every cultural system. Mou managed the tension between cultural differences and commonality by combining Zhu Xi's idea of 'one principle many manifestations' (*liyi fenshu*) with Kantian concepts of the universal and the particular.

According to Mou, the Chinese cultural system first apprehends 'life' in seeking the way of virtue to enhance the lives and welfare of the people. It develops into a system of 'ethical politics' with humaneness (*ren*) as the highest principle: objectively it attempts to edify transformation through a system of rites and music; subjectively it gives rise to personal cultivation grounded in the learning of heart–mind and human nature (*xinxing zhi xue*). In contrast, the Greek tradition first grasps 'nature', which gives rise to a cultural system of the intellect, with the development of logic, mathematics and science. Western culture of Greek origin manifests the spirit in its analytic fulfilment of reason; Chinese culture manifests the spirit in its synthetic fulfilment of reason. While each culture has its particular 'rational' direction, each can learn from the other and expand its own capacity of limited 'manifesting of the universal' by 'turning at the source', developing what has been lacking in its limited historical manifestation. This provides the basis for mutual learning and convergence between Chinese and Western cultures; convergence must however not sacrifice diversity. Unfortunately, such learning has not been the norm in the various attempts at 'Westernization' in Chinese societies.

In Mou's view, Chinese cultural iconoclasts who have vociferously advocated science and democracy suffer from ignorance about culture and infatuation with superficial imports. The result is scientism and intellectualism. They fail to understand that science, as a particular manifestation of human spirit, has its own territory and limits; meaning and value lie outside these limits. Measuring everything by the criteria of science obliterates the ethical and the spiritual. Chinese pursuit of democracy has been equally problematic. Mou considered Western democracy a matter of institutional protection against abuse of power in politics. He criticized those who turn it into a doctrine of social life devoid of discipline and constraint. Introducing 'democracy' into the relations between father and son, between husband and wife, between brothers and friends, would only result in mutual indifference or even mutual antagonism.[10] Mou analysed human life in terms of three domains: knowledge, politics and daily life. Science belongs to the domain of knowledge, but on its own is insufficient to constitute a way of life. Democracy lies in the domain of politics. As a political way of life, it cannot encompass the whole of human life. The remaining domain of ethics and religion provides ways of daily life, and constitutes the driving forces of cultural creation. The strength of Chinese culture lies in this last domain, to which Confucianism belongs. Not being of the same domain, Confucianism does not contradict or oppose science or democracy.

In Mou's view, Chinese culture, of which Confucianism is the mainstream, could be expanded to include science and democracy. Mou did not see this inclusion as 'Westernization', since he viewed science and democracy as rooted in 'universal humanity'. While Western culture has developed those aspects of the human spirit, Chinese culture has been dominated by tradition of the way (*daotong*), exemplified by Confucius' teachings on personal cultivation and the way of the inner sage. This pertains to the realm of daily life, the domain of ethics and religion. Learning in China was subordinated to these ethical and spiritual concerns. Although such learning could be called a tradition of learning in one sense, it develops and relies on the intuition more than the intellect; there has been no tradition of learning (*xuetong*) in the sense of intellectual learning that produces knowledge in the form of logic and science. According to Mou, Chinese culture therefore needs to acquire this tradition of learning to expand its domain of knowledge. This intellectual learning could and must be developed by expanding, not replacing, the ethical and spiritual learning of China's tradition. The tradition of politics (*zhengtong*) in China has evolved from aristocracy to autocracy, with order and chaos alternating. Confucianism has a political philosophy of the 'outer king' (*waiwang*) that accompanies its teachings on the inner sage. In Mou's opinion, the Confucian political ideal, humane (*ren*) government that rules with virtue, has never been realized. Such a government would 'hide the world in the world', which Mou interpreted as an open society, as the world belongs to everyone rather than to the ruler alone. Chinese culture needs to expand its political domain by understanding its own tradition of politics and finding the way forward, which lies in replacing 'subordination' with 'coordination' in human relations. The mission of Confucianism in the present age, its modernization, is to demand a 'new outer king' of virtuous government that recognizes in democracy its own 'formal cause', and requires scientific knowledge as its 'material cause' – it is not an abandonment of the traditional ideal, but a new understanding of the Confucian ideal.

Connecting China and the world: New Confucian participation in global discourses

Third-generation New Confucians continue to reflect on the relevance of Confucianism to modern life, and move on to promote Confucianism as not only important to the Chinese, but also offering rich resources to others. As a representative of that group, Tu Wei-ming has taught in American universities for most of his working life, although he has maintained close links with Asia. As director of the Harvard–Yenching Institute, Tu not only promotes Confucianism in the West; he has brought young PRC scholars to Harvard to join the conversation on new Confucianism. Such institution- and network-building overseas, including in Hong Kong and Taiwan, by New Confucians after 1949 has been instrumental in the flourishing of New Confucianism.

Probably the most influential promoter of Confucianism worldwide today, Tu has devoted most of his work to showing how Confucianism can meaningfully contribute to the cultivation of cultural competence, ethical intelligence and spiritual values not just for the Chinese, but for people in both East and West. Tu views Confucianism as an all-encompassing humanism that regards the secular as sacred and, through self-cultivation and good government, attempts to transform the world from within according to its cultural ideal of unity between heaven and humanity. Tu downplays the role of Confucianism as Chinese imperial state orthodoxy; he insists that 'the gradual expansion of the Confucian cultural movement into different layers of an alien despotic polity and various echelons of society enabled the tradition to become truly influential'.[11] He also rejects 'politicized Confucianism', which is the power of the state over society, politics over economics, and bureaucratization over individual initiative, but affirms Confucianism as a way of life guiding family relations, work ethics and personal cultivation. Tu maintains that Confucian personality ideals – the authentic person (*junzi*), the worthy (*xianren*), or the sage – can be realized more fully in liberal democratic societies than in either traditional imperial dictatorships or modern authoritarian regimes. According to Tu, the lack of ideas of radical transcendence, positive evil, transcendent rationality, and institutional mechanisms against autocracy in the Confucian tradition renders it vulnerable to authoritarianism. Confucianism must therefore creatively transform itself in light of Enlightenment values.

Tu believes that despite several attempts to destroy it, Confucianism remains an integral part of the 'psycho-cultural construct of the contemporary Chinese intellectual as well as the Chinese peasant'.[12] Borrowing Mou's concept of the 'three waves of Confucianism', he looks forward to a 'third epoch' of Confucian humanism, wherein Confucianism is modernized but maintains its continuity with the classical formulations of Confucius, Mencius and Xunzi in the first 'wave', elaborated by Zhu Xi and Wang Yangming in China, and Yi T'oegye and Yamazaki Ansai in Korea and Japan during the 'second wave'. This 'New Confucian Humanism, though rooted in the East, draws its nourishment from the West as well as from Asia'.[13] Tu himself draws widely on the Western Enlightenment in his elaboration of Confucianism, while at the same time expanding the meaning of Enlightenment values. Against Asian exceptionalism that would harness Confucianism as a source of 'Asian values' to challenge and resist the human rights movement, Tu argues for compatibility of Confucianism with the concept of human rights. His support of the universality of human rights is premised on the human rights discourse being dialogical, communicative and, hopefully, mutually beneficial. Human rights, as 'the common language of humanity', need to be expanded and deepened through intercultural exchange. Tu recognizes some shortcomings in the Western Enlightenment mentality: its values do not always cohere into an integrated guide for action, and could degenerate into acquisitive individualism, vicious competitiveness, pernicious relativism, or excessive litigiousness. The Enlightenment project also does not give enough weight to the idea of community. Tu believes that, as Asian intellectuals have learned conscientiously from the West, it is time for European and American intellectuals 'to appreciate what Confucian humanism, among other rich spiritual resources in Asia, has to offer toward the cultivation of a global ethic'.[14] Tu calls for Confucian humanism, in its creative modern transformation, to intellectually challenge the Enlightenment mentality in order to contribute significantly to a new ethics for a global community.

Tu has developed his insights into the tension between the Enlightenment mentality and the Confucian tradition partly in the context of his observation of East Asian modernization. He remarks that Japan and the four mini dragons (Singapore, South Korea, Hong Kong and Taiwan), in achieving their economic successes characterized by mercantilism, commercialism and international competitiveness, have embraced Enlightenment instrumental rationality. His critical examination of the post-Confucian thesis – that Confucian ethics contributed to the economic rise of East Asia, which offers an alternative development model – concludes that Confucian East Asia exemplifies significantly different modernities that are less adversarial, less individualistic and less self-interested than their Western counterparts. In providing the cultural resources for developing East Asian market economies and democracies with their own distinctive features, Confucianism testifies to the role of traditions in shaping the modernization process and defining the meaning of modernity: modernization is culturally differentiated, and there are multiple modernities rather than a singular modernity defined by the West.

Tu Wei-ming's visit to Beijing in 1985 has been regarded as the beginning of 'the return of New Confucianism to its homeland'.[15] New Confucianism was one of the five major phenomena that distinguished the 'culture craze' (*wenhua re*). In debates over modernization, Westernization and cultural tradition, Chinese intellectuals attempted to rediscover 'national essence' in Confucianism with the help of overseas New Confucians. New Confucianism in Mainland China became a way of reconstructing the Confucian ideal to meet the political and cultural needs of the time. Zhang Dainian called for a scientific study 'to promote the democratic essence of Confucianism and fight against its feudal dross'.[16] Chen Lai saw a need for 'rational reorientation' of Confucianism in multicultural China. Others argued over whether Confucianism could serve the needs of modernization in China. Within a few years, New Confucianism became a focal point in the studies of Chinese thought and culture. It laid the groundwork for the 'national studies craze' (*guoxue re*) of the 1990s. Instead of merely researching New Confucianism, some Mainland scholars began to identify themselves as New Confucians. While the CCP attempts to appropriate Confucianism to justify its authoritarianism and legitimate itself as the defender of Chinese culture, New Confucians such as Tu offer an alternative liberal democratic future for Confucianism and Chinese culture. It is still too early to judge the achievement of PRC New Confucianism, but if Confucianism has a permanent place in Chinese culture, its practical and philosophical reconciliation with Mainland China's current modernization must certainly shape modern Chinese culture and transform Confucianism in the process.

Notes

1. Zhang Zhidong, 'Quanxue Pian' [Exhortation to Learn], trans. in Wm. Theodore de Bary (ed.), *Sources of Chinese Tradition*, New York, Columbia University Press, 1960, pp. 82–7.
2. Wm. Theodore de Bary, 'The New Confucianism in Beijing', *The American Scholar* 64, 1995, 175–89.
3. Joseph Levenson, *Confucian China and its Modern Era*, London, Routledge and Kegan Paul, 1958, p. 61.
4. *Ibid.*, p. 64.
5. Kung-ch'uan Hsiao, *A Modern China and a New World: K'ang Yu-wei, Reformer and Utopian, 1858–1927*, Seattle, University of Washington Press, 1975.
6. John H. Berthrong, *Transformations of the Confucian Way*, Boulder, CO, Westview Press, 1998, p. 182.
7. Liu Shu-hsien, *Essentials of Contemporary Neo-Confucian Philosophy*, Westport, Praeger, 2003, pp. 24–6.
8. 'Manifesto for a Reappraisal of Sinology and Reconstruction of Chinese Culture', trans. in Carsun Chang, *Development of Neo-Confucian Thought*, vol. 2, New York, Bookham, 2002, pp. 455–83.
9. Liu, *Essentials*, p. 30. On Liang as a Buddhist, see Hanafin, 'The Last Buddhist: The Philosophy of Liang Shuming', in John Makeham (ed.), *New Confucianism*, New York, Palgrave, 2003, Ch. 7. Among the evidence Hanafin cited for Liang being 'Buddhist' are Liang's own testimony in the 1980s, his use of Buddhist methodology in his works, and his assessment that Buddhism is superior to Confucianism. However, Hanafin admitted the relationship between Buddhism and Confucianism in Liang's work is very complex and Liang is not always consistent, probably indicating a certain degree of ambiguity, even internal conflict, on his part.

10. Cf. Sor-hoon Tan, *Confucian Democracy: A Deweyan Reconstruction*, New York, State University of New York Press, 2004, for discussion of how democracy that is more than political could fit into Confucian culture.

11. Tu Wei-ming, *Confucianism in Historical Perspective*, Singapore, Institute of East Asian Philosophies, 1989, p. 3.

12. Tu, *Confucian Ethics Today: The Singapore Challenge*, Singapore, Curriculum Development Institute of Singapore, p. 80.

13. Tu, *Confucianism*, p. 39.

14. Tu, *The Inaugural Wu Teh Yao Memorial Lectures 1995*, Singapore, Unipress, 1996, p. 19.

15. Makeham, *New Confucianism*, p. 85.

16. *Ibid.*

Guide to further reading

Alitto, Guy S., *The Last Confucian: Liang Shu-ming and the Chinese Dilemma of Modernity*, Berkeley, University of California Press, 1979.

Ames, Roger T., 'New Confucianism: A Native Response to Western Philosophy', in S. Hua (ed.), *Chinese Political Culture*, Armonk, M. E. Sharpe, 2001.

Berthrong, John H., *Transformations of the Confucian Way*, Boulder, CO, Westview Press, 1998.

Bresciani, Umberto, *Reinventing Confucianism: The New Confucian Movement*, Taipei, Ricci Institute for Chinese Studies, 2001.

Chang, Carsun [Zhang Junmai], *Development of Neo-Confucian Thought*, vol. 2, New York, Bookman, 1962.

Cheng, Chung-ying and N. Bunnin (eds.), *Contemporary Chinese Philosophy*, Oxford, Blackwell, 2002.

de Bary, Wm. Theodore (ed.), *Sources of Chinese Tradition*, New York, Columbia University Press, 1960.

   'The New Confucianism in Beijing', *The American Scholar* 64, 1995, 175–89.

Hsiao, Kung-ch'uan, *A Modern China and a New World: K'ang Yu-wei, Reformer and Utopian, 1858–1927*, Seattle, University of Washington Press, 1975.

Levenson, Joseph, *Confucian China and its Modern Fate*, London, Routledge and Kegan Paul, 1958.

Liu, Shu-hsien [Liu Shuxian], *Essentials of Contemporary Neo-Confucian Philosophy*, Westport, Praeger, 2003.

Louie, Kam, *Critiques of Confucius in Contemporary China*, Hong Kong, Chinese University Press, 1980.

Makeham, John (ed.), *New Confucianism*, New York, Palgrave, 2003.

Tan, Sor-hoon, *Confucian Democracy: A Deweyan Reconstruction*, New York, State University of New York Press, 2004.

Tu, Wei-ming. *Confucian Ethics Today: The Singapore Challenge*, Singapore, Curriculum Development Institute of Singapore, 1984.

   Confucianism in Historical Perspective, Singapore, Institute of East Asian Philosophies, 1989.

   Way, Learning, and Politics: Essays on the Confucian Intellectual, New York, State University of New York Press, 1993.

   The Inaugural Wu Teh Yao Memorial Lectures 1995, Singapore, Unipress, 1996.

8

Socialism in China: a historical overview

Socialism in China has a history of almost a century, from its origins in the 1890s to its gradual abandonment by the end of the twentieth century. The Communist Party of China (CCP) still claims to lead a socialist society, but this claim has gradually lost its plausibility since the 1980s. Memories of socialism linger, and the achievements of the socialist revolution are regularly invoked in defence of the Party's legitimacy. But socialism in any meaningful sense has little to do with the everyday lives of the people in a society that has become a workshop of global capitalism, and shows every sign of becoming an integral part of a culture of consumption that characterizes contemporary culture around the world – at least for those who can afford to join in with the relentless urge to consume.

The following overview of socialism in China is guided by two premises that need to be spelled out at the beginning. First, the socialist revolution in China was from the start entangled in questions of nationalism and nation-building. This has encouraged some scholars to view socialism merely as one more expression of a national search for 'wealth and power'. This view, while by no means wrong, is one-sided in that it ignores the utopian hopes that played a part in dynamizing the Chinese revolution, not just the socialist revolution but the revolution in general. Socialism, however, provided a vision that promised to transcend the ills of contemporary society. It also offered a means to this end: social and cultural revolution, which from the origins of socialism appeared as two sides of the same coin. The instrumentalization of socialism in the cause of national revolution coexisted throughout with utopian longings for the creation of a just society that would also transcend the particularism of the nation. The dialectic between these two understandings of socialism, often indistinguishable in the discourse on revolution, is crucial to understanding the contradictions and dynamics of the socialist revolution. Socialism initially appealed to Chinese intellectuals in its utopian guise (especially anarchism). This was to give way in the end to the victory of an instrumentalized version, which is the guise in which socialism appears in contemporary China.

The second premise is not formally part of the discussion below but is important nevertheless in comprehending the fate of socialism in China, which is best understood as part of a regional history of socialism that encompasses, in addition to China, Japan, Korea and Vietnam. Socialism in China flourished as part of a regional search for revolutionary alternatives to Euro/American capitalism. In the earliest period, Japan served as a major – if not the only – source of socialist ideas. Tokyo in some ways played a part in Asian radicalism comparable to the part played by London in Europe. Until the 1920s, works by Japanese anarchists and Marxists such as Kotoku Shusui, Osugi Sakae and Kawakami Hajime provided the major source of socialist ideas for Chinese, Korean and Vietnamese intellectuals. By the 1920s, as Japanese politics became more repressive, Shanghai and Guangzhou emerged as gathering places for Eastern Asian socialists. In the 1930s, Yan'an in northwestern China, by then the headquarters of the Communist Party, attracted radicals not only from Eastern Asia but from as far as the United States. After the victory of Communism in China, needless to say, China itself would lay claims to centrality in a global revolution against capitalism. Throughout, however, socialist movements in the various societies comprising Eastern Asia played an important part in cross-fertilizing one another. We may observe, likewise, that the victory of capitalism in Japan, Korea and Taiwan from the 1970s was a major reason for the decline in the appeal of socialism in those societies and, eventually, in the PRC.

The history of socialism in China is approached below in terms of three major periods. The first period – the origins – covers the years from the last decade of the Qing Dynasty (1644–1911) through the early years of the Republic, to the May Fourth Movement of 1919. This period witnessed the emergence of anarchism and varieties of socialism that sought in state-instituted social policies answers to contemporary problems. The period from 1919 to 1949 witnessed the emergence of Marxist–Leninist Communism as the foremost current in socialism. This period may itself be divided into two phases: an urban revolutionary phase until 1927, and a subsequent rural revolutionary phase. It was in the latter phase that a guerilla revolutionary socialism emerged that would guide the Communist Party to victory in 1949, led by Mao Zedong (1893–1976) who himself achieved supremacy in the leadership of the Party during this period. The last period, from 1949 to Mao's death in 1976, was the time during which a socialist society was established. This period, too, may be divided into two phases. The first phase, the decade of the 1950s, witnessed the establishment of a socialist society modelled very much on the socialism of the Soviet Union. For a variety of reasons, this model was rejected by the late 1950s, and a revolutionary approach to development was revived that was to culminate in the mass social mobilization – a revolution within the revolution – of the Cultural Revolution of the 1960s. In hindsight, the Cultural Revolution was not the beginning of a new revolutionary phase but the last gasp of the Chinese revolution. Following Mao's death in 1976, China turned to 'opening and reform' under the leadership of Deng Xiaoping, which would gradually take the country along the path to capitalism, especially after the Tiananmen Incident of 1989. China may still be viewed as a postsocialist society, where the memories of socialist revolution linger, but the memories are fading fast.

The origins of socialism in China

The term socialism first appeared in China during the late nineteenth century, but it was of little significance politically or intellectually until around 1905, when socialistic ideas were incorporated in the political platform of the Revolutionary Alliance (*tongmeng hui*), the predecessor to the Guomindang, at the urging of Sun Yat-sen, who has been known since then as the 'Father of the Chinese Republic'. At about the same time, two anarchist societies were established by Chinese students abroad – one in Paris, and the other in Tokyo. By 1910, on the eve of the overthrow of the Qing Dynasty, a Socialist Party was established by a maverick intellectual, Jiang Kanghu (1883–?), who had come to socialism through his interest in women's education.

The ideological inclinations represented by these organizations – anarchism and a kind of social policy socialism – would dominate the socialist scene in China over the next decade. The socialism of the Revolutionary Alliance addressed most directly state-building efforts that were underway in these years, as the Qing Dynasty sought to convert the old monarchy into a modern nation-state. Its goal, quite Bismarckian in intent, was to establish policies that would forestall the social inequalities that Sun Yat-sen believed would inevitably accompany China's incorporation into the world of capitalism. These policies, reflecting the thinking of contemporary analysts of capitalism in Europe and North America, consisted most importantly of state regulation of the ownership of land, as well as control in the public interest of large-scale industrial undertakings that were deemed to be particularly vulnerable to monopoly ownership. Such measures were intended not to revolutionize society, but to anticipate and prevent the social revolution that at the end of the nineteenth century seemed to have become inevitable in Europe.

Of less importance politically but possibly more influential intellectually was Jiang Kanghu's Chinese Socialist Party (*Zhongguo shehui zhuyi dang*), established in 1910. Jiang would pursue his own kind of socialism over the next three decades. His career included a brief period teaching at the University of California–Berkeley, as well as work as a librarian at the Library of Congress in Washington, DC. By the early 1910s, the Chinese Socialist Party claimed to have thousands of members. With its many branches across China, however, the Party was more like a study society than a political party. Jiang's socialism itself is most interesting as an effort to organize into one comprehensive system the conflicting currents in European socialism that Chinese intellectuals encountered in the early part of the century.

It was during this period that anarchism also emerged as a distinct current within the burgeoning socialist movement among Chinese intellectuals. Following the Boxer Uprising in 1900, the Qing government sent students abroad in large numbers as part of its reform movement. Anarchism flourished initially among students in France and Japan. The New World Society, established in Paris in 1906, began in 1907 to publish a journal, *The New Era*, which for the next three years would serve as a major source of anarchist theory, as well as information on the anarchist movement in Europe. Its guiding light was Li Shizeng (1881–1954), who had gone to France to study biology and converted to anarchism through his acquaintance with the family of French anarchist geographer Elisee Reclus. *The New Era* promoted a revolutionary futuristic anarchism, and was among the first Chinese publications to openly attack native traditions, in particular, Confucianism.

An anarchist society established in Tokyo at almost the same time, the Society for the Study of Socialism, by contrast promoted an anti-modernist anarchism influenced by Leo Tolstoy, and stressed the affinity between anarchism and philosophical currents in the Chinese past, especially Daoism. Led by the classical scholar Liu Shipei (1884–1919) and his wife, He Zhen (?), this society published its own journals, *Natural Justice* and *Balance*. Interestingly, these Tokyo publications evinced a more radical stance on contemporary issues than their counterpart in Paris, especially on issues of anti-imperialism and feminism. The publications also promoted Kropotkin's ideas on the combination of agriculture and industry in social organization, and the social and ethical benefits of combining mental and manual labour, which were to have a lasting influence in Chinese radicalism.

Anarchism put down deeper roots among radical Chinese intellectuals on the Chinese Mainland after the revolution of 1911 that led to the establishment of the Republic. Chinese anarchists, like all anarchists in Eastern Asia, suffered from police interference because of their 'dangerous ideas'. Still, they had greater space for action in the turmoil following the fall of the Qing Dynasty in 1911. Anarchist activity was visible in the burgeoning labour movement in South China. Paris anarchists brought their activities home, and were especially influential in educational circles. And a new generation of anarchists appeared in South China around the figure of an assassin turned anarchist, Liu Sifu (1884–1915), better known by his adopted name of Shifu. The Cock-Crow Society that Shifu established in 1912 and its journal, *People's Voice*, served in the mid-1910s as the most important organs of anarchism in China. Shifu promoted the social anarchism of Kropotkin, and while not a particularly original thinker, played an important part in his polemics with the socialist Jiang Kanghu in clarifying differences between anarchism ('pure socialism') and other currents in socialism. It was above all his seriousness of purpose that impressed his followers and others, so that by the 1920s his ideas would achieve the status of an 'ism', Shifu'ism. Shifu died in 1915 but his followers carried on the activities of the Society he had founded.

By the late 1910s, educational reform activities were under way in Beijing that would culminate in the New Culture Movement of the late 1910s and early 1920s, which was to play a seminal role in the cultural revolution in modern China. Paris anarchists and their associates were to have an important part in these reforms; they were joined enthusiastically by the younger anarchists who had received their training under Shifu's tutelage. Anarchist ideas on the family, youth and women, the communal experiments that they promoted, and their concern for labour, acquired broad currency in the culture of a new generation, even though not many were aware of their anarchist origins in the Chinese context. Anarchists also played a part in the founding of the first Bolshevik groups in China, which eventually culminated in the founding of the Communist Party in 1921. These gradually overshadowed the anarchists, and marginalized them. Among those to come under anarchist influence was Mao Zedong who, like many later Bolsheviks, expressed enthusiasm at the time for European anarchists and their ideas. It is arguable that the initial anarchist inspiration remained with Mao long past his conversion to Bolshevism.

During the first two decades of the twentieth century, socialism was most important in Chinese thought and politics for drawing attention to the social dimension of political change. While this was true of all socialists, it was anarchists who were responsible for introducing into Chinese the idea of 'social revolution' that would have a lasting influence in subsequent years. Anarchists believed that significant political change could not be realized unless it was based on social transformation. While some anarchists were attracted to violence as a means of social transformation, others repudiated violence in favour of peaceful methods, especially universal education. But they all shared a belief that society, and social forces, were determinants of politics, and must provide the point of departure for any meaningful change. The fact that anarchist ideas of social revolution also had strong implications of cultural revolution makes their advocacy all the more interesting, as these twin ideas would emerge in later years as driving forces of the Chinese revolution. They would have a strong impact on the thinking of the May Fourth generation a decade later. This generation would also produce the first generation of Marxist Communists in China.

Ideas and values that had their origins in East Asian intellectual and political traditions, which might have helped to produce original reformulations of anarchism, were to play little part in the historical development of anarchism in East Asia or elsewhere. The more modernist anarchists (most importantly, the Paris anarchists) simply rejected native legacies as backward. Those inclined toward some kind of synthesis did not have much success in achieving their goal. This was due mainly to a seeming preference on the part of anarchists (East Asian or otherwise) simply to appropriate those values for anarchism, or, conversely, to appropriate anarchism for East Asian values. The articulation of native legacies and anarchism in full recognition of their differences might have produced an 'East Asian anarchism'. Anarchists who were inclined to nativism, however, seemed to be satisfied simply to identify native legacies and anarchism on the basis of superficial resemblances, and made no effort toward such articulation.

In spite of its apparent kinship with a variety of native legacies, anarchism was motivated by historical and social concerns that bore upon them the stamp of their origins in the European Enlightenment. Anarchist ideas when they first appeared in East Asia represented a different comprehension of political space from that which had existed in East Asian societies earlier. Scholars of anarchism in East Asia have attempted to locate anarchism within various legacies of the past – from neo-Confucianism to Daoism and Buddhism. Such an effort is more a product of a culturalism that pervades studies of East Asia than of the concrete historical circumstances surrounding the appearance and assimilation of anarchism. It eschews a clear distinction between historical causation and the appropriation of the past for a historical consciousness that had its sources elsewhere. It not only conflicts with the anarchists' self-images as revolutionaries, but also with historical evidence. Anarchism, and the social revolutionary consciousness it promoted, were products of a new historical situation created by capitalist modernity, and the political reorganization it called for in the form of the nation-state. European anarchists such as Kropotkin were among the foremost advocates of Enlightenment promises of science and democracy. Anarchists in East Asia for the most part subscribed to similar ideas in defiance of native traditions, which brought to them no end of trouble. Where they discovered anarchism in native traditions, it was with a new consciousness of politics, and it entailed the reinterpretation of the past through the demands and consciousness of the present.

Marxism in the Chinese revolution

Following the October Revolution in Russia, anarchists found a formidable competitor on the left; Bolshevik Communists who commanded better organizational abilities were therefore more effective in organizing the growing labour movements, and, not incidentally, received backing from the new Soviet Union. By 1927, Chinese anarchists, in their anti-Bolshevism, devoted their efforts mainly to fighting Bolshevik ideological and labour activity, some in collusion with the most reactionary elements in Chinese politics. Communism, associated earlier with anarchism, came to be identified in the 1920s with Marxism and Bolshevism.

While politically irrelevant after the mid-1920s, anarchists continued with cultural and educational activities. In the cultural arena, the most important contributions were those of Li Feigan (Bajin) (1904–), the novelist who for a long time was the only Chinese anarchist of stature known in anarchist circles abroad. Paris anarchists were instrumental in 1927 in establishing a Labour University in Shanghai, which for a period of five years sought to put into practice the anarchist belief in the need to combine mental and manual labour in education. This belief, and the Kropotkinite insistence on combining agriculture and industry in social development, had become part of radical culture during the New Culture Movement. These anarchist contributions to Chinese radicalism would outlast the anarchist movement and appear after 1949 as important elements in the conflicts over Bolshevik bureaucratism.

Regional interactions also played an important part in the origins and unfolding of Marxism and the Communist movements it informed from the 1920s. As had been the case with anarchism, Marxism found its first adherents in Japan, which then served as a major, if not an exclusive, source of Marxist theoretical literature and, in the late 1910s, of Communist activism. As early as the first decade of the century, the Marxist Katayama Sen was active in the Second International, and among the Japanese community in the United States. In the 1910s, Marxism gained important adherents such as Kawakami Hajime in Japanese academia. Kawakami's theoretical writings would provide the first Marxists in China with their knowledge of Marxism.

Marxist ideas, as filtered through social democracy and social reform movements in the United States and Europe, had reached radicals in China in the early 1900s in conjunction with the growing nationalist movement. Guomindang theorists such as Hu Hanmin and Dai Jitao acquired a more sophisticated understanding of Marxism in the 1910s, while Sun Yat-sen and his close associates were in 'exile' in Japan. It is revealing that during these two decades, the radicals who found some relevance in Marxism were those who were located in Japan, in constant contact with Japanese radicals such as Kawakami Hajime. When the Guomindang relocated on the Chinese Mainland in around 1920, Guomindang theorists were among the first to initiate discussions of Marxism. They were quickly joined by a new generation of radicals who, having gone through an anarchist phase, increasingly turned to Marxism following the May Fourth Movement of 1919. It was these radicals who, with the help of advisors dispatched by the newly founded Soviet Union, established the Communist Party of China in July 1921. The Party grew quickly after the May Thirtieth Movement of 1925, which was sparked by the killing of Chinese workers and students demonstrating against imperialism. Communists were successful in assuming leadership of the nation-wide labour strike that followed the incident, although in South China, where the centre of gravity for the Communist movement moved after the alliance with the Guomindang in 1924, unions associated with the Guomindang and the anarchists remained powerful, leading to serious divisions within the labour movement, as well as the Guomindang suppression of Communism in 1927.

During this initial phase, Soviet and Communist International agents played an important part in the revolutionary movement, which was concentrated mostly in urban areas, especially Shanghai and Guangzhou. The revolutionary movement was also largely guided by V. I. Lenin's analyses of contemporary capitalism and imperialism, and took the overthrow of feudalism and imperialism as its main targets. It was on this basis that the Communists collaborated with the Guomindang, which itself continued to express socialist aspirations through Sun Yat-sen's principle of people's livelihood (*minsheng*) which, along with nationality and sovereignty, made up Sun's 'Three People's Principles' (*sanmin zhuyi*). The Communists, however, increasingly also emphasized the emergent urban bourgeoisie, arguing that since the interests of the Chinese bourgeoisie were closely linked to foreign capital, only a social revolution that also targeted the bourgeoisie could serve the goal of national autonomy, which was to be not just political but economic as well. Conflict over the issue of class struggle in the national revolution was an important ideological factor that brought the alliance to an end in 1927.

The Communist Revolution was to take a rural turn after 1927, even though the Communist Party never lost its contact with urban areas. It was during this period, especially after the Long March of 1934–5, that Mao Zedong emerged as the leader of the Party. And it was under Mao's leadership, aided by a new generation of military leaders and ideological theorists, that a new strategy was devised for the Communist Revolution that may best be described as a 'guerilla socialism', as it was the necessities of guerilla warfare against the much stronger Guomindang government that shaped both the policies and the thinking of the new leadership. The goals of the revolution remained the same: the anti-feudal anti-imperialist struggle aimed at national liberation. Nevertheless, the forced retreat to the rural areas, and the conditions under which the Communists survived, necessitated a shift in focus from the earlier period of Communism. There was a noticeable intensification of nationalism during this period in contrast to the cosmopolitanism and internationalism that had attracted many to the Communist movement in the 1920s. The necessities of guerilla warfare also called for closer integration between the Party and the military (the Red Army, later the People's Liberation Army, PLA), which has been an enduring feature of Chinese Communism since then.

Theoretically, the Party sought to adjust Marxism to the realities of Chinese society, which was to culminate in Mao's so-called 'sinicization of Marxism' (*Makesi zhuyide Zhongguohua*, literally, 'making Marxism Chinese'). This did not mean subjecting Marxism to Chinese philosophical principles, or abandoning the fundamentals of Marxism – such as the priority given to material circumstances of revolution or class struggle. Two aspects of 'sinicization' were, however, of considerable significance. One was what may best be described as the 'vernacularization' of Marxism; the rephrasing of Marxism in a Chinese and local idiom that would make it comprehensible to the vast numbers of peasants who were to provide the backbone of the Communist military victory. The other was the centrality of the concept of 'contradiction', which had been taken up earlier by Soviet philosophers but was elevated in Mao's thinking to a status of supreme theoretical importance, primarily because it allowed for the kind of intricate and concrete analysis that a calculation of forces required under circumstances of guerilla warfare. Marxism, in Mao's hands, became a hermeneutic, a guide to the analysis of society. The shift provided a powerful tool. It also presented a predicament, for theory ceased to be a sure guide to the outcomes of socialism. Interpretation without a frame of reference could also lead to arbitrary outcomes, since any situation could lend itself to more than one interpretation. This predicament required for its resolution the elevation of the role of the Party in guaranteeing progress toward the socialist vision, which further required intensified ideological discipline within the Party itself, as well as a leadership that would maintain both the vision and the discipline. The Party had to be able at all times to work as a unit, a well-disciplined team. The Communist Party was able to achieve such a unity in the 1940s, which gave it a political edge over the Guomindang. In the long run, however, it also distanced the Party from its constituents, and reinforced tendencies that were already implicit in Lenin's formulations on Bolshevism, to substitute the Communist Party for the proletariat and the peasantry whose interests the Party claimed to represent and safeguard.

By the 1930s, most important Marxist writings were available to Chinese intellectuals. Moreover, Mao was surrounded by a number of Party intellectuals who were familiar with theoretical developments in the Soviet Union and elsewhere, and who were theorists in their own right. But the 'sinicization of Marxism' reflected Mao's insistence on the priority of praxis (transformative political and ideological practice), or at the very least his view that theory without practice was little more than empty intellectual talk and obscurantism. The view was also useful in discrediting Mao's Soviet-trained rivals whose personal familiarity with Soviet Marxism gave them at least some theoretical edge over Mao's autodidacticism.

The immediate consequence of Mao's 'sinicization of Marxism' was the reformulation of Party revolutionary strategy, which was given an urgency with the Japanese invasion of the Chinese Mainland in July 1937. The invasion provoked popular demands in urban areas for the suspension of hostilities between the Guomindang and the Communist Party, and led to the re-establishment of a united front between the two parties. The united front, however brief, culminated theoretically in Mao's idea of 'New Democracy', which articulated a strategy that would bring the Communist Party to power in 1949. Mao outlined his idea in an essay of that title published in January 1940. What is interesting about the essay is the distinction that Mao drew between the Chinese situation and those of advanced capitalist societies as well as the Soviet Union. As a semi-feudal semi-colonial country, he argued, China needed to follow its own path of revolution, which required an additional stage between capitalism and socialism that he called 'new democracy'. New democracy would be characterized by a mixed public/private economy, an alliance of advanced classes (the proletariat and the peasantry, the bourgeoisie and the petit-bourgeoisie) socially and politically, and a culture that would be created by filtering the national culture of the people – the masses – through the principles of Marxism.

'New Democracy' in many ways represented an appropriation or rephrasing of Sun Yat-sen's 'Three People's Principles' for the Communist Party with an eye to claiming that the Party was more faithful to Sun's legacy than the Guomindang itself. Indeed, the Communists made an effort in these years to articulate their ideology to the Three Principles.

The route to revolution and development that the idea suggested would also prove appealing to many Chinese intellectuals, especially those with an inclination to milder forms of socialism, of whom there were many, including some in the Guomindang. Some of these intellectuals had already begun to lean towards the Communist Party with the National Salvation Movement, which got underway from 1936, as they believed that the Communists were more serious than the Guomindang about fighting Japan. Even many businessmen were attracted to Mao's promise of continued support for private enterprise, albeit within the framework of what may best be described as bureaucratic capitalism. During the civil war that ensued following the defeat of Japan in 1945, these non-party groups, by then dubbed the 'Third Force', were to shift their support to the Communist Party, which guaranteed legitimacy to the Communist victory in 1949. Officially speaking, the victory of the Communist Party in 1949 was the victory not of Communism, or even socialism, but of New Democracy. It is interesting in hindsight to note that when China again turned to 'reform and opening' after Mao's death, the developmental policies of the Deng Xiaoping leadership were initially quite reminiscent of New Democracy. The fate of those policies may also be taken as indicative of the instabilities of the compromise represented by New Democracy, which were to be resolved by renewed revolutionization in the late 1950s, and the turn to capitalism in the 1990s.

The experience of rural revolution was also important in providing a model for development on an agrarian basis that was developed during the so-called Yan'an Period after 1937, when the Communist movement came to be centred in Yan'an in northern China. Surrounded by Guomindang affiliated forces, and subsequently by the Japanese, the Communists in Yan'an developed – from the sheer need for survival – policies of 'self-reliance', which included supplementing agriculture with small industries to meet the needs of the population and, most importantly, of the People's Liberation Army. The policies, reminiscent of ideas that anarchists had derived from Kropotkin earlier in the century, would resonate with policies instituted during the Great Leap Forward in the late 1950s, as well as the township industries that played an important part in the initial phase of development in the 1980s. They were to provide an ideal, in these later years, of a course of development that provided an alternative to the Soviet-style urban-based heavy-industry path of socialist development.

Socialism under the socialist state

If the Communist Party in power offered anything of theoretical interest, it was with the Cultural Revolution of the 1960s. The policies of New Democracy were largely responsible for the claims of the new state for legitimacy, but the contradictions built into New Democracy became apparent almost immediately. The Party undertook land reforms to put an end to 'feudalism', which was consistent with the New Democratic promise to redistribute land to the landless to achieve some measure of equity in the countryside. In the cities, rather than abolishing private ownership, the effort took the form of enhancing labour and bureaucratic regulation. These policies almost immediately produced their own contradictions: how to prevent the reconcentration of land, or to balance the needs of individual entrepreneurship against public needs and control. Politically, these contradictions raised the question of how deeply the Party would penetrate society in the control – if not the resolution – of these contradictions, calling into question the promise of class alliance and democracy.

Given the Party's ideological commitment to socialism, it may have been a foregone conclusion that these contradictions would be resolved toward greater concentration of political and economic power in the hands of the Party, accompanied by more forceful intervention in the economy. If so, the tendencies inherent in the ideology were further reinforced by the developmental path that the Party chose after 1953, which was modelled on the development of the Soviet Union, with priority given to the development of heavy industries. This choice no doubt had a lot to do with the political alliance with the Soviet Union against the hostility that the People's Republic faced almost immediately from the capitalist world, with the United States leading the way in the conflict over the Korean peninsula that began almost immediately after the end of World War II. Soviet aid in developing an industrial base for the new regime was of crucial importance, as was the mobilization of internal resources for an all-out effort in the building of heavy industries – most importantly, agriculture. Given the low level of technology available for agricultural development, collectivization was to lead to an immediate enhancement of agricultural production, reinforced once again by the ideological appeal of collectivization in the establishment of socialism. By 1956, the Chinese countryside was largely collectivized, and from late 1957, it was reorganized into communes. The abolition of private property in industry accompanied collectivization in the countryside.

Within less than a decade, China moved from New Democracy through socialism to the verge of Communism, or so the leadership claimed.

The achievements were impressive, but so was the disaster that an accumulating impatience created by the end of the decade, when revolutionary mobilization for development proved disastrous for the welfare of the people. The conflicts created by this eventuality were largely responsible for the intensification of struggles within the Communist Party itself over the appropriate path to be followed in achieving socialism. These struggles were largely responsible for intra-Party conflicts that would find an outlet in the mid-1960s in the so-called Great Proletarian Cultural Revolution.

While it did result in factional struggles within the Party, the Cultural Revolution raised fundamental questions not only about developmental policies, but about revolution itself as a means to socialism. It was already apparent from the experience of socialism in the Soviet Union that a Communist Party in power did not guarantee the achievement of socialism, but instead created a new power structure that could best be described as bureaucratic capitalism, which ushered in all the ills of an uncontrolled bureaucracy without abolishing the problems of inequality and exploitation associated with capitalism. The new socialist state, in other words, itself appeared to be an obstacle to further development toward socialism. Against the 'de-radicalization' of the revolution, the Cultural Revolution raised the necessity of renewed class struggle. The struggle was directed against the new power structure. Mass cultural revolution to this end was also conceived by Maoists as a means to creating cultural habits appropriate to socialist commitments and existence. This revolution within the revolution, the necessity of which became a cornerstone of Maoism, introduced important new insights into socialist political theory, but also highlighted the importance of culture – as opposed to material change – as a dynamic force in the creation of socialism. In hindsight, these insights appear also to be insights into the impossibility of socialism as it had been imagined by more than a century of socialist thinking, from utopian socialists in the early nineteenth century to Marx, Lenin and postwar socialists: a total transformation of society not only in its economic and political, but also in its social, cultural and even psychological constitution. Contemporary efforts to malign the Cultural Revolution disguise its importance in the history of socialism – even as its last gasp.

Following Mao's death in 1976, the revolutionary phase of socialism in China was to come to an end. Beginning in 1978, under the leadership of Deng Xiaoping, China was to enter a period of so-called 'reform and opening' (*gaige kaifang*), which would gradually lead to incorporation in an emergent global capitalism. As noted above, the decade of the 1980s was marked by the hesitations and contradictions of policies that were reminiscent of the policies of New Democracy of the 1940s and early 1950s. The contradictions of these policies were brought to a head in June 1989, which brought the Party into open conflict with its urban constituencies. Once the conflict was over, the contradictions were resolved this time by a headlong plunge into capitalism from the early 1990s, which has brought great developmental success to the People's Republic, but at the risk of betraying all the promises of socialism which the Party continues to invoke as a source of legitimization. Chinese society today suffers from all the inequalities of capitalist societies, but its claims to 'socialism with Chinese characteristics' are still not to be dismissed out of hand, as memories of socialism linger, and are integral to the vocabulary of politics, if not to its grammar.

The present has broken with the revolutionary socialist past, but still contains that past as a lingering – residual – element of its present. Despite incorporation in a global capitalism, the PRC may still be described best as a postsocialist society; no longer moving toward socialism in any recognizable way, but still shaped in so many ways by its socialist revolutionary past. The Communist Party describes the present as the initial stage of socialism or, to use the vocabulary of native utopianism, a 'small welfare' (*xiaokang*) society. A movement has recently been launched, possibly in response to increasing inequality and unrest, especially in rural areas, to establish a 'harmonious society' (*hexie shehui*). A new developmental plan, based on a so-called 'scientific development outlook' (*kexue fazhan guan*) takes 'humans' (*ren*) as the premise and the goal of development. But the Party under the leadership of Hu Jintao remains wedded to resolving the problems of development through further development, rather than reconsidering the path of development that has produced the social and cultural contradictions, as well as the enormous ecological challenges, that have emerged as the PRC has turned into 'the workshop of the world'.

A concluding observation

As the PRC has changed, so has the world. The world of contemporary global modernity is no longer the world of the early twentieth century, when socialism appeared both as a vision of the future and a practical ingredient of nation-building. It is not the world of imperialism against which socialism promised national liberation and autonomy. Neither is it the world of the Cold War, which pitted capitalism against socialist efforts to keep it at a distance. It is the world of a global capitalism that is willing to accommodate socialism as long as it plays by the rules of capitalism. And it is a world in which the meaning of capitalism itself is sufficiently blurred to allow self-professed socialists a modicum of ideological self-respect in their claims to socialist commitments even as the societies they lead are progressively reshaped by the forces of capitalism. Whether or not the accumulating crisis of global capitalism will once again inject vitality into this socialism remains to be seen. If so, it is likely to be socialism of a different kind from the one that was born of the struggles of a century or more of imperialism, nation-building and Euro/American cultural hegemony.

What radical activity there is presently is dominated not by socialisms of the Bolshevik kind, with centralized parties aiming at centralized states, but by loosely connected grassroots movements – the so-called new social movements – in which socialist goals informed by Marxist theoretical critiques of capitalism are articulated through organizational forms that share in anarchist suspicions of centralized power and cultural hegemony. There is a logic to these movements – the logic of struggle against a global capitalism that itself seeks flexibility of domination by conjoining the global and the local in its operations. Chinese socialism, in its commitment to central power, still seems to operate outside this logic. How long it can do so is an open question, the answer to which depends in some measure on the choices the leadership makes concerning social justice and environmental consciousness, both internally and in its quest for integration into a world of global capitalism.

Guide to further reading

Bernal, Martin, *Chinese Socialism to 1907*, Ithaca, NY, Cornell University Press, 1976.
Bernstein, Gail, *Japanese Marxist: A Portrait of Kawakami Hajime, 1879–1946*, Cambridge, MA, Harvard University Press, 1976.
Chan, Ming K. and Arif Dirlik, *Schools into Fields and Factories: Anarchists, the Guomindang and the Labor University in Shanghai, 1927–1932*, Durham, NC, Duke University Press, 1991.
Cumings, Bruce, *The Origins of the Korean War*, Princeton, NJ, Princeton University Press, 1981–1990.

Dirlik, Arif, *Marxism in the Chinese Revolution*, Lanham, MD, Rowman and Littlefield, 2005.

> *Anarchism in the Chinese Revolution*, Berkeley, CA, University of California Press, 1991.

> *Origins of Chinese Communism*, New York, NY, Oxford University Press, 1989.

Dirlik, Arif, Paul Healy and Nick Knight (eds.), *Critical Perspectives on Mao Zedong's Thought*, Atlantic Heights, NJ, Humanities Press, 1992.

Dirlik, Arif and Maurice Meisner (eds.), *Marxism and the Chinese Experience: Issues in Contemporary Chinese Socialism*, Armonk, NY, M. E. Sharpe, 1989.

Friedman, Edward, Paul Pickowicz and Mark Selden, *Chinese Village, Socialist State*, New Haven, CT, Yale University Press, 1991.

Hinton, William, *Shenfan*, New York, NY, Random House, 1983.

> *Fanshen: A Documentary of Revolution in a Chinese Village*, New York, NY: Monthly Review Press, 1967.

Johnson, Chalmers A., *Peasant Nationalism and Communist Power: The Emergence of Revolutionary China*, Stanford, CA, Stanford University Press, 1962.

Knight, Nick, *Li Da and Marxist Philosophy in China*, Boulder, CO, Westview Press, 1996.

> *Mao Zedong on Dialectical Materialism: Writings on Philosophy, 1937*, Armonk, NY, M. E. Sharpe, 1990.

Kraus, Richard. *Class Conflict in Chinese Socialism*, New York, NY, Columbia University Press, 1981.

Krebs, Edward, *Shifu: Soul of Chinese Anarchism,* Lanham, MD, Rowman and Littlefield, 1998.

Lang, Olga, *Pa Chin and his Writings: Chinese Youth between the Two Revolutions*, Cambridge, MA, Harvard University Press, 1967.

Lee, Hong Yung, *The Politics of the Chinese Cultural Revolution*, Berkeley, CA, University of California Press, 1978.

Lin, Chun, *Transformations in Chinese Socialism*, Durham, NC, Duke University Press, 2006.

Meisner, Maurice J., *Mao's China: A History of the People's Republic*, New York, Free Press, 1997.

> *Marxism, Maoism and Utopianism*, Madison, WI, University of Wisconsin Press, 1982.

> *Li Ta-chao and the Origins of Chinese Marxism*, Cambridge, MA, Harvard University Press, 1967.

Notehelfer, Fred G., *Kotoku Shusui: Portrait of a Japanese Radical*, Cambridge, Cambridge University Press, 1971.

Riskin, Carl, *China's Political Economy: The Quest for Development*, Oxford, Oxford University Press, 1987.

Scheiner, Irwin, *Christian Converts and Social Protest in Meiji Japan*, Berkeley, CA, University of California Press, 1970.

Schwartz, Benjamin A., *Communism and China: Ideology in Flux*, Cambridge, MA, Harvard University Press, 1968.

> *Chinese Communism and the Rise of Mao*, New York, Harper and Row, 1958.

Selden, Mark, *The People's Republic of China: A Documentary History of Revolutionary Change*, New York, Monthly Review Press, 1979.

> *The Yenan Way in Revolutionary China*, Cambridge, MA, Harvard University Press, 1971.

Stanley, Thomas, *Osugi Sakae, Anarchist in Taisho Japan: The Creativity of the Ego*, Cambridge, MA, Harvard University Press, 1982.

Van de Ven, Hans, *From Friend to Comrade: The Founding of the Chinese Communist Party, 1921–1927*, Berkeley, CA, University of California Press, 1991.

Zarrow, Peter, *Anarchism and Chinese Political Culture*, New York, NY, Columbia University Press, 1990.

*Interested readers would also be advised to check writings by Chinese leaders – Mao Zedong, Deng Xiaoping, Jiang Zemin, Hu Jintao – which are readily available in numerous collections.

9

Chinese religious traditions from 1900–2005: an overview

This chapter discusses the rituals and beliefs of the Han Chinese majority, their local communities, indigenous popular religious sects, Daoism and Buddhism, as well as Roman Catholic and Protestant Christianity. After many years of suppression, since the 1980s these traditions have been revived in many areas of the country, community festivals in honour of local gods are again being carried out, Daoist and Buddhist clergy are once again being ordained, and there are more Protestant and Roman Catholic Christians than ever before. As for Confucianism, its ethical principles permeated late traditional Chinese culture, and have had considerable influence on the beliefs and values of the practitioners of other religious traditions and on the veneration of ancestors by families and lineages. In Taiwan there are still temples dedicated to Confucius, and some popular sects for which he is the chief deity, but during much of the twentieth century he was attacked on the Mainland as a symbol of all that was out-moded and backward. In recent decades, however, there has been an attempt by some intellectuals in China to rediscover his teachings, and the shrine and tomb in his hometown in Shandong Province have been restored.

Before we explore these religions, however, a few words should be said about Islam in China. Muslim merchants reached China by both land and sea by the late seventh century, and eventually settled in many parts of the country, mostly in the northwest. There are now at least 20 million Muslims in China, both scattered in small communities and as parts of many ethnic groups. They have had their own organizations, leaders, mosques and schools, and encourage pilgrimages to Mecca and contacts with Muslims in other countries, so they have retained a strong sense of their own identity. As Dru Gladney writes, 'Muslims in China live as minority communities amid a sea of people, in their view, who are largely pork-eating, polytheist, secularist, and kafir ("heathen").[1] Their numbers have gradually increased both naturally and through intermarriage. For the most part Chinese governments have allowed them their own organizations and customs, but in response to economic difficulties and the teachings of some Islamic leaders there were several Muslim rebellions in the eighteenth and nineteenth centuries. The most important was an uprising in Shaanxi, Gansu and Xinjiang provinces that lasted from 1862 to 1877 before being put down by Qing forces. Calls for Muslim autonomy in Xinjiang continued in the twentieth century. Both the Republican and Communist governments have included Muslims among the 'five great peoples' of China, along with Mongols, Tibetans, Manchus and the Han majority.

There are ten major groups of Muslims in China, the largest of which are the Hui, Uyghurs and Kazakhs; all maintain their own customs and religious practices and support different sects. Since the end of the 'Cultural Revolution' in 1976 the government on the whole has sought to be supportive by providing funds for the repair of mosques and the reprinting and distribution of the Qur'an, actions intended in part to strengthen relations with predominantly Muslim countries in Asia and the Near East. Muslim leaders have become active again, people are attending services at mosques, and everywhere one finds Muslim food stores, restaurants and butcher shops that provide mutton and beef. However, because of the discovery of oil in Xinjiang, and its proximity to non-Chinese Muslims in Central Asia, the Chinese government has been concerned to suppress any groups in this area that might support some form of independence, but the complexity of intra-Muslim relations and attitudes has so far prevented a cohesive movement in that direction.

Historical background

As indicated in Chapter 2 of this volume, China suffered a series of catastrophes such as the Opium Wars, the Taiping Uprising and the Boxer Rebellion in the nineteenth century. One result of China's successive defeats by foreign powers was an effort by some intellectuals to reform and modernize the country, an effort that included turning temples into schools. In the past the state had attempted to control religious activities by publishing the names of approved temples and deities in 'registers of sacrifices' published by the Ministry of Rites, which were intended to regulate proper etiquette, customs and rituals. Such approval was based on advocacy of local deities by officials in their areas; gods and temples not included in the official registers were considered illicit and could be subject to suppression by particularly zealous officials. But late nineteenth-century reformers, influenced by Western ideas, considered worship of such deities to be fundamentally irrational and superstitious. This more serious threat to traditional religious activities intensified periodically during the twentieth century, both in the Republican period (1911–49) and in the People's Republic that followed it. As a result of successive 'anti-superstition' campaigns, many temples were destroyed or converted to other uses, large-scale rituals suppressed, and Daoist priests and Buddhist monks forced to return to lay life. However, these campaigns were effective mostly in cities; people in rural communities where the great majority of the population lived clung tenaciously to their traditions of ritual and belief, and where possible rebuilt their temples and revived their festivals, with family and community heads continuing as ritual leaders.

During the long War of Resistance against Japan that began in 1937, many temples were used as army barracks or destroyed in the fighting, as they were later in the civil war between Nationalists and Communists that did not end until the People's Republic was established in 1949. As order was gradually restored, for a short time some temples and festivals revived, but soon government control of all levels of society increased to a degree previously unknown. This control included the confiscation of temple lands, the return of their resident clergy to lay life, the expulsion of foreign missionaries, and the establishment of a Religious Affairs Bureau to regulate religious activities. Only the five traditions of Buddhism, Daoism, Islam, Roman Catholicism and Protestantism were recognized as legitimate, and offices were set up to control them and ensure that they supported the new regime. This meant that local community rituals and beliefs, the ancient foundation of Chinese religion, were considered 'feudal superstition' and thus illegal. However, religious activities continued in many areas until the Cultural Revolution. During this period almost all such activities ceased, and temples, churches and mosques were closed.

In 1978, some rituals, temples and churches began to resurface, and in 1982 the Communist Party issued 'Document 19', which stated that its policy on religion was to protect and respect freedom of religious belief, but also guaranteed the freedom not to believe; it also reaffirmed that only the above-mentioned five religions were legitimate. Although this document continued the old emphasis on control, compared to the Cultural Revolution it seemed a limited liberalization, and religious activities began to revive around the country. In some places local officials continued the old suppression, but in others they began to support the restoration of temples and festivals. It is interesting to note that in around 1980 Chinese scholars began to write about local religious activities for the first time in several decades, calling them 'folk beliefs' rather than 'feudal superstition'.

The situation of religion on the Chinese Mainland was sharply different from that in Taiwan, and in Hong Kong before its 'handover' to China in 1997. In Hong Kong freedom of religion prevailed until 1997 and has continued since. During the Japanese occupation of Taiwan from 1895–1945, religious activities in local communities and Christian churches were for the most part permitted to continue, as was the case after the Nationalist forces took over the island after the end of the war. After the Communist victory in 1949 the Nationalists made a point of allowing freedom of religion in contrast to its suppression on the Mainland. The main exceptions to this were popular religious sects such as the Way of Pervading Unity (*Yiguan dao*) and the Presbyterian Church, the latter because of its support for indigenous Taiwanese culture and language. However, these restrictions were eased after the abolition of martial law in 1986, and today the religious scene in Taiwan is very lively indeed.

Local community traditions of ritual and belief

For thousands of years the great majority of the Chinese people have lived in rural villages and towns, sustained by agriculture, manual labour, handicrafts and small shops. Among their activities have been ritual offerings to ancestors and deities, carried out in homes, lineage shrines and local community temples, sometimes in cooperation with those of other communities. These offerings of incense and food are believed to strengthen relationships between people and their ancestors and gods, and thus cause them to be more responsive to prayers for aid. Despite much local variation, similar temples, images, offerings and festivals can be found everywhere, all supported by practical concerns for divine aid to deal with the problems of everyday life. These local traditions have their own forms of organization and institutionalization, with their own types of leaders, deities and beliefs. There are Daoist, Buddhist and government influences on these traditions, but they must be adapted to the needs of local communities. It is the villagers who build temples and organize festivals, but priests or monks may be invited to recite their scriptures in honour of the gods. All members of the community are expected to participate and contribute, regardless of their class or economic status.

Chinese local religion also shares a common set of theoretical assumptions, its own 'theology', which is based on the belief that the living and the dead – gods, humans and ghosts – are all connected by bonds of mutual influence and response; bonds of mutual obligation that are based on a sense of a moral universe in which righteousness, respect and destructive behaviour eventually bring their own retributions or rewards. Promise, efficacious response and gratitude, disrespect, cheating and punishment – all of these are manifested in specific material ways and provide the basic assumptions underlying ritual and divination. People expect the gods to be efficacious, *ling,* able to answer their prayers. The human counterpart and stimulus for such divine response is sincerity, *qiancheng,* in prayers and offerings, a sincerity based on faith that the gods really exist and can indeed respond. This is reinforced by the belief that many of the gods were once humans; that humans can become gods; that deities and the dead can respond to divination or appear in dreams, and can speak or write through spirit mediums; and that the dead live in an underworld from which they can be called up or to which their living relatives can go in séances to see them. Through geomancy, *fengshui,* and intercession with the gods, the natural world is also part of this system of influence and response. Siting of graves and buildings that recognizes and respects the flow of power in the landscape brings blessings; proper worship of the gods is believed to bring rain or stop floods. It is this network of relationships that provides the underlying logic and coherence of local cults.

Chinese local religion is based on family worship of deities and ancestors on home altars, but also involves large-scale festivals in which members of the whole village or township community participate, on occasions such as the birthdays of the gods, or to seek protection from droughts, epidemics and other disasters. In all cases such festivals invoke the power of the gods for practical goals to 'summon blessings and drive away harm'. The major ritual activity of these three- to five-day celebrations involves processions carrying images of the gods through the villages. Operas based on traditional stories and values are performed every day and evening. Festivals are intended to be lively and *renao* 'hot and noisy', a kind of 'collective effervescence', to use Durkheim's words, formed by the presence of tens of thousands of worshippers and onlookers crowded tightly together. All of the local gods are also believed to be present to enjoy the offerings of incense and food, and to enjoy the operas. In addition, merchants come from the surrounding area to display their wares. Worshippers pray for healing and success for their families and vow to repay the gods with new robes or opera performances if their prayers are answered. They also consult the diviners and spirit-mediums who gather at these festivals. Similar local rituals have long been carried out in Taiwan and Hong Kong, and in Chinese communities in Southeast Asia; the gods and some practices may differ, but everywhere such traditions are a basic aspect of Chinese culture and identity. Of course, Chinese local rituals and beliefs are similar to those of ordinary people in many other cultures, whatever their larger political and intellectual contexts; wherever one looks, one sees people praying and making sacrifices to their gods or saints for help in dealing with their problems, appeals that can also involve festivals and processions. Viewed in this way, the Chinese traditions are part of a worldwide practical religion.

Indigenous popular religious sects

Popular religious sects are also a worldwide phenomenon. The term 'sect' refers here to voluntary religious associations that have their own founders and leaders, deities, organizations, rituals, scriptures and beliefs. Most Chinese sectarian associations were obscure and peaceful, but the scriptures of some proclaimed that this sinful world was about to end with the descent of a saviour, who would establish a new paradise on earth, with new rulers of its own. This was of course anathema to the government, which sought to suppress such groups, some of which staged violent uprisings, and eventually all sects were prohibited by law. Nonetheless, some sects continued to be active, and by the eighteenth century had even reached Taiwan, and later, Southeast Asia. Such groups continued to be active in the Republican period and in the People's Republic until the Cultural Revolution. However, recent research in north China has discovered some sects functioning quietly as community traditions in villages. In Taiwan, Hong Kong and Southeast Asia, by contrast, such groups have established large public temples, and distribute tracts in their vegetarian restaurants to attract new members.

In Taiwan there are also many 'new religions', some similar to those in Japan, founded by charismatic leaders who claim supernormal powers of healing and the ability to communicate with gods and the spirits of the dead. On the Mainland there have been some small groups like this that were quickly suppressed, but in 1992 a new sect known as the Falungong, the 'Cultivation of the Wheel of the Teaching' was founded by a practitioner of *qigong* ('energy cultivation') named Li Hongzhi. (*Fa* originally referred to the *dharma*, the teaching of the Buddha). *Qigong* had been practised for a long time in China by individuals and small groups as a form of meditative exercise and healing, but Li used it as the basis of a book in which he claimed to be a moral teacher with supernormal powers. This book was eagerly received as a new revelation, and by 1996 had sold nearly a million copies that were read in study groups all over China, groups that it was claimed had a combined membership of millions of people. In that same year the government banned the sale of the book and started to refer to the Falungong as a 'heretical cult'. Li Hongzhi fled to the United States in 1998, and on 25 April 1999 more than 10,000 sect members, each holding a copy of Li's book, assembled in a peaceful demonstration outside the Communist Party headquarters in Beijing to protest government opposition to their group. This demonstration surprised and shocked the government, which outlawed the Falungong in November of that year, arrested thousands of its members, and burned books and tapes of Li's teachings. Since then the group has been suppressed in China, but it continues to be active elsewhere, and strongly criticizes the government through the Internet and Falungong newspapers.

Daoism

Daoism is fundamentally a religion of *qi*, the vital breath from which nature, the gods and humans evolve. The source and order of this vital substance is the Dao, the ultimate power of life in the universe. The gods are personified manifestations of *qi*, symbolizing astral powers of the cosmos and organs of the human body with which they are correlated. Under the conditions of existence, *qi* becomes stale and worn out, so it must be renewed through ritual processes that restore its primal vitality. These rituals consist essentially of visualizing and calling down the cosmic gods to re-establish their contact with their bodily correlates. In this way the adept or priest ingests divine power and recharges his bodily forces for healing, rejuvenation and long life. Priests are believed to be able to release their cosmic powers through ritual actions that revive the life forces of the community around them. Since the fifth century, Daoist beliefs and practices have been written down in hundreds of scripture texts believed to have been divinely revealed. These texts are concerned throughout with moral discipline and orderly ritual and organization.

Several schools of Daoism developed over the centuries, led by men who claimed to have received new revelations of sacred texts, but after the Song period (960–1179) the most important new developments were the establishment of the monastic Quanzhen Complete Perfection School and the closer relationships of local priests with the ritual traditions of local communities. Quanzhen was founded by a scholar named Wang Zhe (1113–70), who claimed to have received revelations from two superhuman beings, whereupon he gathered disciples and founded five congregations in northern Shandong. After his death several of his leading disciples continued to proclaim his teachings across north China. While some Quanzhen beliefs and rituals are similar to those of other Daoists, its organization and institutions are distinctive, primarily because they are based on celibate lineages of masters and disciples with their own monasteries and ordination rituals. The Quanzhen Movement spread across China by establishing monasteries and networks of temples, and by increasing the number of places where ordinations could be carried out.

The major centre of Quanzhen training and ordination has long been the White Cloud Temple (Baiyunguan) in Beijing, where periodic ordination rituals were held until the establishment of the People's Republic. The first such ritual to be carried out after that was in 1989. By 1996 there were over 4,000 Quanzhen monks and around 2,300 nuns in Beijing, Shanghai and several provinces. The use of spirit-writing in Quanzhen lay communities was one of the sources of the rapid spread of this practice among many popular religious sects during the nineteenth century, but the major Daoist influence on local community religion has been rituals carried out by married priests living at home, called *huoju Daoshi* (lit. 'living by household fires'), who are not affiliated with Quanzhen. These priests are trained as disciples in the homes of masters. They live there for several years learning texts and rituals until they are ready to practise on their own. Disciples can also inherit the position from their fathers.

Local communities hired Daoist priests (or Buddhist monks) to assist with annual temple festivals or periodic *jiao* festivals of renewing the life force of the community. They did so by reciting scriptures and conducting rituals known only to such specialists. The status and power of community gods could be enhanced by having scriptures written that related them to Daoist deities. All of this encouraged the development of a Daoist priesthood devoted primarily to conducting rituals in local communities. During the Ming dynasty (1368–1644) this home-dwelling priesthood was officially designated as the Zhengyi (Correct and Unified) Order to distinguish it from Quanzhen, although in fact it involved many local variations and master/disciple lineages. Zhengyi priests are ordained by the authority of Zhang Tianshi, Celestial Master Zhang, who the faithful believe is a descendant of the founding Zhang lineage in the Han period.

Along with those of other religions, many Daoist temples were destroyed during the nineteenth and twentieth centuries, beginning with attacks by rebel armies during the Taiping Uprising of 1851–64 mentioned above. Later, many other temples were converted into schools, military barracks, storehouses and government offices, a process that culminated in the Cultural Revolution, when any remaining priests were returned to lay life and their ritual activities ceased. However, the National Daoist Association, originally founded in 1957, was re-established in 1980 and began to restore some temples. From that time, Daoist temples and rituals, like those of other religions, were revived in many areas as part of the new period. After a hiatus of several decades, in 1995 around 200 Zhengyi priests were ordained. Although large-scale rebuilding and rituals must still be approved by local officials, in many areas Daoism appears to be re-established.

Taiwan and Hong Kong Daoism

The Quanzhen school has never been strong in Taiwan, but there are groups that practise the ancient tradition of the inner circulation and refinement of the 'vital force' of *qi*. However, Zhengyi Daoist priests have been present in Taiwan since the Qing period with their own 'professional domains' based in communities of residents whose ancestors moved to the island from areas of the Mainland, mostly in Fujian and Guangdong provinces. Daoist activities in Taiwan are recognized by the state and have continued essentially uninterrupted since the beginning. The priestly vocation is passed on in families; novices move into the homes of masters where they are trained as disciples for several years, reading sacred texts and learning how to perform rituals. They are initiated by these masters and taught the secret traditions for the transmission of texts and ritual talismans. After initiation they may be invited by local people to perform rituals in their homes and community temples. These rituals are for temple and annual festivals, exorcism to drive away harmful forces believed to cause illness and epidemics, changing the destiny of those afflicted with troubles, and funerals. The basic structure of the rituals is the same, beginning with purification involving abstinence from sexual relations, writing a formal announcement of the time, place and nature of the ritual, preparation of altars with scrolls depicting the chief Daoist deities, putting on elaborate robes and caps with symbolic decorations, inviting gods to descend to the altar by reciting their names from scriptures, and performing symbolic gestures and dance steps. A few leaders may be invited into the sacred area in front of the Daoist altar to represent the community in the rites, but the remainder of the people carry out their own worship of local deities with incense, offerings and processions, venerate special tablets for their ancestors set up at the festival, and watch festival operas.

There are two main types of Daoists in Hong Kong, which here refers to the entire Special Administrative Region – local versions of Zhengyi priests who perform funeral rituals and liturgies to renew life forces at community *jiao* festivals, and temples derived from the Quanzhen tradition devoted primarily to the deity Lü Dongbin. Zhengyi-type priests living with their families who came to Hong Kong from Guangdong are called Nahm-mouh lao; they came in the 1940s to escape wars and repression in China. There are now around 500 Nahm-mouh lao active in Hong Kong, with what Daoism scholar Lai Chi Tim calls their own 'liturgy performing halls' and professional organization. In response to invitations from families or community leaders, in *jiao* festivals they write memorials inviting the gods to descend, and make offerings and read scriptures before temporary altars to Daoist deities, as in such rituals in Taiwan. The names of those who have contributed funds for the festival are included in these memorials, which are both posted on walls and announced repeatedly before being burned at the end of the festival. The priests also perform penance rituals for the community, feed hungry ghosts and expel harmful forces. Similar rituals are performed by priests in coastal communities of Hakka speakers who originally moved to Hong Kong from areas of Fujian province. As in Taiwan, while the priests are reciting their scriptures and performing specialized rituals, the people are viewing operas, venerating their ancestors and bearing their gods through the community in processions.

The Quanzhen tradition and the worship of Lü Dongbin were brought to Hong Kong from Guangdong during the 1920s and 1950s by groups of lay devotees who consulted the god through spirit-writing for spiritual advice and medical prescriptions. Many of the shrines built for Lü Dongbin are small, but there are also several large and elaborate temples for him and other Quanzhen deities in Hong Kong, where rituals are performed by resident priests. These rituals, based on numerous scripture texts, include those for initiation of new devotees, confession, annual festivals for the gods, funerals and memorial services. There are lay members of these temples, but they are open to worshippers from the whole area, not just from particular communities. Some Lü Dongbin/Quanzhen temples serve as mausoleums, with large mortuary halls filled with thousands of tablets and niches for the ashes of the dead, for which their families must pay substantial fees. At ceremonies to ease the passage of the dead through purgatory, priests in elaborate robes read scriptures in the presence of both these altars and groups of grieving relatives. Colourful paper houses, furniture, automobiles and clothing are ritually burned to convey them to the underworld. The income from mortuary fees and rituals is used to support the temple and its other activities. In recent decades some of the major temples have used some of this income to establish schools, orphanages, senior centres and clinics, similar to those set up by Hong Kong Buddhist and Christian groups.

Buddhism on the China Mainland, Taiwan and Hong Kong

Some Buddhists moved from India to Central Asia by the first century BC, and there is evidence for this tradition in China by the first century AD, during the Eastern Han dynasty, 25–220. By the second century, Buddhist images were worshipped and scriptures began to be translated into Chinese. Communities of monks and lay worshippers gradually spread across the country, supported by Indian and Central Asian missionaries, and, beginning in around 400, by Chinese pilgrims returning from trips to India and Central and Southeast Asia, bringing with them more scriptures to be translated. The translation of rules for monastic life led to the establishment of groups of celibate monks and nuns devoted to worship, the recitation of scriptures, and meditation. As in India before, these monastic communities relied on support from the communities around them and from the state. In some times and places they were supported by rulers and officials, and in others they were not, which began a long history of alternate periods of acceptance and repression, a history that continues today. Opposition to Buddhism occurred on the grounds that all groups owed primary allegiance to the state, and that celibacy violated the obligation to continue the family line. However, Buddhist ideas of karma, individual moral cause and effect over successive lifetimes, associated with ideas of paradise for the pious and purgatory for sinners, soon became the basis for the beliefs and practice of Chinese devotees.

From the beginning, Buddhist monks and nuns had been in close contact with people in the communities around them on whom they depended for food, labour and new recruits to the monastic life. Lay people attended lectures expounding the scriptures, and monks and nuns performed rituals in monasteries, community temples and homes, particularly for funerals and during annual temple festivals. These rituals involved the recitation of scriptures that invoked the help of Buddhas and bodhisattvas by name, so the people had ample opportunities to learn basic concepts and moral teachings. Groups of lay devotees led by monks raised funds for images and the printing of scriptures and tracts. Some of these devotees gave formal allegiance to the Buddha, his teachings and the monastic order, and took vows not to kill, steal, lie, drink alcoholic beverages or commit immoral sexual acts, and thus became disciples of monks. For most people, however, Buddhism has meant faith in the power of Buddhas and bodhisattvas to respond to prayers and the gaining of karmic merit through piety and good deeds. The transfer of knowledge from monasteries to communities was greatly facilitated by the teachings of the Pure Land School that developed in the Tang period (618–907), because this school taught that salvation could be obtained simply by reciting in faith the name of the Buddha Amitabha, who presided over a paradise in the west. By the succeeding Song period (960–1279), there appeared lay societies devoted to reciting the Buddha's name. At first these groups were connected with monasteries and led by monks, but later some became independent. It was from such associations that the popular religious sects discussed above eventually developed.

Buddhist monasteries continued to be active in succeeding periods until the mid-nineteenth century, when many were destroyed during the Taiping Rebellion. Some monasteries were later rebuilt, and new monk leaders appeared, but Buddhism was furthered primarily by lay devotees, who continued to establish associations and reprint scriptures. In response to the late Qing political reformers, Buddhist reformers established academies for training monks and nuns, set up regional and national Buddhist associations, and employed modern printing methods to publish scriptures, tracts and newspapers. Buddhist monasteries and lay societies had long carried out some charitable activities, but now efforts were made to emulate Christians by establishing clinics, orphanages and retirement homes. Lay associations for worship and study continued to be active, with many set up in vegetarian restaurants that distributed free devotional literature, thus setting an example for the indigenous popular sects discussed above.

Statistics from the Chinese Buddhist Society in 1930 estimated that at that time there were about 738,000 Chinese monks and nuns living in 267,000 temples, most of them small but a few large enough for complete monastic organization and periodic ordination rituals. In 1947 it was estimated that there were 4,620,000 Buddhists in China, including lay supporters. Again, many Buddhist temples were destroyed in battles with warlords, by the Japanese occupation of 1937–45 and Chinese resistance to it, and by the civil war between Nationalist and Communist forces. After the People's Republic was established, land reform confiscated the land on which monasteries had depended for income, monks and nuns were ordered to return to lay life, and Buddhist practices and institutions were attacked in the successive campaigns used by the new government to establish control. In the Qing and Republican periods restrictions on Buddhism were not strictly enforced, but in the PRC they were, culminating in thorough-going suppression during the Cultural Revolution. Some rituals and festivals had continued to be practised until 1966, when everything came to a halt for ten years. However, as we have seen, from the early 1980s religious activities began to revive, including those of the Buddhists. This revival naturally depended on what texts and images had been preserved, and on what older monks and nuns remembered of past practices. A key problem was that as younger people joined, a whole middle generation of leadership was missing because recruitment and training had ceased during the Cultural Revolution.

The Manchu rulers of the Qing dynasty favoured Tibetan Buddhism, and throughout the twentieth century Tibetan monks travelled about China to lecture and teach the gestures and incantations of their Tantric tradition. Chinese monks have also gone to Lhasa to study. This interchange resumed in the 1980s, and today continues to function as an unofficial link between Tibet and Chinese Buddhists, a link the government allows as another form of Buddhist-based diplomacy, similar to its long tradition of encouraging contacts with Buddhists in Southeast Asia.

By the end of the twentieth century Buddhist monasteries, training academies and ritual activities had been restored in many areas of China, with monks and nuns receiving small monthly stipends. They are also permitted to go on pilgrimages to sacred sites and travel to other monasteries to study, so this ancient tradition is active once again.

Taiwan

Some Buddhist beliefs and practices, particularly devotion to the bodhisattva Guanyin, have existed in Taiwan since Chinese people began to migrate there in the seventeenth century, but very few ordained monks and nuns were present during the Qing period. In their absence, in Qing Taiwan it was *zhaijiao* 'vegetarian sects', some with married leaders, that attracted most people interested in religious activities other than those carried out in homes and community temples. These groups were Taiwan forms of the popular religious sects discussed above. Buddhist monasteries were not established until after the beginning of the Japanese Occupation in 1895, when Japanese Buddhists began proselytizing on the island with government support. This was done primarily by establishing associations sponsored by Japanese Buddhist denominations, such as the Patriotic Buddhist Association by the Soto sect, but these associations were not very effective in reaching out to the Taiwanese people. More important for them was the coming to Taiwan of several Buddhist masters from Fujian province who set up monasteries and carried out ordination rituals in Taiwan for the first time.

Many Buddhists came to Taiwan in the migrations from China after the end of Japanese Occupation in 1945 and the 1949 defeat of the Nationalist forces in the civil war. In 1947 the Buddhist Association of the Republic of China was organized, led by refugee monks from the Mainland, who considered Taiwan Buddhism to be disorganized, because of lingering Japanese influence and the activities of the vegetarian sects. Among these monks were several followers of the reformer Yinguang (1861–1940), who promoted a revival of Pure Land practice. In the 1960s new reformed organizations were established that emphasized the importance of Buddhist activities in the world, following the example of Taixu (1889–1947). One of these was Foguangshan, Buddha's Light Mountain, founded by Xingyun (b. 1927); another was the Ciji gongdehui, the Compassionate Relief Merit Society, established by a nun whose Buddhist name is Zhengyan (b. 1937). A third new organization is Fagushan, Dharma Drum Mountain, founded by Shengyan (b. 1930). Foguangshan's goal is to realize the Pure Land on earth through the good deeds of lay devotees, which include participation in political activities. Ciji is best known for its charitable relief activities and Fagushan for its emphasis on meditation and religious self-development. All of these groups include many lay leaders and members. Their scale, sophistication and outreach are new in the history of Chinese Buddhism, and are a credit to the tradition. As on the Mainland, Tibetan Buddhism is also popular in Taiwan, in part because of the presence on the island of exiled Tibetan monks as well as visits by the Dalai Lama.

Hong Kong

Although there were small Cantonese Buddhist temples in isolated areas earlier, the real growth of Hong Kong Buddhism came with the migration of northern monks after the establishment of the People's Republic. From that time, the development of this tradition was shaped by rapid population growth, urbanization and industrialization, the shortage of land for burials, and the need to compete with Christianity. There are two types of Buddhist temples in Hong Kong – small convents established by monks or nuns for their own residence, rituals and meditation, and large public temples with imposing images and pagodas that provide rituals for lay people, primarily funerals and memorial services. As with Hong Kong Daoist temples, many Buddhist temples include large rooms lined with niches for the ashes of those whose families have rented them. Monks or nuns recite scriptures to generate merit to transfer to the spirits of the dead to ease their passage through the underworld and help ensure a good rebirth. There is a Hong Kong Buddhist Association, formed in 1945, that manages a hospital, schools, homes for the aged and sick, and youth organizations. Monks also perform large-scale rituals in honour of the birthdays of the Buddha Sakyamuni and such popular Buddhas or bodhisattvas as Amitabha, the Buddha of Healing, and Guanyin. All of these activities are organized in cooperation with lay devotees, and in response to their needs, a response that has led to the development of Buddhist marriage ceremonies that are unknown elsewhere. In Hong Kong lay men and women can also enter monasteries for a short time before returning to their homes, a custom influenced by similar practices in Thailand and Taiwan. Since the mid-1980s Hong Kong monks and nuns have visited and lectured at Buddhist centres on the Mainland.

Since the handover of Hong Kong to the People's Republic in 1997 the Hong Kong government has indicated its support for Buddhism by declaring Buddha's Birthday a public holiday. Since that time the University of Hong Kong has established a Buddhist Institute and the Taiwan-based Foguangshan has established a Buddhist Studies Centre at the Chinese University of Hong Kong. In 1998 the large Chilin Nunnery was built in Tang-dynasty style in the Diamond Hill area with business and government support, and has since proved an important new site for worship and tourism.

Roman Catholic Christianity

After Buddhism, the earliest foreign religious traditions to reach China were Judaism, Islam, Manichaeism and Nestorian Christianity, all of which arrived during the Tang period (618–907). Franciscan monks from Italy arrived in the fourteenth century, but both their tradition and that of the Nestorians failed to take root and disappeared by the fifteenth century. It was Italian Jesuits in the sixteenth century, led by Matteo Ricci (1552–1610), who first built churches, made converts and gained some recognition from the Chinese state. After a year of study in the Portuguese colony of Macau, Ricci was eventually able to move into China, and reached Beijing in 1601. He gradually made a name for himself by teaching about European mathematics, astronomy and mechanics and by showing the clocks the missionaries had brought with them. He learned to speak, read and write Chinese, and dressed as a Confucian scholar. He also made some influential converts who paved the way for other Jesuits to obtain positions as court astronomers and to do missionary work, so that by Ricci's death in 1610 there were around 2,500 baptized Chinese Christians. The church continued to grow in the following centuries, although it was still technically illegal for Chinese to convert to this foreign religion, and Christianity was classified as a heretical sect.

At the local level there were disputes between Christian villagers and their neighbours over support for community festivals, a tension that has been somewhat resolved by the development of predominantly Roman Catholic villages where Christians could build churches, carry out their own forms of worship, funerals and weddings, and venerate their ancestors. On the whole, such villages were left alone by the state unless they were implicated in unrest related to other popular religious sects. It was in this village form that the Chinese Roman Catholic tradition entered the nineteenth century. During that century the situation of Christianity in China was radically changed by the treaties imposed on China by Britain and France after they defeated the Chinese in wars intended to open the country to foreign trade. These treaties forced the Chinese to admit Christian missionaries as well as merchants. Permission for the Chinese to practise Roman Catholicism was granted in 1844 and 1846. An 1858 treaty guaranteed the toleration and protection of Christianity, with the implication that such protection also extended to Chinese converts. In the civil wars with the Taipings and Boxers many missionaries and Chinese Christians were killed and churches destroyed, but by 1900 many missionaries had returned and Catholicism continued to be based in predominantly Christian villages, where churches and schools were built and priests taught the people to attend mass on Sundays, maintain family prayers before images of Christ, Mary or saints, abstain from opium, and replace traditional festivals with those of the Christian year. So the tradition persisted in the twentieth century through all the upheavals that occurred up to the Communist victory in 1949.

The history of Roman Catholic and Protestant Christianity in China entered a new phase after the establishment of the People's Republic, which expelled all missionaries and forbade outside support. A Religious Affairs Bureau was established to control all religious activities through state-approved 'mass associations', including the Catholic Patriotic Association (CPA), set up in 1957; only leaders and activities approved by that Association were allowed. The CPA proceeded to appoint priests and bishops without Vatican approval. However, in 1949 the Vatican had prohibited all Chinese Catholics from cooperating in any way with the new Communist regime, which put church members in a very difficult position. The result was that the majority of Catholics continued their traditional practices in an unauthorized 'underground church' with its own priests and bishops, and refused to recognize the officially sponsored church. Some underground bishops and priests have been imprisoned for long periods, but are seen as martyrs by their followers, who will not attend masses said by government-approved priests. This split continues today. As noted above, government policies toward religion began to change in 1979, which has resulted in increased numbers of temples, churches and religious participants; in the Catholic case, from around 3 million in 1949 to 12 million in 2001, perhaps 6 or 8 million of these unofficial, but restrictions on unauthorized activities remain. From around 1979 some priests and bishops were released from prison, and some churches rebuilt and seminaries reopened. There have been times when Beijing and the Vatican have appeared to be working toward a compromise, but the government refuses to allow what it considers foreign interference in a Chinese religion, and the Church maintains that only ordinations that it approves are valid, in some cases excommunicating bishops appointed by the government. The situation is exacerbated by the Vatican's continued diplomatic recognition of Taiwan. In 2006 the Church refused to recognize several new Chinese bishops, while the Vatican appointed Hong Kong Bishop Joseph Zen Ze-kiun as a Cardinal, which enraged Beijing. In the meantime, however, most Chinese Catholics continue to worship in their villages as before, organizing themselves and led by lay leaders if priests are unavailable.

Roman Catholicism in Taiwan

Beginning in 1628 Spanish Dominican missionaries from the Philippines established churches in northern Taiwan, and despite opposition from some aboriginal groups eventually converted around 4,500 people to Christianity. However, in 1642 the Spanish presence on the island was ended by the Dutch, who were in turn expelled by the Chinese general Zheng Chenggong (Koxinga) in 1661. Subsequent attempts to re-establish the mission failed until the treaties with the foreign powers forced the Chinese to open ports in Taiwan in 1869. Local opposition to the missionaries persisted, but by the early years of the Japanese occupation, new churches and schools had been built and the work of the missionaries began to take hold, so that by 1938 there were 9,000 Catholics in the province. After the defeat of the Nationalist forces on the China Mainland in 1949, large numbers of priests and nuns fled to Taiwan to continue their work. They were welcomed by the government, which continued to have diplomatic relations with the Vatican. There were soon hundreds of Chinese priests, with the first Chinese Cardinal appointed in 1960. As a result the Church grew rapidly, and by 2001 there were 1,135 Catholic congregations in Taiwan, with a total of around 300,000 members. Thus, due in part to recognition and support from the Vatican, the Church has prospered along with other religious traditions in Taiwan. There is no split in Taiwan between official and unofficial activities as there is on the Mainland. If Vatican support for the Taiwan Church could be disentangled from its diplomatic recognition of the government there, a major obstacle to the work of the Church in China would be removed.

Protestant Christianity

The first Protestant missionary on the China Mainland was the Presbyterian Robert Morrison (1782–1834), sent by the London Missionary Society, who arrived in Guangzhou in 1807. With the help of Chinese assistants, Morrison and other Europeans began to translate the Bible and Christian tracts into Chinese. The first converts took such tracts from Guangzhou into other parts of China. During the first decades of the nineteenth century foreigners were not allowed to travel in China, and could only live in Guangzhou and Macau, so the work of Chinese converts was vital.

Despite these early efforts, by 1840 there were still only around twenty Protestant missionaries in China from Britain and the United States and fewer than 100 Chinese converts, but the mission situation changed dramatically after the 1842 Treaty of Nanking ended the first 'Opium War'. As noted above, treaties that followed later Chinese defeats by foreign invaders opened up more of the country to both trade and missionary work. Another result was the increased importation of opium, which was deplored by some missionaries, although some served as interpreters at treaty negotiations and all rejoiced in the new opportunities for their work as they moved deeper into the country. Most such work was devoted to converting as many Chinese as possible to Christianity, a task that continued to emphasize translating, printing and distributing the Bible and Christian tracts. However, the Protestants also established schools, not only for boys, but also for girls, which was an important departure. They also built hospitals, clinics and printing presses, so some of the Protestant contributions to China had already begun in this early period. All of this encouraged the rapid growth of Protestant missions, with 498 mission stations established by 1890 in every province except Hunan. It is estimated that there were around 80,000 Chinese Protestants by 1900, but Protestants were still far outnumbered by Roman Catholics, of whom there were around 720,000 at that time.

During the Boxer Uprising, around 1,900 Chinese Protestants and 188 foreign missionaries were killed, mostly in mission stations in the north but also elsewhere in the country. However, much of the destruction that took place during this period was the work of the foreign armies that invaded China to put down the Boxers; to this day, some local records in the north recall the devastation not only of Beijing, but also of villages and their temples.

After 1901 established mission groups expanded rapidly, and new ones were introduced, including recently established evangelical groups that proclaimed the imminent end of the world and the second coming of Christ, thus preparing the way for the indigenous Chinese Christian sects that developed a few decades later. Nonetheless, despite such growth, the total number of Christians in China still accounted for less than 1 per cent of the total population. In the 1920s and 1930s, mission work in China was repeatedly threatened by sporadic warfare, banditry and a decline in local administrative control, all much exacerbated by the Japanese invasion. All of this encouraged the further development of new Protestant churches founded and led by the Chinese themselves, a movement that began in around 1906 when Yu Guozhen, a Presbyterian pastor in Shanghai, established with his colleagues the Chinese Christian Union (Jidujiaohui) and formed an independent Chinese congregation, which led to a federation of over 100 similar groups that was later emulated elsewhere. Between 1917 and 1919 a Pentecostal Chinese movement appeared – the True Jesus Church – proclaiming the imminent return of Christ and claiming the powers of healing and speaking in unknown tongues. This group was anti-foreign and insisted that Chinese Christians renounce their old churches. Another indigenous church, known as the Assembly Hall, or the 'Little Flock', appeared in the mid-1920s, led by the evangelist Ni Tuoshen. It was also anti-foreign, but stressed personal holiness rather than Pentecostal practices. Another Pentecostal tradition, the Jesus Family, which began in rural Shandong province in around 1927, practised communal living and eating, including several hours of worship each day and shared work and child care. This group believed that its members could receive divine messages while in a trance. There were other similar groups, all influenced not only by similar Western traditions, but by the old Chinese sectarian hope for the coming of a divine saviour. In none of these groups did missionaries have a formative influence; these sects were in effect a second declaration of independence by Chinese Christians after the abortive attempt by the Taipings sixty years earlier, and helped prepare the way for the self-support needed during the Japanese Occupation and after 1949.

A major goal of the Japanese Occupation government that ruled large areas of north and east China from 1937 to 1945 was to replace Western colonial influence with its own rule, including doing away with the missionary-dominated Church of Christ in China that had been established in 1922 to coordinate the activities of the major denominations. Japanese attempts to unify the churches in a new organization were not successful; the real impact of Japanese rule was to force the churches to become self-supporting, which helped them survive after the Communist takeover. Thus, the old goal of freedom from control by foreign denominations was paradoxically realized under two authoritarian regimes.

In 1950 the government of the new People's Republic of China established the 'Three Selfs' policy for Christianity in China – Self-Government, Self-Support and Self-Propagation. This led to the severing of ties with foreign missions, whose representatives had mostly left by 1952. Independent Chinese churches were also suppressed, and some of their leaders imprisoned. A national Three Self Patriotic Movement Committee was established to control church activities; when all Protestant denominations were abolished in 1958, it became the only legal church organization, but, like the Roman Catholics, many Protestants sought to avoid it through unauthorized worship in 'house churches'. Protestant Christians had to endure the same PRC political campaigns as all other religious people, but after the 1979 change in government policy, their numbers also rapidly increased. There had been around 750,000 Protestants in China in 1949, but by government estimates, in 2000 there were at least 25 million, including participants in autonomous house churches. This represents a 33-fold increase, and for the first time there are more Chinese Protestants than Catholics. Some of the autonomous groups have hundreds of members, who meet openly in large church buildings. Protestant churches can be found everywhere in China, in both cities and the countryside, with unofficial evangelical groups that promise healing and direct personal experience of God growing most rapidly, as is also the case elsewhere. More than twenty theological seminaries and Bible schools are now training church leaders. In addition, the academic study of Christian ideas by ostensibly non-Christian scholars has developed in universities and research institutes, to study values and ideas that are believed to have contributed to the development of capitalism and modernity. Some foreign evangelical groups are illegally providing radio broadcasts, Bibles, tracts and funds to their Chinese counterparts, and Chinese Protestant leaders see their work as part of a world movement, but the church is now a Chinese religion, fundamentally independent and poised to continue its success.

Protestant Christianity in Taiwan

After the expulsion of Dutch missionaries in the seventeenth century, the first Protestants to work in Taiwan were English Presbyterians, who began to visit the island from their base in Fujian in 1859 and established a church there in 1865. In 1871 a Canadian Presbyterian, George L. Mackay, began to work in northern Taiwan among both Han Chinese and aboriginal peoples. Mackay and his successors translated the Bible into the Southern Min dialect spoken by Han Taiwanese, established schools and a hospital, and negotiated on behalf of the people with the Japanese. The Presbyterians also founded a theological college in the old city of Tainan, and promoted self-rule by the Taiwan church.

After the expulsion of the Japanese from Taiwan in 1945, Chinese Nationalist forces fleeing the Mainland took over, missionaries began to return, and church activities resumed, with the Presbyterians identified with the Taiwanese rather than the newly arrived mainlanders. Although by 1949 the Guomindang Nationalist government had lost a long and bitter civil war with the Communist forces under Mao Zedong, it continued to insist that Mao was just a 'bandit' and that it remained the legitimate government of all of China, the whole structure of which it moved to Taiwan. The island was put under martial law, and native Taiwanese were treated as second-class citizens. Mandarin became the official language, and it was made illegal to publish Bibles in Romanized Min dialect, as the Presbyterians had been doing. By 1945 Taiwan had not been part of China for fifty years, so many Taiwanese resented the sometimes heavy-handed Nationalist administration, and on 28 February 1947 large-scale riots broke out against the government after the police beat up a woman who was selling cigarettes illegally. The governor of Taiwan accepted a list of thirty-two demands drawn up by a group of Taiwanese leaders, but two months later Nationalist troops attacked, with the result that around 10,000 people were killed or died in prison, most of them lawyers, teachers, newspaper editors and Presbyterian ministers. This event is still remembered as *Ererba*, 2/28. In the long run this traumatic event led many to support the cause of Taiwan independence, and further consolidated the position of the Presbyterian Church.

In 1946 the government officially welcomed missionaries from a variety of Protestant denominations, including Lutherans, US Southern Baptists and Pentecostal Assemblies of God; many who had been in China moved to Taiwan, but worked primarily with Mandarin speakers from the Mainland, so the Presbyterians continued to concentrate on the Taiwanese, and support their language and political rights. The government imprisoned some Presbyterian leaders, confiscated their publications, suppressed their news magazine, and tried to close their theological college. However, in 1986 the government lifted martial law, legalized political opposition, and moved toward establishing real political and individual freedoms. A variety of Christian groups had been active since 1946, but they now began to grow even more rapidly, so that by 2001 there were 3,609 Protestant congregations with 2,566 ministers, 1,097 missionaries and 605,000 members, over 220,000 of whom were Presbyterians. These groups contributed to public life by establishing schools, universities, hospitals and relief agencies. Together with the other religious groups discussed above, the Protestants have made Taiwan a veritable hothouse of religious activity. Religion in Taiwan is a standing refutation of the old idea that religion will recede as modernity advances.

Concluding comments

The economy and society of China are now undergoing massive changes, and its cities are growing rapidly, all in a context in which economic and political concerns are dominant. In the midst of this process millions of people are trying to recover some of their traditional values, beliefs and practices. This recovery depends not only on families, but also on a variety of religious traditions, such as those discussed in this chapter. These traditions provide a social space between family and state; they have economic dimensions, particularly in the case of the community festivals, but they are not essentially economic activities, so they give people room to be and do something else. For better or worse, for many people around the world religion seems to be a basic part of being human, so in that sense religious activities in China provide people with a further opportunity to be human, rather than merely part of an economic and political system. In China as elsewhere, religion does not go away as modernization progresses, so all of this has profound implications for the future of Chinese society and its potential for eventual democratization, as well as for China's relationships with other countries.

The local community traditions discussed here remind us of some of the deeply rooted practices and attitudes that are contributing to the economic success of China today, particularly their practical emphasis on what works, their complex organization, and their involvement of people in volunteer work that benefits the whole community. Community festivals provide a model of ordinary folk reaching out beyond the local village to involve tens of thousands of people from the surrounding area, bringing with them their gods, opera troupes and merchants. Local officials may be asked for permission to hold processions and to ensure that there is enough electricity for all the planned activities, but the organization, trade, food and security are all arranged by the people themselves, and in many areas such activities have been going on for hundreds of years. Against this background, the success of Chinese entrepreneurs today should be no surprise!

Notes

1. Dru Gladney, 'Islam in China: Accommodation or Separatism?', in Daniel L. Overmyer (ed.), *Religion in China Today*, Cambridge, Cambridge University Press, 2003, p. 145.

Guide to further reading

Bays, Daniel H. (ed.), *Christianity in China from the Eighteenth Century to the Present*, Stanford, CA, Stanford University Press, 1996.

Chang, Maria Hsia, *Falun Gong: The End of Days*, New Haven and London, Yale University Press, 2004.

Chen, Kenneth K. K. S., *Buddhism in China: A Historical Survey*, Princeton, NJ, Princeton University Press, 1964.

Clart, Philip and Charles B. Jones (eds.), *Religion in Modern Taiwan: Tradition and Innovation in a Changing Society*, Honolulu, University of Hawai'i Press, 2003.

Gladney, Dru, 'Islam in China: Accommodation or Separatism?', in Daniel L. Overmyer (ed.), *Religion in China Today*, Cambridge, Cambridge University Press, 2003.

Goossaert, Vincent. 'The Quanzhen Clergy, 1750–1950', in John Lagerwey (ed.), *Religion and Chinese Society*, Hong Kong, Chinese University Press and Paris, Ecole Francaise d' Extreme-Orient, 2004, vol. 2, pp. 699–771.

Lai Chi Tim, 'Daoism in China Today', in Daniel L. Overmyer (ed.), *Religion in China Today*, Cambridge, Cambridge University Press, 2003, pp. 107–21.

Lagerwey, John, *Taoist Ritual in Chinese Society and History*, New York, Macmillan Publishing Company; London, Collier Macmillan Publishers, 1987.

Latourette, Kenneth Scott, *A History of Christian Missions in China*, Taipei, Ch'eng-wen Publishing Company, 1970. First published in London in 1929.

Lipman, Jonathan N., *Familiar Strangers: A History of Muslims in Northwest China,* Seattle and London, University of Washington Press, 1997.

Madsen, Richard, *China's Catholics: Tragedy and Hope in an Emerging Civil Society,* Berkeley, University of California Press, 1998.

Overmyer, Daniel L. (ed.), *Religion in China Today*, Cambridge, Cambridge University Press, 2003.

Rossabi, Morris, 'Islam in China', in Mircea Eliade (ed.), *The Encyclopedia of Religion*, New York, Macmillan Publishing Company, 1987, vol. 7, pp. 377–90.

Thompson, Laurence G., *Chinese Religion: An Introduction,* 5th edition, Belmont, CA, Wadsworth Publishing Company, 1996.

Tong, Hollington K., *Christianity in Taiwan: A History*, 2nd edition, Taipei, China Post, 1972.

Welch, Holmes, *The Practice of Chinese Buddhism, 1900–1950*, Cambridge, MA, Harvard University Press, 1967.

Yang, C. K., *Religion in Chinese Society: A Study of Contemporary Social Functions of Religion and Some of their Historical Factors*, Berkeley, Los Angeles and London, University of California Press, 1970.

10

Languages in a modernizing China

A recent estimate put the number of native speakers of Chinese globally at 1,110 million in 1995, with English a distant second at 372 million; more significantly, the same estimate put the number of native speakers of Chinese aged 15–24 in 2050 at 166 million, and the number of speakers of English at 65 million, after Hindi/Urdu (73.7 million) and Arabic (72.2 million).[1] These statistics derive from the fact that Chinese is the official language of the most populous country on earth – China, with a population of 1,300 million in 2006 – and is also used by overseas Chinese communities scattered extensively around the world, with a total population estimated to be in the vicinity of 30–40 million. What we know as Chinese, however, comprises dozens or hundreds of mutually unintelligible dialects. These fall into nine major groups, each of which in turn consists of a number of subgroups. The names of the major groups of Chinese dialects, their populations and geographical distribution in China are presented in Table 1.

As Table 1 shows, Mandarin is by far the largest group of Chinese dialects in terms of population and geographical distribution. All of the other dialects apart from Jin – notably Wu, Cantonese, Min and Hakka – are often referred to as Southern dialects because they are mostly spoken in areas south of the Yangtze River. The origin and path of evolvement of the Chinese dialects is currently a field of robust research in historical linguistics and dialectology, and there are still many unresolved issues and unanswered questions.[2] However, it is generally recognized that the dialectal diversity of Chinese may date back as far as the earliest written record of Chinese civilization. While the base dialect of Chinese originated in the Yellow River region in the north of China thousands of years ago, what later came to be known as Cantonese, Wu and Xiang may have

Table 1. *Distribution of the Chinese language in China*

Name	Approximate Number of Speakers (millions)	Major Areas
Mandarin	660	
Beijing Mandarin		Beijing
Northeastern Mandarin		Heilongjiang, Jilin, Liaoning
Jiao-Liao Mandarin		Shandong, Liaoning
Ji-Lu Mandarin		Hebei, Shandong
Central Plains Mandarin		Henan, Shaanxi, Shandong
Lan-Yin Mandarin		Gansu, Ningxia
Southwestern Mandarin		Sichuan, Yunnan, Guizhou
Jiang-Huai Mandarin		Jiangsu, Anhui, Hubei
Jin	45	Shanxi
Wu	70	Shanghai, Southern Jiangsu, Zhejiang
Hui	32	Southern Anhui
Xiang	25	Hunan
Gan	40	Jiangxi
Kejia (Hakka)	40	Guangdong, Fujian, Jiangxi
Yue (Cantonese)	62	Guangdong, Guangxi, Hong Kong
Min	60	Fujian, Guangdong, Hainan, Taiwan

(based on information from S. A. Wurm, *et al.* (eds.), *Language Atlas of China*, Hong Kong, Longman Group (Far East) Ltd., 1987; R. Li, 'Chinese Dialects in China', in S. A. Wurm *et al.* (eds.), 1987, A-2; and J. Hou, (ed.), *Xiandai Hanyu fangyan gailun*, Shanghai, Shanghai Jiaoyu Chubanshe, 2002)

developed in the southeast of China before the Qin Dynasty (221–206 BC), most likely as an outcome of close contact between the Chinese-speaking Han, the largest ethnic group in China, and indigenous people speaking other languages. Affinity varies between the major contemporary Chinese dialect groups, and also between sub-groups within the same group. Cantonese and Min, for instance, are more different from Mandarin than are other dialects, and Cantonese is at least as different from Mandarin as English is from German. Cantonese and Min are also the most heterogeneous of all the dialect groups, each containing a large number of mutually unintelligible dialects.

Modern Standard Chinese is given different names in the major Chinese-speaking communities. It is called *putonghua* (common speech) in Mainland China and Hong Kong, *guoyu* (national language) in Taiwan, and *huayu* (Chinese language) in Singapore. Allowing for some regional variations, all of the Chinese-speaking countries and regions, broadly speaking, look to Beijing Mandarin for norms of pronunciation, and the broader Northern Mandarin for basic vocabulary and grammar. Modern Standard Written Chinese, on the other hand, is by and large the written form of standard spoken Chinese.

The Chinese script is characterized as a logographic writing system, with each basic writing symbol – known as a character – indicating both sound and meaning. This contrasts with a phonographic writing system, in which basic writing symbols typically indicate sound only – a phoneme in the case of an alphabet, and a syllable in the case of a syllabary. Chinese is the only writing system in the world that has been in continuous use for at least 4,000 years. Chinese characters fall into four broad categories according to their graphic formation and composition at the time they first took shape – pictographic, ideographic, compound indicative, and phonetic–semantic compounding. Pictographic characters follow as much as practical the physical shape of the objects they stand for, such as 人 *ren* (person), 山 *shan* (mountain) and 口 *kou* (mouth). Ideographic characters indicate in a diagrammatic manner concepts and objects that do not usually have a physical appearance. Some examples are 一 *yi* (one), 二 *er* (two), 上 *shang* (up) and 下 *xia* (down). Compound indicative characters are formed by joining two or more pictographic or ideographic characters to depict a new concept or object based on the semantics of the components. An example is 休 *xiu* (rest), which consists of a person 人 leaning against a tree 木. Another example is 伐 *fa* (attack), composed of a person 人 and a dagger-axe 戈 *ge*, which originally meant attacking a person with a dagger-axe. Phonetic–semantic compounding characters are composed of two parts, one indicating the phonetic pronunciation and the other the semantic category. Examples are 桐 *tong* (plane tree) and 桃 *tao* (peach [tree]), with the left part 木 'tree' being the semantic indicator, and the right parts 同 and 兆 the phonetic indicator.

The Chinese terms for the Chinese language are *zhongwen* (Chinese writing) and *hanyu* (the language of Han). 'Han' in the second term derives from the name of by far the largest ethnic group in China, the Han. There are fifty-five other officially recognized ethnic groups in China, usually referred to as *shaoshu minzu* (ethnic minorities). Table 2 shows the genetic affiliation, population of speakers and geographical distribution of the major non-Chinese languages in China.

Table 2. *Distribution of non-Chinese languages in China*

Genetic Affiliation (major languages)	Major Areas
Sino-Tibetan	
Chinese	
Tibeto-Burman (Tibetan, Yi, Bai, Hani, Tujia)	Tibet, Yunnan, Sichuan
Kam-Tai (Zhuang, Dong, Boyei, Dai)	Guangxi, Yunnan, Guizhou
Miao-Yao (Miao, Mian, Bunu)	Hunan, Guangxi, Guizhou, Sichuan
Altaic	
Turkic (Uyghur, Kazak, Kirgiz)	Xinjiang
Mongolian (Mongolian, Dongxiang, Daur)	Inner Mongolia, Xinjiang, Gansu
Manchu-Tungus (Xibe, Ewenki)	Xinjiang, Heilongjiang
Austro-Asiatic (Va, Blang, Deang)	Yunnan
Austronesian (Gaoshans)	Taiwan
Indo-European (Tajik, Russian)	Xinjiang, Inner Mongolia
Status undecided (Korean, Jing)	Jilin, Heilongjiang, Liaoning, Guangxi

(based on information from Wurm *et al.* (eds.), *Language Atlas*, and M. Fu and J. Wang, 'Minority languages in China', in Wurm *et al.* (eds.), 1987, A-4)

Some ethnic languages, most notably Mongolian, Tibetan and Uyghur, have their own writing system and a time-honoured literary tradition, although many did not have a fully fledged writing system until the second half of the twentieth century.[3] A few of these ethnic minorities, such as the Hui and Manchurians, have all but abandoned their original native language and adopted Chinese as their mother tongue. Most, however, have maintained their own language and, in some cases and to varying degrees, their own writing system.

Chinese language in premodern times

Rather than being valued as a symbol of national pride and identity that was important in the formation and advancement of nationalism as was the case in most European nations, the Chinese language was perceived in mainstream intellectual and political circles from the late nineteenth century as grossly inefficient and a serious obstacle to modernization. If China was to become a modern state, it was argued, the Chinese language must undergo drastic and wide-ranging reform.[4] The following century witnessed an attempt at language reform on a scale unparalleled in human history in terms of the size of population involved and the extent of changes to the way the language was used. Tremendous efforts have been exerted to make the Chinese language more in tune with a modernizing society.

In the eyes of the intellectual and political elites of the time, as well as a considerable proportion of the general public, the Chinese language suffered from three major shortcomings at a time when China embarked on the course of modernization in the late nineteenth century. First, China, with its vast land area, large population and great dialectal diversity, did not have a national spoken standard that would be appropriate for formal purposes and for easy communication across dialects. Secondly, standard written Chinese was essentially based on Old Chinese from the time of Confucius (551?–479? BC), and was completely divorced from the contemporary spoken language. Thirdly, the traditional Chinese script was regarded as a very difficult system to learn and to use, and was considered the main reason for an illiteracy rate as high as 95 per cent in China at the turn of the twentieth century. In the remainder of this section, I will examine each of these problems more closely, and also consider initiatives and measures that were proposed and implemented toward their solution.

The Chinese dialects listed in Table 1 display great diversity, most notably in pronunciation but also to a considerable extent in vocabulary and grammar. There was in effect a lingua franca that evolved throughout Chinese history since the earliest times, based mainly on the dialects of the capitals of successive imperial dynasties, mostly in north China. As it was often used by officials, it was called *guanhua* (speech of mandarins), and it is from this that the large group of northern dialects, Mandarin, derived its name.[5] There is still debate over which regional varieties of Mandarin served as the dialectal base of the lingua franca in pre-modern times. Recent research suggests that it was Nanjing Mandarin, a variety of Jianghuai Mandarin, from the beginning of the Ming Dynasty (1368–1644), and Beijing Mandarin from the second half of the nineteenth century onward.[6] The lingua franca that was used, as far as we can tell based on the limited evidence available, was an ill-defined hybrid, with speakers in other dialectal areas incorporating any number of features from local dialects into the Mandarin they employed. As could be expected, it did not enjoy the prestige usually associated with a modern standard language, and was even despised by some scholars as only fit for people of lower status such as housemaids. Its use was also highly limited, mostly confined to oral communication between speakers of mutually unintelligible dialects. There was no attempt at codification or standardization of the lingua franca as a standard form of spoken Chinese for the general public. It was not taught at school; nor did it serve as the medium of instruction. The number of people who attained any degree of proficiency in it was minimal in areas of southern dialects. As a result, dialect diversity posed a huge linguistic barrier to effective oral communication in China.

In a country of such great dialectal diversity, the written language and the writing system in which it was recorded served as the most reliable means of communication, and, combined with other customs and values, played a bonding role for the Chinese as a nation throughout Chinese history until modern times, primarily for the literate but also for other sectors of society. Until the early twentieth century, the standard written Chinese, known as *wenyanwen* (classic literary language), was mainly based on classics in Old Chinese from the period up to the Qin (221–206 BC) and Han dynasties (206 BC–AD 220) in terms of grammatical and lexical norms. Alongside *wenyanwen*, a new style of written Chinese known as *baihuawen* (vernacular literary language) began to develop from the late Tang dynasty (618–907). This new written form was much closer to the contemporaneous vernacular in Mandarin areas in the north of China. Many popular novels such as *Shuihu zhuan* [*Heroes of the Marshes*] and *Hong lou meng* [*Dream of the Red Mansion*] and dramas were composed in *baihuawen* in the subsequent Song (960–1279), Yuan (1206–1368), Ming (1368–1644) and Qing (1616–1911) dynasties. It was also extensively used for informal purposes such as diary writing and book-keeping. For formal and official functions in education, administration and legal proceedings, however, traditional written Chinese – *wenyanwen* – was the undisputed norm. As it was increasingly divorced from spoken language after the Han dynasty, it took much more time and effort to acquire literacy in *wenyanwen* than in a writing style based on the daily vernacular.

Two features of the Chinese script made it an ideal writing system for the Chinese language for thousands of years. First, it contains a large number of homophonous characters with different graphic shapes to differentiate homophonous words and morphemes, in much the same way as we write *two*, *too* and *to* in English to differentiate words. What makes Chinese substantially different from English in this respect is that the number of homophonous expressions is much larger in Chinese. Take the syllable *ji* for example: when it is pronounced in the first, second, third and fourth tones, which are meaning-distinguishing pitch variations of syllables, it is represented by 47, 33, 12 and 45 distinct characters respectively in the *Modern Chinese Dictionary* (1998), and these encode at least as many different words and morphemes in Modern Chinese. Secondly, the graphic shape of characters does not indicate in a direct and straightforward manner their actual pronunciation in any Chinese dialect. These two features have enabled the Chinese script to be used across times, dialects and even languages, as is the case with Japanese and Korean. On the other hand, the same features are generally regarded as the underlying cause of the considerable difficulty encountered by contemporary learners and users of Chinese script.

In terms of graphic structure, around 90 per cent of Chinese characters commonly used in Modern Chinese are the so-called phonetic–semantic compounding characters. While an alphabetic writing system typically has no more than a few dozen letters as its basic units, Chinese has around 1,300 distinct basic symbols that are used as sound-indicating components of characters, and 250 that are meaning-indicating components. As almost all of the characters were first composed more than a thousand years ago, many have undergone considerable change in pronunciation and meaning, so that characters with the same sound-indicating component may now have quite different pronunciations. In addition, the semantic affinity of characters that share the same meaning-indicating component is not always as straightforward as it was when the characters were originally composed. Literacy in Chinese is measured in terms of the number of characters learned. One needs to know at least 1,800 distinct characters as the essential prerequisite to basic reading and writing skills in Modern Chinese, while a primary-school graduate is expected to have learned around 3,000 characters. With the mnemonic value of sound- and meaning-indicating components greatly reduced by historical attrition, literacy acquisition in Chinese demands much more time and effort on the part of learners, at least in the early stages, than phonographic writing systems such as English. A comparative study has found that the reading materials of Chinese schoolchildren up to Grade 4 are only around one sixth in volume of those at the comparative level in countries that use a phonographic writing system. The reason for the differential is attributed to the much greater amount of time spent on learning the Chinese script in Chinese schools before children can read and write competently in Chinese.

Language reform in twentieth-century China

Language reform in China has mainly aimed to address these three problems. Reform started in the late nineteenth century as an integral part of the national drive for modernization, and has focused on three major aspects – the establishment and promotion of a standard spoken language as the national language, reform of the traditional Chinese script through simplification and phonetization, and replacement of *wenyanwen* by a new, modernized *baihuawen* as the base of Modern Written Chinese.

Establishment of a standard national language

The concept of a standard national language for China was borrowed from Japan, which pursued modernization during the Meiji Period (1868–1912) and achieved considerable success in social and political reform, leading to the general advancement of its economic and military strength in comparison to its Asian neighbours. Inspired by Japan's success in promoting the Tokyo dialect as the national language, early Chinese advocates of a national language called for the unification of the Chinese dialects in the form of a national spoken standard, and also for the unification of speech and writing, in the early years of the twentieth century. This was later known as the National Language Movement.

The first issue was to decide which dialect should be taken as the basis for the standard national language. Despite the fanfare surrounding the proposal of a few Southern dialects as possible candidates, Beijing Mandarin was chosen. This came as little surprise, largely because the *guanhua* based on Northern Mandarin had served as a de facto lingua franca for centuries, in spite of its ill-defined nature and relatively small number of fluent speakers in non-Mandarin areas. What language reformers set out to do next was to define precisely the phonological, lexical and grammatical features of the national language, based on Beijing Mandarin, and promote it across the country. Specifically, they needed to decide which features of Beijing Mandarin should be taken as constituents of the national language, which should be left out, and which features of other dialects should be included. The consensus in the first years of the movement was that while the national language was to be based broadly on Beijing Mandarin it should also incorporate features from other dialects. In a resolution on the unification of the national language adopted by the national language planning institution in 1911, it was decided that the constituent features of the national language should be 'correct, elegant, and logical', which opened the way for heated debate over the exact meaning of these attributes as guiding principles in the codification of the national language.

The standard pronunciation of the national language was defined in terms of the pronunciation of around 6,500 characters that were in common use. Members of a special Commission for Unifying Reading Pronunciation voted in 1913 on the pronunciation of each of these characters, and the results were coded in the *Dictionary of National Pronunciation* published in 1919. This represents what was later called *lao guoyin* (Old National Pronunciation). Whereas around 90 per cent of the characters followed their pronunciation in Beijing Mandarin, *lao guoyin* also incorporated features from other Chinese dialects, features from earlier periods of Chinese, and some artificial distinctions not attested to anywhere in actual speech. All of the features that were not part of contemporary Beijing Mandarin were chosen on the grounds of allegedly being 'correct, elegant and logical' and to accommodate speakers of other dialects. The outcome was an artificial, hybrid system that was actually spoken by no one. Chao Yuan Ren, an eminent Chinese linguist, remarked half jokingly that he and another scholar were the only two people in China who spoke the national language correctly when they were commissioned to make gramophone records of the system for educational purposes.

The artificiality of Old National Pronunciation caused confusion among users and prompted calls for change. The proposal that the pronunciation of the national language be based exclusively on Beijing Mandarin gradually gained widespread support, and finally led to a considerably revised edition of the *Dictionary* being published in 1932. It contains 12,219 characters, with their pronunciation following the general convention in Beijing Mandarin. The system used in the 1932 dictionary was known as *xin guoyin* (New National Pronunciation), which represented the standard pronunciation of the national language of China. In 1956, *putonghua* replaced *guoyu* as the name of the national language of the People's Republic of China, and was defined as follows:

> *Putonghua* is the standard form of Modern Chinese with the Beijing phonological system as its norm of pronunciation, and Northern dialects as its base dialect, and looking to exemplary modern works in *baihuawen* for its grammatical norms.

There are some features of Beijing Mandarin that have not been admitted as part of *putonghua*, as contained in standard reference works such as the *Modern Chinese Dictionary*. They are relatively few in number, and usually of restricted use in Beijing Mandarin. From this perspective, *putonghua*, like other standard languages in the world, is a theoretical abstraction that is not to be equated with any actual linguistic code. On the other hand, it should also be noted that Beijing Mandarin is by far the closest of all the Chinese dialects to *putonghua* – not only in pronunciation, but also in vocabulary and grammar.

Script reform

The reform of the traditional Chinese script since the late nineteenth century has been the most arduous – and the most controversial – area of language reform in China. Generally speaking, there have been two major approaches to script reform – simplification and phonetization.

Simplification of the traditional Chinese script is achieved mainly through reducing the number of component strokes in characters, and by reducing the number of characters in common use. In the first case, a component of a character is replaced by one with fewer strokes, or a character is replaced by one of its component parts, or by another – usually homophonous – character with fewer strokes. Examples are 氣 → 气, and 臺, 颱, 檯 → 台. In the second case, one of the variant graphic forms of a character is selected as the authorized standard, and all other forms are abolished. Examples are 烟, 煙, 菸 → 烟. Simplified characters have always been popular among users throughout the history of the Chinese script, as they meet the natural inclination towards reduced effort on the part of writers. Historically, however, they have almost always been confined to informal uses and not allowed on formal occasions. Generally speaking, what language planning institutions have done in script simplification is to grant official recognition to the simplified characters that have already been in popular use in handwriting, and to replace complicated characters with their simplified counterparts in school education and in print.

A list of 324 simplified characters was promulgated by the Nationalist government in 1935 for use in schools and publications. However, it was withdrawn in the same year due to strong opposition from some government officials, which was a striking illustration of the longstanding traditional reverence for Chinese script in Chinese society and the accompanying abhorrence of any attempt to meddle with the official writing system. Script simplification resumed in the 1950s under the new government of the People's Republic of China. The first scheme of simplified characters, promulgated in 1956, comprised 515 simplified characters and 54 basic components of characters. A complete list of 2,236 simplified characters was published in 1964, comprising all of the simplified characters in the first scheme, as well as all characters that have one or more of the simplified characters as their component parts. With some other characters replaced by simpler homophonous ones, a total of 2,264 traditional characters have undergone simplification in this process. The average number of strokes in the traditional characters involved has been reduced from 15.6 to 10.3, which, in the great majority of cases, has made the characters easier for general users to both write and recognize. The simplified script has since replaced the traditional script as the official writing system in China. Singapore adopted the same simplified script as Mainland China in 1976, but Taiwan and Hong Kong have retained the traditional script. While this difference may cause some inconvenience to readers from the other areas, it would be an exaggeration to claim it has seriously hindered effective written communication between the two groups. As noted earlier, a large number of simplified characters have long been in widespread use in handwriting in Taiwan and Hong Kong, as well as in Mainland China, as part of *caoshu* (cursive style) or *xingshu* (running style), much in the same way as different fonts are used in print and handwriting in English. The choice of the official script in Taiwan stems principally from political considerations of differentiation from the Mainland, rather than the technical adequacy of the writing system.[7]

Phonetization involves the design of a new phonographic writing system for writing Chinese. The first phonetic writing in Latin script for Chinese was designed by Jesuit missionaries stationed in China in the late sixteenth century, mainly for the purpose of facilitating Chinese learning by Westerners, but this new way of writing Chinese was destined to extend its function beyond language pedagogy. With more Western missionaries working in China in the second half of the nineteenth century, it was realized that the phonetic writing used by foreigners to learn Chinese could also be used by native Chinese to write their own dialects, and its acquisition usually took only a fraction of the time needed to learn the traditional script. Dozens of schemes in Latin script were designed by Western missionaries to write all the major Chinese dialects and used to translate the Bible and other proselytizing material. The first phonetic scheme designed by a native Chinese was published in 1892 by Lu Zhuangzhang to write his native dialect of Xiamen, a Min dialect. In all, more than a thousand phonetic schemes have been proposed over the past century to write standard Chinese and its various dialectal varieties.

Schemes of phonetic writing for Chinese have been designed to serve one of two major purposes. One is to play an auxiliary or supplementary role to the Chinese script, providing learners and users of Chinese characters with a tool for sound annotation, transcription and indexing. Like the International Phonetic Alphabet, this is not meant to be used as a bona fide writing system. On the other hand, some schemes are designed to function as a fully fledged writing system that may be used as an alternative to the traditional script for those who cannot afford the time and effort to learn characters, or that may supersede the traditional script altogether for all functions and purposes.

The first scheme of phonetic writing of Chinese, *zhuyin zimu* (sound-annotating alphabet) – later renamed *zhuyin fuhao* (sound-annotating symbols) – was promulgated in 1918 by the Ministry of Education of the Republic of China for use in annotating the pronunciation of Chinese characters.[8] Instead of adopting Latin script, the basic symbols of *zhuyin zimu* were adapted from simple Chinese characters or character components, in much the same way as *kana* symbols were formed in Japanese. This played a very useful role in facilitating the learning of the standard spoken Chinese in the following decades. It was replaced by *hanyu pinyin* (Chinese phonetic writing) – or shortened as *pinyin* – in Mainland China from 1958, but has been in continuous use in Taiwan. The first scheme in Latin script, *guoyu luomazi* (national language romanization), was promulgated by the government in 1928. It superseded other schemes in Latin script, such as the Wade-Giles and Postal systems, as the standard scheme of romanization of Chinese characters to be used in transcription of Chinese names, indexing, and so on. Like *zhuyin zimu*, it has been in continuous use in Taiwan in revised versions, but has been replaced by *hanyu pinyin* on the Mainland. In 2001, the Ministry of Education of Taiwan published another phonetic scheme, *tongyong pinyin* (general phonetic writing), which was intended to replace *guoyu luomazi* as the official phonetic scheme of Chinese in Taiwan, but has not been well received by the general public.[9] In fact, there are several phonetic schemes in current use in Taiwan, including Wade-Giles, *guoyu luomazi*, *hanyu pinyin* and *tongyong pinyin*. The following are the transliterations of

'Chinese script' in Wade-Giles, *guoyu luomazi, hanyu pinyin* and *tongyong pinyin* respectively – *chung kuo wen tzu, jung guo wen tz, zhong guo wen zi,* and *jhong guo wun zih*.

The most influential scheme of phonetic writing of Chinese in Latin script is *hanyu pinyin*, which was promulgated by the Chinese government in 1958, and has since been in widespread use in China and elsewhere in the world as the standard phonetic scheme for Chinese. It was designed to represent the pronunciation of Chinese characters in *putonghua*, but has also been adapted for some southern Chinese dialects such as Cantonese. Like *zhuyin zhumu* and *guoyu luomazi*, pinyin was intended to serve an auxiliary role to the conventional writing system. Its main functions include the annotation of the pronunciation of characters to facilitate the learning of *putonghua*, transcription of Chinese names, indexing, and so on. As it is written in Latin script, pinyin was also intended to serve as the basis for the design or reform of writing systems of other ethnic languages in China. It has fulfilled all of these functions – and more – successfully in the fifty years since its publication. It has been adopted by many international organizations, including the International Standardization Organization and the United Nations, as well as by a growing number of other institutions such as universities and libraries outside China, as the standard form for the transcription of Chinese names and words. A pinyin-based input/output system is also arguably the most popular system for Chinese word processing.

Most designers of phonetic writing schemes for Chinese started with the intention of replacing the traditional Chinese writing system with their new design in due course, and this was also the case with pinyin. A close reading of the literature on script reform in the early 1950s shows that phonetization of Chinese was firmly on the agenda of the language planning institutions of the new Chinese government. There was debate over the desirability and feasibility of replacing the Chinese script with a new phonographic writing system, and on the technicalities of the various schemes designed to fulfil such a role. Dominant opinions at the beginning, including those of the government leadership, were in favour of introducing a new phonetic scheme that would be used as a fully fledged writing system for Chinese, either to replace the Chinese script as soon as practical, or as an alternative to be used alongside the traditional writing system during a long transitional period. When pinyin was finally published, however, there was no mention of its immediate or potential use as a bona fide writing system for Chinese,

to the disappointment of many enthusiastic advocates of the phonetization of Chinese.

All of the efforts and attempts to replace the Chinese script with
a phonetic writing system have failed so far, not because of lack of enthusiasm on the part of language planners, but due to several seemingly insurmountable linguistic and non-linguistic obstacles. As noted
above, there are large numbers of homophonous words and expressions
in Modern Chinese, which are graphically differentiated by different
characters, but would assume the same written form in a phonographic
system such as pinyin. Furthermore, as the only writing system that has
been in continuous use for more than 4,000 years, the Chinese script is
the written medium of a tremendous amount of literature that has been
a defining part of the Chinese civilization. The abolition of Chinese characters would in effect deny the great majority of Chinese access to their
rich literary heritage and deprive them of a good part of what has made
them Chinese. The overwhelmingly negative arguments against the
Chinese script and many other traditional Chinese values that marked
much of the twentieth century have been subjected to more critical
scrutiny recently. An increasing number of scholars are of the opinion
that quite a few of those views are lopsided, and at times too radical to
be of real benefit for the Chinese nation. With general self-confidence
gradually being restored after decades of strong economic growth, it
seems that the Chinese are re-examining their own history and cultural
heritage, including the Chinese writing system, in a more objective and
balanced way.

Reform of Modern Written Chinese

The replacement of Old Chinese-based *wenyanwen* with a new vernacu-
lar-based *baihuawen* as the standard written Chinese has been credited
largely to a group of Western-trained scholars in the so-called New Culture Movement of the late 1910s, with Hu Shi (1891–1962) their most visible and eloquent advocate. What happened in China was comparable to
similar events in Renaissance Europe, when speakers of English, French
and Italian switched from Latin to new literary written languages based
on their vernaculars. Citing European examples for the Chinese to emulate, Hu Shi summarized his proposals succinctly in terms of *guoyu
de wenxue, wenxue de guoyu* (literature in National Language and a literary National Language), which laid down the basic principles for the
development of a new written Chinese based on Modern Chinese, and

the development of a national language in a refined literary style. The proposal won widespread support across Chinese society, and within the relatively short period of a decade or two *wenyanwen* was replaced by a new written style in *baihuawen* as the standard written Chinese for the great majority of uses and functions.[10] In present-day China *wenyanwen* as a written style is confined to special circumstances, and texts wholly in *wenyanwen* are rarely composed by contemporary writers.

It would be wrong, however, to assume that *wenyanwen* has totally disappeared from everyday life in China. Old Chinese is still being taught as an important language subject in schools, partly because it is the language of literary heritage, and partly because of the nature of Modern Written Chinese. While based broadly on Beijing Mandarin, Modern Written Chinese has also incorporated a large number of features from other Chinese dialects, foreign languages, and in particular Old Chinese. Many words and expressions in Old Chinese are still in active use, and constitute an indispensable part of the repertoire of Modern Written Chinese because of their stylistic effect of terseness and formality and their special cultural connotations.[11]

Language use in present-day Chinese society

The first Chinese law on language and script, the People's Republic of China Common Language and Script Law, was enacted by the National People's Congress of China in 2000, and took effect from January 2001. The law outlines the goals and objectives of language planning in China, and also specifies measures to be taken in implementing the law. What the terms 'common language and script' refer to here are *putonghua* and the simplified script, the use of which is the main focus of management and monitoring by official language planning institutions affiliated with the various government departments. It is also stressed in the opening section of the law that, as a fundamental principle, the use of the common language and script in China should help to safeguard state sovereignty and national dignity, contribute to national unity and ethnic solidarity, and facilitate the material, cultural and moral progress of the socialist society. While providing a general framework for the management of language-related issues in various sectors of the community, the 2000 law is also an encapsulation of the guiding principles, major targets and achievements of language policy and language planning in China since the late 1950s.

The PRC government has paid much more attention to language policy and language planning, and placed it under tighter government control, than did pre-1949 regimes. An authoritative language planning institution at the national level, the Chinese Script Reform Commission – renamed the State Language and Script Commission in 1985 – was established in 1954, and given responsibility for all issues relating to language reform and use in the country. The National Conference on Script Reform convened the following year marked the beginning of an era in which language reform and management were fully integrated into the agenda for the modernization of the nation. Script simplification, design of *hanyu pinyin* and promotion of *putonghua* were identified at the conference as the three major tasks for language planning in China. Apart from the tumultuous years of the Cultural Revolution (1966–76), great efforts have been made to achieve the goals set for each of the three tasks. With the backing of the strong political will and efficient administrative apparatus characteristic of an all-powerful government, considerable success has been achieved since the late 1950s.

Putonghua is now the national standard in all television and radio broadcasting services, and in film and other mass-media productions in China. Broadcasting in other major Chinese dialects such as Wu, Min and Cantonese is also available in dialect areas to accommodate people in the older generation, but is normally restricted to several hours a day and local news and weather forecasts. *Putonghua* is stipulated as the standard medium of instruction in school, and it is mandatory for all teachers to pass a proficiency test as part of their qualifications. Compliance, however, varies between regions. As would be expected, school teachers in major cities are much more likely to be proficient in *putonghua* than those in rural and mountainous areas. This difference in terms of the quality of school teachers, combined with a difference in school attendance rates, has had a major impact on the rate of *putonghua* acquisition. The latest survey, in 2004, established that overall 53.05 per cent of the population in China speaks *putonghua* with reasonable fluency, with the percentage considerably higher in cities and townships than in the countryside (66.03 per cent compared to 45.06 per cent). In most non-Beijing Mandarin areas, *putonghua* has become what is known in sociolinguistics as a High Language, fit for use for formal purposes in business, education and public administration, whereas the local dialect is a Low Language, customarily used on informal occasions among family and friends. In some dialect areas, particularly the Wu and Min areas, dialect attrition is becoming a concern. It has been reported that an increasing number of youngsters are less fluent in their local dialect than in *putonghua*, with some losing their dialectal skills altogether. Teenagers in Shanghai tend to use *putonghua* both in and outside the home. A recent study of language use by 6 to 14 years olds in Jinhua, a large Wu-speaking city in Zhejiang province, found that while all speak *putonghua*, half could no longer speak their local dialect. This has prompted calls for action, with suggestions that a certain number of hours should be set aside at school to teach subject matter in the local dialect as part of measures to preserve the local dialect and culture.

Bilingualism in Chinese and the predominant local ethnic language(s) is the goal of language policy in areas with a sizeable proportion of ethnic minorities such as Inner Mongolia, Xinjiang and Tibet. It has been legislated at the state, provincial and lower levels since the 1950s that ethnic minorities have the right to learn and use their own languages and scripts for various purposes. At the same time, they are encouraged to learn Chinese, while Han people living in these areas are urged to learn the local ethnic languages. Bilingualism is fairly common in Inner Mongolia, Qinghai and Guangxi, where ethnic minorities have intermingled with the Han for centuries. On the other hand, in Tibet and Xinjiang, around 70 per cent of non-Han local residents, mostly farmers and herdsmen, are unable to communicate in *putonghua*. This is because the Tibetans and many ethnic minorities in Xinjiang have a robust tradition of education in their own languages and scripts, and did not come into close contact with the Han until relatively recently. However, the situation is changing. Ethnic minorities in these areas, especially people of the younger generation, are motivated by social mobility and financial advantage to acquire high proficiency in Chinese. It has been reported that the demand for bilingual education in Chinese and ethnic minority languages far outstrips the supply provided by the public education system, and that parents in ethnic minorities use private funding to set up more schools for bilingual education for their children.[12] It is safe to assume that the accelerating economic development in the provinces with sizeable populations of ethnic minorities will be accompanied by a significant increase in the number of bilingual speakers of *putonghua* and local ethnic languages. At the same time, it should also be noted that there has been a steady decline in the number of speakers of certain ethnic languages, some of which are on the verge of extinction. One such example is Tujia, a Tibetan-Burmese language spoken mainly in Sichuan, Hunan and Hubei provinces in China. Among the Tujia population of around 8 million, fewer than 3 per cent still speak the Tujia language, with the remainder having switched to Chinese as their first language.

The simplified script has been firmly established as the official standard in China, and has also been increasingly recognized around the world as the most popular, if not the sole standard, script of Chinese. There are occasionally calls for reverting to the traditional complicated script, on the grounds of facilitating written communication with Taiwan and Hong Kong and better access to historical literature. The PRC Common Language and Script Law states that the complicated script may be used, but only for highly restricted functions and purposes such as handwritten shop signs and artistic works. It is very unlikely, however, that the government will revoke the simplification reform and revert to the older script. With the last generation of children who learned the complicated script in primary school now almost sixty years old, the great majority of the Chinese population has grown up in the new writing system that has been in place since the late 1950s. Generally speaking, there is little nostalgia for the complicated Chinese characters in the present-day Chinese community; nor is there any enthusiasm for a new fully fledged phonographic writing system for Chinese, except perhaps among a tiny number of calligraphers, academics and professional language planners. So firmly entrenched has the current writing system become in China that, in all likelihood, it will remain relatively stable for the foreseeable future.

Conclusion

The development of an efficient, supra-local means of oral and written communication for all regions and areas of the country and mass literacy for the population are integral to the multi-faceted process of national modernization. In a developing and modernizing society such as China has been since the late nineteenth century, when people leave the rural villages to which the elder generations had been confined for hundreds of years, they tend to find dialectical diversity a serious impediment to communication with people from other parts of the country, and feel an urgent need for an overarching standard in which they can communicate with others with ease and efficiency. Mass literacy, on the other hand, is indispensable to any country aspiring to the ranks of industrialized modern nations. Broadly speaking, all the efforts of language reform and language planning in China over the past century or so have aimed at these two major objectives – a national spoken and written standard to facilitate communication, and an improved writing system to facilitate mass literacy.

The current situation in relation to language form and language use in China, as described in this chapter, is both the outcome of spontaneous evolution over hundreds or even thousands of years, and, more significantly, the effect of meticulous design and active management as part of the unremitting endeavour for national modernization since the late nineteenth century. A de facto lingua franca across dialectal barriers evolved largely on the basis of the dialect of the capital cities of successive imperial dynasties in Mandarin areas before modern times. Through the process of codification and standardization, it developed into a national standard language that has been effectively promoted and extensively used in China since the first half of the twentieth century. Similarly, a vernacular style of writing, *baihuawen*, which was confined to casual uses before the twentieth century, has replaced the formal written language of *wenyanwen* as the basis of Standard Modern Written Chinese as a result of the New Culture Movement of the late 1910s. The current Chinese writing system is likewise a hybrid of tradition, reform and innovation. Broadly speaking, simplification of the traditional Chinese script is nothing more than official recognition and standardization of the simplified forms of characters that had been in widespread use in handwriting over hundreds of years. Phonetization of Chinese, on the other hand, was initiated by Western Jesuits in China in the late sixteenth century and has greatly facilitated the acquisition and use of Chinese characters in China and elsewhere, although it has not achieved the objective entertained by some language reformers of providing a fully fledged alternative writing system for the language.

Notes

1. Graddol, David, 'The Future of Language', *Science* 303, 2004, 1329–31.
2. See Norman, Jerry, *Chinese*, Cambridge University Press, 1988; and Hou, Jingyi (ed.), *Xiandai Hanyu fangyan gailun*, [Introduction to Modern Chinese dialects], Shanghai, Shanghai Jiaoyu Chubanshe, 2002.
3. Zhou, Minglang, *Multilingualism in China: The Politics of Writing Reforms for Minority Languages 1949–2002*, Berlin and New York, Mouton de Gruyter, 2003.
4. See Chen, Ping, 'China', in Andrew Simpson (ed.), *Language and National Identity in Asia*, Oxford, Oxford University Press, 2007, Chapter 7 for an in-depth account.

5. *Guan* in *guanhua* is also interpretable here as 'general public', so *guanhua* can also mean 'speech of the general public'.

6. Chen, Ping, *Modern Chinese: History and Sociolinguistics*, Cambridge, Cambridge University Press, 1999.

7. See Chen, Ping, 'Policy on the Selection and Implementation of a Standard Language as a Source of Conflict in Taiwan', in Nanette Gottlieb and Ping Chen (eds.), *Language Planning and Language Policy: East Asian Perspectives*, London, Curzon, 2001, pp. 95–110.

8. See Chen, *Modern Chinese*, for a detailed account of *zhuyin zimu* and the other phonetic schemes discussed below.

9. This is yet another example that highlights the major consideration on the part of the official language planning institution in Taiwan, which is to differentiate Taiwan from Mainland China as much as possible. Whether ideology will prevail over pragmatism with the general public on language and script issues is another matter.

10. It should be pointed out that as the Modern Standard Written Chinese is based on northern Mandarin, its acquisition is relatively easier for Mandarin speakers than for speakers of southern dialects. Historically, as well as in contemporary China, writing in southern dialects has been rare, despite the large numbers of speakers of these dialects. For details, see Chen, *Modern Chinese*, Chapter 7.

11. See Hodge, Bob and Kam Louie, *The Politics of Chinese Language and Culture: The Art of Reading Dragons*, London and New York, Routledge, 1998 for an account of social meanings associated with use of expressions in Old Chinese and dialects.

12. Chen, 'China', Chapter 7.

Guide to further reading

Chen, Ping, *Modern Chinese: History and Sociolinguistics*, Cambridge, Cambridge University Press, 1999.

    'Policy on the Selection and Implementation of a Standard Language as a Source of Conflict in Taiwan', in Nanette Gottlieb and Ping Chen (eds.), *Language Planning and Language Policy: East Asian Perspectives*, London, Curzon, 2001, pp. 95–110.

    'China', in Andrew Simpson (ed.), *Language and National Identity in Asia*, Oxford, Oxford University Press, 2007, Chapter 7, 139–67.

Fu, Maoji and Jun Wang, 'Minority Languages in China', in S. A. Wurm *et al.* (eds.), 1987, A-4.

Graddol, David. 'The Future of Language', *Science* 303, 2004, 1329–31.

Hodge, Bob and Kam Louie, *The Politics of Chinese Language and Culture: The Art of Reading Dragons*, London and New York, Routledge, 1998.

Li, Rong. 'Chinese Dialects in China', in S. A. Wurm *et al.* (eds.), 1987, A-2.

Norman, Jerry, *Chinese*, Cambridge, Cambridge University Press, 1988.

Wurm, Steven A., B. T'sou, D. Bradley *et al.* (eds.), *Language Atlas of China*, Hong Kong, Longman Group (Far East) Ltd., 1987.

Zhou, Minglang, *Multilingualism in China: The Politics of Writing Reforms for Minority Languages 1949–2002*, Berlin and New York, Mouton de Gruyter, 2003.

11

The revolutionary tradition in modern Chinese literature

This *Companion* provides the opportunity to devote equal attention to modern China's revolutionary and involutionary traditions. Involutionary (inward-looking) literary practices such as modernism, popular fiction and pastoral nativism are often defined in opposition to a simplistic, monolithic conception of revolutionary literature. Here we have a chance to instead explore the complexities of the revolutionary tradition in Chinese literary history. However inflated the place of revolutionary literature may be in standard Mainland literary histories, and no matter how self-important leftist writers and critics may have been, the social realist and critical realist approaches in fiction, drama and film, and the rhetoric of revolutionary romantic fervour in poetry and music had a central shaping influence on the development of modern Chinese literature.

Change is the defining feature/theme of all of the significant types of literary creativity in modern China. The wide spectrum of modern literary impulses in China, including the vernacularization of writing, anti-traditionalism in ideology, the depiction of modes of consciousness or lifestyles never written about before, the investigation of social problems in the field (sometimes involving the author's participation), the desire to transform the consciousness of the reader, to devote literary creativity to fulfilling political aims, or to completely reject political aims – all this grand variety of literary difference boils down to the impetus to create something new, and is the heart of modernity in Chinese literature.

It began when scholars near the end of the Qing dynasty perceived that the challenge of imperialism was not merely a test of economic and military might, but a traumatic encounter with an entirely different philosophy of society and history than China had faced before. In the later decades of the nineteenth century, the Chinese could observe their neighbour Japan, felt by many as an inferior tributary state, in an aggressive and successful process of modernization after the accession of the Meiji emperor in 1868. Many Chinese intellectuals and officials felt that to rise to the challenge of the Japanese and stave off the threat of Western imperialism, the Chinese would need to appropriate not only the military and industrial technology of Western powers, but the modes of thought that were their basis: science, competition, liberalism.

Chinese have traditionally looked to scholars for social, political and moral guidance. Their hard-won possession of literacy gave them unique access to the legacy of the ancients as well as to foreign cultures in the form of translated texts. Thus they looked to literature and writers for their role in Japan's success, and surmised that Japan's success in spiritual modernization was due in part to the development of a new literary form, the political novel. However inaccurate this perception may have been, the emergence of the modern novel in Japan was certainly a momentous phenomenon. Because the sociopolitical role of the scholar intellectual in China was familiar, as millennia of poetry, essays, political philosophy and historiography attest, the Chinese of the late nineteenth century were prone to view the vernacular, historically and socially conscious novels that accompanied Japan's modernization as important engines of that process. The political novel, in the eyes of reformers such as Liang Qichao, Yan Fu and Xia Zengyou, looked to newspapers, the public sphere and constitutional monarchy as the answers or at least the methods for achieving the goals of wealth, power and democracy for modern China.[1]

There are at least two important assumptions at work at the birth of modern Chinese literature: (1) scholars, intellectuals and the literati, who had traditionally been the leaders of society, would continue to play this role by guiding the development of new literature; and (2) the use of literature was more than ever to act directly as an engine of social change.

Fiction would be a particularly important form for its mimetic and affective capacities, because it could document or model important changes happening in China and elsewhere in the world. The aesthetics of realism and contemporaneity attributed to the realistic novel could have the effect of helping readers relate the world of the novel more closely to the world of their own social lives, thus ensuring the political novel's influence on the reader's thinking. This was the vision, in any case, the promise that modern literature was supposed to hold in

China for national salvation and even radical social change. These two elements: the centrality of the intellectual to social change and the function of literature as an agent of that change, created a foundation for the emergence of revolutionary literature in China.

The idea of a 'revolutionary tradition' may seem oxymoronic, but literature enlisted by political activists or Communist Party officials in the process of social change, political indoctrination, or the radicalization of readers' consciousness develops conventions of plot, rhetoric and character that are distinctive from literature written for other purposes or informed by other visions of literature and its relationship to history and social life. In fact, in the Chinese case, revolutionary literature was often prone to 'conventionality', except when certain authors were able to stretch or depart from existing practices.

While it developed within a larger literary context from the early years of the twentieth century to the assumption of national power by the Chinese Communist Party, Chinese revolutionary literature was able to maintain a dynamic vitality as it struggled for readers' attention with popular novels and a growing and diversifying involutionary tradition of literature, including works with traditionalist and modernist elements. Many literary histories of modern China make revolutionary literature the protagonist of that history, gradually gaining dominance of the literary scene, and finally achieving victory over reactionary and feudal forces in 1949 with the Chinese Communist Party's accession to power. Most recent scholarship, however, demonstrates that, in the Republican period, while always very influential due to the prominence of authors such as Lu Xun, Ba Jin and Ding Ling, revolutionary literature was one position in a complex and diverse literary field, and it often struggled for readership with other forms that were more popular or thought to be artistically superior, or that for other reasons better satisfied readers' expectations for literary modernity. Nevertheless, the revolutionary literary tradition is one of China's most distinctive contributions to world literature, and produced most of the best-known works in the modern Chinese literary canon.

Chinese revolutionary literature is often described in terms of its perspective as deriving from a class-based worldview, in terms of its themes as anti-capitalist, antifeudal and anti-imperialist, and in terms of style as naturalist or realist (in the case of fiction, drama and film). What is missing from this conventional configuration is the essential feature of revolutionary literature: its operative quality. A truly revolutionary literature is a literature that has social effects, affecting readers' consciousness, prompting controversy and debate, and promoting social engagement and activism. If the Chinese Communist Party is distinctive for the importance it places on artistic and literary expression (and, as an ironic result, has been particularly repressive of artists and writers), it is precisely because its leadership and cultural authorities understand the potential revolutionary social effects of literature.

Revolutionary literature is more than just literature that has a social effect; a novel such as Lao She's *Luotuo xiangzi* [Rickshaw, 1937], in its vivid articulation of the plight of the poor on the streets of Beijing, was widely read and helped spread sympathy for the downtrodden, but it is not quite revolutionary in that it does not cast the light of revolutionary consciousness on contemporary social experience. By contrast, Ba Jin's novel *Jia* [Family, 1931] provides the reader with an array of different ideological positions, some of which – like that of the youngest son Juehui – are revolutionary, and a discernible tendency on the part of the author in favour of the revolutionary stance.

Revolutionary consciousness in Chinese literary practice is the conscious awareness of contradictions among classes in one's own society and one's own position within that class structure, particularly the awareness of alienation and victimhood (often mediated across classes through a structure of empathy), and the conviction that such alienation and victimhood demand immediate and decisive action.[2] The construction and articulation of such a revolutionary worldview and its transmission to readers is the definitive operative feature of revolutionary literature and art. Especially in the wake of the proletarian literary movement of 1930, revolutionary literature evolved into a coordinated writing process in which writers not only learn techniques and conventions, but articulate and thus acquire and convey revolutionary consciousness, developing a peculiarly revolutionary understanding of what literature is and how it fits into social practice.[3] This understanding ensures that literature has these social and political operative factors, and that it gestures beyond the text both through its references to the world and through its agency in affecting, influencing and even constructing the consciousness of the reader. Through these connections, the work of revolutionary literature is meant to have a socially transformative effect. This is accomplished in several different ways: transforming the consciousness of readers; stimulating constructive debates on contemporary social issues; mobilizing collective radical social actions such as strikes and political demonstrations; and providing educational and organizational assistance to labourers, peasants and soldiers. Such literature accomplishes these things in part by documenting the effects of imperialism, traditional 'feudalism' and class conflicts, and also by constructing revolutionary personalities either as characters or through the first person point of view (as in poetry).

Revolutionary literature must articulate a relationship between itself (meaning the political position of the author, his or her political and social aims, or the world of the revolutionary literary work as a reflection of such positionality) and local and national political authority. How this plays out depends on whether the political authority is perceived as (or is required to be perceived as) revolutionary by the author. If not, then the literary work needs to critique that political authority and pave the way for its subversion by the victims of its oppression. But when the political authority asserts itself to be revolutionary, as in the case of wartime border areas such as Yan'an and the People's Republic of China, the revolutionary path for literature is trickier. This is because in order for a literature to be revolutionary in a socialist regime it must also be subordinated to the revolutionary political authority. That is, officially speaking, social change must not involve the subversion of the revolutionary authority, but in principle it cannot advocate the maintenance of the status quo either. It might solve this problem by extolling socialism and the Party while paying lip service to revolutionary change, but that would no longer be truly revolutionary. On the other hand, more truly revolutionary literature under socialism might pay lip service to the Party's authority while advocating change and transforming consciousness through critique. This is dangerous and often costly to the author, but may be the only way to be a revolutionary writer under socialism, because it is the only way that preserves the operative quality of literature.

In the remainder of this chapter, to move beyond the complementary tendencies to simplify revolutionary as one homogeneous block or to look at each writer as an idiosyncratic individual, I will compare different types of revolutionary writing, each exemplified by representative authors, both in the context of a pluralistic society and under the socialist regime. Each type is defined by an attitude about the relationship of literary practice to revolution and a certain revolutionary aesthetic and form in practice. I will classify each type as though it were a kind of writer, keeping in mind that one writer may write different types of revolutionary literature, or may not always write revolutionary literature.

Radical, independent social critic

Lu Xun (1881–1936) represents a stance on the author's part of unprecedented, radical social and cultural critique, as well as the deft manipulation of form and literary conventions to articulate a revolutionary consciousness, particularly through his unique creation of unreliable fictional narrators and his attendant cultivation of alienation on the reader's part in his short stories. To put it in the terms outlined above, the operative quality of Lu Xun's fiction lay in the awkward, alienated position in which the reader is left, when made to identify with dubious, unreliable narrators. Not all of Lu Xun's short stories are revolutionary, and even those that clearly are, such as 'Zhu fu' [New Year's Sacrifice, 1924] and 'Yao' [Medicine, 1919], contain clues to the author's ambivalence about their revolutionary significance. In the end, however, by questioning even revolution so radically, Lu Xun comes across as a consummately revolutionary writer. Any discussion of Lu Xun as a revolutionary writer should not neglect a major portion of his literary output, the *zawen* or miscellaneous essay (Lu Xun's works have caused the term to mean 'satirical essay'). Whether Lu Xun turned from short fiction to the *zawen* for revolutionary reasons, there is no question that it represents a form of literary struggle against conservative forces.[4] He published these works prominently in newspapers and magazines, thus returning to the portals of the public sphere opened by Liang Qichao. Lu Xun's *zawen*, though not always such carefully wrought works of art as his short stories and prose poems, do exhibit some of the same imagery conventions and rhetoric as revolutionary literature. Thus they belong just as much to this tradition as does his fiction.

The dedication to an individual radical aesthetic was promoted after Lu Xun's death by the Marxist critic and editor Hu Feng (1903–85), who helped develop a theory of national forms during the war against Japan (1937–45), and as editor of *Qiyue* (July) during the war nurtured a cohort of revolutionary novelists and essayists such as Lu Ling, Ah Long and Cao Bai, with confident personal vision.[5]

Realist/naturalist literary craftsman

Another kind of revolutionary writer subordinates his independent viewpoint to the realistic depiction of society and characters and the contradictions within and among them. For such writers, literature is art and not a tool, and the operative quality of fiction for them lies in the impression it gives of a close connection with the contemporary world and the author's careful attention to character psychology. Many members of the *Wenxue yanjiu hui* (Literary Association, est. 1921), publishing their work in the *Xiaoshuo yuebao* [*Short Story Monthly*], belong to this category, but not all Literary Association writers and works are revolutionary.[6] For these writers, the aesthetics of the nineteenth-century European realistic novel and drama are the conduit to literature's social efficacy: the realistic depiction of contemporary life would to them naturally focus on *wenti* (problems or issues) and a structure of resonance is established between the implied author and the reader, whereby the reader is led to see the problem in the same light, engendering a desire to do something about it. In the early 1920s, this generally took the form of short stories about women and men trying to escape from arranged marriages, suicides related to conflicts with this and other traditional social norms, and the encounters of upper-class characters with peasants or workers, whose suffering overwhelmed them. If one were to rigidly define revolutionary literature as a literature that explicitly provides the answer to social problems in the form of collective action and social revolution, these stories would not be revolutionary. But they are operative in the sense that they recast a commonly experienced situation as a 'problem' and thus create disequilibrium in the reader, making him or her wish to intervene in some way and resolve the problem. Thus the literature's operative quality connects the text and the reader to social practice.

As this Literary Association cohort became more mature, novelists gradually created longer works throughout the 1920s, and representative authors such as Ye Shengtao (1894–1988) and Mao Dun (1896–1981) added aesthetic depth to problem fiction. The effect of lengthening the fictional text, as can be observed in Mao Dun's 1928 novellas, 'Huanmie' [Disillusion], 'Zhuiqiu' [Pursuit] and 'Dongyao' [Vacillation] and Ye Shengtao's *Ni Huanzhi* [*Schoolmaster Ni Huanzhi*, 1928] is to depart from the raw directness and authorial emotional involvement of the earlier problem stories to create more sophisticated fictional worlds with greater psychological complexity, more distance between the author and the world of the text, the use of symbolic and lyrical structures as well as realist aesthetics, and a broader social and historical purview. Yet rarely do these aesthetic strategies turn the author or reader away from society; on the contrary, they endeavour to deepen the literary work's engagement with the pressing issues of the day and with the subjectivity of the reader. This is how these writers realized the motto associated with them, *wei rensheng er yishu* ('art for life's sake').

Proletarian/organizational

The literary scene became more politically galvanized after the Nationalist Party's purge of Communist Party members in January 1927, when the Northern Expedition reached Shanghai. Shortly after this, the literary and political scene in Beiping (Beijing) became inhospitable to socially engaged literature, and many progressive writers fled south. Over the next two years, what had been a fragmented and divisive left-wing literary scene, including elements of the banned *Taiyang she* (Sun Society) and *Chuangzao she* (Creation Society) and followers of Lu Xun came together to form an umbrella organization with no explicit ties to the Chinese Communist Party called the *Zhongguo zuoyi zuojia lianmeng* (League of Left-wing Writers) in 1930.[7] One advantage of the timing of the Left-wing League's formation was that it coincided with the high tide of the international proletarian literary movement. Originating in the Soviet Union but spreading quickly through metropolitan centres in Weimar Germany, France, the USA and Japan among many others, the significance of the proletarian movement was its internationalism. Literary organizations in each country used translation projects, the promotion of Esperanto, proletarian literacy and literary campaigns, and the promotion of new genres such as reportage to engage the working classes in the production of revolutionary culture with the ultimate goal of universal revolution and the liberation of the working classes from oppression.

The preceding several years on the Chinese literary scene had created unusually fertile soil for the promotion of the proletarian literary movement, and this became the primary task of the League of Left-wing Writers. Because of the gap between ideals and realities, the limited abilities of the largely upper-class writers and critics who made up the Left-wing League membership, and political repression under the Nationalist government, the International Settlement government in Shanghai, and the powerful connections of large corporate factory owners (domestic and foreign), little was achieved specifically in the area of worker literature and art in actual practice. But the campaigns, committees and activities organized by the Left-wing League led to the emergence of a particular style of urban working-class literature practised by certain representative authors such as Ding Ling (after 1929), Hu Yepin and Xia Yan, a playwright whose narrative of a day in the life of a teenage country girl indentured to work in a textile factory, 'Baoshen gong' [Indentured Worker, 1936], became the most famous piece of Chinese reportage literature.

In terms of social effect, or the operational quality of the literature, Chinese proletarian literature works in much the same way as literature from the Literary Association, by bringing its readers face to face with social issues, particularly lower-class suffering, and providing at least the elements of a theoretical explanation for that suffering and the means of stopping it. What is different is that the setting has entered into the life-world of the lower class; even authors are of a privileged background, but they are (hopefully) proletarianized through the process of research and composition. The proletarian literary movement operated as a means of training revolutionary writers, especially by requiring them to experience the everyday life (especially in the workplace) of workers, peasants and soldiers, and by requiring them to work collectively, devaluing individual vision in the creative process. Thus another important difference is the intended transformation of the writer through the experience of writing. The transformation of Ding Ling's fiction from writing about the ennui and frustration of sophisticated, privileged urban women and men in 1928–9 ('Shafei nüshi de riji' [Diary of Miss Sophia, 1928], 'Yige nüren he yige nanren' [A Woman and a Man, 1928] to writing the anatomy of a peasant uprising in the aftermath of a flood in her 1931 story 'Shui' [Water], is representative of the aims of the proletarian type of revolutionary literature.

Voices of the people

The active period of the League of Left-wing Writers coincided with the elevation of violent tensions with Japan, flaring up in the Shanghai Incident of 1932 and coming to a head with the outbreak of war in July of 1937, when the Japanese invaded Beijing. Thus an unexpected benefit of proletarian literary practice in China was its applicability to the battlefield in and outside the city.[8] That is, the creative method of organizing groups of writers to go 'on location', interviewing, researching, even living and working with the subjects of their work, lent itself well to the conditions of war and the reading interests of a broader public than had been interested in proletarian literature *per se*. Reportage, fiction and dramatic texts written using this method were also characterized by confrontational aesthetics of alienation, and graphic violence, designed to shock and enrage the reader.[9]

However, as the Communist Party line shifted in the mid-1930s from an urban-centred, proletarian revolutionary strategy (influenced by the cosmopolitan international Communist movement) to a rural strategy of peasant mobilization under the leadership of Mao Zedong, literary policies also began to change. In the face of a de facto civil war just as China was bracing for Japanese attack, it was particularly important to the Communist Party to enlarge the audience that was receiving political indoctrination through cultural products. In debates on cultural policy that extended into the war years, a consensus was reached even among fellow travellers that previous revolutionary literatures in China were too Europeanized, cosmopolitan and elitist, and that to reach the broader Chinese masses it would be necessary to adopt and adapt *minzu xingshi* (national forms) such as traditional local theatre, drum singing and storytelling. One of the earliest examples of this shift in policy was the organization of travelling theatre troupes who moved through the countryside, experimenting with forms sometimes derived from traditional performing arts to convey modern messages of national salvation and resistance to imperialism.[10] At first, the performers and writers of such material were all urban intellectuals, often students who had come long distances to battle areas or Communist bases to contribute to the war effort. Prominent writers engaged in the war effort through the activities of the All China Resistance Association of Writers and Artists (est. April 1938) in Wuhan and Chongqing included Lao She, Wu Zuxiang and Tian Han. In the case of the famous novelist Lao She, who was the nominal leader of the Association, these debates caused him to shift his literary attention to popular performing arts and drama, represented by his increased attention to propaganda plays such as *Canwu* [*Lingering Fog*, 1939], *Mianzi wenti* [*The Problem of Face*, 1941] and *Guojia zhi shang* [*The Country Above All*, 1943].

But in time, in the process of penetrating the masses in the countryside, especially in the relatively stable context of the Communist base areas such as Yan'an, voices would emerge even from among the peasantry, the most successful of whom is Zhao Shuli (1906–70). Zhao emerged on the literary scene shortly after the appearance of Mao Zedong's 1942 'Talks at the Yan'an Forum on Literature and Art', which established and guided the literary policy of the Chinese Communist Party for the following three decades.[11] Mao's 'Talks' emphasized that literature in the service of revolution should no longer reflect urban experience unfamiliar to peasants, that it should not cultivate a personal, individual vision but reflect the variety and vitality of the peasant and soldier masses, and that in all cases of contradiction between the author's vision and Communist Party policy, authors would have to defer to the authority of the Party: literature for life's sake had become literature in the service of politics, in the service of the people.

While for many prominent writers such as Ding Ling and Mao Dun this created obstacles and limitations, it also paved the way for a new kind of writer. Although he was well enough educated to already be involved in publishing and journalism, Zhao Shuli's peasant background and keen interest in local storytelling and performing arts (national forms) inspired him on encountering Mao's 'Talks' to cultivate a kind of fiction that featured colourful local characters and language based on this background, with a humorous tone and protagonists who were skilful at talking. He produced works such as 'Xiao Erhei jiehun' [The Marriage of Xiao Erhei, 1943], 'Li Youcai banhua' [The Rhymes of Li Youcai, 1943], and 'Fugui' [Lucky, 1945], which alternately reflected the simple moral goodness of the peasantry (an important requirement of the new literary policy) and the inhumanity of the old society, contrasted in broad strokes with the healthy optimism of life under Communist rule. While this adoption of national forms can be said to constitute a further immersion in the life-world of the lower class, this new mode is actually less socially effectual than those discussed above, and moves away from our definition of revolutionary literature.

Party loyalist

This returns us to the difficulty of creating a revolutionary literature in the service of the Communist Party. Absent the revolutionary mandate to critique and reject political authority, orthodox socialist literature seeks its operative quality in the modelling of heroes, in channelling enthusiasm into politically correct structures of feeling – in short, in the creation of a convincing new socialist person from the inside out. This posture was not common before the Yan'an period (i.e. before 1934), but under Communist rule before and after 1949 there was a need to envision a positive working-class existence rather than shocking indictments of class exploitation. While there had been some writings of this type since the 1920s, it was not until the Yan'an period that extolling contemporary life became one of the principal tasks of literature. Liu Baiyu was one of the most devoted to this task. His *Yan'an shenghuo* [*Life in Yan'an*, 1946] is a typical example of this kind of positive socialist literature. Like many of Zhao Shuli's stories, *Life in Yan'an* revolves around narratives (presented here in chapter categories in vignette form) contrasting an individual's past in the old society with his successes under socialism.[12]

Critic of socialist society

As revolutionary literature continued to develop an orthodox aesthetic in the PRC, the declining tension between published literature and political authority ensured a decrease in the literature's operative quality, despite its supposed revolutionary character. At the same time, other forms of writing took on operative qualities, shifting the operative role away from literature, perhaps because of the close official scrutiny and sponsorship of literature. Having been educated in revolutionary thought since the 1930s, however, enthusiastic young people would still be looking for objects of criticism and struggle, armed with the faith instilled in them by Marxist and especially Maoist rhetoric learned in school, that society could improve without limit through struggle and criticism. It is necessary here to tease out the features of orthodox revolutionary literature, because it inherits some of the characteristics of revolutionary literature prior to Communist leadership and loses others. The characteristics that are preserved, due to their endorsement by political authority, became those most explicitly associated with the term 'revolutionary', while those lost, principally the socially operative quality, shifted to non- or less-artistic forms such as big character posters, newspaper editorials and reportage literature.

After Mao's 1942 'Talks', it was established Communist Party policy that literature would serve politics, which meant that it not only had to refrain entirely from social criticism when writing about contemporary life, but that it would also have to assist in the promotion of government policies and politically correct values and attitudes. Moreover, the 'Talks' also included the expectation that literature reflect the life-world of workers, peasants and soldiers, thus making intellectuals, clerks and managers – those collectively referred to as the petit bourgeoisie and the bourgeoisie in Party jargon – inappropriate subjects for literature. Thus, the characteristics of publishable literature under these circumstances were the almost exclusive use of rural or factory settings (or battlefields in the case of the civil war and the Korean War), collectivism on the part of the authors and characters (at least the protagonist and the positive characters), clarity of utterance and themes, often involving the simplification of complex situations, and a deliberate modelling or demonstrative function. These characteristics can be observed in major works including Ding Ling's *Taiyang zhao zai Sanggan he shang* [*The Sun Shines on the Sanggan River*, 1949] and Hao Ran's 1966 novel *Jinguang dadao* [*The Golden Road*, made into a film in 1975]. They can also be observed in the *geming yangbanxi* (revolutionary model operas) of the late 1960s. Authored collectively, model operas used some of the dramaturgy of Peking Opera to achieve the goals of clarity and simplicity in depicting key moments in modern Chinese revolutionary and military history. All of these works extol heroes who are imbued with the determination to struggle and an unerring moral compass, but in order for them to have an object against which to struggle, they require settings outside the socialist regime, or characters who embody traditional values, capitalist or Western values, or imperialism. This creates a tension for the reader because the celebration of struggle stimulates their enthusiasm, and yet the work has to contain that energy through a kind of revolutionary catharsis, rather than encouraging the reader to satisfy the yearning for social engagement in their everyday life, as was previously the case with revolutionary literature. 'Revolution' thus becomes reified, alienated or alienating.

By the mid-1950s, the same tension was unfolding in the Soviet Union, where on the one hand there was fiction and reportage about contemporary life that featured young energetic characters filled with revolutionary zeal grappling with problems in their work units and communities, and on the other hand there were reportagers such as Valentin Ovechkin writing pieces critical of official corruption and inefficiency in the Communist Party apparatus. Ovechkin was a young Soviet journalist in the 1950s who was promoting the use of feature articles with literary embellishment (called *oçerk*) to reveal social problems. A young Chinese journalist named Liu Binyan (1925–2005) happened to meet Ovechkin in the mid-1950s, and this marked the resurgence of reportage literature in China. From Ovechkin, Liu Binyan learned that it could be viewed as a kind of revolutionary zeal to seek out corruption and social inequity within a socialist system and expose it through fact-based narrative that used artistic techniques.[13] Liu Binyan's 'Zai Qiaoliang gongdi shang' [On the Bridge Construction Site, 1956] did just this, exposing the selfish and corrupt practices of a local official in charge of an important construction project in which cutting corners in quality could be a public menace; Liu's other piece the same year, 'Benbao neibu xiaoxi' [Inside News of the Newspaper], took on restrictions to freedoms in his own field. Liu's work emerged in the context of the Hundred Flowers Campaign, in which intellectuals and artists were encouraged by government leaders (particularly Mao Zedong) to air their grievances and criticisms. Mao's rhetoric tied the initiative to a revolutionary spirit (courage, truthfulness, looking difficulties in the face, not bowing to authority), but as we know, the outcome of the campaign was the persecution of large numbers of these outspoken intellectuals through imprisonment or re-education through labour.

Liu's reportage, which would probably not have been published but for the patronage of a senior editor named Qin Zhaoyang, sparked fierce criticism and heated debate about the limits of criticism, as well as about Liu's journalistic ethics (naming names, yet embellishing his story for dramatic effect), and he was expelled from the Communist Party and eventually sentenced to years of re-education through labour. Like many persecuted in the anti-rightist campaign, Liu's activities were also restricted during the Cultural Revolution, and he was only restored to normal social status in 1978 at the time of Deng Xiaoping's rise. Immediately Liu began to write more reportage, pursuing the same agendas as he had in his early work.[14] Although consistent with the more liberal mood of the times, Liu's new work was still highly controversial, because by focusing on officials in power, there were implications that not all of the problems of the Cultural Revolution had yet been solved, which was not consistent with the Deng Xiaoping regime's self-image.

Nevertheless, Liu Binyan's re-emergence on the Chinese literary scene stimulated an unprecedented outpouring of *baogao wenxue* (reportage literature) in the early 1980s, and this became one of the most distinctive features of the cultural scene. Liu himself maintained that his writing was not literature and he did not want it to be read as such, but many critics and imitators felt differently. The genre was treated as literary by scholars who wanted to place the contemporary trend in the context of the genre's entire history in the twentieth century back to the 1920s and 1930s, and new practitioners of the form including Su Xiaokang, Jia Lusheng and Qian Gang often felt strongly that its artistic qualities were essential to driving the truth home using facts. Given the considerable, intentional social effects of such works and the artistic agenda of their authors, the reportage of the 1980s may have been the last wave of Chinese revolutionary literature.

In this chapter, I have isolated various types of revolutionary writing to begin to unpack the complexities of this important aspect of the Chinese literary legacy. The operative quality of revolutionary literature opens the experience of literature outward from the circuit of author–text–reader to include society or the reader's life-world as a site for the completion of the aesthetic transaction. In China, this connection of reader and society has been part of literary modernity since before the May Fourth Movement. Although the emergence (or persistence) of involutionary modes of writing created a tension with this paradigm, that tension animated the development of Chinese literature throughout the twentieth century.

Notes

1. C.T. Hsia, 'Yen Fu and Liang Ch'i-ch'ao as Advocates of New Fiction', in Adele Austin Rickett (ed.), *Chinese Approaches to Literature from Confucius to Liang Ch'i-ch'ao*, Princeton, Princeton University Press, 1978; Leo Ou-fan Lee and Andrew Nathan, 'The Beginnings of Mass Culture: Journalism and Fiction in the late Ch'ing and Beyond', in David Johnson, Andrew J. Nathan and Evelyn S. Rawski (eds.), *Popular Culture in Late Imperial China*, Berkeley, Los Angeles and London, University of California Press, 1985, pp. 360–95.

2. Jing Tsu, *Failure, Nationalism, and Literature: The Making of Modern Chinese Identity, 1895–1937*, Palo Alto, Stanford University Press, 2005.

3. Charles A. Laughlin, *Chinese Reportage: The Aesthetics of Historical Experience*, Durham, Duke University Press, 2002.

4. Mary Louise Scoggin, 'Ethnography of a Chinese Essay: Zawen in Contemporary China', PhD dissertation, University of Chicago, 1997.

5. Kirk Denton, *The Problematic of Self in Modern Chinese Literature: Hu Feng and Lu Ling*, Stanford, Stanford University Press, 1998.

6. Michel Hockx, *Questions of Style: Literary Societies and Literary Journals in Modern China, 1911–1937*, Leiden and Boston, Brill, 2003.

7. Wang-chi Wong, *Politics and Literature in Shanghai: The Chinese League of Left-Wing Writers, 1930–1936*, Studies on East Asia, Manchester, Manchester University Press, 1991.

8. Qian Xingcun (ed.), *Shanghai shibian yu baogao wenxue*, Shanghai, Nanqiang shuju, 1932.

9. Laughlin, *Chinese Reportage*.

10. Charles J. Alber, 'Ting Ling and the Front Service Corps', in Fondation Singer-Polignac (ed.), *La littérature chinoise au Temps de la Guerre de résistance contre le Japon (de 1937 à 1945)*, Paris, Éditions de la Fondation Singer-Polignac, 1982 pp. 117–30; David Holm, *Art and Ideology in Revolutionary China*, Oxford, Oxford University

Press, 1990; Charles A. Laughlin, 'The Battlefield of Cultural Production: Chinese Literary Mobilization during the War Years', *Journal of Modern Literature in Chinese* 2, no. 1, 1998, 83–103.

11. Bonnie McDougall, *Mao Zedong's 'Talks at the Yan'an Conference on Literature and Art': A Translation of the 1943 Text with Commentary*, Ann Arbor, Michigan Papers in Chinese Studies, 1980.

12. Laughlin, *Chinese Reportage*.

13. Rudolf Wagner, 'Liu Binyan and the *Texie*', *Modern Chinese Literature* 2.1, 1986, 63–98.

14. E. Perry Link (ed.), *People or Monsters? – and Other Stories and Reportage from China after Mao*, Bloomington, Indiana University Press, 1983.

Guide to further reading

Alber, Charles J., 'Ting Ling and the Front Service Corps', in Fondation Singer-Polignac (ed.), *La littérature chinoise au Temps de la Guerre de résistance contre le Japon (de 1937 à 1945)*, Paris, Éditions de la Fondation Singer-Polignac, 1982, pp. 117–30.

Denton, Kirk, *The Problematic of Self in Modern Chinese Literature: Hu Feng and Lu Ling*, Stanford, Stanford University Press, 1998.

Hockx, Michel, *Questions of Style: Literary Societies and Literary Journals in Modern China, 1911–1937*, Leiden and Boston, Brill, 2003.

Holm, David, *Art and Ideology in Modern China*, Oxford, Oxford University Press, 1990.

Hsia, C. T., 'Yen Fu and Liang Ch'i-ch'ao as Advocates of New Fiction', in Adele Austin Rickett (ed.), *Chinese Approaches to Literature from Confucius to Liang Ch'i-ch'ao*, Princeton, Princeton University Press, 1978, pp. 221–57.

Hsia, T. A., *The Gate of Darkness: Studies on the Leftist Literary Movement in China*, Seattle, University of Washington Press, 1968.

Laughlin, Charles A., 'The Battlefield of Cultural Production: Chinese Literary Mobilization during the War Years', *Journal of Modern Literature in Chinese* 2, no. 1, 1998, 83–103.

    Chinese Reportage: The Aesthetics of Historical Experience, Durham, Duke University Press, 2002.

Lee, Leo Ou-fan and Andrew Nathan, 'The Beginnings of Mass Culture: Journalism and Fiction in the Late Ch'ing and Beyond', in David Johnson, Andrew J. Nathan and Evelyn S. Rawski (eds.), *Popular Culture in Late Imperial China*, Berkeley, Los Angeles and London, University of California Press, 1985, pp. 360–95.

Link, E. Perry (ed.), *People or Monsters? – and Other Stories and Reportage from China after Mao*, Bloomington, Indiana University Press, 1983.

    The Uses of Literature: Life in the Socialist Chinese Literary System, Princeton, Princeton University Press, 2000.

Liu Kang and Tang Xiaobing (eds.), *Politics, Ideology, and Literary Discourse in Modern China: Theoretical Interventions and Cultural Critique*, Durham, Duke University Press, 1993.

McDougall, Bonnie, *Mao Zedong's 'Talks at the Yan'an Conference on Literature and Art': A Translation of the 1943 Text with Commentary*, Ann Arbor, Michigan Papers in Chinese Studies, 1980.

Qian Xingcun (ed.), *Shanghai shibian yu baogao wenxue*, Shanghai, Nanqiang shuju, 1932.

Scoggin, Mary Louise, 'Ethnography of a Chinese Essay: Zawen in Contemporary China', PhD dissertation, University of Chicago, 1997.

Tsu, Jing, *Failure, Nationalism, and Literature: The Making of Modern Chinese Identity, 1895–1937*, Palo Alto, Stanford University Press, 2005.

Wagner, Rudolf, *Inside a Service Trade: Studies in Contemporary Chinese Prose*, Cambridge, MA, Harvard University Press, 1992.

'Liu Binyan and the *Texie*', *Modern Chinese Literature* 2.1 (1986), 63–98.

Wong, Wang-chi, *Politics and Literature in Shanghai: The Chinese League of Left-Wing Writers, 1930–1936*, Studies on East Asia, Manchester, Manchester University Press, 1991.

12

The involutionary tradition in modern Chinese literature

The abolition of the imperial examinations in China in 1905 heralded, among many other things, a significant change in the Chinese practice and understanding of literature. Prior to 1905, knowledge of literary texts and the ability to compose essays and poems were crucial components of the education of any man wishing to advance himself in society, as well as of the home education of many women from gentry families. After 1905, this direct link between literary reading and writing on the one hand and social status and power on the other gradually disappeared, as did the privileged access of men to public education. Although literature continued to be accorded high value within modern culture, its position in modern society became more marginal, but at the same time more autonomous. A literary scene emerged, populated by literary figures, including an increasing number of women, who were no longer literati, or scholar officials, but 'literary intellectuals' (a term coined by Bonnie S. McDougall and Kam Louie[1]).

Despite the increasing marginality of literature within society as a whole, many literary intellectuals continued to attach great social and political value to literary work. A very influential modern view of literature, first articulated by Liang Qichao at the start of the century, saw writing and especially fiction as a useful tool for transforming readers' mentalities and thereby bringing about social and political reform, or revolution. Indeed, early statements of modernity in Chinese literature seem to have centred on the notion of revolution. Liang Qichao proclaimed a 'poetry revolution', a 'fiction revolution' and a 'drama revolution'. Even more famous is the 'Literary Revolution' proclaimed by Chen Duxiu in 1917, which has in the past often been the starting point of histories of modern Chinese literature. The significance of revolutionary views of literature for writing produced between 1949 and 1976, during the heyday of Communist rule, hardly needs explaining. The revolutionary tradition in modern Chinese literature is the topic of Chapter 11 in this book. The present chapter deals with what can be considered the opposite of the revolutionary trend – i.e. those writings that were based on a view of literature as valuable in and of itself, that were inward-looking in the sense that they allowed for continuity with Chinese cultural tradition, and that were on the whole less concerned with bringing about social or political change. Following David Der-wei Wang,[2] I refer to this tradition as the involutionary tradition.

Contrary to the revolutionary tradition, which has often been described in terms of a mainstream development that progressed logically and seamlessly towards the triumph (and later downfall) of socialist realism, involutionary trends appear more scattered and less 'representative' of the tumultuous changes taking place in twentieth-century China. Nevertheless, in terms of literary value and lasting reader appreciation, the involutionary tradition is as important as the revolutionary tradition. Most of the older authors, works, groups and genres discussed below were popular in their own time, and were often ignored by critics and scholars during the first decades after 1949, but have in recent decades again found their place within the modern Chinese literary canon. For more recent writings, canonization processes are inevitably still under way, and truly 'revolutionary' writing has become scarce, although there is still a strong body of opinion in favour of literature and writers playing a social or political role. For the contemporary period, I have therefore focused on those trends that seem most obviously opposed to, or distinct from, social or political engagement, either because they seemingly unconditionally surrender to market forces, or because they occupy smaller, more independent literary spaces.

Changes in print culture and the emergence of a literary scene

During the late nineteenth century, modern print culture was introduced to China. For culture in general and for literature in particular this development had far-reaching consequences. The introduction of steam printing meant that printed matter could be produced much more efficiently than in the past. New printing techniques also meant that illustrations, and soon photographs, could be reproduced at low cost. Large publishing companies were quick to emerge, first and foremost in Shanghai, which soon became the hub of China's printing and publishing industry.[3] The new industry brought career opportunities in publishing, editing, translation and journalism which, together with the cosmopolitan image of semi-colonial Shanghai, attracted many literary intellectuals to the city. By the 1910s, a range of different literary magazines had emerged that were professionally produced and distributed to subscribers in cities across the country. Most of the magazines paid for contributions and thus helped to introduce the phenomenon of the 'professional writer' to the literary world. Meeting places, salons, clubs and other organizations for literary activity were quick to emerge, and an at times very public 'literary scene' (*wentan*) came into being. The vast majority of writers, including the most revolutionary ones, were active on this scene until it was scattered during the War of Resistance and subsequently brought under state control after the Communist takeover, until its re-emergence in tandem with economic reform from the 1980s onwards. Many of the works and trends discussed in this chapter were (or still are) of intrinsic value to the members of this specialized literary community, or had their main impact within that community.

Terminology and genres

During the late empire and the early years of the Republic, writers and thinkers contributing to the new literary magazines brought about a remarkable conceptual change, as a result of which literature came to be defined no longer as any and all writing by a member of the literati class, but specifically as a type of writing that is aesthetic and creative in nature. Documentary texts such as histories, memorials or official treatises ceased to have value within this new concept of literature. Narrative writing (*xiaoshuo*) and especially the novel moved to the centre of a new genre hierarchy. The literary magazines of the 1900s and 1910s were full of narrative texts, most of them in prose, some in rhymed form, many in the vernacular, many still in the classical language, some original, some translations, and many of them a mixture of both – all were categorized as *xiaoshuo*, and for literature as a whole the term *wenxue* eventually became widely accepted. Long novels such as Liu E's *The Travels of Lao Can* (1907) and Wu Jianren's *Strange Events Eyewitnessed in the Past Twenty Years* (1910) were originally serialized in these journals and are considered to be among the first major works of modern Chinese literature. Both were long chapter novels in the tradition of older Chinese fiction, but what makes them modern (apart from the publication mode) are things such as the emphasis on the individual experience of the protagonist and, in the case of Wu Jianren, the use of a first-person narrator rather than an omniscient story-teller. Both novels are also modern in the way in which they express concerns about a crisis in society and culture brought about by the many changes that have come with the impact of the West and the many changes that have taken place in urban centres such as Shanghai.

The Travels of Lao Can describes the adventures of the male protagonist, Lao Can, as he travels through various realistic and imagined landscapes where he encounters other characters that represent a wide range of classes and professions in the Chinese society of the late imperial period. The novel is especially powerful in its exposure of the lack of integrity and the corruption of officialdom. As such, the novel is indicative of the emergence of a new type of literary intellectual, occupying an autonomous stance in their critique of contemporary society and no longer pursuing a career in the imperial bureaucracy. Apart from its political and social messages, *The Travels of Lao Can* has been highly praised for its (vernacular) style and for its author's vivid imagination.

In *Strange Events Eyewitnessed in the Past Twenty Years*, Wu Jianren (also known as Wu Woyao) presents what his narrator claims to be the memoirs of a character called Jiusi Yisheng ('Nine Lives'). Written in first-person narrative, the memoirs consist of roughly a hundred episodes that are claimed to be eyewitness accounts of various types of corruption, deceit and debauchery in late imperial Shanghai. Many of the episodes are grotesquely funny, but the underlying serious message about the state of contemporary society is clear. Neither Wu Jianren nor Liu E makes any attempt to connect their exposure of social ills with any call for political revolution.

Countless subgenres of *xiaoshuo*, based on content and theme, were distinguished in the pages of literary magazines of the first decades of the twentieth century – these included detective fiction, science fiction and especially romance fiction. Much of the fiction of this early period, like the magazines in which it was published, has an experimental, at times playful nature. Although many of the stories expressed serious concerns about the state of the nation and the value of traditional Chinese culture in a modern world, traditional forms and sensibilities, as well as traditional moral values, were to be found alongside new and imported ideas. Even with the advent of a younger generation of more iconoclastic writers onto the Shanghai scene in the 1920s, this older type of modern fiction remained relatively popular with the kind of elite readership that would read literary magazines in the first place. Eventually referred to by its opponents as 'Mandarin Ducks and Butterflies Fiction', this style of writing represented a less programmatic approach to modernity in literature, enjoying all that Shanghai culture and its literary scene had to offer. As such it is, although not considered 'high literature', part and parcel of the involutionary tradition.

The involutionary aspect of this particular kind of modern fiction is clearly present in a novel that many consider to be its epitome, Xu Zhenya's (1889–1937) *Jade Pear Spirit*, first published in 1912. Unlike most Chinese novels, whether traditional or modern, Xu Zhenya's work is not written in the vernacular but in classical Chinese. It tells the tragic love story of a young widow and her son's teacher, which results in an inevitable confrontation with Confucian morality (which expected widows not to remarry), leading to the female protagonist's suicide. The novel, which became a successful film in 1924, clearly deals with realistic problems confronted by men and women in a modernizing yet often still morally conservative society. What makes it different from works in the revolutionary tradition, apart from the use of classical language, is its refusal to connect the story with a clear message in favour of social change, free love and women's emancipation.

New Literature, its genres and its critics

From the late 1910s onwards, a type of writing known as 'New Literature' (*xin wenxue*) became popular among young urban intellectuals. Writing of this type heralded even more changes to the concept of literature, especially to literary language and genre norms. Its writers were committed to reducing as much as possible any impact of earlier Chinese literature on their own work, turning instead to Western and Japanese examples. The language of New Literature, especially in the 1920s, is a Europeanized version of the modern Chinese vernacular. It contains many loanwords from Western languages (often borrowed from the Japanese rendering into Chinese characters of those words), as well as some Westernized grammatical structures, or previously unknown written distinctions, such as different characters for 'he' and 'she' (both pronounced *ta* and thus indistinguishable in speech). The Europeanized vernacular is also different from the older vernacular in its use of punctuation.

The forms of New Literature are the short story, the spoken drama, the familiar essay, the psychological novel and the free verse. For many of its authors, adhering to a programme of Westernization and de-traditionalization of literature was an act of principle and part of a wide-scale revolution in culture known as the 'New Culture Movement' (*xin wenhua yundong*). However, the notion of a New Culture devoid of con-tinuities with the past did not appeal to everyone. An especially bitter debate raged in the early 1920s about the value and status of vernacular free verse.

Of all the genres of New Literature, New Poetry was soon considered to have the least revolutionary potential. By the early 1920s, most New Poets had come to conceive of poetry first and foremost as a means of individual expression, not of social or cultural transformation. They did, however, insist on the freedom to express their emotions with-out being bound by traditional prosody. The popularity of free verse (*ziyou shi*) was problematic for those who considered poetry to be by definition a type of prosodic writing. Most vocal in their opposition to New Poetry (and, *in extenso*, to all New Literature) was the group around the Nanjing-based journal *The Critical Review* (*Xueheng*). Founded by a group of returned students from the USA who had studied under Irving Babbitt at Harvard, the *Critical Review* writers (Wu Mi, Mei Guangdi and others) championed an inward-looking understanding of literature aimed at preserving, rather than denying, the literary achievements of the past, especially in the highly revered genre of classical poetry. They were not in any way opposed to Western influence or Westernization, but they did not consider that continuing a glorious literary tradition was opposed to or in conflict with the introduction of Western thought. They launched attacks on New Poetry and New Poets in their own and other journals.

Some New Poets themselves, such as the famous poet and critic Wen Yiduo, agreed with the definition of poetry as prosodic writing, but disagreed that the forms and idioms of classical poetry should be continued into the modern era. Instead they tried to design new pros-odies that they considered to be more applicable to the cadences of the modern vernacular. In the mid-1920s, Wen achieved fame with a highly regular type of poetry, based on lines containing the same number of 'feet' (*dun*), which appeared like rectangular blocks of text on the printed page, and were therefore half-jokingly referred to as 'the dried beancurd style' (*doufugan ti*). Wen Yiduo's most famous poem in this style is 'Dead

Water' (1926), a description of a dirty, stinking ditch filled with rubbish and leftover food that is full of images of decadence and suggestions that squalor might bring forth beauty. The poem is somewhat reminiscent of Baudelaire and makes no explicit references to any particular context, but it is nonetheless traditionally read as an allegory for the state of China in the mid-1920s.

Of all poets writing in bound forms in the first half of the twentieth century, Xu Zhimo is the most famous and has enjoyed the most lasting reputation with a wide readership. His highly romantic verse, coupled with his activity on the literary scene and his romantic lifestyle, made him a literary celebrity. Most well known is his elegantly written 'A Second Farewell to Cambridge', in which he melancholically describes his sentiments during his final days at the famous British university.

Throughout the twentieth century modern Chinese poets have continued the search for ideal prosodies for a modern poetry, maintaining the traditional formalist definition of poetry and thus preserving a level of continuity with traditional Chinese concepts of literature that is not found in other genres, with the exception of certain types of prose writing, which will be discussed more below.

Zhou Zuoren and the prose essay

Zhou Zuoren (1885–1967), a Beijing University professor and leading cultural reformer of the late 1910s, became famous in the 1920s and 1930s for his idiosyncratic prose writings, in a genre referred to by the traditional term *xiaopin wen* ('vignettes'). In a conscious move away from the revolutionary tradition that he initially helped to create, Zhou preferred the mildly ironic, conversational tone of the vignette to the biting sarcasm of the *zawen* ('critical essay') for which his older brother Lu Xun (pseudonym of Zhou Shuren, 1881–1936) was famous. Zhou deliberately chose to write about the most mundane or abstruse topics that caught his fancy, angering some of the revolutionary writers with essays with titles such as 'On Flies' and 'On Reading on the Toilet'. More importantly, and typical of the involutionary tradition, Zhou used his essays to discuss his wide readings in classical Chinese texts, interspersing descriptive passages in simple modern vernacular with obscure quotes in difficult classical Chinese. To this he added knowledge and interests acquired through his readings in foreign literatures, ranging from Ancient Greek to modern Japanese.

Despite the blemish of collaboration with the Japanese occupiers of Beijing during the War of Resistance, for which he was later convicted and which caused serious critical reception and scholarship of his work to cease until the mid-1980s, Zhou Zuoren continues to be respected for the beauty of his prose style, for his originality and erudition, and for the staunchly individualistic stance he took in the 1920s and 1930s in opposition to the overly programmatic, collectivist trends within the New Culture Movement.

Shen Congwen and native soil fiction

Whereas the revolutionary tradition in modern Chinese literature often goes hand in hand with a push towards setting national standards (national language, national culture, national forms and so on), writers advocating involutionary aesthetics often find themselves drawn to the regional or the local. Zhou Zuoren would often dwell on local customs in his essays, and even more famous in this respect is the fiction of Shen Congwen, one of the most prolific authors of the Republican period.

The region that serves as the setting for most of Shen Congwen's stories is West Hunan, in the heartland of what was in ancient times the Kingdom of Chu. Chu culture, especially the classic poem 'Encountering Sorrow' (*Li sao*) and its myth-making author Qu Yuan, has for centuries been conceived of as an alternative to the Confucian mainstream. In his fiction, Shen Congwen often refers to the cultural roots of West Hunan and the representation of Chu culture in literature through the ages. At the same time, his stories are populated with characters from humble backgrounds – peasants, sailors, prostitutes – whom he manages to portray as simple and backward on the one hand, yet on the other hand living an unaffected and often idyllic life, far away from the centres of modernization and globalization. Refusing to subscribe to the revolutionary tradition's narrow focus on the peasantry as an oppressed class in need of enlightenment and leadership, Shen Congwen mixes awareness of the problems of rural communities with nostalgia for their disappearing lifestyle.

Shen Congwen's most famous work of fiction is the novella *Border Town* (1934). Set among the Miao people of West Hunan (an ethnic minority to which Shen Congwen himself belonged), *Border Town* tells the story of the young girl Cuicui and her grandfather, who raises her. Shen

Congwen's description of Cuicui's youth and beauty is matched by his depictions of the idyllic landscape, but the story taking place within this setting is that of a sad love triangle between Cuicui and two brothers, one of whom eventually commits suicide, while the other is prevented by Cuicui's grandfather from marrying her.

In the 1930s, Shen Congwen was undoubtedly one of China's most highly regarded and most popular writers of serious fiction. After 1949, his approach to literature in general and his attitude towards the countryside in particular were criticized, and his work was left out of the canon until the 1980s, when he was rediscovered. He is now again seen as one of the greatest modern Chinese writers, and his work was a major inspiration to contemporary authors, including the 1980s 'searching for roots school' (*xungen pai*), about which more later.

Shi Zhecun and modernism

Modernist writing, with its emphasis on the individual experience of the fragmented reality of modern existence, its rigorous adherence to aesthetic autonomy, its mistrust of collective ideology, and its preference for formal experiments, epitomizes yet another aspect of the involutionary tradition. Modernist writing almost literally turns inward on itself, as it encourages the reader to return to the text again and again, penetrating deeper and deeper in an attempt to construct some sort of unified interpretation.

The most outstanding modernist Chinese writer of the Republican period is Shi Zhecun (sometimes spelled 'Shi Zhicun'), who was active on the Shanghai literary scene in the 1930s. Shi Zhecun's short stories typically explore the subconscious desires and suppressed libido of individual urbanites, sometimes combined with plots that betray the influence on his writing of English gothic horror novels as well as traditional Chinese tales about ghosts and fox fairies. A typical example is the short story 'Sorcery', in which the protagonist is a man travelling from the city to the countryside to visit a friend. At various moments during his trip he sees what he believes to be a witch (about which he has read in Edgar Allan Poe stories and other Western books). Suffering what seems like a nervous breakdown, worsened by his suppressed desire for his host's wife, he eventually collapses. When he has recovered and returned to the city, convinced that he had only imagined all the bad omens, he receives word that his young daughter has died.

Shi Zhecun also rewrote old stories about well-known heroes from popular premodern fiction, enriching them with detailed modernist narration of the protagonists' psychological states. An example is the story 'Shi Xiu', in which the story of the sworn brothers Shi Xiu and Yang Xiong, from the classical novel *The Water Margin*, is rewritten with strong emphasis on Shi Xiu's suppressed desire for Yang Xiong's wife.

Shi Zhecun's stories often move back and forth between reality and fantasy, the mundane and the grotesque, leaving it to individual readers to decide what they will or will not believe. Shi's interest in psychoanalysis, sexuality and individual perceptions of reality all testify to his inward-looking, modernist approach to writing, even though formally speaking his works are not very experimental. Although Shi Zhecun's period of literary activity in the 1930s was relatively short and his output limited, and although like Zhou Zuoren and Shen Congwen he was subsequently ignored until the 1980s, his unique brand of modernism has since attracted considerable critical and scholarly attention.

Zhang Ailing and anti-romanticism

Like Shi Zhecun, Zhang Ailing (also known as Eileen Chang) was active as a writer for only a short time. The stories and essays she produced during the 1940s as she lived in occupied Shanghai are however among the most widely read and loved in the entire Chinese-reading world. Superficially, many of her stories appear to be romance fiction, describing complicated love stories between men and women of Shanghai's (and occasionally Hong Kong's) upper classes. The plots of her stories are laden with references to high-society life, including detailed descriptions of beautifully dressed women and their dashing young suitors, providing the reader with many of the ingredients and formulas that make popular romance fiction so attractive to a wide readership. Upon closer reading, however, most of Zhang's works are complicated by the presence of a profoundly detached narratorial voice, which succeeds in turning the various idyllic romances into mundane struggles by insecure men and women in search of social and economic stability. Zhang excels at characterization. In beautiful language and with a supreme eye for detail, she has managed to create some of the most memorable protagonists in modern Chinese literature. The juxtaposition of glamorous decadence and down-to-earth pragmatism in most of her stories and characters is intended to drive home the idea that true happiness is often short-lived, usually hard-fought and sometimes plain ugly, but at least it is 'real'. For this reason, Edward Gunn[4] in his study of wartime literature describes her work using the term 'anti-romanticism'.

Zhang Ailing's stories, as well as her essays, highlight gender issues, especially as they relate to the status of women in polite society in cities such as Shanghai, often expressing mildly cynical views about the possibility for women to advance themselves without the help of men. Her most famous work is the long story 'Love in a Fallen City', which describes the courtship of Bai Liusu, a Shanghai divorcee, and Fan Liuyuan, an overseas Chinese man, against the backdrop of the mounting Japanese invasion of Hong Kong. The development of their relationship, narrated mainly from Liusu's point of view, is constantly described in battle terms and images, with Liusu approaching the affair strategically with the aim of securing marriage. Set against the backdrop of glamorous Shanghai dance halls and Hong Kong hotels, yet displaying a profoundly anti-romantic attitude, the story reaches its climax when the Japanese invade Hong Kong and the couple find real intimacy among the ruins of the fallen city, becoming 'just another married couple'.

Zhang Ailing's mistrust of idealism and, perhaps more importantly, her apparent lack of interest in writing about the war that was all around her, resulted in her work being completely ignored after 1949, until the mid-1980s or so. Because Zhang herself had moved to Hong Kong in the early 1950s, and later to the USA, she continued to be widely known among Chinese communities outside China, especially in Taiwan, where she influenced an entire generation of (women) writers. Nowadays, she is also immensely popular with readers in Mainland China, if not always with critics, some of whom continue to be suspicious of the popular literature aspects of her style.

The early decades of the PRC and underground literature

From 1949 to 1976 the involutionary tradition in modern Chinese literature lay dormant in the PRC, at least in public. Newly created works of literature published after 1949 were subject to strict censorship on the basis of Communist Party policy which demanded of literature that it supported political movements. Authors and critics who suggested, however cautiously, that more individual expression ought to be allowed, were generally silenced or persuaded to retract their statements. Moreover, for most of the 1950s and at least part of the 1960s, a majority of authors were in support of the new system, both for idealistic reasons (i.e. they believed in the Communist Party's policies) and for pragmatic reasons (they enjoyed the status of 'cultural workers' and were generally well paid for writing and publishing).

As mentioned above, leading writers such as Zhou Zuoren, Shen Congwen, Shi Zhecun and Zhang Ailing had been removed from the canon. Their works were available only to those considered ideologically advanced enough to be impervious to the 'corrupting' influences of these authors, mainly party cadres and some academics. These same readers were also allowed to own and consult limited editions of translated works of modern Western literature, known as the 'brown cover books' (*huang pi shu*), containing such works as J. D. Salinger's *Catcher in the Rye* and Samuel Beckett's *Waiting for Godot*. During the Cultural Revolution, copies of these 'brown cover books' started circulating among rusticated youths, often the children of party cadres with reading privileges. The more talented writers among these youths, inspired by these foreign works and spurred on by disillusionment with officially published writing, created a lively underground literary scene during the 1970s. The best of their writings emerged above-ground during the Democracy Wall Movement of the late 1970s and eventually found their way into official literary journals in the early 1980s, in some cases more than a decade after they were written. Most famous were the so-called 'obscure' (*menglong*) poems by young authors such as Bei Dao, Shu Ting, Mang Ke, Gu Cheng and Yang Lian, most of whom have since gone on to international fame.

In the early years after the Cultural Revolution, 'obscure poetry' was a shock to the Communist Party literary system because of its relatively apolitical content and its occasionally difficult imagery. Nevertheless, it is difficult to decide whether or not this poetry should be seen as part of the involutionary tradition. In what was to become the flagship poem of the genre, Bei Dao's 'Huida' [The Answer], the unusual imagery and individual expression are put into the service of the inflated ego of a speaker who purports to represent all those who have been victimized and all those who challenge and doubt what they are told to believe. The central stanzas of the poem read as follows:

> 'I am telling you, world
> I DO NOT BELIEVE
> there may be a thousand challengers under your feet
> but you can count me as number one thousand and one

I don't believe the sky is blue
I don't believe in the echo of thunder
I don't believe that dreams are false
I don't believe that death goes unpunished.

The poem ends with a reference to the age-old Chinese characters (a symbol of national culture), with the announcement that change is on its way and with an expression of hope for all future generations of Chinese people.

Although it is undeniable that obscure poetry brought about a massive change in the perception and appreciation of poetry in China in the late 1970s and early 1980s, and although authors such as Bei Dao demonstrated considerable courage in defending this kind of writing in the face of initial establishment criticism and attempts at suppression, most of the poems in the genre do not look inward, but reach out to the millions of people, especially intellectuals, who suffered during the Cultural Revolution, and deliver an urgent plea for political, social and cultural change.

Once basic literary liberties had been restored, more introspective literature soon emerged. Bei Dao himself turned to more apolitical work and, since his decision not to return to China after the events of 4 June 1989, his poetry has become more and more dominated by themes of solitude, alienation and exile, presented in sparse language and simple, juxtaposed images – a modest kind of poetry that no longer attempts to speak on anyone's behalf. In China itself, too, younger poets enjoying the liberties fought for by the likes of Bei Dao yet disenchanted with the political aspects of the obscure poetry movement have turned to writing typically modernist work, characterized by a focus on language and imagery (rather than form and meaning), by rich intertextual references, and by an appeal to intellectual depth rather than to emotional response. Arguably the leading representative of this type of poetry in China nowadays is the Beijing-based poet Xi Chuan. Other recent trends in poetry are discussed later. But first we return to the 1980s to discuss developments in fiction.

Avant-garde and root-seeking

During the second half of the 1980s, literary policies had relaxed enough for some experimental works of fiction to appear in the official literary magazines. Currently famous writers like Yu Hua and Su Tong made their debuts during this period. Their stories were labelled 'avant-garde' (*xianfeng pai*), a term that is slightly misleading given the fact that, rather than being radically opposed to the literary establishment, these authors actually relied on that establishment to condone their work. After all, despite the relaxed policies, publication in the official literary magazines in the 1980s was still only possible with establishment approval. Nevertheless, the authors involved managed to shock their readership with their radical narrative experiments, as well as with the content of their work, which often featured hair-raising scenes of violence, described in a detached, almost matter-of-fact tone. Most experimental (and arguably most 'avant-garde', since he never made it far on the official circuit) was the author Ma Yuan, whose stories feature highly unreliable narrators as well as extensive use of meta-fictional devices, drawing the reader into the text yet at the same time making any and all coherent interpretation unsustainable, and leaving no doubt about the fact that any representation of 'reality' is always the construction of a particular individual. Ma Yuan's stories flew in the face of the (socialist) realist paradigm, which had been state policy in the PRC for decades, and paved the way for new approaches.

A typical Ma Yuan story, featuring all his favourite narrative devices, is 'Fabrication', a fragmented account of a Han Chinese man's stay in a lepers' village in Tibet and his encounters with various inhabitants of the village. The story starts out with the narrator introducing himself as 'the Han Chinese author Ma Yuan', reminding the reader of the fabricated nature of what one is about to read. Later, some of the storylines are narrated twice with completely different conclusions, while the 'author' keeps reminding the reader not to believe anything that is being said. The story ends with the narrator waking up outside the village and finding that in reality only one day has passed, and the date just happens to be 'May Fourth' – more than a wink to the literary and political tradition and ideology that Ma Yuan opposes.

Another much-discussed avant-garde writer of this period is Can Xue. Her short stories depict dreamscapes full of grotesque images of fear, violence and surreal transformations of people, animals and objects. Can Xue's work, often compared to that of Kafka, is devoid of any references to any real time or place, yet in some of her best work, such as the short story 'The Little Hut on the Mountain', she succeeds in conjuring up scenes of fear, terror, isolation and alienation that are as real as the scenes in which they are set are imagined.

Experimental techniques involving unreliable narration, fragmentation and, especially, the use of different language registers and dialects were also characteristic of another type of 'avant-garde' writing, sometimes considered a separate 'school' (*pai*), commonly known as 'searching for roots' (*xungen*). The published agenda of the roots seekers, drafted by their main representative, the author Han Shaogong, announced their interest in exploring alternative Chinese cultures, including the culture of Chu mentioned above, as well as popular religion and the cultures of ethnic minorities, in an attempt to dig up 'roots' that lay outside the mainstream Confucian tradition. This search for roots was inspired in part by the authors' experiences as rusticated youth during the Cultural Revolution, and especially in Han Shaogong's stories of the period, the life, language and customs of remote countryside communities are often described through the eyes of an out-of-place young intellectual narrator. These themes merge in Han's often-anthologized story 'The Homecoming', which features a male protagonist travelling to a remote village where he is eventually convinced that he is someone else, a person who stayed in the village years earlier and committed a crime there. The language and customs of the villagers are represented in minute detail and made to seem very exotic, whereas the identity conflict of the protagonist is clearly hinted to be that of the lost generation of rusticated youth.

A good example of the combination of experimental technique and roots-seeking themes is Gao Xingjian's novel *Soul Mountain*, written for the most part in China during the 1980s and highly typical of literature of that period. The identity conflict of the contemporary Chinese intellectual is made palpable in *Soul Mountain* through the threefold narrative perspective (the 'I', the 'you' and the 'he'), representing different sides of the protagonist who travels through remote areas of China in order to record exotic languages and customs, but also to come to terms with his own identity and with his position as a writer under a regime that attempts to prescribe the correct relationship between writing, reality and 'truth'. As mentioned above, some of the roots seekers hark back in their writing to the regionalism found in Shen Congwen's pre-1949 stories and novellas, especially in their use of idyllic settings and their occasional references to the culture of Chu.

After the 1980s, most of the 'avant-garde' writers discarded their more extreme narrative experiments, focusing on more readable historical and psychological fiction in more conventional form. The 'root-seeking' writers discarded their programmatic search for an alternative cultural heritage and concentrated increasingly on what was always their strongest trait: setting stories in remote village communities. Some of the best Chinese novels of the 1990s, such as Han Shaogong's *Dictionary of Maqiao*, Yu Hua's *Chronicle of a Blood Merchant* and Mo Yan's *The Republic of Wine*, combine elements from both 'avant-garde' and 'root-seeking' trends with altogether realist and story-driven prose.

Recent developments

In the last ten years or so, involutionary trends have moved into new territory by explicitly renouncing the various links between writing, enlightenment, social and political change, the Nation and modernity, which pervade so much of modern Chinese literature. Perhaps the most significant characteristic of these trends is that they no longer perceive themselves in opposition to, or as an alternative to, the revolutionary tradition. Instead they flaunt their disrespect for any kind of literature that takes itself too seriously and irritate the establishment (even the 'involutionary establishment') with their shameless pursuit of money and fame, or their refusal to provide their works with any kind of 'depth'. The exponential growth of the book market (including a large black market and an even larger 'second channel' of semi-official publishing houses) and the rapid development of literary space on the World Wide Web since the late 1990s have also contributed to this trend.

Perhaps the first sign that something was really changing in the modern Chinese literary field was the arrival on the scene of a self-styled 'Generation X', led by the Shanghai-based young female writer Wei Hui. In 2000, her novel *Shanghai Baby* achieved huge popular success first in China and later on the international book market. In what is arguably one of the most culturally offensive scenes in the whole of modern Chinese fiction, Wei Hui describes how her protagonist submits herself completely to a foreign man, allowing him to use her body as he pleases during a long, painful sexual encounter, and how as a result of this the protagonist realizes she is in love with him. To make matters worse, she then dumps her Chinese boyfriend, who commits suicide. The Chinese critical establishment was outraged and condemned the book, which was subsequently also hit by a government ban (increasing the novel's market value on the black market and offering a good marketing strategy for the English translation, which bore the slogan 'Banned in China!'

on its cover). Seldom has a Chinese novel evoked so much anger and aggression from both government and literary circles, with a number of authors who themselves had been the victims of persecution in earlier decades openly calling for Wei Hui to be silenced. Apart from various anxieties relating to national pride and male insecurity, the underlying reason why Wei Hui's work was considered offensive may well be the fact that she did not acquiesce to being seen as a trash writer, but continued to claim that she represented the aesthetic of a new generation.

In poetry since the 1990s, apart from the modernists already referred to above, the main innovative voice is that of Yu Jian. His long poems, written in highly colloquial language, featuring often absurd dialogues and conversations, and striving for a complete absence of metaphor, aim for the complete deconstruction of language as a carrier of any kind of deeper meaning, instead presenting human speech as a ritualistic, performative activity, with occasional references to the emptiness of those 'going through the motions' trying to produce politically correct statements in Party-speak. As a poet, Yu Jian represents what has become known as the 'people's poets' (*minjian shiren*) who, in a widely publicized debate around the turn of the twenty-first century, confronted the 'intellectuals' (what I have called the 'modernists' above) for their elitist attitudes towards writing and their supposed snobbish adherence to outdated literary forms and practices. Many 'people's poets' have also taken to the World Wide Web to publish and discuss their work.

The rise of web literature (*wangluo wenxue*) has arguably been the biggest shock to the state-regulated system of production and consumption of literature. Both aspiring new writers and established older writers contribute profusely to Internet discussion forums (*luntan*, also known as 'BBS') that allow for unprecedented levels of interaction between authors and their readership, as well as for the creation of collective works consisting of contributions by various writers to one and the same 'thread' that slowly grows into a literary work. Many niches have been created inside cyberspace for writers and literary groups of various persuasions, ranging from sites for classical poetry to extremely avant-garde groups that set out to shock their audiences with sexually and otherwise explicit writing. As long as no overt stance of political dissidence is taken, most of these spaces are tolerated by the state apparatus. Web literature and related practices have also proved commercially successful, often leading to their republication in print and in some cases to their authors achieving celebrity status.

Epilogue

At the beginning of the twenty-first century, the revolutionary tradition in modern Chinese literature has dwindled. Involutionary approaches to writing have become the mainstream, mirroring their position in other parts of the world, yet the intervention of new market principles, new technologies and an increasingly haphazard censorship system have made these approaches discover new directions. In many cases, these directions involve the unlikely combination of provocative, avant-garde-like styles with writing for (real or imagined) mass audiences. Whether or not this will ever lead to renewed attempts to produce revolutionary appeal remains to be seen.

Notes

1. Bonnie S. McDougall and Kam Louie, *The Literature of China in the Twentieth Century*, London, Hurst, 1997.
2. David Der-wei Wang, *Fin-de-siècle Splendor: Repressed Modernities of Late Qing Fiction, 1849–1911*, Stanford, Stanford University Press, 1997.
3. Cf. Christopher A. Reed, *Gutenberg in Shanghai: Chinese Print Capitalism, 1876–1937*, Vancouver, University of British Columbia Press, 2003.
4. Edward M. Gunn, Jr, *Unwelcome Muse: Chinese Literature in Shanghai and Peking, 1937–1945*, New York, Columbia University Press, 1980.

Guide to further reading

Lau, Joseph S.M., and Howard Goldblatt (eds.), *The Columbia Anthology of Modern Chinese Literature*, New York, Columbia University Press, 1995.

13

Music and performing arts: tradition, reform and political and social relevance

This chapter takes up some of the main genres of modern Chinese culture that come under the general heading of music and performing arts. The traditional forms include traditional theatre (*xiqu*); traditional dance; folk songs (*min'ge*); narrative singing (*shuochang* or *quyi*); and traditional instrumental music (*qiyue*).[1] Modern forms include the modern spoken play called the *huaju*; several other forms that were influenced greatly by the Chinese Communist Party (CCP), such as opera (*geju*, literally 'song drama') and 'dance drama' (*wuju*); and music introduced from outside China, especially the West. Some attention will be given to how the main forms have developed since the early years of the twentieth century, and to how these forms interacted with the society and the politics of the day. The chapter will adopt a basically, though not entirely, chronological structure. However, it will make no attempt at a consolidated discussion of all these genres. Rather, it will use examples from them to illustrate important themes.

Since the early years of the twentieth century, three in some ways related themes have dominated China's music and performing arts. These are: how to reform or preserve them to maintain their popularity and relevance; the ability of the performing arts to change society; and the dichotomy between Chinese traditional and Western or Soviet forms. Some new genres have emerged under Western influence, but they have not simply followed the original models exactly. Although many traditions persist into the twenty-first century, no previous century has witnessed more thorough-going change in China's music and performing arts than the twentieth century.

Another theme of considerable interest is the dichotomy between urban and rural performing arts. Referring specifically to folk music, one specialist refers to 'the gulf between rural and urban music-making, between the music of the *yiren* [artists] in the villages and that of the urban professional troupes'. He continues that '[d]espite the contacts between town and country, as long as the urban professional scene dominates our image of Chinese music, we need to adjust our perspective'.[2] He is referring specifically to the late years of the twentieth century, but his comments might also apply to other periods. In fact, most of the developments discussed in this chapter originated in the cities, and it was there that they had their greatest impact. However, we would do well to remember the living traditions that still exist in the countryside and away from the main centres.

The social and political context is covered elsewhere in this volume, but I note here that the reforms of the last decade of the Qing dynasty (1644–1911), the May Fourth Movement of 1919, and the Japanese Occupation and the various revolutions of the twentieth century have all exerted profound influence on music and the performing arts, although they have also generally left the traditions with a substantial following. The need to bring a degree of modernization to China has affected the arts since the late nineteenth century and accelerated since then, although not consistently. The impact of the modernization push since the 1970s may turn out to be even greater than that of the revolutions that preceded it, and in the early years of the twenty-first century has still far from run its course.

Late Qing reform

In traditional China, elite society despised drama (*xiqu*) and its practitioners. As the main branch of popular literature, along with the novel, popular drama was so coarse that almost all traditional scholars regarded it as demeaning to be seen at a performance. But reformist thinkers such as Liang Qichao (1873–1929) took a different view. In a piece published in 1902 Liang claimed that reform of drama and the novel was essential to undertaking the reform of the country, as well as of its ethical standards, religion, customs, learning and 'people's hearts and characters'. His reason was simple: 'popular literature wields incredible influence over the way of the world'.[3] Meanwhile, scholars such as Wang Guowei (1877–1927) began to take traditional theatre very seriously as an area of scholarship. His 1912 work on the history of Chinese drama in the Song (960–1279) and Yuan (1280–1368) periods, *Song Yuan xiqu kao* [*Enquiry into Song and Yuan Drama*], proved both seminal and highly influential. According to one contemporary scholar, 'it is fair to say that it represented the first systematic Chinese-authored insertion of Chinese literature into the discourse of "world literature".[4] The idea that the popular arts influenced the minds of the people gathered momentum during the twentieth century. Research was interrupted several times, for instance during the war against Japan and more particularly the Cultural Revolution, but drama and other performing arts remained a respectable area of study, and the twentieth century produced an enormous amount of path-breaking work.

In the Chinese theatre itself reform was well under way by the time the Qing Dynasty fell in 1911. Reform was prominent in several of the traditional *xiqu* forms, including the most famous, the *jingju*, often translated as either Beijing Opera or Peking Opera. In August 1904, the reformist *jingju* actor Wang Xiaonong (1858–1918), who had taken to the stage after being dismissed from a position as county magistrate for his love of song, put on a new-style piece that reflected the dire situation in China at the time. The item, called *Guazhong lanyin* (literally 'melon seeds, cause of the orchid'), was about an ostensible war between Poland and Turkey, which ended in Poland's humiliation and partition.

In fact, Wang Xiaonong's real purpose was closer at hand: he aimed to use the theatre to educate the people in patriotism. In February 1904, Japan had declared war on Russia and the war had been fought on Chinese soil. China's humiliation could hardly have been greater. Wang's supporters believed the theatre should 'force people to think and feel for their country' and 'be a model for awakening our four hundred millions'.[5] His experiment, which he put on in Shanghai because it was considered a comparatively free and open city, proved very popular, both with audiences and reviewers. It showed that people could respond to dramas that concerned contemporary politics, and were willing to accept theatre that departed from the traditional patterns with their endless repetition of stories based on Chinese novels, history, stories and legends.

The last years of the Qing saw the development of the modern form called *huaju* (literally 'words drama'), but more often known in English as 'spoken drama'. This was a new and very important form of drama that followed Western patterns of theatre, mostly transmitted through Japan. Its most prominent feature was that the dialogue was spoken, not sung or intoned, as in the traditional drama. In June 1907 the Spring Willow (*Chunliu*) Society put on a Chinese-language play called *Heinu yutian lu* [*The Black Slave's Cry to Heaven*], which was an adaptation of the American novel *Uncle Tom's Cabin* by Harriet Beecher Stowe (1811–96).

While this first Chinese spoken drama was performed not in China but in Japan, the spoken drama quickly gained a following in China itself, although mainly among the educated. The new form produced a long line of excellent representative examples, a few of which will be mentioned later. Moreover, the first Chinese spoken drama very specifically advocated social reform for the downtrodden masses, because the novel on which it was based, *Uncle Tom's Cabin*, dealt with the oppression of black slaves in the United States. The idea that drama should reflect and help to change society was from the beginning one of the main hallmarks of this new form. One specialist has written that, given 'its inherently public nature and the social views of the writers, spoken drama has been the most assertive form of innovative literature in modern Chinese society'.[6]

We might also note that the first modern-style proscenium stage where both modern and traditional plays were performed and open to Chinese audiences was located in Shanghai's New Stage (*Xin wutai*) theatre, which dates from 1908. This stage could accommodate complex scenery and properties, in contrast to the old-style stages, which had no décor and only very simple props. Instead of sitting around tables, as so often happened in the old-style theatres, the audience faced the proscenium. Although traditional stages are still occasionally used in China, the proscenium stage has become dominant for the theatre. Modern concert halls have also become the norm for musical performances.

The Republican period

The New Culture Movement, which began with the appearance of the journal *New Youth* in 1915, and the May Fourth Movement of 1919 had a tremendous effect on Chinese drama. Western theatre patterns exerted a powerful influence, with many plays translated into Chinese, smoothing the way 'for the new theatre of ideas, in which scripts became the basis of the production; stagecraft became secondary to faithful adherence to a preconceived and unalterable written form; authors dictated to actors; and exhortation replaced entertainment'.[7] An implication of this last point was that the reform movement gathered momentum, with dramatists increasingly convinced that they must use their art to change society for the better and to help roll back the Western and Japanese imperialism they saw as humiliating China.

In the field of music and the performing arts, the New Culture activists faced a dilemma: reform appeared to require them to take new forms and styles from the West, but patriotism implied that their own tradition might have good things to offer. Few people shared the radical view of Qian Xuantong (1887–1939) that traditional Chinese drama should be eliminated altogether, since it was a relic of an evil Confucian past. However, the main beneficiary of May Fourth radicalism was undoubtedly the spoken drama, the Western form that had been introduced to China through Japan. And the literary doctrine guiding the new drama was realism, which required costuming, gestures and actions that resembled everyday life and required 'facing truth and reality, especially the unpleasant truth of unhappy endings',[8] all of which was the direct antithesis of traditional drama.

The May Fourth period led to a very distinguished period in the history of the spoken drama, with a host of distinguished playwrights that included Ouyang Yuqian (1889–1962), Hu Shi (1891–1962), Guo Moruo (1892–1978), Tian Han (1898–1968) and Hong Shen (1894–1955). A good example of this genre is the work of Cao Yu (1910–96), the pen-name of Wan Jiabao. One specialist expresses a typical view when he claims Cao Yu as 'the greatest of all the playwrights China has produced in modern theatre'.[9] Despite his long life, prolific output and in general highly successful career, Cao's best plays were produced in the 1930s. These were *Thunderstorm* [*Leiyu*, 1934], which has been called 'the most famous dramatic work of the pre-war period and possibly the most performed play in the modern Chinese theatre',[10] *Sunrise* [*Richu*, 1936] and *The Wilderness* [*Yuanye*, 1937]. According to one specialist, *Thunderstorm* and *Sunrise* 'attracted unprecedented audiences to the spoken drama and helped establish the first full-time professional company devoted exclusively to spoken drama'.[11] Although Cao Yu's plays are set in China and are an attempt as serious as any in modern Chinese theatre to wrestle with the problems of Chinese society, they certainly show the foreign impact familiar to his times. One writer states that he was 'heavily influenced by and deeply indebted to his great predecessors in the Western theater, particularly Ibsen, O'Neill and Chekhov'.[12]

In terms of the traditional drama, an interesting development in the Republican period was the 'newly written historical drama' (*xinbian lishi ju*). These were new arrangements of old or historical stories in traditional style. The theatre scholar Qi Rushan (1877–1962) wrote some of these for his friend Mei Lanfang (1894–1961), the most famous actor

China has produced. However, it was the CCP writers who paid most attention to this form.

In May 1942, CCP Chairman Mao Zedong put forward from his base in Yan'an in northern Shaanxi the idea that literature and the arts were an essential component in developing revolutionary ideology among the masses. It was important to use them directly for propaganda purposes and to follow a class line, with the arts clearly supporting the masses of workers, peasants and soldiers against the class enemies, especially the landlords, big bourgeoisie and collaborators with the Japanese. Mao's ideas applied to all arts, not just the performing arts, but he was particularly interested in traditional theatre, which became one of the sites he used to push his ideas.

The CCP sponsored a movement to 'weed through the old and push forward the new' (*tuichen chuxin*).[13] For *jingju* an important stage came on 9 January 1944, when Mao saw a newly written historical drama called *Bishang Liangshan* [*Forced up Mount Liang*]. It tells of the rebels of the classical novel *Shuihu zhuan* [*Water Margin*], which is about rebels and feudal ruling-class oppression, because its focal point is that the protagonist Lin Chong is given no choice but to go up Mount Liang and join the rebels there. Mao was very enthusiastic about the drama, praising the actors for 'restoring history's true face' by making positive characters not out of 'lords and ladies' (*laoye taitai shaoye xiaojiemen*) but of rebels and the masses.[14]

Already, a form similar to Western opera, known as *geju* (song drama), was emerging. The first large-scale example among the Han majority of China was *The White-Haired Girl*, which premiered in April 1945 in conjunction with the Seventh CCP Congress. The opera combines Western and Chinese instrumentation, singing style and music, and is largely based on local melodies, but departs from the conventions of the traditional drama. *The White-Haired Girl* is about a village girl who, raped by a landlord, escapes into the mountains where she has a child and undergoes privations so severe that her hair turns white and the local people regard her as a spirit. In the end, the revolution triumphs and she accuses the landlord of his crimes.

The People's Republic of China from 1949 to 1976

When the CCP came to power in 1949, it set about reforming music and the performing arts to suit the needs of the new socialist China, as well as preparing to use these arts for political purposes. In music, the main focus was on the popular arts, including *xiqu*, folk music and *quyi*, because one of the main points of the CCP's doctrine was that the arts should both reach the masses and influence them in the direction of socialism. Several major organizations were set up to cater for the needs of musicians and dramatists, and festivals were held to promote their work. One Chinese account of early PRC activity in the field of *quyi* could apply to other popular music:

> Many literature and art workers took part in *quyi* reform work. On the one hand, they helped folk artists collect and arrange good traditional works, and raised them to new heights from ideological and artistic points of view. On the other hand, they actively created and arranged new works that reflected realistic life.[15]

The 'realistic life' reflected in these new works was geared very definitely to perpetuate the values of the new regime and the policies it was putting forward.

Like all art forms, the *xiqu* was expected to advocate revolt against the feudal system, equality for oppressed groups such as peasants, women and minorities, and patriotism. Some works that appeared to go against such themes were banned, and many 'newly written historical dramas' on traditional themes were developed that followed the CCP line. These used complex décor and stage properties, with the characters of the libretto projected on screens beside the stage. The changes initially left most of the conventions of the *xiqu* intact. However, from 1954 a few conventions that were considered 'unhealthy', such as the old method of imitating the gait of a woman's bound feet, were banned.

In the spoken drama, Cao Yu continued to write new work, and in 1956 the People's Literature Press published his three-act *Bright Skies* [*Minglang de tian*], which concerns American germ warfare during the Korean War. Probably the best representative spoken drama in the early years of the People's Republic is *Teahouse* [*Chaguan*] by the Manchu writer Lao She, pen-name of Shu Qingchun (1899–1966), which was written in 1957 and premiered the following year. The play is unique in the way it sets its three acts in the same place, the Yutai Teahouse in Beijing, but in entirely different periods – the first in 1898, the second soon after the death of China's first president Yuan Shikai in 1916, and the third shortly before the CCP came to power. Lao She regarded Beijing's teahouses as 'a microcosm of society as a whole',[16] which meant that a teahouse could portray a reasonably accurate view of the development of history over half a century.

In 1957, the new form of *wuju* (dance drama), which combined elements of Western ballet with traditional Chinese dance movements and Western and Chinese music, was developed. New theatres were built, official figures claiming that the number rose from 891 in 1949 to over 2,800 in 1959, an early example being the People's Theatre (*Renmin juchang*) in Beijing. Meanwhile, the CCP attempted to raise the social status of actors and musicians, by inviting representatives to join the CCP and even the National People's Congress.

At the same time the CCP did not initially ignore either traditional Chinese or foreign music. It reformed the ancient musical instrument the seven-stringed zither (*guqin*) and sponsored publication of transcriptions of old pieces as well as the training of good *guqin* performers. In 1956 the China National Symphony Orchestra (*Zhongguo guojia jiaoxiang yuetuan*) was established in Beijing. It performed some Western music but also Chinese works written especially for it, some of which used both Chinese and Western instruments. In December 1956 a Chinese opera company put on Giuseppe Verdi's *La Traviata*, which was the first European classical opera to be performed in the PRC.

The Cultural Revolution (1966–76) clamped down on Western music and traditional Chinese music that did not pass the test of being fully revolutionary. For a start, Lao She died under tragic circumstances as a direct result of the Cultural Revolution. The leader of the revolution in the performing arts was Mao Zedong's radical wife Jiang Qing (1913–91). The *xiqu* was restricted to a very small number of 'model dramas' (*yangban xi*), mostly *jingju* but also a few others such as ballets, all set in the revolutionary period from the late 1920s on. Traditional *xiqu* and *quyi* were not allowed to be performed, while records of them disappeared from the shops. All the models were specifically designed to emphasize the class struggle, the leading positive characters being revolutionary heroes and the negative ones class enemies such as landlords or Japanese invaders. One of the few items allowed to be performed by the China National Symphony Orchestra was the *Yellow River Piano Concerto*, composed for it by committee and designed to emphasize the heroism of the Chinese people.

Possibly the best known of the 'model dramas' was the *jingju The Red Lantern* [*Hongdeng ji*], which features three generations of revolutionary heroes set against the background of the Japanese occupation. The story gives full play to the revolutionary heroism of the three protagonists, especially the main hero, the middle-generation Li Yuhe. In addition, the stage properties, gestures and acting allow the characters and heroic class nature of the heroes to be set effectively against the reactionary qualities of the Japanese general and the soldiers and Chinese collaborators who support him. A few Western instruments have been added to the orchestra of this *jingju* to emphasize the heroism, while the music has a staccato style that is part of the mechanism of portraying the class struggle inherent in the story.

Another of the revolutionary 'model dramas' was the war ballet *The Red Detachment of Women* [*Hongse niangzi jun*], which takes up the theme of the oppression of women, but shows them resisting fiercely by forming a women's detachment. Chen Xiaomei comments:

> At first sight, gender differences seem to disappear as women warriors take to the battlefield as ably and courageously as their male counterparts. But it then becomes evident – when we see that women are encouraged to be androgynous but that men's so-called male characteristics remain inviolate – that the unequal power relationship between genders will persist.[17]

The tension to which Chen refers is a very interesting one. However, both in the period of civil war before 1949, when the drama is set, and during the Cultural Revolution, when it reached its greatest popularity, the focus in *Hongse niangzi jun* was inevitably more on the political than on gender struggle. What mattered most was that women should take part in revolutionary struggle along with men and fight as well as men, not that they should in all respects be equal to men.

It would be a mistake to write off the theatre of the Cultural Revolution period completely. Even in the early twenty-first century, the 'models' attract some attention and occasional performance. Moreover, the Cultural Revolution period saw a blooming of theatrical performance in the countryside. Village amateurs were very active, even though they had to follow the tight prescriptions laid down by Mao and his followers. Mao was one of the few leaders in modern Chinese history to place emphasis on rural culture.

The People's Republic of China: reform period since the late 1970s

The Cultural Revolution was probably the most restrictive period for the arts in Chinese history. However, with Mao's death in 1976 and the negation of the Cultural Revolution in 1978, things changed very quickly for music and the performing arts.

The late 1970s ushered in a period of spectacular revival and creativity in the Chinese theatre. The best traditional *xiqu* and *quyi* came back, as did the best 'newly written historical dramas' of the past, even including *Bishang Liangshan*. The *geju* and *wuju*, few of which had been allowed to be performed during the Cultural Revolution, were revived, their tunes regaining popularity throughout much of the country.

In terms of newly created items, the most prominent and controversial items were the spoken dramas and the 'newly written historical dramas'. We can see several major themes in the dramas produced in the 1980s. One was a revival of traditional patterns and a rethinking of Chinese history, of all periods – imperial, modern and contemporary – the last primarily consisting of attacks on the Cultural Revolution and all it stood for. Another theme was Western influence in the theatre. Yan Haiping, one of the best dramatists of the time, as well as a leading commentator, has written that, besides dramatists who reread China's past and examined current conditions in China,

> [t]here emerged another group of playwrights who attempted to break away from what they saw as the alienating, antiartistic, and ultimately illusory role of social and moral leadership with which Chinese intellectuals … seemed obsessed. Looking to the West for inspiration, these playwrights discovered Western modernism in their eager, albeit tentative, pursuit of "the modern".[18]

Perhaps the most innovative dramatist in the field of the spoken drama in the 1980s was Gao Xingjian (born 1940), who was in 2000 to distinguish himself by becoming the first person writing mainly in the Chinese language to win the Nobel Prize for literature. In 1981 he joined the Beijing People's Art Theatre, the leading spoken drama company in China. Between 1982 and 1985 he wrote three notable plays, *Juedui xinhao* [*Absolute Signal*, 1982], *Chezhan* [*Bus Stop*, 1983] and *Yeren* [*Wild Man*, 1985]. The first director for all three plays was Lin Zhaohua (b. 1936), vice-president of the Beijing People's Art Theatre from 1984 to 1998 and one of China's most significant directors. The partnership confirmed the Beijing People's Art Theatre as China's main centre of experimental theatre.

Both *Absolute Signal* and *Bus Stop* show the heavy influence of modern Western theatre. The French newspaper *Le monde* declared that *Absolute Signal* marked 'the birth of avant-garde theatre in China'.[19] *Bus Stop* is regarded as China's first example of theatre of the absurd.[20] About a group of people who wait ten years for a bus that never comes, it is to some extent inspired by Samuel Beckett's *Waiting for Godot*,[21] although we should not underestimate 'the dynamic synthesis of Western and Chinese theatrical traditions present in the play'.[22] In *Wild Man*, Gao turned much more to traditional themes, including Confucianism, Daoism, and folk cultures, as well as to the theatrical style of the traditional drama (*xiqu*).[23]

Although the theatre of the 1980s was incomparably broader in range and creativity than that of the Cultural Revolution had been, the authorities continued to keep an eye on what was happening in the theatre and did not hesitate to ban plays they found offensive to the socialist system. Gao Xingjian was a controversial figure who came under suspicion for the highly experimental nature of his work, which appeared to CCP authorities to depart from or ignore any socialist ideal, as well as for the somewhat negative view of contemporary Chinese society that comes over in his plays. One specialist claims that Gao compromised his endings, making them less bleak than he would have liked.[24] In any case, he left China in 1987, making his home in Paris. In 1991 he declared he would never return to a 'totalitarian China', and in 1998 he became a French citizen.[25]

The 1980s were also an excellent period for the 'newly written historical dramas', indeed probably the best decade since the form emerged. Very good dramas were produced in many of the regional styles. The most represented style was, not surprisingly, *jingju*. However, the most innovative playwright of the period was probably Wei Minglun (b. 1940), who wrote for Sichuan Province's main traditional regional theatre genre, called Sichuan drama (*chuanju*).

Unlike Gao Xingjian, Wei Minglun has continued to live in China – in fact, in Zigong in his native Sichuan Province. His best-known work is *Pan Jinlian*, which will be discussed briefly below, but he has written other innovative dramas. Probably the most notable of these is an adaptation into a *jingju* (1993) and then a *chuanju* of Giacomo Puccini's last opera, *Turandot*, itself set in China. Wei's *Turandot* won him numerous awards at the National Drama Festival held in 1994 in Chengdu, Sichuan's capital.

However, despite some continuing exceptions such as the works of Wei Minglun, the last decade of the twentieth century and the beginning of the twenty-first century have not been as rich as the preceding period for the Chinese performing arts. Xiaomei Chen is quite right when she writes:

> It is important to point out that after the mid-1980s, theatre
> productions declined drastically, losing out to television, film, and
> other mass media. Gone were the days of early post-Maoist China
> when a play could draw large audiences with its pointed critique
> of contemporary society ... Gone also were the 'golden' times of the
> Cultural Revolution, when dramas of model theater like *The Red
> Detachment of Women* were familiar to the majority of the people.[26]

Since the early to mid-1990s the modernization push has had an especially severe impact on *xiqu*. The government has attempted to maintain
it in several ways, such as sponsoring large-scale festivals and making
traditional music, especially *jingju*, into a tourist attraction. Chen's reference in the above quotation to television is particularly interesting, since
China Central Television has set aside an entire channel for the traditional theatre. The medium of television may yet save traditional music.

Although the decline of interest in traditional Chinese music and
performing arts has occurred everywhere in China, it has been most pronounced in the cities. In the countryside traditions of all kinds have retained considerable strength. Rural customs, such as popular festivals,
still survive and draw some interest, and folk peasant musical and drama
troupes remain quite active in many parts of rural China.

One factor of relevance here is religion, the importance of which to
Chinese society is recognized in its allocation of a chapter in this book.
The following comment may be specifically about instrumental music,
but could apply equally to other performing arts, especially those of the
countryside.

> Religion is a major theme: secularization is far from complete, and
> to seek instrumental music almost inevitably leads us to the study of
> ritual. Folk ritual specialists and musicians, serving calendrical or
> life-cycle rituals, are still the major life-force of instrumental music
> in China today. Some village musicians are professional, others
> perform as a social or religious duty. Musicians also meet for their own
> pleasure – notably the string ensembles of coastal southern China.[27]

One of the most remarkable phenomena of the reform period has been
both highly secular and highly urban: the emergence of an active rock
music (*yaogun yinyue*) scene in China. The first rock band, called Wan-Li-
Ma-Wang from the surnames of its four members, was set up in Beijing
in 1980. It performed mainly Western music such as songs by the Beatles
and the Rolling Stones. Since that time, the number of rock bands has

grown exponentially. Beijing remains by far the most active centre of Chinese rock music, with over 200 bands in 1994,[28] but there are bands in other cities such as Shanghai, Chengdu and Guangzhou.[29] The 'father' of Chinese rock is Cui Jian (b. 1961), who has produced many songs that have become popular among China's youth, most notably 'I Have Nothing' [*Yiwu suoyou*], which premiered in May 1986. Although the performance of rock is mainly a male phenomenon, there are some female rock artists, and the first all-female rock band was Cobra (*Yanjingshe*), founded in the spring of 1989.

It is the greater openness to the West that has characterized the reform period which has enabled the growth of a Chinese rock scene. Rock was one of the main cultural products of the sudden and spectacular enthusiasm for everything Western when contacts with the West became permissible after the end of the Cultural Revolution and foreign students, cassettes and television programmes flooded into China. On the other hand, there are significant Chinese elements in the instrumentation and style of Chinese rock. It has even been suggested that Mao Zedong's ideology of rebellion and revolution has made it possible to sinicize rock music effectively.[30]

There are political implications in the introduction of such an art form. Just as in the West, rock is associated with cries for freedom and opposition to the establishment. Cui Jian's 'I Have Nothing', though initially performed at a state-organized concert in the People's Workers' Stadium in Beijing, became a 'student hymn' during the protests of 1989.[31] Most rock artists since then have maintained some anti-establishment flavour. Cui Jian has continued to emphasize individualism and criticize society in his art, and though his early success with 'I Have Nothing' has never been completely replicated he remains recognized both in China and abroad.[32]

The authorities have occasionally stopped rock concerts, on the grounds that they are hostile to the government, at least in flavour and at times directly in content. Yet the rock music industry is thriving, and has produced numerous tapes and CDs. Moreover, rock music remains diverse, including works that range 'from rap, reggae, jazz, World Beat, and heavy metal to punk and even to dance music'.[33]

The reform period has seen the emergence not only of far more Western influence on Chinese theatre but also of performance of Western theatrical and musical pieces. Western music was suppressed more or less entirely during the Cultural Revolution. But the opening up in the reform period has been incomparably broader than during the 1950s or early 1960s. Exchanges with Western countries have meant the regular performance of Western works by foreign groups, sometimes in conjunction with Chinese. Probably the largest in scale of these foreign performances as of 2008 was the Nuremberg State Theatre's production of Richard Wagner's mighty *Der Ring des Niebelungen*. The four operas were performed in Beijing late in 2005, the first time the entire cycle had been performed in China. In Beijing in 1986, this writer saw a Chinese performance, in Chinese and by Chinese performers, of Georges Bizet's *Carmen*. In May 2000 the China Philharmonic Orchestra was established in Beijing, with the German-trained Yu Long as its founding artistic director and principal conductor. It plays the Western orchestral canon, such as the works of Beethoven, Brahms and Mahler, as well as Chinese symphonic items from the 1930s and music newly written by Chinese composers in an idiom heavily influenced by Western styles. One of the channels of China Central Television is dedicated to telecasting concerts of the Western classics, as well as Chinese traditional music and occasionally groups from other foreign countries.

Training in Western music has come to occupy a fairly high place in the Chinese education system, with Chinese-trained musicians doing well on the international stage. Perhaps the most famous is the composer and conductor Tan Dun (born in 1957 in Hunan), who was trained at the Central Conservatorium in Beijing but has lived in New York since 1986. Tan has conducted several of the world's most famous orchestras and is fully conversant with Western musical idiom, but his works combine Western and Chinese styles in what one writer has called 'his search for the core of global musical and artistic experience'.[34]

Some notes on gender in the Chinese theatre

One of the most prominent themes in spoken drama as well as in the reformed *xiqu* has been gender. Progressives have been very keen to use drama as a means of improving the lot of women. Many plays, including those set in the distant past, have pushed the cause of women's emancipation, and we have seen above how Jiang Qing and her followers adapted gender issues during the Cultural Revolution. Illustrative of gender matters are two items about Pan Jinlian, a character in one chapter of the novel *Shuihu zhuan* [*The Water Margin*], as well as in the erotic and pornographic novel *Jin Ping Mei* [*The Golden Lotus*]. Pan was traditionally regarded as an evil woman because she was a nymphomaniac who killed one of her husbands to marry Ximen Qing, the anti-hero of *Jin Ping Mei* and a man even more noted for his insatiable sexual appetite than she.

An early example of a play about Pan, entitled simply *Pan Jinlian*, was written by actor, dramatist and drama historian Ouyang Yuqian, and premiered in 1927, being published in 1928.[35] Originally a spoken drama, it was also performed as a *jingju* with Ouyang himself playing the title role. Despite Pan Jinlian's bad reputation in traditional times, Ouyang Yuqian takes her side and has her voice a plausible defence of her actions as a fighter for women's rights. In Ouyang's hands, she becomes almost a heroic figure, the antithesis of the image traditionalists attributed to her.

Written over half a century later, *chuanju* dramatist Wei Minglun's most important and novel drama is also called *Pan Jinlian*, and according to its creator 'a Sichuan drama of the absurd' *(huangdan chuanju)*. The drama crosses cultural and time barriers by appealing to judgments about Pan by a range of people, including the only female emperor in Chinese history Wu Zetian (who reigned from 684–705), Anna Karenina, Ximen Qing himself, and a female judge of the People's Republic. At the end of the drama, the judge sums up as follows:

> This is the story of a woman's fall –
> Ages of feudalism caused it all.
> I wished to save her, but she'll soon be dead.
> My heart cannot overrule my head.
> We should not follow ways we know are evil;
> The moral of this story's deep and doleful![36]

Wei Minglun does not justify Pan Jinlian's actions. She is no hero, and in that sense he departs from some feminist accounts of Pan, especially Ouyang Yuqian's version. On the other hand, he does transfer the blame away from the woman herself and to the society in which she lived. This is very clear in the judge's summary, especially in her comment that the root cause of her actions was 'ages of feudalism'. Wei wrote of an absurdist dream he had had about the play, in one part telling the French absurdist playwright Eugène Ionesco that in his play Pan 'undergoes enormous transformations, from simple naïveté to complicated worldliness, from trying to fight against the odds to sinking into total depravity, from an innocent victim to a criminal'.[37] Wei's *Pan Jinlian* is actually more about the position of women in contemporary China than it is about the past. But to take the historical characters and use the form of traditional *chuanju* was a brilliant development in the history of *xiqu*. At the end of his absurdist dream Wei heard hostile voices telling him that *Pan Jinlian* would not help revitalize the traditional theatre, but would only hasten its decline. This 'horrible' thought shocked him thoroughly, and he woke to greet 'some light in the eastern sky'.[38] However, if traditional theatre does decline, it will hardly be the fault of Wei Minglun.

A very different way of looking at gender issues in Chinese theatre derives from the ancient practice of cross-dressing, which meant that boys or men played female roles while women played men's roles. The male *dan* or female impersonator existed in almost all local traditional drama styles, and saw its greatest artistic development in the four great *dan* of the *jingju*, most prominent of whom was Mei Lanfang.

The decline of cross-dressing began in the Republican period. Ironically, this was partly because Mei himself took on some female disciples, a highly radical move at the time. This meant that women would begin to play women's roles. The Beiping Private Advanced Traditional Drama School (*Beiping shi sili Zhongguo gaoji xiqu zhiye xuexiao*), established in 1930, was extremely unusual in taking on both male and female students. Meanwhile, in the 1920s women began to play men's roles (*sheng*) in the local style of Zhejiang Province called the *yueju*, often translated as Shaoxing Opera, which became an all-female theatre by the early 1940s.

PRC governments have generally found it unnatural to have men playing female roles or vice versa. They have also condemned as feudal the past practices involved in training the male *dan*, which included the purchase of little boys from desperately poor parents by managers. In 1964, Zhou Enlai stated that cross-dressing of all kinds would gradually be phased out, even though it would continue to be part of actors' training. In practice, what has happened since the Cultural Revolution has been 'the gradual demise of the male *dan* across all forms of regional opera, and the continual flourishing of the female *sheng*', particularly in *yueju*.[39] There is a certain irony in this fact, considering the former importance of male *dan* in performing women's roles.

Conclusion

The balance between Western influence on the arts and the Chinese tradition, whether reinvented or unreformed, has changed greatly over the last few decades, and mostly in the direction of Western influence. It is remarkable to see the tradition in decline at the same time that rock music seizes the imagination of urban young people. Market forces have become much stronger than ever before in the period of reform, and seem to be accelerating since China joined the World Trade Organization at the end of 2001. This will probably affect the situation of music and the performing arts in China, because the government will no longer provide the funds to bail out failed companies.

At the same time, China is becoming demographically more urban than ever before. The 1982 census indicated that 20.91 per cent of the population was urban, but this figure grew to 26.44 per cent in the 1990 census and 36.22 per cent in the census of 2000.[40] Small towns may well remain centres of traditional arts, and it would be a mistake to write off rural or semi-rural traditions. But the balance between urban modern arts and rural traditional arts will continue to shift in favour of the former.

The forces of globalization in music and the performing arts in China are expanding at the expense of those of indigenization, but it is unlikely that the traditions will die out completely. In some contexts, globalization has the effect of reviving traditions, because people do not want to see their own culture swept away in a tide of globalization. But one thing appears fairly cert   revived tradition will be a changed tradition. It may be possible   pure tradition for tourists, a bit like a museu   nothing wrong with museums deeply seated in socie

Notes

1. These five categorie
   cologists in the 195
   tions, Oxford, Clar
2. Jones, *Folk Music*
3. See Liang Qichao
   Fei (ed. and tra
   Present, Ann Arl
4. Patricia Sieber
   Song-Drama, 1:
   lan, 2003, p. 7
5. Quoted in R
   Twentieth Ce
6. Edward M.
   Drama, An

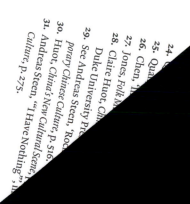

24.
25. Qua
26. Chen,
27. Jones, *Folk M*
28. Claire Huot, *Chi*
   Duke University Pr
29. See Andreas Steen, *Roc*
   porary Chinese Culture,
30. Huot, *China's New Culture*, p.516.
31. Andreas Steen, "I Have Nothing,"
   Culture, p.275.

7. Bonnie S. McDougall and Kam Louie, *The Literature of China in the Twentieth Century*, London, Christopher Hurst, 1997, p. 156.

8. Gunn, 'Introduction', p. viii.

9. Faubion Bowers, *Theatre in the East: A Survey of Asian Dance and Drama*, New York, T. Nelson, 1960, p. 299.

10. McDougall and Louie, *The Literature of China*, p. 177.

11. Gunn, 'Introduction', p. ix.

12. John Y. H. Hu, *Ts'ao Yü*, New York, Twayne Publishers, 1972, p. 137. Joseph S. M. Lau's major study of Cao Yu is entitled *Ts'ao Yü, The Reluctant Disciple of Chekhov and O'Neill, A Study in Literary Influence*, Hong Kong, Centre of Asian Studies, Hong Kong University, 1970.

13. See Hu Dongsheng, Su Yi, Han Xibai, *et al.*, *Zhongguo Jingju shi, zhongjuan* [The history of China's jingju], vol. 2, Beijing, Zhongguo xiju chubanshe, 1990, pp. 244–50.

14. See the passage quoted in Huang Yuchuan (ed.), *Mao Zedong shengping ziliao jianbian, yibajiusannian – yijiuliujiunian* (Brief material from Mao Zedong's life, 1893–1969), Hong Kong, Union Research Institute, 1970, p. 221.

15. Su Ren, 'Quyi wenxue' ['Quyi literature'], in Zhang Geng Yu Lin, Liu Nianzi *et al.* (eds.), *Zhongguo da baike quanshu, xiqu quyi* [China encyclopedia, Traditional theatre, balladry], Beijing, Shanghai, Zhongguo da baike quanshu chubanshe, 1983, p. 324.

16. Lao She, 'In Response to Some Questions about *Teahouse*', in Lao She (trans. John Howard-Gibbon), *Teahouse, A Play in Three Acts*, Beijing, Foreign Languages Press, 1980, p. 82.

17. Xiaomei Chen, 'Introduction', in Xiaomei Chen (ed.), *Reading the Right Text: An Anthology of Contemporary Chinese Drama*, Honolulu, University of Hawai'i Press, 2003, p. 47.

18. Yan Haiping, 'Theater and Society, An Introduction to Contemporary Chinese Drama', in Haiping Yan (ed.), *Theater and Society, An Anthology of Contemporary Chinese Drama*, Armonk, New York; London, England, M. E. Sharpe, 1998, p. xv.

19. See Sy Ren Quah, *Gao Xingjian and Transcultural Chinese Theater*, Honolulu, University of Hawai'i Press, 2004, p. 63.

20. For a translation of *Bus Stop* see Gao Xingjian, trans. Kimberly Besio, 'Bus Stop, A Lyrical Comedy on Life in One Act' in Yan (ed.), *Theater and society*, pp. 3–59.

21. Quah, *Gao Xingjian*, p. 64.

22. Carla Kirkwood, 'Bus Stop', in Edward L. Davis (ed.), *Encyclopedia of Contemporary Chinese Culture*, London and New York, Routledge, 2005, p. 55.

23. See a translation of *Wild Man* in Gao Xingjian, trans. Bruno Boubicek, 'Wild Man', *Asian Theatre Journal* 7, no. 2, [Fall 1990], 195–249.

Quah, *Gao Xingjian*, pp. 85–9.

Gao Xingjian, p. 89.

troduction', p. 51.

sic of China, p. 365.

a's New Cultural Scene, A Handbook of Changes, Durham and London, s, 2000, p. 165.

Music, Rock Bands', in Davis (ed.), *Encyclopedia of Contem-*

pp. 154–5.

Davis (ed.), *Encyclopedia of Contemporary Chinese*

32. Andreas Steen, 'Cui Jian', in Davis (ed.), *Encyclopedia of Contemporary Chinese Culture*, p. 118.

33. Huot, *China's New Cultural Scene*, p. 170.

34. Joanna C. Lee, 'Tan Dun', in Davis (ed.), *Encyclopedia of Contemporary Chinese Culture*, p. 580.

35. For a translation of this play see Ou-yang Yü-ch'ien, trans. Catherine Swatek, 'P'an Chin-lien', in Gunn (ed.), *Twentieth-century Chinese Drama*, pp. 52–75. On Ouyang Yuqian, see McDougall and Louie, *The Literature of China*, pp. 161–4, including brief commentary on *Pan Jinlian* on pp. 162–3.

36. Wei Minglun, trans. David Williams, with the assistance of Xiaoxia Williams, 'Pan Jinlian, The History of a Fallen Woman', in Yan (ed.), *Theater and Society*, p. 188. The whole *chuanju* is translated on pp. 123–88.

37. Wei Minglun, 'I am Dreaming a Very Absurd Dream: Thoughts on *Pan Jinlian*', in Fei (ed. and trans.), *Chinese Theories of Theater and Performance*, p. 197.

38. Wei, 'I am Dreaming a Very Absurd Dream', p. 201.

39. Siu Leung Li, *Cross-dressing in Chinese Opera*, Hong Kong, Hong Kong University Press, 2003, pp. 191–2.

40. See the basic figures from the censuses in National Bureau of Statistics of China (comp.), *Zhongguo tongji nianjian, China Statistical Yearbook 2002*, Beijing, China Statistics Press, 2002, p. 95.

Guide to further reading

Chen, Xiaomei (ed.), *Reading the Right Text: An Anthology of Contemporary Chinese Drama*, Honolulu, University of Hawai'i Press, 2003.

Chen, Xiaomei, *Acting the Right Part: Political Theater and Popular Drama in Contemporary China, 1966–1996*, Honolulu, University of Hawai'i Press, 2002.

Gunn, Edward M. (ed.), *Twentieth-century Chinese Drama, An Anthology*, Chinese Literature in Translation, Bloomington, Indiana University Press, 1983.

Jones, Stephen, *Folk Music of China, Living Instrumental Traditions*, Oxford, Clarendon Press, 1995.

Mackerras, Colin, *The Chinese Theatre in Modern Times from 1840 to the Present Day*, Chinese History and Society, London, Thames and Hudson, 1975.

   The Performing Arts in Contemporary China, London, Boston and Henley, Routledge & Kegan Paul, 1981, reprinted *China: History, Philosophy, Economics* vol. 18, London, New York, Routledge, 2005.

McDougall, Bonnie S. and Kam Louie, *The Literature of China in the Twentieth Century*, London, Christopher Hurst, 1997.

Mittler, Barbara, *Dangerous Tunes, The Politics of Chinese Music in Hong Kong, Taiwan and the People's Republic of China*, Wiesbaden, Harrassowitz, 1997.

Quah, Sy Ren. *Gao Xingjian and Transcultural Chinese Theater*, Honolulu, University of Hawai'i Press, 2004.

Stock, Jonathan P. J., *Huju: Traditional Opera in Modern Shanghai*, Oxford University Press, 2003.

Yan, Haiping (ed.), *Theater and Society, An Anthology of Contemporary Chinese Drama*, Asia and the Pacific; Armonk, New York; London, England, M. E. Sharpe, 1998.

14
_____

Revolutions in vision: Chinese art and the experience of modernity

Since the mid-1990s, contemporary Chinese art has been increasingly visible in European, North American and Australian venues.[1] While the same period has also seen an equally unprecedented interest in the art of many other non-Western countries, indicating a more general waning of Western-centred conceptions of artistic contemporaneity, the sheer abundance of recent Chinese art is particularly striking. While it has long been acknowledged in the West that China has its own highly distinctive visual culture, this has often been presented as a largely monolithic and timeless tradition, distinct from the concerns of Western art. European art has generally been seen as having developed over time, whether the focus has been on the emergence of coherent perspectival space during the Italian Renaissance or on the apparent movement towards abstraction and formal purity in the modern era. Chinese art, at least from the point of view of the non-specialist Western observer, has by contrast seemed relatively static in terms of both its subject matter and its technique. With the irruption of recent Chinese art into Western exhibition venues, both the sense of Chinese art as occurring in some other cultural space and the sense of it as somehow not really having a historical development are no longer tenable. Chinese art now clearly exists in the present tense, rather than offering some unchanging timeless tradition that provides an exotic backdrop against which the historical evolution of Western art can be viewed, and it is perceived as taking place within the same globalized arena for art as that occupied by its Western counterpart.

This chapter will offer a characterization of recent Chinese art as one part of an introduction to twentieth-century Chinese art as a whole. Despite the interest in contemporary Chinese art there has been relatively little exhibition of earlier twentieth-century art outside China itself and also little non-specialist Western critical attention; yet without some consideration of such art any general account of artistic modernism that was written from the present globalized moment would surely remain only parochial.[2] In presenting the distinctive Chinese artistic response to the modern experience, I will adopt a simple tripartite periodization, and the three successive periods will be defined in sociopolitical terms, rather than by reference to any intrinsic art historical logic such as stylistic development. In part this is a recognition that there is no easy counterpart in China to the '-isms' of modern European art history – its succession of style or movement labels – but it is also a recognition that, for China in particular, any consideration of art in isolation from its changing sociopolitical or cultural context would only lead to misunderstanding. The first phase considered here coincides with the period of the Republic of China (1912–49), the second with the era of the People's Republic from its founding until the end of the Cultural Revolution (1949–76), and the third with the period of economic liberalization and cultural opening that followed. If it is only during the first period – following the New Culture Movement (1917–23), with its emphasis on cultural solutions to the problem of national regeneration – that art might potentially have had a role on centre stage, in the latter two phases (where political and then economic solutions to China's ills came, successively, to dominate) it was equally entwined with the events of national life as a whole.

China's artistic trajectory in the twentieth century was marked by the extraordinary degree of social change the country witnessed, with two revolutions – one Republican and one Communist – within less than forty years of each other, and the arguably even more radical effects of the accelerated economic transformation of the past twenty years. Although this has led to many interruptions and historical discontinuities in China's artistic life, justifying the periodization proposed here, there are nevertheless several overarching themes that are relevant to this period as a whole, and that are most usefully specified in advance of the more chronologically organized discussion that follows. While not exactly constituting straightforward continuities, these themes – which to a certain extent interweave – do offer us some way of specifying the particular nature of China's artistic experience over the last hundred years.

Perhaps the most persistent theme in twentieth-century Chinese art was its response to non-Chinese art, and more particularly to Western art. While knowledge of Western art had been brought directly to the

Chinese court or had permeated southern trading cities such as Canton and Macau much earlier, it was only with the twentieth century that Western ways of image making came to be widely seen in China as viable alternative modes for making high art. This moment of cultural or epistemological relativity (one way of defining the experience of modernity in general) also led to an awareness of Japanese art, and the century saw both travel by artists in search of alternative training or artistic sources and a reform of Chinese art education to accommodate the lessons of Western models. From the early Republican period onwards ambitious artists in China began to produce work that made use of media, styles and themes gleaned from Western art. This responsiveness to the West cannot be adequately described as passive influence or abject mimicry, but was at its best an active and selective appropriation guided by concerns specific to the time and place in which a particular Chinese artist was working. Most evident in art that used oil paint, this accommodation to the lessons of Western art can also be seen in ink painting, and even those ink painters whose work seems determinedly native in its sources are in some sense also a product of a modern world in which foreign modes need to be acknowledged, if only as something one consciously chooses to resist or reject.

If the relationship to Western modes of art was problematic, this was no different from the relation of Chinese artists of the modern period to their inherited native tradition. The rich heritage of ink painting and calligraphy in particular was something a great many artists felt a need to accommodate, and since this process is still occurring today it can be considered as the second major theme of twentieth-century Chinese art. Although certain art historical accounts have presented Western and Chinese modes of art-making as opposed to each other, and certain Chinese artists have indeed felt this to be the case, at other times there has been a sense that bridges can productively be built across the divide. The seeming unavoidability of the inherited visual tradition in China, and the difficulty of simply denying or discarding it to achieve modernity without risking some kind of felt deracination (and yet the difficulty of simply continuing to produce the kind of art that had been made in quite different premodern cultural circumstances), marks the Chinese experience of the modern as different from that of most European artists. Whereas for Maurice Vlaminck or Umberto Boccioni, say, artistic modernity consisted quite straightforwardly in a disavowal of the past, such an option rarely seemed adequate in the Chinese context.

This ambivalence between inherited and imported modes has led to a high degree of heterogeneity or pluralism in modern Chinese art, and (another related sub-theme) to much art that can be described as 'hybrid' in nature, even before the more widespread appearance of such art in the West during the era of post-modernism. One reason that the clash of cultures was felt particularly strongly in China was that its context was not merely trade, intellectual exchange and migration in a more neutral sense, but rather foreign invasion and occupation of Chinese soil. Although the impact of imperialism is also found in many other parts of the globe, the particular form it took in China's foreign concessions (where key areas of territory came under foreign jurisdiction but without being altogether cut off from the life of the rest of the country, for example in the French concession in Shanghai) is perhaps worth noting, being a causal factor of two further interrelated themes considered here: the importance of the city in modern Chinese art and the importance of China's margins in its artistic development. To a very large extent, the story of modern art in Republican China was a story of Shanghai. The development of Chinese visual culture during that time occurred primarily in the unprecedented crucible offered by this modern city, connected to the rest of the world through a vibrant port and containing foreign-run areas in which its Chinese citizens could encounter other cultures on home soil. In the present era of openness the major Chinese cities are again the primary sites of artistic experiment, often in response to the challenge of the new forms of urban existence emerging there, but, even in the earlier PRC era, cities can be said to have played a central role. This is because the flame of Chinese modernity was kept alive during this extended period of cultural closure by the cities of Taipei and Hong Kong.

These two cities, existing outside the People's Republic and both in their own ways markedly open to global economic, cultural and information flows, are also good examples of how Chinese artistic modernity grew from the margins rather than from the centre. Although Shanghai, Hong Kong and Taipei can each be thought of as at the edge of China, this theme of the margins only partly overlaps that of the city. Another significant part of China's cultural margin has been its diaspora. If most of the important Chinese artists of the Republican era only sojourned in Japan or the West, the period after the establishment of the People's Republic saw many major artists settling overseas, where the encounter with new developments in Western modernism was intense. In the decade following 4 June 1989, when artistic contemporaneity was newly emergent in the PRC but lacked native opportunities for open exhibition, a further wave of ambitious artists joined the diaspora, finding opportunities for display and sale not otherwise available to them.

A further key theme for twentieth-century Chinese art, as for other areas of Chinese cultural life, is nationalism. Artists of the Republican era began to introduce nationalist themes in their art, and in the PRC era such engagement with national content became a requirement for art that was strictly policed. While this embrace of national content was often found in the work of artists whose choice of medium and style was indebted to Western precedent, it had a particular consequence for ink painting, because that medium itself came during the twentieth century to have national connotations in a way it would never have done in earlier eras. This burden of being a national medium (now that it was thought of in contrast to oil, say) is reflected in the new term '*Guohua*' ('Chinese painting' or 'national painting') that emerged as a common label for ink painting in the twentieth century.

The Republican era (1912–1949)

Many of the most significant artists of the Republican era were those who had gained first-hand exposure to non-Chinese artistic traditions.[3] France was a particularly attractive destination for artists, with painter Lin Fengmian (1900–91), for instance, arriving in 1920 to study in both Dijon and Paris, while Xu Beihong (1895–1953) had arrived there a year earlier, basing himself in the French capital. Japan, which had travelled further down the road of modernization by that time than China, offered an appealing alternative base for study and exposure to cultural otherness in the early part of the century, and one that was rather closer at hand. Gao Jianfu (1879–1951), for instance, spent time there during his formative years as an artist (as well as being involved with the revolutionary movement of Sun Yat-sen), while Fu Baoshi (1904–65) was among those Chinese cultural figures who spent time in Japan during the early 1930s.

For each of these artists, overseas exposure was to influence the style of their art, although resources acquired overseas could not be applied unproblematically in the Chinese context, and some modification was always needed before foreign idioms could become viable in the home environment. For Xu, an oil painter who had developed an academic realist style, the main adaptation lay in applying this manner to Chinese subjects in a way that expressed appropriate national meanings, as in works

1 Xu Beihong, 'Tian Heng and his 500 Retainers', 1928–30

such as *Tian Heng and his 500 Retainers* (1928–30) (see figure 1). In this paint-ing Xu depicts Tian Heng, a heroic figure who chose to commit suicide rather than capitulate to the first emperor of the Han dynasty, as he takes leave of his followers for the last time. Even Xu, however, chose to also produce works in a more stylistically hybrid idiom by creating ink paint-ings that retained a Western-influenced sense of volume (for example, in his many images of horses). Gao Jianfu's output is less heterogeneous at the level of medium than Xu's, and his ink paintings allowed him to in-corporate Western understandings of volumetric form without produc-ing works that looked too obviously non-Chinese. Even Gao was to find difficulties in balancing the desire to retain a sense of relation to the ink-painting heritage (important even for a non-traditionalist painter such as Gao because of its national connotations) and a desire to incorporate modern-life subject matter of a kind not previously seen in Chinese art. In *Flying in the Rain* (1932), for instance (see figure 2), he depicts a group of biplanes (thus introducing connotations that are both explicitly mod-ern and linked to political nationalism due to the fact that Sun Yat-sen had emphasized the importance of aviation for the country's strength), but places them towards the rear of the painting's space lest they disrupt too violently the compositional format expected of a Chinese landscape painting.

In addition to artists such as Xu and Gao, who in their very different ways found the realism of Western art a resource for revitalizing Chinese painting, bringing it back in touch with the real world to a greater

2   Gao Jianfu, 'Flying in the Rain', 1932

degree than they considered it to be, there were Chinese artists of the Republican era who looked to Western modernist developments. In their case the resources of the West were often of interest more for what they had in common with the inherited language of ink painting than as an antidote to its failings. The visible brushwork of European Expressionism seemed equivalent for them to the *xieyi* tradition that had been present in Chinese ink painting from at least the Yuan dynasty, and which treated brushwork as a tool for the spontaneous display of character rather than the meticulous description of things (*xiesheng*). This interest in expression can be found in the painting of Lin Fengmian, for instance, and although his use of bright colour, inspired by Europeans such as Matisse, was without precedent in Chinese art (as was his Impressionism-influenced interest in reflections on the surface of water), overall his works have a more 'Chinese' feel than the oils of Xu. His characteristic favouring of a water-based medium helped produce this effect.

Certain of the possibilities and problems associated with the introduction of Western modes into the Chinese context can be illustrated most clearly through a discussion of the theme of the nude. Lin made use of nudes, so commonly found in Western art, in *Suffering* (1929), completed just three years after his return to China. Although the exact meaning of this now-destroyed work remains unclear, it does seem that Lin was using the naked body to express his response to events in contemporary China, and to carry meanings that are national and public in nature. Xu attempted something similar in *Yu Gong Removes the Mountain* (1940), in which semi-clothed figures, which draw on an understanding of the human body gained in studies from life done in Paris, add vividness to the representation of a well-known Chinese story about an old man who succeeds in the seemingly impossible task of moving a mountain when the heavens reward his determination. Direct depiction of the unclothed body frequently provoked opposition in the China of that time, however, and the use of nude models in art education was a source of conflict on more than one occasion. Liu Haisu (1896–1994) employed nude models at the Shanghai Art Academy (a private art school in Shanghai at which he was the director) as an integral part of European-style life-class training, but this led him into conflict with the warlord Sun Chuanfang in the mid-1920s.

Liu did not travel to Europe until slightly later than Lin and Xu, but like them he played a significant role in the reform of the Chinese art education system. Following their return to China from Europe in the mid-1920s, both Lin and Xu were to serve in turn as President of the Beijing Academy of Fine Arts, and Lin was also to become the founding head of the Hangzhou Academy of Art in 1927. This introduction of Western methods of art education, more important in the long run than the direct experience of Western art through overseas travel, was part of a broader project of educational renewal being undertaken in the Republican period. The arts were seen as playing a particularly important part in this project of national revitalization, and Lin's efforts in this area were inspired in part by the educational philosophy of Cai Yuanpei (who served for a time as Minister of Education following the establishment of the Republic, and who became Chancellor of Peking University in 1916). Cai believed that art could take over the role formerly played by religion in the spiritual life of the population, and Lin (who became personally acquainted with him) displays an analogous understanding of the significance of art in his own writings.

The development of institutions devoted to art education was a significant achievement of the Republican period, offering an alternative to the master-and-pupil training pattern that had been the dominant paradigm. It had the potential to enable people from a broader range of social backgrounds to engage with art, transforming its social basis, and provided a great many of the more interesting artists of this period with a living, thus enabling them to continue in their chosen vocation. These years also saw the development of various other aspects of an emerging public sphere for art, such as the practice of displaying art in exhibitions. The government itself was to arrange a National Art Exhibition in Shanghai in 1929, for instance, with a second exhibition taking place in Nanjing, Shanghai and Guangzhou in 1937. Clearly such arenas in which art could address a nationally conceived public were essential if it was to play a role in the life of the nation, and museums were equally significant tools for propagating national ideology. When the imperial art collection became a museum in 1925, for instance, the art of China's past was being mobilized in a radically novel way – even the old was becoming modern.

In addition to art schools, museums and public exhibitions, an important infrastructural role was played by art publishing. Albums of illustrations and translations of foreign books about art helped the process of understanding Western art and its possible usefulness as a source, while specialist art magazines provided the vehicle for the evolution of a distinctive Chinese art-critical discourse. One important art magazine

3 Lin Fengmian, 'Exercise', c. 1934

of the Republican period was *Yi Feng*, which featured both Western and Chinese art of a variety of styles. Much modernist art was reproduced and discussed in its pages: it published a translation of André Breton's Surrealist Manifesto of 1924, for instance, as well as a colour illustration of Lin Fengmian's *Exercise* (*c*.1934), in which the artist shows awareness of the heightened and non-naturalistic colour schemes of European modernism, and adopts an angular stylization of forms that is reminiscent in particular of Cubism (see figure 3).

Although artists in other parts of China were also to benefit from this growth of a hospitable niche for art as a part of public culture, it was in Shanghai that this new form of art found the most fertile environment. The foreign concessions made for a particularly rich and culturally plural environment in this metropolis, which like other port cities of the world was particularly open to imported culture. Even ink painting without any overt foreign element had thrived in response to the patronage of the city's merchant class. The Shanghai School artists of the late nineteenth century and early twentieth century such as Ren Bonian (1840–95) and Wu Changshuo (1844–1927) were among the first to revitalize inherited painting modes as the dynastic era came to an end. The city also played a leading role in the broader field of visual culture, with the Shanghai cinema, graphic design and advertising art of the Republican era all proving distinct, and the tall, Western-style buildings that gathered along the Bund were quite unlike anything else in Asia. Even in architecture Western modes had their limits when transplanted in China, though, and the American architect Henry K. Murphy (1877–1954), who designed a number of buildings in China during the Republican era and also produced a plan for Nanjing as a Nationalist capital, felt the need to introduce Chinese architectural elements into his buildings, taking inspiration in particular from Beijing's Forbidden City.

Despite the promising start towards a culturally distinctive brand of modernity in China during the 1920s and 1930s, no period of full flowering was to follow. Due to the war that followed in the wake of Japanese invasion and the subsequent period of civil strife that only ended with the establishment of the People's Republic in 1949, the project of establishing a Chinese cultural modernity that gained momentum after the New Culture Movement of the late 1910s and early 1920s remained incomplete. Shanghai's position near the coast, the very factor on which its economic growth had depended, made it particularly vulnerable, and artists from the city were to join many others displaced inland as the conflict spread. Fu Baoshi was among several artists to spend time in the Nationalist wartime capital, Chongqing, where he started to develop a subjective and frequently pessimistic style that sprang from the particular political conditions of that time of national crisis. Zhang Daqian (1899–1983) travelled even further inland, finding resources for the development of his own art by making copies of the ancient Buddhist wall-paintings at Dunhuang (evidence that the past as well as the foreign could be a source of the new). Other artists joined the Communists in exile elsewhere in China's interior, helping to forge a new visual culture that before long would return to the coastal cities in triumph. When Mao Zedong gave his 'Talks at the Yan'an Forum on Literature and Art' in 1942, he was effectively announcing the end of the post-May Fourth era of artistic modernism and pluralism. From that time onwards, art was to be required to take the point of view of the masses, and to be subservient to political goals.

From the founding of the People's Republic to the end of the Cultural Revolution (1949–1976)

Although the Republican period saw Chinese artists responding to both realist and modernist tendencies in Western art, only the former remained of interest after the founding of the People's Republic.[4] In the hands of Xu Beihong, who had trained in an academic tradition, 'realism' in art was already at some remove from the socially critical role it had played in the work of the French painter Gustave Courbet (1819–77), and after 1949 an even greater distance was to open up. Courbet deliberately challenged the visual clichés that were found in the academic art of his time, representing the nude or the subject of rural labour in uncomfortably demystifying ways. The socialist realism that came to predominate in Mao's China, however, was a pliant tool for relaying approved ideological positions, and nothing more.

With political solutions to China's problems in ascendancy, the state assumed a far greater role in the cultural sphere than it had in the preceding period. It became the major actor, exerting control through cultural organizations even as it provided artists with assurances of a livelihood and a social role. In a strange way art was to achieve the ambition it had been sketching out for itself in the 1920s and 1930s, finding at last a national audience and national meanings to convey to that audience.

The politicization of life in the People's Republic meant that art was frequently called upon to directly represent political events, albeit in the most carefully sanitized way. *The Founding of the Nation* (1952–3) by Dong Xiwen (1914–73), for instance, depicts the founding ceremony of the new state, with Mao given full prominence, but revisions to the work later proved necessary as certain figures in the painting subsequently fell from political favour. Mao's centrality was repeatedly affirmed in other works too. A well-known example from the Cultural Revolution era, *Chairman Mao goes to Anyuan* (1967) by Liu Chunhua (b. 1944), features the early political life of the leader. Apart from promoting the cult of Mao himself, painters also produced a great many upbeat and idealized representations of agricultural labour, industrial production and infrastructure development. Such works tend to emphasize the productivity of collective labour, but individuals can also make an appearance in order to serve as positive role models, often shown heroically triumphing over adverse weather conditions for the common good. One such example is *I am Seagull* (*c.*1972) by Pan Jiajun (b. 1947), which features a female linesman calling in her code name after having successfully carried out a repair. Brimming with youthful energy, she appears completely undaunted by the heavy rain in which she has been working.

Oil paint proved to be the most effective technical means for art of this kind, but photography also played a role in this propaganda imaging because of the medium's inherent sense of veracity. The images of Mao by Hou Bo (b. 1924) are among the most well-known Chinese photographs of this period, but the medium of photography can sometimes prove too truthful, too replete with detail, providing an excess of information that enables images to be read against their grain in more recent historical moments as documents of barbarism. This is the case with certain of the images of Li Zhensheng (b. 1940), who worked as a photojournalist for the *Heilongjiang Daily* during the Cultural Revolution years, and who stored a large number of his more sensitive negatives under the floorboards until they could be brought out for exhibition and publication from the late 1980s onwards. Perhaps an awareness of the potential all images retain to some extent to be read against their grain lies behind the coupling of political slogans with the images of mass-reproduced propaganda posters of the Maoist era. In this way the meaning of the images was pinned down and made specific, divesting them of much of their residual ambiguity.

The Cultural Revolution period saw an intensification of the political control of art that had been in place for some time, and resulted in a serious narrowing of Chinese visual culture. Certain images of Mao (such as the portrait found in the front of the 'little red book' of his collected thoughts, but also Liu Chunhua's *Chairman Mao goes to Anyuan*) were reproduced and circulated in enormous quantities during this time, playing a role not altogether dissimilar to that of religious icons in other cultural contexts. In addition to appearing in public places, images of Mao also found their way into homes, sometimes even occupying the place that would previously have been reserved for the family shrine.

But this image of a homogeneous culture needs to be qualified to some extent. The foreign influences that had played such a role in the Republican era did not disappear entirely, for instance, but took new forms. In the early years of the PRC, before a political breach developed, influences from Russian art were to replace contact with Western European models. Exhibitions of Soviet art were held in China, and Chinese students were able to study with Russian teachers both in Russia and in China itself. For more established artists too there were opportunities for travel within the Communist bloc: Li Keran (1907–89), for instance, travelled to East Germany in 1957.

Although lacking the heterogeneity of style found in the previous period, painting of the PRC era did retain pluralism in one respect, in that ink-based works that drew on the native brushwork heritage continued to be produced alongside works in oil. Valued because of its potential for signifying national uniqueness even in an era so often given to eradicating all that was old, this inherited medium did of course need to bow to the political agenda of the times, and realistic representation tended to take the place of ink play. Nevertheless, it is fair to say that ink painting retained more possibilities for artistic expression than oil had, and certain works of genuine artistic merit were created during this time, belying reductive images of Maoist China as devoid of interesting or complex art.

The realist tendency in ink painting exemplified during the Republican era by Gao Jianfu was to prove a useful resource for the state's goal of producing a modern socialist art. Although in certain respects Gao's Japanese-influenced style proved problematic as a basis for a national idiom after that country developed imperial ambitions against China, Guan Shanyue (1912–2000) was able to employ it to produce a landscape painting that celebrated the new China as optimistically as many oil painters. Li Keran also attempted to develop a realist mode of ink painting during the early PRC era, although from the late 1950s on he was tempering the more narrowly descriptive tendency of his work up to that time to produce paintings that on occasion have a richer poetic strength. These works were not exactly a 'return to tradition' since their inky blackness and use of shading can sometimes betray a debt to Western artists such as Rembrandt, and their scale and monumentality address them to a public audience unknown to literati painting.

Painters such as Li were able to produce works that at first appear to be pure landscapes, far removed from the servitude to propaganda found in most oil paintings, but such apparent freedom was frequently gained by making topographical reference to locations of revolutionary or national significance. This is the case with *Fighting in Northern Shaanxi* (1959) by Shi Lu (1919–82), which contains the small but recognizable figure of Mao himself, gazing out from the edge of a cliff at the landscape beyond, as if during a pause in the revolutionary battle (see figure 4). Room for manoeuvre was also created by inscribing images with poetry by Mao, or taking a painting's theme from his poems. Both of these strategies

4 Shi Lu, 'Fighting in Northern Shaanxi', 1959

are found in the work of Fu Baoshi, who produced many paintings of great poetic richness that illustrate Mao's words, such as *Heavy Rain falls on Youyan* (1961) (see figure 5), an earlier version of which had lines from Mao's poem 'Beidaihe' inscribed upon it. Li also uses this tactic of referencing Mao's poetry in *Ten Thousand Crimson Hills* (1964), which introduces Communist signification through extensive use of red paint in the depiction of autumnal trees. Compared to this work, Fu's *Heavy Rain falls on Youyan* seems a much less straightforward embodiment of Maoist ideology. A rather pessimistic image of rain falling on the sea executed in free and expressive brushwork, it corresponds to the earlier part of Mao's poem. However, it fails to provide any counterpart to the revolutionary optimism that suddenly appears at the poem's end to trump

5 Fu Baoshi, 'Heavy Rain Falls on Youyan', 1961

the apparent negativity of the first stanza, or clarify it as a reference to a now-surpassed historical era.

Even painting that failed to make the partial (and maybe deliberately self-protective) accommodation to Communist ideology found in the works of Li and Fu was able to be produced in the Maoist era, as the case of Lin Fengmian attests. This veteran modernist could not continue to produce the kind of ambitious public images he had undertaken in the Republican era, but rather than pliantly adapting his manner to the needs of the new political order he was largely to retreat into a more private mode of image making, creating powerfully expressive and atmospheric landscapes. While successfully retaining or creating a space for the artistic assertion of subjectivity in this way, Lin was not, however, able to escape criticism. In 1964 his works were attacked by Shi Chongming in an article in the art magazine *Meishu* for being mournful and desolate, and lacking a healthy socialist spirit. In the ensuing Cultural Revolution period, when criticism of such supposedly 'black' painting as counter-revolutionary reached a new pitch, Lin was left with no option but to destroy his own work.

Although Shanghai had been the most exciting crucible for cultural experiment in the Republican era, Beijing was to become the undisputed centre of the new state – indeed, from its first moment, with the establishment of the People's Republic being announced from Tiananmen, the gate at the front of the Forbidden City. This political logic of appropriating the locus of power of the imperial age for the new society was to have strong architectural consequences for the city. Although the Imperial Palace itself remained intact, the area in front of the gate, Tiananmen Square, was to be transformed into a massive gathering space focused on Tiananmen itself, on which Mao's portrait was displayed. Major buildings of national significance, the Great Hall of the People and the Museum of Chinese History (both completed in 1959), were constructed on either side of the Square, which functioned as a symbolic focus of the national topography. Mao himself, on his death, was to be interred within the Square in a Memorial Hall (completed in 1977), and with a Monument to the People's Heroes having already been placed in the Square in 1958, this further served to saturate the site with socialistic national meaning. Sculpture and painting also played their part in this process, whether in the form of paintings installed inside the Great Hall of the People, such as Fu Baoshi and Guan Shanyue's massive landscape based on a poem by Mao, *This Land so Rich in Beauty* (1959), or in the form of the sculptural reliefs around the base of the Monument to the People's Heroes that depicts canonical moments from Revolutionary history, created by a team of artists under the direction of Liu Kaiqu (1904–93), who had studied in France during the Republican era. Although an alternative plan for post-revolutionary Beijing supported by architect and architectural historian Liang Sicheng (1901–72) had envisaged preservation of the old city and construction of a new centre of power outside the historic city walls, this failed to find favour, and the walls, along with much else of historic Beijing, largely disappeared.

China after Mao

Although China became relatively culturally homogeneous under Mao, as has been argued here with certain qualifications (particularly with regard to ink painting), it should be remembered that in one respect the creation of the People's Republic saw an institutionalizing of cultural pluralism in the country. This is because Nationalist China did not disappear altogether, but retreated to the island of Taiwan, which became the Republic of China. The Nationalists took with them the Imperial art collection, which they used to bolster their claims to legitimacy, deploying it in the service of a distinctly non-Communist national cultural discourse in which continuity with tradition was emphasized. In the British colony of Hong Kong, equally excluded from the PRC but (unlike Taiwan) not constituted politically or culturally as a national space, further non-Communist expressions of Chineseness were to be found in art.

Cultural as well as economic openness to the West in both these marginal locations led to a renewal of the dialogue with Western art that had been such a prominent part of artistic life in the Republican era. Indeed, certain significant Chinese artists were to migrate to the West in the face of the state of turmoil that prevailed for so long in China or because of the triumph of Communism. Zhao Wuji (b. 1921), for instance, was to base himself in Paris from 1948, while Zhang Daqian was to live in South and later North America, migrating to Taiwan only in the last years of his life. Such extended stays or permanent migration were a completely different phenomenon from the brief and usually educationally related visits made to the West by earlier artists such as Xu Beihong and Lin Fengmian. As a consequence, different artistic results were to come from these later encounters, with Zhao (whose name is often romanized in the West as Zao Wou-ki) playing a significant role in the cultural life of his adopted homeland.

The renewal of Chinese art from its margins in the post-World War II era was not simply a matter of easier access to Western art, however. Perhaps even more important was the fact that Western modernist art – and particularly painting – had itself changed in significant ways. New York had replaced Paris as its centre of gravity, and the brushy, linear abstractions of the American Abstract Expressionists seemed much closer in spirit to the inherited language of Chinese painting and calligraphy – and thus more available – than the geometric abstraction of an artist such as Piet Mondrian had been. Dialogue now seemed possible on more equal terms, especially since certain Western artists of this era had consciously borrowed from Asian art and culture themselves. An engagement with Western modernism no longer necessarily entailed cultural deracination, and Zhao Wuji, for instance, was able to incorporate an influence from Chinese calligraphy in developing his painting style towards greater abstraction, as in the case of *Wind* (1954).

The new proximity between Chinese tradition and Western modernity still left gaps to be bridged, however, and cultural hybridity was a common characteristic of the new Chinese painting that emerged, such as that of Lu Shoukun (Lui Shou-kwan, 1915–76), Han Zhixun (Hon Chi-fun, b. 1922) and Wang Wuxie (Wucius Wong, b. 1936) in Hong Kong, or that of Liu Guosong (Liu Kuo-sung, b. 1932) in Taiwan. Lu combined prominent calligraphic ink strokes that self-consciously invoke the

6   Zhu Ming, 'Taichi Single Whip', 1985

Chinese brush heritage with allusions to the work of contemporary Western artists such as Adolph Gottlieb and Pierre Soulages, while Han, Wang and Liu have all on occasion deliberately juxtaposed calligraphic or ink painting references with geometric elements that recall aspects of Western modernism such as American hard-edged abstraction. While the historical trajectories of Taiwan and Hong Kong were in certain respects similar in the postwar period, the sense of living in a place where 'East meets West' seems to have been particularly strong in late colonial-era Hong Kong, and the paintings of Lu, Han and Wang appear at times to be grappling with both the possibilities and difficulties of such perceived cultural hybridity.[5] Something similar seemed to be happening in sculpture. Whereas on the Mainland this medium produced such pliant vehicles of propaganda as *The Rent Collection Courtyard* (1965), a 'realist' presentation of the iniquities of pre-Revolutionary landlords produced by a team of artists from the Sichuan Academy of Fine Arts, in Taiwan we find Zhu Ming (Ju Ming, b. 1938) creating abstracted images of figures in Tai Chi poses that are dynamic equivalents to those of Henry Moore (see figure 6), while Hong Kong's Wen Lou (Van Lau, b. 1933) treated the very 'Chinese' subject of bamboo in a geometric vocabulary of forms indebted to European constructivism.

The recreation of a culturally open or pluralistic art environment on the Mainland only became possible following the economic opening

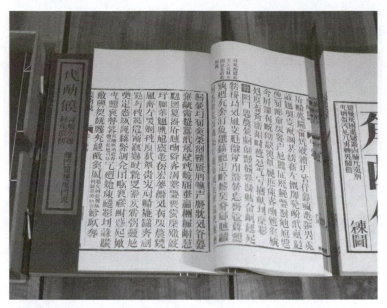

7   Xu Bing, 'Book from the Sky' (detail), 1988

that occurred in the 1980s. Before the end of that decade a great deal of artistic experimentation had taken place, such as that in the supportive environment offered by the Hangzhou Academy of Art, and in 1989, shortly before the crackdown in the wake of the student protests of that year, there was a large-scale breakthrough exhibition of avant-garde work at the China Art Gallery in Beijing.[6] Xu Bing (b. 1955) had by this time already created his *Book from the Sky* (1988), a conceptual installation in which thousands of well-formed but meaningless Chinese characters are printed from hand-carved wooden blocks onto the surface of paper (see figure 7). Following the Tiananmen massacre this head-on Dada-like confrontation with tradition was imbued with further, more explicitly political, layers of connotation, and a cynical mood was often to be found in the art that was produced in the early to middle 1990s, a fertile time for art production, even if display of such experimental work within China itself was all but impossible until much later. The paintings of Fang Lijun (b. 1963) were peopled with aimless, clone-like figures, completely at odds with the new official mood of optimism over economic growth (e.g. *Series II, No. 2*, 1992; see figure 8), while Wang Guangyi (b. 1956) produced a series of canvases that directly addressed the newly emerging consumer society. Juxtaposing the now-obsolete visual

8 Fang Lijun, 'Series II, No. 2', 1992

imagery of Maoism with that discovered in the equally rhetoric-loaded vocabulary used to advertise imported brand names, Wang's consciously hybrid images (e.g. *Great Criticism Series: Pepsi*, 1992) echoed and helped to specify the curiously heterogeneous urban environments rapidly coming into being in China at the time.

Due to the post-1989 crackdown, several of the most interesting of the emerging contemporary artists in Mainland China chose to relocate to more hospitable climes. Xu Bing was among this wave of émigrés, settling in New York, which was also home to Gu Wenda (b. 1955) and Zhang Hongtu (b. 1943), who had left China in 1982. Art that could not be widely exhibited at home became increasingly valorized overseas, and each of these artists responded to their new residential and display environments by producing works that dealt with the meeting of cultures. Xu Bing, for instance, developed his 'New English Calligraphy', a way of writing the words of Western languages in the strokes of Chinese calligraphy that he used in various artworks, while Zhang Hongtu began his 'Repaint Chinese Shan Shui Painting' project in which a series of well-known Chinese ink paintings are repainted using oil in the style of

European modernists. In *Fan Kuan – Van Gogh* (1998), for example, a well-known Song dynasty landscape by Fan Kuan is redone in the style of Vincent Van Gogh (see figure 9).

Such works by Xu and Zhang, like those of certain other Western-based Mainland artists, choose to deal with well-established symbols of Chineseness, and take a binary approach to cross-cultural issues that is not dissimilar except in its degree of self-consciousness or irony from that of Wang Wuxie or Liu Guosong. In the art of Hong Kong during the corresponding mid-to-late 1990s period, however, an increasing concern for issues of local cultural identity is found, transcending the binary East–West language of earlier Hong Kong ink painting. Specifically a response to the approach of the city's 1997 handover to Chinese rule, this politicized evocation of the local was often effected by means of references to the Cantonese dialect or to specifically Hong Kong symbols borrowed from the city's popular culture. Such emphasis on local expression had a counterpart in Taiwanese art following the end of martial law in 1987 and the process of political liberalization that saw the first non-GMD president elected in 2000. In both cities non-traditional art media became increasingly the means of choice for ambitious work, with photography and installation art – neither tainted by association with national discourse – gaining new prominence.

Only in the new millennium did the kind of open artistic arena enjoyed by artists in Hong Kong and Taiwan or in the diaspora show signs of reappearing on the Mainland. The Shanghai Biennales held at the Shanghai Museum of Art (with the first involving international curators and artists being held in 2000) and the Guangzhou Triennials held at the Guangdong Museum of Art from 2002 played a key role in this change.[7] With the now well-established penetration of Mainland Chinese cities by global capitalism and consumer culture, and the massive transformation of the built environment of Beijing, Shanghai and other cities in progress, new sites for art have opened up in the increasingly heterotopic fabric of the major urban centres. One particular concentration of art spaces occurred in the former factory district of Dashanzi in Beijing, for instance, while Shanghai has seen something similar in the Suzhou Creek area. Artists from all parts of China have moved to its urban centres, with Beijing as the capital city proving particularly attractive, even in some cases for cultural workers who had spent a decade or more outside China. All kinds of media and styles, from ink to video, are now actively employed by Chinese artists, and – more importantly – there is

9 Zhang Hongtu, 'Fan Kuan – Van Gogh', 1998

also a great heterogeneity in terms of content. Consequently, art offers one of the most prominent sites in China today in which refusal of the meanings promoted by the state or the marketplace is to be found, even if pressure towards normalization will undoubtedly be felt as such new art finds an increasingly visible place in both publicly funded and for-profit venues.

Notes

1. One important American exhibition was *Inside Out: New Chinese Art*, which had its first showing in New York at the Asia Society galleries and at P. S. 1 in 1998. For the catalogue of this show, see Gao Minglu (ed.), *Inside Out: New Chinese Art*, University of California Press, 1998.
2. For recent Western exhibits of modern Chinese art see Julia F. Andrews and Shen Kuiyi, *A Century in Crisis: Modernity and Tradition in the Art of Twentieth Century China*, New York, Guggenheim Museum, 1998; and Jo-Anne Birnie-Danzker, Ken Lum and Zheng Shengtian (eds.), *Shanghai Modern, 1919–1945*, Ostfildern-Ruit, Hatje Cantz Verlag, 2004. Previous studies of Chinese artistic modernity as a whole include David Clarke, *Modern Chinese Art*, Oxford, Oxford University Press, 2000; Maxwell K. Hearn and Judith G. Smith, *Chinese Art: Modern Expressions*, New York, The Metropolitan Museum of Art, 2001; Michael Sullivan, *Art and Artists of Twentieth Century China*, University of California Press, 1996. A study that considers China as part of the broader story of Asian artistic modernity is John Clark, *Modern Asian Art*, Sydney, Craftsman House, 1998.
3. On art of the Republican era, see Birnie-Danzker *et al.* (eds.), *Shanghai Modern, 1919–1945*; and Ralph Croizier, *Art and Revolution in Modern China: The Lingnan (Cantonese) School of Painting, 1906–1951*, University of California Press, 1988.
4. On art during the PRC era, see Julia F. Andrews, *Painters and Politics in the People's Republic of China, 1949–1979*, University of California Press, 1994; and Ellen Johnston Laing, *The Winking Owl: Art in the People's Republic of China*, University of California Press, 1988.
5. For a study of Hong Kong art see David Clarke, *Hong Kong Art: Culture and Decolonization*, North Carolina, Duke University Press, 2002.
6. Concerning avant-garde art in Mainland China see Valerie Doran (ed.), *China's New Art, Post-1989*, Hong Kong, Hanart TZ Gallery, 1993; Martina Köppel-Yang, *Semiotic Warfare: The Chinese Avant-Garde. 1979–1989, A Semiotic Analysis*, Hong Kong, Timezone 8, 2003; Gao, *Inside Out*; and Wu Hung, *Transience*, Chicago, The David and Alfred Smart Museum of Art, University of Chicago, 1999.
7. For the catalogue of the First Guangzhou Triennial, see Wu Hung, Wang Huangsheng and Feng Boyi (eds.), *The First Guangzhou Triennial. Reinterpretation: A Decade of Experimental Chinese Art*, Guangzhou, Guangdong Museum of Art, 2002.

Guide to further reading

Andrews, Julia F., *Painters and Politics in the People's Republic of China, 1949–1979*, University of California Press, 1994.

Andrews, Julia F. and Shen Kuiyi, *A Century in Crisis: Modernity and Tradition in the Art of Twentieth Century China*, New York, Guggenheim Museum, 1998.

Birnie-Danzker, Jo-Anne, Ken Lum and Zheng Shengtian (eds.), *Shanghai Modern, 1919–1945*, Ostfildern-Ruit, Hatje Cantz Verlag, 2004.

Clark, John, *Modern Asian Art*, Sydney, Craftsman House, 1998.

Clarke, David, *Hong Kong Art: Culture and Decolonization*, North Carolina, Duke University Press, 2002.

Modern Chinese Art, Oxford, Oxford University Press, 2000.

Croizier, Ralph, *Art and Revolution in Modern China: The Lingnan (Cantonese) School of Painting, 1906–1951*, Berkeley University of California Press, 1988.

Doran, Valerie (ed.), *China's New Art, Post-1989*, Hong Kong, Hanart TZ Gallery, 1993.

Gao Minglu (ed.), *Inside Out: New Chinese Art*, Berkeley, University of California Press, 1998.

Hearn, Maxwell K. and Judith G. Smith, *Chinese Art: Modern Expressions*, New York, The Metropolitan Museum of Art, 2001.

Köppel-Yang, Martina, *Semiotic Warfare: The Chinese Avant-Garde. 1979–1989, A Semiotic Analysis*, Hong Kong, Timezone 8, 2003.

Laing, Ellen Johnston, *The Winking Owl: Art in the People's Republic of China*, University of California Press, 1988.

Sullivan, Michael, *Art and Artists of Twentieth Century China*, University of California Press, 1996.

Wu Hung, *Transience*, Chicago, The David and Alfred Smart Museum of Art, University of Chicago, 1999.

Wu Hung, Wang Huangsheng and Feng Boyi (eds.), *The First Guangzhou Triennial. Reinterpretation: A Decade of Experimental Chinese Art*, Guangzhou, Guangdong Museum of Art, 2002.

15

Cinema: from foreign import to global brand

Cinema arrived in China as a foreign import a little over a century ago. Today, 'Chinese cinema' travels the world as a culturally defined national brand. The turnaround can be traced quite precisely. It originated with the breakthrough screening of *Yellow Earth* [*Huang Tudi*], directed by Chen Kaige and shot by Zhang Yimou, at the 1985 Hong Kong International Film Festival. This launched the Fifth Generation of Chinese films and filmmakers as an arthouse line for the 'Chinese cinema' brand. (The term 'Fifth Generation' is generally understood as referring to the 1982 graduates of the Beijing Film Academy.) Unlike other export moments, such as Bruce Lee in the 1970s, *Yellow Earth* opened the door for various kinds of Chinese films. The works of Taiwan New Cinema directors such as Edward Yang and Hou Hsiao-hsien found themselves on the same arthouse shelves as those of the Fifth Generation. Nearby, Hong Kong action films associated with John Woo and stars such as Chow Yun-Fat established a cult niche alongside the Bruce Lee kung fu corner. More recently, Ang Lee's *Crouching Tiger Hidden Dragon* [*Wohu Canglong*, 2000] has taken the martial arts blockbuster out of the niche market and into the multiplex theatres.

However, it is not clear if the people of China, Taiwan and Hong Kong also think of this internationally branded cinema when they hear the phrase 'Chinese cinema'. They are more likely to think specifically of films produced within the borders of the People's Republic – not least because the government of the People's Republic defines Hong Kong and Taiwan films as 'foreign films'. The definition of 'Chinese cinema' is contested now and always has been. It differs according to both nation-state politics and different cultural definitions at different times.

Some scholars have tried to get around these complications by coining the term 'Chinese-language cinemas' (*huayu dianying*). However, some Taiwanese independence supporters contest the idea that the Hokkienese-derived language most commonly spoken on the island is a kind of 'Chinese language', and claim that Taiwanese is sufficiently distinct to be treated as a language in its own right. Moreover, English or other languages sometimes dominate films made in the diaspora, even though the characters may be of Chinese background and the cultural setting Chinese.

This chapter examines film produced in the lands of what was the Qing dynasty (1644–1911) prior to the ceding of territories to Western powers and Japan in the late nineteenth century. But its aim is not to define 'Chinese cinema'. Instead, it narrates the Chinese cinema to show how, since its beginnings, it – just like its definitions – has shaped and been shaped by questions of the nation-state and national culture. Perhaps this is not so surprising. Both cinema and the territorial nation-state came to the lands ruled by the Qing as part of a package called 'modernity' that was not produced locally but delivered unsolicited from the West. The appropriation of both the cinema and the nationstate has been part of the desire to 'catch up', and not only become fully modern but also make modernity fully Chinese. Of course, this experience of modernity is not unique to China. Indeed, the sense of not being fully national or modern is not even unique to the non-Western world, however accentuated by the history of imperialism. No nation-state measures up to the conceptual ideal of unity, coherence and eternal stability, and being fully modern is always deferred into the future perfect tense. While the approach adopted here is only one way of tracing a line through the history of Chinese cinema, hopefully it will help to bring out some connections to broader developments.

However, the ways in which Chinese cinema has negotiated its intersection with issues of the national under the sign of modernity are specific. This chapter examines some key episodes. First, it considers the effort to respond to the perceived threat of foreign cultural invasion by sinicizing both the cinema and modernity in various ways. Secondly, in the 1930s and 1940s, when unprecedented waves of both foreign culture and foreign troops were moving across China, the desire to respond provoked debate about the role of cinema and how to modernize Chinese culture. The contradictions of this time are condensed in the figure of the 1930s female star, Ruan Lingyu, treated here as a case study.

After the civil war that followed Japanese defeat, two models of nation-state were implemented, each with its own national cinema form, designed to complement different projects of national modernization. In the People's Republic of China, there was Chinese socialist realism. On Taiwan, the Republic of China responded with healthy realism. Meanwhile, in Hong Kong, cinema was shaped by the lack of nation-state status. Hong Kong's situation as a colony and a site of exile led to the development of a particular consciousness, expressed and developed in the cinema, of the territory's liminal status. In the 1980s, new waves in both the People's Republic and Taiwan criticized and re-examined the history of nationalist modernization in both places, seeing it not as progress but as ruination. Finally, the globalization of the film industry has completely reconfigured the relationship between the national and the cinema. The triumphant Chinese cinema export brand has been one part of this process, but the collapse of cinema as a national cultural institution has been another facet of the process. In its place are a series of quite separate cinemas appealing to distinctive audience segments within and outside Chinese territories.

Making the cinema Chinese

The first films in China were foreign imports that were shown in 1896. At that time, China was a declining dynastic realm that had already ceded Hong Kong to Britain and Taiwan to Japan. The screenings took place in Hong Kong and Shanghai, cities born with the arrival of the West that went on to become main centres of film production. As elsewhere, attempts to determine exactly when and where the first screenings occurred rely on faint traces, such as notices in newspapers. As Pang Laikwan points out, one such notice indicates a January 1896 screening at the Old Victoria Hotel in Hong Kong. Another more specific advertisement is for a screening in the Xu Gardens in Shanghai on 11 August of the same year.[1]

The choice of screening venues indicates that cinema was understood in relation to existing practices. This localized or sinicized the foreign technology and culture of the cinema. Film was inserted into variety shows in existing entertainment venues. Pang Laikwan has emphasized the importance of the public garden, and Zhang Zhen has examined teahouses as sites for these variety shows.[2] The public garden was itself a response to modernity, transforming the private garden from a space for promenading and looking at the view into an urban public form. In the teahouse, the idea of early cinema as an 'attraction' in the West achieved a Chinese manifestation.

The first Chinese film production was not until 1905. It took place neither in Shanghai nor in Hong Kong, but in Beijing. *Dingjun Mountain* [*Dingjun Shan*] was named after the famous Chinese opera episode it recorded. The decision to film something as distinctively Chinese as an opera scene manifests anxiety about cinema as a foreign form. It tries to inoculate against the perceived dangers to agency and identity posed by an invasion of foreign technology and culture, by making the modern in general and the cinema in particular Chinese. This pattern continues through much of Chinese cinema history. Several cinema 'firsts' are operatic. The first two films made in Hong Kong in 1909 – *Stealing a Roasted Duck* [*Tou Shao Ya*] and *Right a Wrong with Earthenware Dish* [*Wa Pen Shen Yuan*] – were also derived from opera scenes. When Zhang Shichuan directed the first sound film in 1931 in Shanghai, this film – *Sing-Song Girl Red Peony* [*Genü Hong Mudan*] – was filled with opera music and scenes. The first Cantonese-language film was a Cantonese opera, *White Gold Dragon* [*Bai Jin Long*, 1933]. The first colour film – *Remorse at Death* [*Sheng Si Hen*] – was an opera film shot in 1948 and starring Mei Lanfang, who had toured with the Beijing Opera to the Soviet Union, Japan and the United States in the years between the two world wars. And the first Taiwanese-language film was a local opera film. However, whether this credit should go to *Six Scholars of the Western Chamber* [*Liu Caizi Xi Xiangji*, 1955] or *Xue Pinggui and Wang Baochuan* [*Xue Pinggui yu Wang Baochuan*, 1956] is disputed. This is because not only was the earlier film a flop, it was also filmed by a troupe from the Mainland.

As a scene of martial choreography, *Dingjun Mountain* is the ancestor of the modern martial arts film. The cultural heritage of martial arts also drove the first major boom in Chinese cinema in Shanghai in the 1920s. After a fire at the photo shop where *Dingjun Mountain* was made, production in Beijing petered out. In the early 1920s, various comedies and melodramas about contemporary issues were made in Shanghai, but in the second half of the decade the 'martial arts and magic spirit' (*wuxia shenguai*) genre became wildly popular. Over 200 such films were made between 1927 and 1931 alone. Twenty-eight of these were episodes in a series called *The Burning of the Red Lotus Temple* [*Huo Shao Hong Lian Si*]. Rather like Indiana Jones's Temple of Doom, the Red Lotus Temple was full of traps that posed exciting challenges for the films' protagonists. One 20-minute segment from this series survives, but most scholarship on early cinema is necessarily based on original stories, scripts, stills and newspaper reports.

This research tells us that martial arts and magic spirit films featured both heroes and heroines. They benefited from trick photography and the other technical marvels of the cinema that enabled them to vault buildings and fly through the air in their efforts to bring justice to the ordinary citizenry. In her chapter on these films in *An Amorous History of the Silver Screen*, Zhang Zhen argues that these narratives can be understood as a response to the fascination with science and technology, which seemed almost magical to many Chinese. The films represent a literal command over technology – the technology of the cinema. Their stories also represent the local realization of the promise of science and technology, filtered through established forms of Chinese narrative.[3]

Making the Chinese modern

However, the fate of this cycle of martial arts and magic spirit films demonstrates that it was not enough to make the cinema Chinese. It had to be modern, too. These films might represent a colloquial and optimistic apprehension and imagination of modernity for scholars today, but at the time not everyone agreed. The GMD Nationalist government overcame warlordism and unified the nation-state in 1927. It responded to the growing popularity and influence of the cinema by establishing the first National Film Censorship Committee in 1931. One of the first acts of this body was to ban martial arts and magic spirit films. To the GMD, they represented the persistence of unscientific superstition and were therefore an obstacle to the establishment of a modern new China.

Enmity between the GMD and the Chinese Communist Party was unremitting, but this was something they agreed on. The 1949 establishment of the People's Republic did not lead to martial arts films being made again until the general cultural relaxation of the 1980s. The first new star to emerge was Li Lianjie – soon to move to Hong Kong and become Jet Li – in films such as *The Shaolin Temple* [*Shaolin Si*, 1982] and *Shaolin Kids* [*Shaolin Xiaozi*, 1983]. However, these films featured none of the 'superstitious' and humanly impossible leaps and bounds of the swordplay sub-genre of martial arts films. Instead, they emphasized plausible athletic feats, mostly in the kung fu style.

Xiao Zhiwei has shown that, as well as banning martial arts and magic spirit films, the GMD's censors also intervened against three other kinds of films. Two were predictable: films that they had political objections to and foreign films that they felt maligned China, such as von Sternberg's *Shanghai Express* (1932). A final category reveals another aspect of the drive to establish a modern nation-state.[4] Sound was introduced to Chinese cinema gradually during the 1930s. In pursuit of the cultural unification also held to be a prerequisite for a modern nation-state, it was decreed that the only spoken language permitted in the cinema would be the 'national language' (*guoyu*).

Language in China is quite different from the languages of Europe, where the concept of the modern nation-state was developed. European-language scripts are phonetic. This means that each spoken language has a corresponding written language. Language difference was one of the ways of determining ethnic groups and the territorial boundaries of nation-states upon the dissolution of polyglot monarchical formations such as the Austro-Hungarian Empire. However, because the written form of the Chinese language is not based on the transcription of sounds, the circumstances there are different. So long as the cinema remained silent, there was no problem. However, the advent of sound threatened a veritable Babel of different local spoken languages. Beijing or Mandarin Chinese was designated as the 'national language' and all other local spoken languages were termed 'dialects'. This was an effort to force-fit the Chinese language into the European-derived idea of national modernity that China and the rest of the world were struggling to attain.

Like the policy on martial arts and magic spirit films, this language policy continued under the Communists until very recently. In 1993, Li Shaohong's film about the fate of prostitutes around the time of the 1949 Revolution, *Blush* [*Hongfen*], was made in a Shanghai dialect version, but for release in Shanghai alone. In 2006, however, the Sichuan-based comedy *Crazy Stone* [*Fengkuang de Shitou*] could be seen across the whole country in Chongqing dialect with subtitles. Nonetheless, the vast majority of films in the People's Republic continue to be made and circulated in Mandarin.

The substantial differences between spoken 'dialects' and the 'national language' in China had important implications for Chinese cinema. In

Europe, most dialect speakers can understand their national language. However, this was not the case in China in the 1930s. This meant that, despite the ban, many producers were still motivated to make films in local languages, especially Cantonese, which is very different from Mandarin and the language most commonly spoken in the diaspora. The GMD censors' decisions about both superstition and language gave an unintended boost to film production in Hong Kong. The British colonial authorities had no concern about transforming Hong Kong according to the standards of a modern nation-state. As an ironic result, martial arts film productions and Cantonese-language cinema developed there. With the advent of sound, Cantonese opera films produced in Hong Kong also proved very popular.

While the popular fantasy cinema prospered in colonial Hong Kong, in Shanghai in the 1930s realism dominated. Realism not only corresponded to the secularism, rationality and science that supposedly characterize modernity, but also offered the possibility of representing the modern national society the GMD wanted to build. Again, the Communists agreed, and they promoted realism, too. However, in many other ways, their vision of that modern nation-state differed. With the benefit of hindsight, clear distinctions have been made between ordinary 1930s films and the 'leftwing' cinema, which the People's Republic has eagerly claimed as its heritage. More recently, however, arguments have proliferated. How strong were the cinematic left's links to the Communist Party? How identifiable were left-wing films at the time? In the 1930s itself, there was a major critical debate over 'hard' and 'soft' cinema. The former pressed for social engagement, whereas the latter insisted on cinema as entertainment. However, this polarization cannot be mapped directly onto the right- and left-wing opposition that became all-important later.

Perhaps one way to think of cinema's relationship to modernity and the existing cultures it encountered is as a sort of sieve. Certain things were to be sieved out as feudal or otherwise inappropriate to modernity. Other things were to be sieved into the national culture. 'National culture' is a modern construct like the nation-state itself. But by projecting its elements back into an eternity without origin, it helps to ground the newness of the national form in 'tradition'. From this perspective, many of the narratives of 1930s films appear to manifest the contradictions of the era as a tension between Confucian and Western values, and a tension over what to keep and what to discard.

Case study: Ruan Lingyu

One figure who encapsulates this complexity is the silent film star, Ruan Lingyu. Ruan committed suicide on International Women's Day in 1935 at the age of only 24. This simultaneous act of protest and submission sums up the contradictions of her life, career and image. From a poor background, Ruan had become involved with her mother's employer's son, but after they separated she became involved with a wealthy businessman. As Andrew Field has shown, when the phenomenon of the female star first appeared in Chinese culture, the public made sense of it through the image of the concubine. In a culture with few female actors and in which acting and prostitution had long overlapped, this was the most logical framework.[5] By the 1930s, stars were beginning to set themselves apart from the image of the concubine, but Ruan's affiliation with the married businessman threatened to invoke that older image. None of this would have mattered had her private life not become public. However, her first husband used her new relationship to sue her for adultery and demand alimony – a very modern concept. Small wonder that her suicide note contained the comment that 'Gossip is a fearful thing'.

The details of Ruan's life are documented in Stanley Kwan's 1991 bio-pic, *Centre Stage* [*Ruan Lingyu*]. Kwan also emphasizes Ruan's role as head of an all-female household comprised of her mother, herself, and her adopted daughter. Ruan is shown as a modern career woman, obsessively keeping the household accounts. But she is also an embodiment of Confucian virtues in her devotion to her family. And yet her suicide is an abandonment of both modern and Confucian values of the responsible/filial parent and child.

Similar contradictions appear in her screen image. She played a dizzying range of roles, ranging from country girls, women workers, prostitutes, Buddhist nuns and maids to female students. One of her most famous roles, as the title character in *The Goddess* [*Shennü*, 1934], contains strange echoes of her own life. She is the devoted mother of a little boy, the ideal role for a woman according to Confucian values. Her devotion is linked to the theme of nationalism, because her determination to pay her son's school fees is motivated by hope that he will do great things for his country. However, it also leads her to prostitute herself in order to pay these fees – completely the opposite of the Confucian virtuous woman. This character and the image of Ruan herself are remarkable condensations of the contradictory anxieties and hopes about modernity and

10 Still from *The Goddess*

Chineseness circulating at the time. These concerns include continuing Confucian values, the quest for national modernity, capitalism and the commercialization of life, ideas about free love, and women's social autonomy.

Lurking in the background of many of Ruan's films was another historical development. Invasion by the Japanese trumped internal tensions and divisions. When the Japanese took over all of Shanghai apart from the foreign concessions in 1937, the Chinese cinema's first golden age was over. Hong Kong thrived temporarily. But once the Pacific War broke out in 1941, the Japanese invaded not only the 'orphan island' of the Shanghai concessions but also Hong Kong. Some filmmakers fled inland with either the GMD or the Communists. As Fu Poshek has traced in his recent book on the topic, others remained in Shanghai and continued to work through the occupation.[6]

A 'second golden age' of 'social realist' dramas flowered in Shanghai after the defeat of Japan. It included such classics as the epic of wartime corruption versus self-sacrifice, symbolized by the hero's two wives, in *A Spring River Flows East* [*Yi Jiang Chunshui xiang Dong Liu*, 1947]. This period also produced Fei Mu's unique postwar psychological drama, *Spring in a Small Town* [*Xiaocheng zhi Chun*, 1948]. Criticized by leftists for its lack of political engagement, this film is nonetheless often nominated as the best Chinese film ever made.

Competing Chinas, different national cinemas

The establishment of the People's Republic in 1949 forced the GMD to retreat to Taiwan, where it re-established its Republic of China. Each regime had its own vision of China as a modern nation-state. And each regime tried to deploy the cinema to help it realize that vision.

On the Mainland prior to 1949, cinema had been an urban phenomenon associated with the petit bourgeoisie. The majority of the population were farmers, and they had never seen a film. The Communist Party based itself among them. Indeed, its great innovation in revolutionary theory was to extend the definition of the revolutionary masses to encompass farmers as well as the proletariat. One of its leading cultural policies was therefore to extend cinema across the whole nation. Studios were established one after the other in many provinces, and a huge programme of movie theatre building was embarked upon. Mobile projection teams of men on bicycles with film equipment and sheets took cinema to the villages and, later, to the communes.

The Party was eager to harness cinema as a pedagogical tool in the socialist transformation of the country. Therefore, by the mid-1950s, it had nationalized all film production. Under the centralized planning system, the pre-revolutionary genre system of market-driven entertainment cinema disappeared. In its place came a system of thematic categories corresponding to messages the Party wanted to direct to certain population sectors – 'youth films', 'rural films', and so on.

The new socialist nation-state not only determined the cinema as an institution and the themes of the films it made, but also determined its style. Although both the GMD and the Communist Party approved of realism, each developed its own specific variant. At first, the Communists adopted socialist realism from the Soviet Union, but after the break with the Russians in the late 1950s, they pursued a 'combination of socialist realism and revolutionary romanticism'. Romanticism highlighted optimistic idealism and faith in the future. How was this Chinese socialist realism like any other realism, and how was it distinctive? And how was this style linked to the Communist vision of the modern nation-state?

Gina Marchetti has noted similarities between socialist and Hollywood realism. Despite the deadly opposition of the Cold War, they shared an underlying secular, rational and scientific understanding of the world.[7] This not only banished 'superstition' from the screen, but also dictated that all events in narratives should be explainable in terms of the logic of the observable world. Their shared faith in human perfectibility also led them to prefer linear narrative structures directed towards the resolution of problems and the famous 'happy ending'. In the case of Chinese socialist realism, unhappy endings were only permitted in historical films set before the Party could have plausibly saved the day.

However, there were also important differences. Hollywood tended to trace problems back to individual psychology, in line with the ideology of American capitalism. Understanding the state as an obstacle, Americanism both empowers and places responsibility on individuals (including corporations, which the American legal system treats as individuals). By contrast, both Soviet and Chinese socialist realism saw class as the primary determinant of character and behaviour, and class struggle as the primary determinant of historical progress. Having gained control of the state, the political leadership sought to maximize its power to ensure the correct outcome of the class struggle and accelerate progress. This class logic also shaped the representation of the nation in the cinema of the People's Republic. Not all Chinese people were depicted as part of the 'people' in the 'People's Republic'. Those classes on the wrong side of the class struggle – class enemies – were excluded.

The first narrative feature film made after the foundation of the People's Republic, Wang Bin's *Bridge* [*Qiao*, 1949], emphasized national unity but showed that certain classes were more reliable than others. The narrative concerns a steel plant commissioned to supply repair materials for a bridge needed in the war effort. The factory's engineers – in other words, its bourgeois intellectuals – doubt the order can be filled. But, fired by patriotism and support for the Communist Party, the factory workers – its revolutionary masses – overcome the problem. In this case, the engineer is inspired by their achievements. But in later films in which there is no war enemy to unite everyone, class enemies take their place. For example, the 1962 comedy *Li Shuangshuang* is a rural tale about women's participation in labour. The eponymous Li is eager to work outside the home, but her husband is unwilling to share the household chores. Persuaded by petit bourgeois class enemies to think of his family rather than the commune, he is putting all his spare time into illegal sideline activities. Because the husband's class background is sound, in the end Li and the Party secretary make him see the error of his ways. But the class enemy lurks on the fringes of the commune, and the film warns the population of the national community to look out for such enemies within.

This logic of the class-based nation also mediated ethnic difference in the cinema of the People's Republic. 'Han' Chinese constitute by far the largest ethnic group in China. But many minority nationalities such as Tibetans, Koreans, and the Uyghurs of Central Asia live in strategically important borderlands. One of the tasks of the cinema was to help integrate these different groups into one nation-state. Class was used as the common language across ethnic difference. A good example is the 1964 film about the Chinese takeover – or liberation, depending on one's politics – of Tibet, Serfs [Nongnu]. It opens with a depiction of Tibet as a feudal class-based society divided between the monks and abbots of the monasteries and the local landlords on one hand, and the exploited serfs who work the lands and pay taxes and tithes to them on the other. The main character is Jampa. Forced to work from childhood as a human horse, he carries his master around the high plateau. Jampa rebels repeatedly. But the film shows that the class struggle in Tibet can only succeed with the support of the People's Liberation Army. In this way, it legitimates the Chinese takeover on the basis of shared class position.

In Taiwan, the GMD responded to socialist realism with what it called 'healthy realism' in the 1960s. During the 1895–1945 Japanese occupation, little film production had occurred. In the 1950s, the GMD was still recovering from defeat. It established various state-owned studios, but the first cinema boom originated with privately owned companies. These mostly produced films in the local version of Hokkienese, especially local opera films. Forgotten for many years, these films have recently been reclaimed as part of the national cultural legacy by supporters of the independence movement. However, a high degree of local culture did not correspond to the GMD's vision of Taiwan as an entirely integrated part of a unified Chinese nation-state. The GMD therefore favoured films in the Mandarin 'national language' with financial incentives.

Such policies led to the eclipse of Taiwanese-language cinema in the 1960s. The government-owned studios specialized in healthy realist films, which the GMD saw as its national cinema. These glossy tales in Mandarin resembled socialist realism in their emphasis on building a better future with hard work and self-sacrifice. However, they eulogized small-scale capitalism based on the family unit rather than condemning it, in the manner pursued by *Li Shuangshuang*. Examples included the prolific Lee Xing's *Oyster Girl* [*Kenü*, 1964], *Beautiful Duckling* [*Yangya Ren-jia*, 1965], and later *He Never Gives Up* [*Wangyang zhongde yitiao Chuan*, 1978]. The first two are farming films and the third is a triumph-against-the-odds melodrama about a disabled man. All three are often understood as national allegories for the Republic of China.

Hong Kong as the outlaw world

The cinemas of both the People's Republic and the Republic of China were shaped by their different projects of modernization via the nation-state. However, Hong Kong's cinema was shaped by its status as a colony – another kind of modern space but one outside the logic of the nation-state. We have already seen how censorship in the 1930s established Hong Kong's emphases on Cantonese-language cinema, martial arts cinema, and Cantonese opera films. Although the culture of these films was specifically Cantonese, premodern settings and emphasis on fantasy made them quite different from the realist vision of contemporary nation building. Furthermore, Hong Kong cinema was not aimed only at the Hong Kong market. In fact, its main market was diasporic Chinese, for whom Chinese culture formed a site of nostalgia distinct from the societies they lived in. As a result, these films were also made in languages other than Cantonese, including Mandarin and various Hokkienese languages. The main exception to this overall pattern was the small-scale and relatively short-lived leftist realist cinema of the 1950s. Associated with the Southern China Film Industry Workers' Union, this cinema included films such as Li Tie's *In the Face of Demolition* [*Weilou Chunxiao*, 1953], which focused on overcrowded housing in a colony overwhelmed by refugees.

Hong Kong cinema's diasporic audience implied a metaphor that grew in importance over the years to come. This was the image of an outlaw world outside civil society and outside the national community. It was also called the 'rivers and lakes' (*jianghu*), a term drawn from Chinese popular fiction and in particular martial arts fiction. Filmmakers who fled the Mainland and established themselves in Hong Kong often perceived themselves as exiles, and this manifested itself in their films. A minority of these were direct representations of the situation. For example, the Chinese title of Zhu Shilin's 1952 *The Show Must Go*

On, Jianghu Ernü, literally means 'children of the rivers and lakes'. The film follows an acrobatic troupe that tries to eke out a living in Hong Kong after the revolution. However, exploited and bullied in the land of the 'rivers and lakes', they return to the Mainland at the end of the film.

However, as Stephen Teo has pointed out in his chapter on postwar cinema in Hong Kong, a more frequent pattern for exiled filmmakers was to avoid all mention of Hong Kong. At first, they often set their films in the Shanghai they pined for. Later filmmakers working in popular genres such as martial arts also chose times and settings appropriate to their sense of Hong Kong and the diaspora as a space of exile.[8] King Hu's extravagant martial arts classic *Dragon Gate Inn* [*Longmen Kezhan*, 1967] is a prime example. The film concerns a family fleeing persecution by the state in the period of the early Qing dynasty. The father has already been executed because he was a minister in the late Ming dynasty, and the fighting takes place in the *jianghu* borderlands. The Qing were Manchus, and the Ming was the last ethnically Chinese dynasty. The metaphor is of patriotism and opposition to Communism, with the *jianghu* standing in for the diaspora.

In the 1970s and 1980s, the first generation to have grown up in Hong Kong with little experience of Mainland China came of age and entered the cinema. Contemporary Hong Kong became a more frequent setting for their films. However, their colonized status meant that it was still a space over which they had no political control . This was made painfully clear when British Prime Minister Margaret Thatcher negotiated directly with Deng Xiaoping's government in Beijing in 1984. Without consulting the people of Hong Kong, they agreed on 1997 as the date for the handover of Hong Kong to the People's Republic. In these circumstances, although the new generation imagined Hong Kong as home rather than as a space of exile, the metaphor of the *jianghu* outlaw land persisted. But now, instead of being coloured by nostalgia for a lost homeland, it was accented by an anticipatory nostalgia for a home-in-the-outlaw-land that would soon be lost. This cultural condition is what Ackbar Abbas calls the *déja disparu*, or the 'already disappeared'.[9]

Many of the now iconic films from this period feature Hong Kong as simultaneously home and *jianghu* – borderland, outlaw space and transit point. In John Woo's *The Killer* [*Diexue Shuangxiong*, 1989], not only does the film take place in a liminal space occupied by gangsters and the police, but both the main cop and the main gangster break the rules of their own brotherhoods, becoming outlaws from the *jianghu* itself. In

11 Still from *The Killer*

one key scene, Chow Yun-Fat's character waxes nostalgic about how the old codes of the brotherhood are disappearing, as he stands high on hills overlooking Hong Kong. In Wong Kar-wai's *Chungking Express* (1994), a similar pattern of doubling occurs. Instead of the cop and the criminal being similar, there are two cops who each fall in love with two women – an old girlfriend and a new one. Not only are these cops in transit in their love lives, but the spaces of the city are constantly being made over. Hong Kong is less their home than a stepping stone on the way to somewhere else, as indicated by the repetition of the song 'California Dreaming'.

Does the 1997 handover mean that this sense of liminality has disappeared in post-1997 cinema? Hardly. Hong Kong cinema is still structured by Hong Kong's condition as 'not a nation'. It is now designated a 'Special Administrative Region' in which none of the key legal, political and administrative structures will change until 2046. This deferred liminality is explored in Wong Kar-wai's *2046* (2004), which tracked forward in science fiction but also backward to room 2046 in a structure that conveyed simultaneous worry about the future and nostalgia for the past. Meanwhile, films such as Johnnie To's *Election* [*Hei Shehui*, 2005] make a mockery of Hong Kong's supposed civil society. *Election* uses triad elections as an allegory for the contemporary state of the *jianghu* that Hong Kong remains in the imagination of many viewers.

The new wave critique of the nation and modernity

The new generation of Hong Kong filmmakers associated with a sceptical critique of modernity's pretensions to freedom, democracy and equality is sometimes known as the Hong Kong New Wave. In 1980s Mainland China and Taiwan, parallel new waves developed a similar critique of Communist and GMD high modernity. In the process, they produced some of the most heavily awarded Chinese films ever made.

The Mainland new-wave filmmakers are known as the Fifth Generation. The demarcation of preceding generations remains disputed, but the Fifth Generation graduated from the Beijing Film Academy (BFA) Directing, Cinematography, and Art Directing departments in 1982. *Yellow Earth* created such a sensation in Hong Kong in 1985 because it was so different from anything that had previously come out of the People's Republic. The Fifth Generation came from divergent social backgrounds. Some were the children of the Communist cultural elite, such as the director of *Army Nurse* [*Nüer Lou*, 1985], Hu Mei, whose father was a composer, or Tian Zhuangzhuang, who went on to make *Blue Kite* [*Lan Fengzheng*, 1993]. His father was a director and his mother an actress who had become a studio head. Others, such as Zhang Yimou, came from humble backgrounds. In Zhang's case, this included political problems that dogged his childhood.

What these filmmakers shared was the experience of the Cultural Revolution. They had been encouraged to rebel against their parents and teachers out of loyalty to Mao. Chen Kaige has stated that the scene of betrayal by the adopted son in *Farewell, My Concubine* [*Bawang Bieji*, 1993] is based on his betrayal of his own father. When the Cultural Revolution got out of hand, this generation was sent down to the countryside, where they discovered a less utopian reality than they had witnessed in the socialist realist cinema. The resulting disillusion spawned a cycle of films in which national modernity appeared as ruination. In *Yellow Earth*, the Communist soldier cannot save the girl; in *Army Nurse*, the disciplinary demands of the PLA ruin the love between a young nurse and a soldier; and in *Blue Kite*, a little boy sees his father and every other man in his mother's life destroyed by Party politics.

By the late 1980s, the rise of a market system was being felt. Many commentators see Zhang Yimou's debut film *Red Sorghum* [*Hong Gaoliang*, 1987] as marking the end of the Fifth Generation phenomenon. However, its theme song was adopted by the Tiananmen students in 1989. In the aftermath, life became difficult for Fifth Generation filmmakers. Many compromised in the face of government pressure. Wu Ziniu, who had made such films as the exposé of the prison system *Evening Bell* [*Wanzhong*, 1988], was soon making patriotic military films. Others stopped making films altogether. Hu Mei's psychological films had never made money, and she disappeared from view, only to reappear later as a successful director of television series.

In Taiwan, as Emilie Yueh-yu Yeh and Darrell William Davis have discussed, the Taiwan New Cinema appeared in the 1980s. Much as in Hong Kong, this new wave was driven by waning connections to the Mainland and the rise of filmmakers who had only known life on the island. Like those of their Hong Kong counterparts, their films focused on local life and rejected commercial fantasy in favour of realism. However, as with their Mainland counterparts, the sceptical excavation of the history of the GMD's modern nation-state project also featured heavily in their work.[10]

The primary representatives of the Taiwan New Cinema are Hou Hsiao-hsien and Edward Yang. Hou's early New Cinema works such as *Summer at Grandpa's* [*Dongdong de Xiaqi*, 1984], *Dust in the Wind* [*Lianlian Fengchen*, 1986] and *A Time to Live and a Time to Die* [*Tongnian Wangshi*, 1985] mixed autobiography and biography to represent Taiwan during the childhoods of Hou and his screenwriters. The resulting images were at once nostalgic and accusatory. They savoured the sad memories of earlier generations who either felt themselves to be in exile or to have been exploited by both the Japanese colonizers and the export-led capitalist order that followed.

Following the relaxation of censorship with the end of martial law in 1987, Hou moved from personal history to Taiwan history. His 1989 *City of Sadness* [*Beiqing Chengshi*] details the fate of a family caught up in the 28 February Incident of 1947. Long taboo, this incident had occurred due to tensions between islanders and the newly arrived GMD, and led to a massacre sometimes compared with the events of 4 June 1989 on the Mainland. This tragic event could be seen as a traumatic origin for the Taiwanese independence movement. Yet Hou presents it at a distance, focusing less on events in Taipei than on their repercussions. In other words, instead of substituting one vision of nation-state based modernity for another, he invites us to see the classic unified nation-state of modernity as impossible in Taiwan and as a ruin.

This perspective is also found in Edward Yang's own historical epic, *A Brighter Summer's Day* [*Guling Jie Shaonian Sharen Shijian*]. Made in 1991 and perceived by many as complementary to *City of Sadness*, this film takes a true event at a high school and relates it to the impact of the Cold War and the White Terror that dominated life on Taiwan during the 1950s and 1960s. Like Hou, Yang eschews turning this into one of the wounds

of Taiwanese national history at the hands of outsiders. Instead, his focus on teenagers and ordinary suburban life portrays the events of the
film as the devastating impact of nation-state modernity on ordinary
citizens, be they of islander or mainlander background.

Just as commercialization brought the Fifth Generation phenomenon
to a premature end in the Mainland, box office problems also had an impact on Taiwan New Cinema. However, these difficulties were not confined to art and alternative cinema. They are part of a general restructur-
ing of the Chinese film industries as they have undergone globalization
over the last two decades. The re-examination of history in the new wave
cinemas of Taiwan and the People's Republic may have helped to divorce
cinema from the classic projects of nation-state modernization by reimag-
ining progress as ruination. However, the structural processes of globalization have played a stronger role in shaping the new configuration of the
relationship between Chinese cinema and the national in the current era.

The national in the transnational

The introduction to this chapter discussed the evolution of Chinese cinema as a global brand over the last twenty years. This final section puts
that phenomenon in the larger context of globalization and the recon-
figuration of the Chinese cinema in general. This process has produced
disjuncture. Chinese filmmakers are no longer necessarily making films
primarily for Chinese audiences, and Chinese audiences are no longer
primarily watching Chinese films. Chinese cinemas are no longer simply
divided according to territorially based industries and markets. Instead,
they correspond to a variety of different markets defined according to
taste structures that correspond to class, culture and infrastructure. To
understand this, we can use Arjun Appadurai's model of globalization as
composed of 'scapes' that organize such disjunctures as flows.[11]

Before the 1980s, Chinese cinema was mostly produced in territorially defined markets by filmmakers from within that territory and for
audiences in that territory. The People's Republic was one such territory. Whether Taiwan should be understood as another such territory, or
whether it and Hong Kong are best understood as film production centres
in a larger territory of Chinese diasporic culture outside the Mainland is
open to debate. But within this model, exports outside Chinese culture
were secondary. There was a reasonably high degree of cultural and territorial homology between producers, industry and audiences.

The more recent development of the Chinese cinema global brand shows that the situation has changed. The filmmakers may be of Chinese background, but the primary audiences may not be, and they may be dispersed across territorial borders. Under the sign of Chinese cinema, one of the product lines is festival films. Adopting Appadurai's terminology, the circulation of films through film festivals can be considered as a transborder flow on the global cinemascape. These festival films are often funded by transborder investment sources, and seen by relatively few people within their territories of production as well as a specialist audience that gathers at film festivals around the world.

A good example of Chinese cinema's participation in this festival flow is the so-called Sixth Generation cinema that appeared in Mainland China in the 1990s. These 1989 Beijing Film Academy graduates had to try to distinguish themselves from the Fifth Generation in the face of post-Tiananmen Massacre increases in censorship. Some gave up and went straight into the mainstream industry. But others decided on a new route – going 'underground'. In China, 'underground' means not submitting films for censorship prior to distribution and exhibition inside China. In other words, the Chinese market is forsaken. This results in low budgets and dependence on income from overseas.

After making his first film, a drama about the difficulties of disabled children in China called *Mama* (1990), Sixth Generation filmmaker Zhang Yuan went underground with *Beijing Bastards* (1992), a film about the rock scene. His colleague Wang Xiaoshuai started out underground with *The Days* (1993), and He Jianjun debuted with *Red Beads* (1993). Both films are about depressed young artists in Beijing. These filmmakers were later joined by other young underground filmmakers who are associated with the Sixth Generation. These include Jia Zhangke, who debuted with *Xiao Wu* (1997), a film about the life of a small-town pickpocket. In recent years, these filmmakers have gone 'above ground', but so far they have had limited market and critical success with their new works.

In Taiwan, the situation of Tsai Ming-liang and other filmmakers who have emerged since the 1990s can be compared with that of the Sixth Generation. The main difference is that the Taiwanese do not have problems with state censorship. But the Taiwan distribution and exhibition market is now largely tied in to Hollywood. It is almost impossible for local films to get screening slots, and local audiences show little interest in them. Tsai may be big in Paris, but in Taipei he has to hawk his films to movie theatres and audiences in person.

Another product line, so to speak, consists of martial arts blockbusters. These are seen by mainstream audiences around the world, including in their territories of production, and are part of the transborder flow that is global entertainment cinema. However, it cannot be said that Chinese audiences are the primary audience for these films, because their main revenue comes from North America, followed by Europe and Japan. In other words, this is still an export-led phenomenon, and it often drives a tourist fantasy of Chinese national culture.

This does not mean that there are no Chinese filmmakers working primarily with local audiences in mind. But even so, it is doubtful those audiences can be defined as national audiences. Take the example of Feng Xiaogang, whose urban comedies such as *Cell Phone* [*Shouji*, 2003], about the intersection of technology and adultery, and *Big Shot's Funeral* [*Dawan*, 2001], about the commercialization of a celebrity funeral, poke fun at Mainland China's new market economy. Such films are released for the Chinese New Year holiday every year, and are very successful. However, they are not uniformly successful. Southern Chinese show relatively little interest in them, and their market is confined largely to the urban middle classes. Likewise, other films appeal to other audience segments.

In these circumstances, there is a double dispersal of Chinese national cinemas occurring. On the one hand, there is local fragmentation of the former national market. Much of that market is now given over to foreign films, and in particular Hollywood cinema. Meanwhile, local films are reorganized into types that appeal to particular audiences in particular localities. On the other hand, there is dispersal outwards, as other kinds of Chinese cinema find their place in the flows of the global cinemascape. The situation is currently in dynamic flux, and the future is unclear.

Notes

1. Pang Laikwan, 'Walking in and out of the Spectacle: China's Earliest Film Scene', *Screen* 47, no. 1 (2006), 66–80.
2. Zhang Zhen, 'Teahouse, Shadowplay, Bricolage: *Laborer's Love* and the Question of Early Chinese Cinema', in Zhang Yingjin (ed.), *Cinema and Urban Culture in Shanghai, 1922–1943*, Bloomington, Indiana University Press, 1999, pp. 27–50.
3. Zhang Zhen, *An Amorous History of the Silver Screen: Shanghai Cinema, 1896–1937*, Chicago, University of Chicago Press, 2005.
4. Xiao Zhiwei, 'Anti-imperialism and Film Censorship during the Nanjing Decade, 1927–1937, in Sheldon Hsiao-Ping Lu (ed.), *Transnational Chinese Cinemas: Identity, Nationhood, Gender*, Honolulu, University of Hawai'i Press, 1997, pp. 35–57.

5. Andrew Field, 'Selling Souls in Sin City: Shanghai Singing and Dancing Girls in Print, Film and Politics, 1920–1949', in Zhang Yingjin (ed.), *Cinema and Urban Culture in Republican China*, Stanford, Stanford University Press, 1999, pp. 99–127.

6. Poshek Fu, *Between Shanghai and Hong Kong: The Politics of Chinese Cinemas,* Stanford, Stanford University Press, 2003.

7. Gina Marchetti, '*Two Stage Sisters*: The Blooming of a Revolutionary Aesthetic', *Jump Cut* 34 (1989), 95–106.

8. Stephen Teo, *Hong Kong Cinema: The Extra Dimensions*, London, British Film Institute, 1997.

9. Ackbar Abbas, *Hong Kong: Culture and the Politics of Disappearance*, Minneapolis, University of Minnesota Press, 1997.

10. Emilie Yueh-yu Yeh and Darrell William Davis, *Taiwan Film Directors: A Treasure Island*, New York, Columbia University Press, 2005.

11. Arjun Appadurai, *Modernity at Large: Cultural Dimensions of Globalization,* Minneapolis, University of Minnesota Press, 1996.

Guide to further reading

Berry, Chris and Mary Farquhar, *China on Screen: Cinema and Nation,* New York, Columbia University Press and Hong Kong, Hong Kong University Press, 2006.

Bordwell, David, *Planet Hong Kong: Popular Cinema and the Art of Entertainment,* Cambridge, MA, Harvard University Press, 2000.

Chow, Rey, *Primitive Passsions: Visuality, Sexuality, Ethnography, and Contemporary Chinese Cinema,* NY, Columbia University Press, 1995.

Hu Jubin. *Projecting a Nation: Chinese National Cinema before 1949,* Hong Kong, Hong Kong University Press, 2003.

Lu, Sheldon Hsiao-peng (ed.), *Transnational Chinese Cinema: Identity, Nationhood, Gender,* Honolulu, University of Hawai'i Press, 1997.

Ni, Zhen, *Memoirs from the Beijing Film Academy: The Genesis of China's Fifth Generation* (trans. Chris Berry), Durham, Duke University Press, 2002.

Yau, Esther C. M. (ed.), *At Full Speed: Hong Kong Cinema in a Borderless World,* Minneapolis, University of Minnesota, 2001.

Zhang Yingjin and Xiao Zhiwei (eds.), *Encyclopedia of Chinese Film,* New York, Routledge, 1998.

16

Media boom and cyber culture: television and the Internet in China

Media and communications have played a crucial role in China's historic transformation since 1979, especially as China has become increasingly involved in the globalization process. Revolutions in information and communication technology have both empowered and weakened the state, and China's reform and opening up policies have ushered in an era of unprecedented autonomy and diversity in Chinese media and communication, influencing public opinion, public policy, political, ideological and socioeconomic changes in this country of over 1,300 million people. Once a complete propaganda vehicle of the ruling Chinese Communist Party (CCP) and the state, media in China have now become increasingly market oriented and profit driven. Television is arguably the most important medium in China's social and cultural life, providing over one billion viewers with news, information, entertainment, points of view and lifestyles. The emergence and phenomenal growth of the Internet in China, on the other hand, promises to bring the information revolution to bear on social change in a more intense, often unpredictable fashion. The number of Chinese Internet users has grown from around 100,000 in 1996 to over 120 million in 2006 (an annual growth rate of more than 200 per cent). Surrounded by controversy and at times outrage from Western societies over the state's censorship and crackdowns on political dissent in cyberspace, the Internet has become an indisputable alternative medium, providing news and voicing public opinion largely unavailable in the state-owned media. Moreover, the electronic and digital forms of television, the Internet and cellular phones have undoubtedly helped to shape a new urban youth culture distinct from those of all previous generations.

Television: history and structures

China had no television during the Republican period (1911–49), and it took nearly ten years for the first television station, Beijing Television, to appear after the People's Republic of China was founded in 1949. On 1 May 1958, Beijing Television, the state network, started experimental operation with black and white signals. The programming consisted of news, documentary films and some entertainment programmes, lasting two to three hours a day, four times a week. A month later, Shanghai Television Station was established. This was the time of the Great Leap Forward (1958–61), when Mao Zedong, leader of the CCP, called on the whole country to build a Communist society that would catch up with, and then surpass, the socioeconomic development of the West in only ten to fifteen years. Television, like any other form of media and culture, was perceived by Mao to be a tool of ideological purification and political propaganda. At first, China saw the rapid spread of television across the country, with twenty stations established by the end of 1960 and thirty six by 1961. However, this rapid growth in the number of stations was followed by a sharp decline, due to the debacle of the Great Leap Forward and the famine of the early 1960s. Stations began to creep back into production after 1964. When the Cultural Revolution (1966–76) broke out, China's media and cultural institutions suffered a severe setback. By 1967, about six months into the Cultural Revolution, all but two Chinese TV stations had stopped broadcasting. Broadcasts resumed in 1969, but with content even more political than that of the earlier broadcasts. China gradually began to build television stations across the provinces, and in 1973 Beijing, Tianjin and Shanghai broadcast colour programmes; by the early 1980s, all television transmission was in colour.[1]

The reform and opening up that took place from 1979 was a turning point for Chinese television. In 1978 there were only 3.04 million television sets in China for a population of around 800 million. This lack of interest was largely due to the programming provided during the Cultural Revolution. Reform again began with Beijing TV, whose name and role were officially changed on 1 May 1978. China Central TV (CCTV) became the new nucleus of Chinese broadcasting. CCTV began to broadcast international satellite feeds in colour on two channels in 1980. As a result of this and other reforms, television audiences grew rapidly. By the end of 1980, the number of television sets had doubled, reaching almost 6 million. The period of reform not only brought economic prosperity, but also created an insatiable desire among the public to know more about China and the world, and to have more fun in life. Television soon became the most popular medium for both news and entertainment.

As heir to Mao's legacy of the Communist propaganda state, the post-Mao leadership under the aegis of Deng Xiaoping was quick to recognize the need to use television to promote the reform agenda while encouraging the growth of the television industry as an economic entity. In 1983, the Chinese government restructured the television system. New television stations were established at 4 levels: national, provincial, prefecture and county. CCTV is the national broadcaster, and currently has 16 channels. Television stations mushroomed in the 1980s. While only 52 stations existed in total in 1983, 422 stations appeared in 1988, with an additional 811 'relay' stations set up by local governments of provinces, municipalities and counties.[2] By the end of 2005, the number of television stations had dropped to 309, with CCTV as the national broadcaster, 34 provincial stations, and 274 municipal or city stations. In addition, there were 53 educational television stations run by national, provincial or city governments. Apart from these full-blown television stations, there were 1,919 relay stations at county level, which did not produce their own programmes except brief local government announcements. These stations (the national, the provincial and city) offered a total of 2,262 channels, and broadcast 25,611 hours of programming every day. In April 1983, China launched its first telecommunications satellite, bringing CCTV's programmes to regions as remote as Tibet and Xinjiang. By 2005, there were 60 satellite channels in China.[3] In 1978, around 2 per cent of Chinese households had TV sets, which broadcast to around 80 million viewers. By 2005, Chinese households had 370 million TV sets, covering 95.29 per cent of the population of 1.3 billion. A survey in 2004 put the number of television viewers in China at 1.2 billion. An average viewer watches 3 hours of TV per day, and 20 channels per day (60 minutes of national TV, 48 minutes of provincial, and 70 minutes on local channels). He or she watches on average 38 minutes of TV drama, 31 minutes of news, 21 minutes of special programmes, 13 minutes of movies, 11 minutes of entertainment, 9 minutes of sports, 4 minutes of cartoons, 3 minutes of musical programmes, 2 minutes of theatre, and 50 minutes of other programmes.[4]

The number of cable TV subscribers had reached 116 million by 2005. Cable television appeared in the late 1970s and grew rapidly in the 1980s. In 1990 the government issued a unified plan for cable television development, and the central government has approved 1,300 cable stations since that date. The most recent developments include digitization of cable television and IPTV (Internet television). Rather than switching broadcasting over-the-air television and cable television from analogue to digital all at once, China began to digitize cable television programmes from 2002 as its strategy for developing DTV (digital television). Shanghai Media Group (SMG, or Shanghai Television Station) now has a digital cable system broadcasting 112 sets of digital programmes daily, and over 24 hours digital programming amounts to nearly 50,000 hours.[5]

All Chinese television stations are owned by the state. In 1985, the national government established the Ministry of Radio, Film and Television (MFRT), which changed its name in 2000 to the State Administration of Radio, Film and Television (SARFT). Its tasks include: approving the content of radio and television programmes as well as films; overseeing film imports and stipulating the time allotted for foreign TV programmes; overseeing the operation of Chinese Central Television (CCTV); and controlling the access of satellite and cable networks as well as supervising their operations. Provincial, city and county television stations come under the control of local bureaus of radio and television. However, in a wave of media conglomerations that began in 1999, attempting to transform bureaucratic agencies into modern business corporations, the provincial bureaus of radio and television changed their names to become corporations/conglomerates/groups. This move was largely unsuccessful, and in 2004, SARFT stopped accepting applications from local bureaus to become conglomerates, and in February 2006, SARFT again announced that it would no longer approve provincial media conglomerates. This abortive attempt at structural change reveals deep-seated, intrinsic problems in Chinese media in general and television in particular.

After nearly thirty years of reform, Chinese television has experienced a profound transformation from a propaganda tool of the state to a profitable business sector, while retaining its essential characteristic of being the 'mouthpiece' of the Chinese Communist Party. On the one hand, the television sector is still firmly under the control of the CCP (the SARFT and all local bureaus fall under the control of the Propaganda Departments of the CCP). On the other hand, the Chinese government (both national and local) has over the years reduced its state funding and subsidies for media organizations to a minimum, and allowed them to function more and more as profit-making enterprises in the overall context of market reform. Advertising, once despised, now 'help(s) link producers and consumers by supplying important economic information and providing "scientific guidance" '.[6] The industry grew at a rate of 41 per cent between 1981 and 1992, and became China's fastest growing industry at that time.

Financial autonomy and dispersion boosted not only the growth of television stations and channels, but also production of programmes that were more entertaining and began to reflect the popular political sentiments of the time. The CCP's imperatives of maintaining absolute control of the 'media orientation' (*yulun daoxiang*) and at the same time maximizing profits from the media industry have led to several significant changes. First, for the television sector (and for other media as well), ratings have become the most important indices for advertising revenue or economic success. The US-based AC Nielsen Media Research group began to make inroads into China in the early 1990s, and by 2005, sophisticated, large-scale ratings surveys drawing on models from the USA, Western Europe, Japan and Hong Kong had become standard measures of the performance of TV stations.

Second, television stations began to practise the separation of programme production and broadcasting (*zhibo fenli*) in the early 2000s. Previously, for Chinese television stations, programme production and broadcasting were all under the same umbrella. In order to increase economic efficiency, television stations began to outsource, subcontract, and purchase a high proportion of their programmes – mostly entertainment programmes such as TV dramas and variety shows – from production companies. As a result, the number of private media production companies has proliferated since 2000, producing a large quantity of entertainment programmes.

The biggest issue for the structural reform of the television sector (and other media sectors) lies in the transformation from government bureaucracy to business enterprise. The stalemate in the conglomeration of media organizations points to the larger dilemma of China's reform in the state-owned sector. A particular challenge for the media sector arises in defining the nature of the reformed agency. Media organizations in China, like educational and health institutions (schools and hospitals), are labelled with the peculiar term 'public service entities/organizations' (*shiye danwei*), as opposed to profit-making business enterprises (*qiye danwei*). In a 2001 CCP decree, television organizations were defined as 'public service entities run as business enterprises'. The situation became even fuzzier with a 2005 CCP decree in which the CCP called for the formation of more powerful and competitive cultural industrial–business conglomerates. To put this rather oblique decree into more straightforward language, it means that Chinese media (television included) must now serve the dual bosses of the CCP and the market, like other state-owned business enterprises such as China Petroleum Co., China Telecommunication Co. and Air China. The crucial role of television (and the media in general) as a public forum for delivering news to the general public and for voicing public opinion is simply sidestepped here. This is perhaps the greatest dilemma that Chinese television and other media sectors now face.

Television news programmes

Television news bulletins are the most important programmes for television stations, and the second most popular with Chinese viewers (after television dramas). Starting with CCTV-1, each television station must have a comprehensive channel to broadcast important news. CCTV-News Channel was established in 2003, broadcasting news 24 hours a day. CCTV's domination of news programming is shown by its prime-time Network News (*Xinwen lianbo*), broadcast daily from 7:00 to 7:30 pm Beijing time. The Chinese government requires all local stations to broadcast this programme simultaneously. CCTV Network News establishes a model and standard for practically all Chinese television news programmes, and serves as one of the most important news outlets for the CCP, in addition to the newspaper *People's Daily* (*Renmin ribao*) and the Central People's Radio Station (*Zhongyang renmin guangbo diantai*). Until now, the format of the Network News has remained unchanged since its first day of broadcasting on 1 January 1978.

CCTV Network News has two presenters, one male and one female (there are two to three pairs of presenters who rotate on a daily basis). These presenters are merely announcers, not news anchors like the late Peter Jennings of ABC News or Tom Brokaw of NBC News in the USA, who have the editorial power to determine the selection of news. The editorial board of CCTV Network News consists of the most senior officials at CCTV, supervised directly by CCTV's President. The Network News invariably begins with the public activities of China's top leaders, in order of their rankings in the highest political body, the Standing Committee of the Political Bureau of the CCP. The first appearance is reserved for the

General Secretary of the CCP, who is also the President of the People's Republic. Conferences, meetings with foreign visitors, tours and speeches involving these top leaders usually take up about ten minutes or one third of the thirty-minute programme. The next ten minutes consist of economic news from across China, and sometimes the segments are pre-recorded and produced weeks or even months ahead. Most news stories consist of positive reports of growth, development and technological advances, and are mainly produced by local television stations.

The CCTV Network News model is true to the CCP's media theory and guidelines. Television should first and foremost serve as the mouthpiece of the government and the CCP, and should mainly cover the successful aspects of Chinese political and economic reform and the positive features of government, and not spread negative thinking and low morale via the news.[7] This media policy is closely tied to the political and ideological agenda in the CCP. Insofar as the CCP has not embarked on any fundamental change to the political structure of a one-party state, it has not shown any willingness to relinquish its firm hold on the media in the foreseeable future. Radical change of the CCTV Network News format is unlikely, and any changes are incremental and gradual.

In 1993 CCTV launched a news magazine, *Oriental Horizon* (*Dongfang shikong*), followed by another news magazine *Focus* (*Jiaodian fangdan*), as part of the network's reform of its news programmes. *East Time and Space* (or *Oriental Horizon*) is a one-hour morning news magazine broadcast at 7:00 am, before most of the audience go to work or school. It contains several segments canvassing events in the daily lives of ordinary citizens and portraits of well-known figures, reporting on a single issue with some depth. The programme is hugely popular, some even claiming it caused a 'silent television revolution in the daytime'. *Focus* is a thirty-minute current affairs programme broadcast in prime time (7:38 pm). It touches on a wide variety of hot topics in China and the world, providing background analysis, on-the-spot reporting and in-studio interviews. The issues covered by *Focus* usually have significant social impact and are of considerable interest to both the government and the public. Some of the sensitive issues concern corruption and rising social disparities and injustice, and these are exposed using an investigative reporting style. Such exposures have brought *Focus* enormous popularity. It achieved the second highest national viewer ratings of 23.8 per cent among all CCTV programmes, trailing only the Network News which has a rating of 45.6 per cent.[8] In 1996, CCTV produced another news magazine show, *News Probe* (*Xinwen diaocha*), a weekly programme that provided in-depth investigative reporting of sensitive social issues. It was similar in many ways to *Focus* but longer, at forty-five minutes. It is broadcast on CCTV-1 for the first time at 10:30 pm each Monday, and rebroadcast on CCTV-News channel on the following Tuesday, Saturday and Sunday, all in non-peak time. Sometimes the issues exposed and criticism of social problems in *News Probe* are more poignant than those covered in *Focus*, partly because it is aired away from prime time, and therefore has less widespread impact, according to the calculations of the editorial board.

Indeed, news programmes such as *Focus* and *News Probe* are often the products of a very complicated and difficult process of selection, negotiation, framing and censorship. The former director of *Focus*, Sun Yusheng, conceded that for each programme he had to carefully weigh up the question of its possible 'negative effects' on 'political stability' in general and on the resolution of the problems it uncovered in particular.[9] In order to please the government and at the same time satisfy the public's demand to know the truth behind incidents, disasters and crimes, journalists and editors need to walk a fine line, or in one critic's words, 'dance with chains'.[10] Their work is an example of the courage, ethical standards and professionalism of Chinese journalists, and reflects an inevitable and irrevocable trend towards more accurate, balanced and fair news reporting in an increasingly open society. In October 1998, Chinese Premier Zhu Rongji met with *Focus* editors and reporters, and left an inscription paying tribute to the programme and expressing the hope that it would serve to provide 'public supervision, [function as] people's mouthpiece, government's mirror, and vanguard of reform'. Changing from the 'CCP's mouthpiece' to the 'people's mouthpiece' is a significant shift, especially when articulated by a top leader. While no substantial reorientation occurred at the CCTV after this visit, local television stations took the cue from Zhu's inscription in their efforts towards reform.

A diverse range of television news programmes and news magazine shows continued to appear on local television stations, devoting more attention to local issues that have direct impact on the everyday lives of ordinary citizens. On 1 January 2002, Jiangsu Television Station's City Channel launched the prime-time news programme *Nanjing Zero Distance* (*Nanjing lingjuli*) which screened from 6:00 to 7:30 pm (overlapping with CCTV Network News, obligingly broadcast by Jiangsu TV-1).

It ushered in a new type of 'news of people's lives' (*minsheng xinwen*), dealing almost exclusively with the everyday events and issues that concern Nanjing residents. Because it is the provincial capital, events in Nanjing have implications for all of Jiangsu, one of the most prosperous provinces on China's east coast. The programme's ratings soon soared, and it attracted the highest Nielsen rating (17.02 per cent) of all television programmes in Nanjing and vicinity (with a population of 6 million).[11] More than 10 programmes of this type emerged in Jiangsu and Nanjing in the next few years, dominating television broadcasting and ratings. Across China, similar news programmes appeared on provincial and city television stations, creating a 'TV war of "news of people's lives"'. Such local news programmes meet the needs of a public with ever-growing concerns about public affairs issues that affect their individual rights and well-being, and are in keeping with the current leadership's policy priority of building a 'harmonious society'.

Television drama, New Year's Gala, and other entertainment programmes

Entertainment programmes dominate Chinese television. Television dramas (*dianshi ju*), a unique form of television serial, have consistently garnered the highest share of ratings of all television programmes since 2000. In 2004, television drama accounted for 29.4 per cent of all programme ratings, followed by news programmes (16.8%), variety shows (7.9%), special features (7.7%), sports (7.0%) and films (5.6%). In 2004, 505 television dramas comprising a total of 12,265 episodes were produced and released onto the market. By comparison, in the same year China produced 212 feature films, the highest number produced since the 1990s. (The average number of films produced each year during the 1990s was fewer than 100.) In 2004, 156 channels operated by 33 city television stations broadcast 1,598 television dramas totalling 183,123 episodes.[12] The average length of a television drama in the early 2000s was 20 episodes, but since 2004, the figure has increased to 26. Many television dramas have as many as 50–60 episodes. (Each episode is approximately 38 minutes long.) Among all types of programmes, television dramas have garnered the largest amount of television advertising revenue. In 2004, advertising revenue from television dramas reached 44.1 per cent of all television advertising revenue. In that year, total television advertising revenue amounted to over 150,000 million yuan Renminbi.

By comparison, the box office revenue of the Chinese film industry in 2004 was 360 million yuan, including domestic revenue of 250 million yuan (of which 100 million came from television broadcasting) and 110 million yuan in international revenue.[13]

Both the number of television dramas produced and broadcast and their advertising revenue indicate that television drama, not film, is the foremost form of entertainment in today's China. The first Chinese TV drama, a 30-minute play, *A Veggie Cake* [*Yikou cai bingzi*], was produced and aired live on the Beijing Television Station on 15 June 1958. From 1958 to 1966, the *zhibo qi* ('direct telecast period') produced nearly 200 single-episode TV dramas. All were produced, performed and telecast live. Television drama production ceased during the Cultural Revolution and did not resume until 1978. In the early 1980s, Chinese television stations broadcast a number of foreign television serial plays, from Japan and the USA, but it was not until the success of *Yearnings* [*Kewang*, 1990], a 50-episode television drama, that television drama or *dianshi ju* came into its own. *Yearning* captured a Chinese audience of hundreds of millions with its melodramatic portrayal of the lives of ordinary citizens during the Cultural Revolution – their loves, lives and families, and how they were subjected to political vicissitudes.

Today not only does television drama boast the highest ratings; it also covers a rich diversity of subject matter and genres. In 2004, the most popular television drama genres were ranked as follows: romance, domestic drama, martial arts, romantic and youth idol drama, crime, revolutionary drama, history, and so on. There are various ways of categorizing the drama genres. Romance can include fictional historical drama, the most popular genre. Within this genre, Qing dynasty (1640–1911) themes account for a significant majority. *Prime Minister Hunchback Liu* [*Zaixiang Liu luoguo*, 1996], the story of a legendary witty and upright Qing prime minister fighting corrupt imperial officialdom, and *Iron-toothed Ji Xiaolan* [*Tiechi tongya Ji Xiaolan*, 2001], a comic fiction about a Qing scholar who bravely challenges the lies and betrayals of the emperor, touch on popular sentiments against corruption and age-old expectations of *qingguan* (upright, honest officials). Another type of romance is romantic stories that incorporate historical figures such as Qing emperors, princes and princesses, in totally fictional plots. The enormous popularity of *Princess Pearl Returned* [*Huanzhu gege*, 1999], with its depiction of a mischievous and rebellious teenage heroine, reflects radically changed social stereotypes and expectations of Chinese girls.

Of the other genres, worth mentioning are the historical dramas that focus on famous Chinese emperors such as the *Great Han Emperor Wudi* [*Han wu dadi,* 2004], *Yongzheng Dynasty* [*Yongzheng wangchao,* 1999] and *Kangxi Dynasty* [*Kangxi wangchao,* 2003], recapturing China's past imperial glory. Revolutionary dramas such as *Years of Burning Passions* [*Jiqing ranshao de shuiyue,* 2002] remind the Chinese public of the powerful revolutionary legacy that is part of modern Chinese history. Another popular genre is adaptations of Chinese classical novels such as *Dream of the Red Chamber* [*Hong loumeng,* 1987], *Journey to the West* [*Xiyou ji,* 1986] and *Romance of Three Kingdoms* [*Sanguo yanyi,* 1995], and of popular martial arts novels by Jin Yong such as *Dragon's Eight Tribes* [*Tianlong babu,* 2004]. In recent years, imported Korean television dramas have also achieved high ratings, creating a Korean cultural boom among urban youth. This has caused unease among SARFT officials and television drama producers. Although China's imports of television dramas have remained quite small (only around 5 per cent of all dramas in 2004), more intense cultural and media exchanges are likely to increase imports (and exports) of television dramas.[14]

If there is a single television entertainment programme that can attract the largest audience in the world, it is CCTV's *Spring Festival Gala* or celebration show (*chunjie lianhuan wanhui*). The Gala debuted in 1983. A spectacular variety show filmed in CCTV's giant studio that includes dance and musical performance, sketch comedy, and cross talks with appearances by national celebrities, it is broadcast live on Chinese New Year's Eve, the traditional time for family reunions, from 8:00 pm till after midnight – New Year's Day. In the twenty four years since its debut, the programme has boasted ratings of more than 90 per cent, or approximately 1,000 million viewers. It has now become part of the Chinese New Year celebrations – a new custom. The most popular part of the Gala is the comic sketches (*xiaopin*), often mild satires of social life and its anomalies. Every year, the Gala production crew tries hard to incorporate everything from popular culture forms such as hip-hop songs and street dances to folk music and traditional Peking Opera, while also satisfying the CCP's demand to make the show a comprehensive representation of mainstream, official ideologies. For instance, Yang Liwei, China's first astronaut, appeared on the 2004 Gala to symbolize China's achievements in science and technology. Because of its magnitude in scale and in advertising revenue, the Gala's behind-the-curtains scenes are often rife with scandals and power struggles. Zhao An, a former director of the Gala, was sentenced to ten years in prison in 2004 for taking bribes. There has been mounting criticism of CCTV's monopoly over New Year's television shows, as the CCTV Gala now has to compete with a greater variety of entertainment forms, some of which were unavailable when it first started. However, it has so far remained the highest-rating television programme in the world. As a cultural ritual with widespread appeal to the Chinese population, it does not yet seem to be past its use-by date.

Challenges to CCTV's monopoly over entertainment programmes have surged in recent years. Hunan Satellite TV, from China's agrarian, hinterland province, has recently captured the hearts of young, especially teenage, viewers across China with its enormously successful entertainment programme *Supergirl* [*Chaoji nusheng*], which first began in 2004. Modelled after the popular US television show *American Idol*, *Supergirl* is a blend of reality show, singing and dancing contest, and beauty pageant, as well as incorporating popular votes from viewers through cellular phones (over 300 million viewers cast their votes by cell phone in 2005), attracting thousands of millions of young teenage girls and their families to apply, participate, and vote for their favourite singers. In 2005, a *Supergirl* craze swept across China, ending in the final selection of the three winners. Two of the three (the first-place getter, Li Yuchun, and the second, Zhou Bichang) were widely regarded as amateurs with poor singing skills and musical talent, who nonetheless managed to stand out with their alternative, often defiant and androgynous (tomboy-like) style. There was harsh criticism from mainstream and academic circles, charging the *Supergirl* show with vulgarity and 'bad taste' sensationalism and populism. CCTV has adamantly refused to allow any of the *Supergirl* winners to appear on its programmes. Nevertheless, because of the huge popularity and enormous profitability of the show (in 2005 Hunan Satellite TV was ranked by CMS Media Research – China's most authoritative media survey company – second in overall viewer ratings after CCTV), many local television stations followed suit. In 2005, Dragon TV, the satellite TV channel of Shanghai Media Group (SMG), introduced two shows similar to *Supergirl* – *My Hero* [*Hao nan'er*], a type of 'Superboy' with all male contestants, and *My Show* [*Wo xing wo Show*], which included both male and female contestants. In fact, CCTV also has its own versions of musical talent contest shows, and there has been fierce competition in this genre across China since 2006.

In addition to the unwaveringly high ratings of television dramas, popular entertainment shows such as *Supergirl* indicate that entertainment is playing the most vibrant role in the Chinese television industry, with far-reaching implications for the future of Chinese media. Chinese television, despite finding itself caught between political pressure from the CCP and market competition, has rapidly developed into a profit-making cultural industry. As part of consumer popular culture, its impact on changing social values and lifestyles is most visible in China's urban youth who have grown up since the beginning of the reform period in 1978. As IPTV, digital television and other new forms of technological innovations become the priorities for China's television sector, incorporation of the Internet and other new forms of telecommunication has accelerated the process of Chinese media's embrace of globalization.

The Internet: alternative media and public forum

The Internet has become a dynamic force in China's cultural landscape today. As a medium, the Internet exemplifies the borderless world of globalization. Globalization not only brings China closer to the world economic system and market, but also generates new forms of culture and social interaction. While information technology boosts economic growth, the Internet has ignited a social engine in China mainly in the political, ideological and cultural arenas. 'Crossing the Great Wall, walking towards the world' [*yueguo changcheng, zouxiang shijie*] (www.cnnic.net.cn/policy/5.shtml) was the first email ever sent from China. It was delivered on 20 September 1987 through China Academic Network (CANet) from Beijing to Germany. In March 1993, the Institute of High Energy Physics (IHEP) established a dedicated data line linked to Stanford University. In January 1995, China began its first public Internet service operated jointly by Sprint in America and China Telecom. In 1996, there were only 100,000 Internet users, but by the end of 1998 the number had reached 2.1 million. One year later, that figure had doubled, reaching more than 4 million in December 1999. By 30 June 2006, the number of Internet users had reached 123 million, and there were 788,400 websites registered in China.[15] In 2006, the United States had 200 million Internet users (19% of the world total), and China ranks second with 11% of users. The third is Japan (86 million users, 8% of the world total), followed by India (60 million users, 5% of the total) and Germany (50 million users, or 4.7%).[16]

Although Internet penetration of China (9.4%) is far behind that of the US (69%), the impact of the Internet on its predominantly urban users (almost 99%) is enormous, especially on urban youth. The overwhelming majority (70%) of Chinese 'netizens' is under the age of thirty. Of all Chinese users, 31.6% are high-school students, 18% are below high-school age, and 50% are college students or have a bachelor's degree. An entire generation, born in the 1980s and afterwards, have grown up in the digital age of the Internet. Most Chinese Internet users engage in the following online activities: reading news (66%), writing and reading emails (64%), browsing BBS chat rooms and forums (43%), obtaining information on jobs, services, commercial products, health care and government services (39%), watching/downloading videos (35%) and blogging (30%).[17] Americans, by comparison, use the Internet mainly as a convenient way of communication and business: writing and reading email (91%), researching products and services (78%) and online shopping (67%) are the major online activities.[18]

The most important role of the Internet in China is as an alternative news medium. The Internet creates a new press, which links to the global communications network. It crosses the boundaries between the state-owned, centralized press and the commercially oriented local press, and between international press and national press. On 20 December 1995, *China Trade Daily* became the first Chinese news medium to have an online version on the Internet. By the end of 1995 only seven Chinese news media outlets had an online service, although the news media were among the first entities in China to develop websites. Meanwhile, major commercial portal companies such as sina.com (*xinlang*), netease.com (*wangyi*) and sohu.com (*souhu*) all created their own news web pages, which achieved tremendous popularity for their faster, often localized news reports in comparison to the state-owned media.

Another major online source of alternative news is BBS (bulletin board service), an online discussion forum and chat room, where a great number of news reports and stories drawn from international sources and the Hong Kong and Taiwan press are posted, along with commentaries by participants in the forum.

BBS and chat rooms for the most part serve as a cyber public forum for discussion of political and socioeconomic issues. The state-owned media were the first to experiment with forms of bulletin boards, chat rooms, online polls and online opinion columns as ways to enhance online interactive journalism and commentaries. The most important example currently is the *People's Daily* online chat room, Strong Power Forum (*Qiangguo luntan*) (bbs.people.com.cn), established in the wake of NATO's bombing of the Chinese Embassy in Belgrade in 1999. It has since grown into one of the hottest public political forums, offering a blend of public debate, news stories, and opinion letters that cover a wide range of issues. Some of these postings are highly contentious and politically sensitive, and the print and electronic media would find it difficult to publish them. Tianya Community (*Tianya shequ*) (www.tianya.cn) located in Hainan is one of the most popular BBS in Chinese language. There are also numerous Chinese-language BBS located outside China, but they are often blocked by the Chinese Internet censorship agencies. Subject to constant and rigorous censorship, the BBS and chat rooms have nonetheless become a vibrant public forum for political and social debate. In March 2003 the murder of college graduate Sun Zhigang by staff at Guangzhou local detention centre triggered a nation-wide protest against the detention system, largely through Internet forums. The State Council (China's Cabinet) changed its regulations governing the detention system in June 2003 in response to the protests.[19]

When the Severe Acute Respiratory Syndrome (SARS) crisis broke out in March 2003, the Chinese government at first totally suppressed any media coverage and instead circulated misinformation on the issue. When the news leaked out and China was confronted with international outrage, the government changed its policy to allow the media to cover the SARS issue extensively. During the SARS crisis, Internet forums attracted a great deal of discussion on China's public health system and freedom of the press. Apart from social issues such as the legal and health systems, Internet chat rooms often attract contentious debate and argument over China's relationships with other countries (the US and Japan in particular), its role in globalization, and the issues surrounding China's rise as a world power. Nationalistic fervour was often expressed in discussion forums concerning the NATO bombing of the Chinese Embassy or the tension over the Taiwan Straits. However, issues such as the Tiananmen crackdown (1989), the outlawing of the Falungong Movement by the Chinese government, human rights, religious freedom and suppression in Tibet, and so on, are strictly censored and prohibited from Chinese-language online discussion forums and web sites.

The Internet and new urban youth culture

Primarily as a medium for urban youth, the Internet has become a major venue for self-expression for the younger generation. At the same time it is a force that helps to shape their values and lifestyles. As a multi-media platform, the Internet provides visual and audio materials as the dominant forms of popular culture, flowing mostly from the USA, Japan and Western Europe, with widespread circulation and influence around the world. Chinese youth, mostly those born since the 1980s, are the main beneficiaries of reform in terms of material and economic prosperity, but they also bear the brunt of the social transition – confusion and the loss of values and ethical norms – as the revolutionary idealism of Mao's era has been rapidly replaced by consumerism and egotism. The beginning of the twenty-first century marks the coming of age of the new generation. A distinct urban youth culture is taking shape, nurtured largely by an electronically based consumer culture. As such, this youth culture is the embodiment of globalization: it draws its icons, styles, images and values mainly from the 'global' (read: Western) consumer culture and entertainment industry. In the meantime, the younger generation has a much stronger desire for a distinct cultural identity and marking their individual differences than did their parents' generation, who were Mao's children, born in the 1950s.

The Internet serves as an interface between the self-identities of urban youth, consumer culture, global fashions and cultural trends. Urban youth today are much more inclined to pleasure-seeking, sensuous or aesthetically pleasing lifestyles and self-expression. The Internet hence provides these techno-savvy youth, who sometimes label themselves Newer New Humanity (*xinxin renlei*), with a much freer and trendier (or 'cooler') venue for self-expression in artistic and literary forms. The recent proliferation of e-fiction sites and the rise of several 'e-fiction star writers', whose writings were published first as Internet literature and then turned into bestselling printed books, have constituted a thriving cyberspace literary field. Beauty-baby authors (*meinu zuojia*) are the products of the Internet and the consumer bestselling market. Wei Hui's novel *Shanghai Baby* [*Shanghai Baobei,* 2000] is generally considered the most well-known work of the 'beauty-baby writers'. The novel depicts sex, lust and drugs among contemporary young Shanghai women who have both leisure time and money, creating a subgenre of 'body writing' (*shenti xiezuo*) – i.e. writing about feminine bodies or using (displaying) feminine bodies as tools for writing.

The Newer New Humanity often finds e-fiction an ideal form for their audacious and trendy pursuit of happiness in romantic adventures and sensuous experiences. In 2001, the e-fiction *The First Intimate Touch* [*Di yici qinmi jiechu*] by Taiwanese cyber writer Bum Cai (Pizi Cai) marked the beginning of vibrant online writing filled with Internet slang and 'cool' language invented by young Internet users. The cyber writing that Bum Cai's e-fiction initiated has since created a 'liberating' language that mixes English acronyms with Chinese shorthand and swear words, and even obscenity with high-tech jargon. The interactive nature of the Internet allows young users to experiment freely with newly invented cyber slang or colloquialisms.[20] Blogs have thus gained tremendous popularity in China, as the blog (*boke*) provides users with a space in which to freely write and post multi-media materials (photos, sound bites and other forms) through hyper links about their personal experiences and opinions in diary form. Blogs are more personalized or customized than BBS or public forums. As a media form, blogs in China also tend to focus on individual experiences and feelings of love, romance, leisure and entertainment, as opposed to BBS and chat rooms, which primarily deal with issues of public interest. From their first appearance in China in 2003, by August 2006 there were over 33 million blogs and 17 million bloggers. Major blog portal companies include Xinlang Blog (http://blog.sina.com.cn), China Blog (Zhongguo bokewang, www.blogcn.com), Sohu Blog (http://blog.sohu.com) and Blogging China (www.blogchina.com). One survey shows that bloggers have a strong desire to circulate their blogs to a wide audience, and quite a few well-known writers, public figures and celebrities use their blogs as a way of addressing the public directly. The new wave of Internet blogs indicates the rise of individualized media for greater freedom of self-expression. Of the 17 million bloggers in China, 70 per cent have a college-level education, and the average age of bloggers is between 20 and 35.

While the blogs provide a much freer space for self-expression by well-educated Chinese youth, the rapid development of cellular phones provides thousands of millions of Chinese with an instant, flexible and affordable means not only of communication but also of entertainment. Mobile cellular phones first appeared in China in the mid-1990s, as a luxury (and often a status symbol) for newly rich businessmen. However, the Chinese telecommunications industry has rapidly expanded its production of cellular phones since 2000, creating a market that has exhibited phenomenal growth. By 30 September 2006, China had 369 million fixed-line phone subscribers, while the number of mobile phone subscribers had reached an astounding 443 million.[21] Not surprisingly, young people are the most active users of cellular phones. They use the cellular phone not simply to call each other, but to exchange a good deal of information and entertainment. Cellular phones can be connected to the Internet, to allow the users to download popular music as ring tones, obtain flashes from the web, and, above all, text messages.

Text messages in China contain anything from simple greetings and personal communications, to comic passages or jokes (*duanzi*), mostly on politics and sex (often combined), to domestic and international news and commentary. The political and sex jokes poignantly denigrate corrupt and inept bureaucrats and satirize social phenomena from rampant egotism to moral degeneration, extramarital affairs and prostitution. As writing such *duanzi* becomes profitable, a sizeable number of professional text message writers have emerged in China in recent years. Hired by the Internet websites that sell text messages to users for a mere 10 fen Renminbi (or 1.3 cents US) each, these text message writers earn a decent monthly income (about 4,000 yuan Renminbi), comparable to that of a computer programmer or an accountant. As inexpensive as a single text message is, the market as a whole is immense. During the seven-day holiday break for Chinese New Year in 2005, 12,000 million text messages containing greetings were transmitted. China Mobile, one of the two giant cellular phone service providers (the other is China Unicom), transmits 700 million text messages per day. If we include China Unicom as well, approximately 14,000 million text messages are circulating around China every day.[22] Now that Chinese Internet companies and television stations are focusing on the new technologies and markets of IPTV and mobile phone TV, the digital network of communication, information, news and entertainment has opened up not only a market with staggering economic potential but also a formidable social space. Cellular phone text messages pose a new challenge for the Chinese government: as a newly developed medium allied closely with the Internet and television, it is more difficult to screen, filter and censor the content of text messages.

Censorship, challenges, and new opportunities

The Chinese government has long realized the double-edged nature of digital communications, and has continued to enhance its censorship technology and mechanisms. The government has adopted complicated measures and technologies, first through control of media organizations including all Internet service providers and Internet media websites, secondly by control of access to Internet websites, and finally through censorship of Internet content. The Chinese government has set up offices at the central and provincial levels to regulate, control and censor the Internet, and has also passed laws and rulings regulating the Internet. In January 1993 the State Council passed the Temporary Regulation for International Computer Information Network, but not until February 1996 was the regulation formally announced. In September 2005, the Chinese government announced newly amended and verified Regulations on the Information Services of the Chinese Internet to replace the 1993 ruling. In the meantime, the government stepped up its measures to censor and crack down on Internet companies, websites and individuals whose actions were considered to violate the regulations. Crackdowns on the Internet have often brought outrage and condemnation from international human rights groups and Western parliaments and governments critical of China's suppression of press freedom and violations of human rights. Google.com's business dealings with the Chinese and the censorship issue that followed created a major controversy in the USA, prompting a Congressional hearing in January 2006.[23]

Insofar as the Chinese Communist Party views the media as a vital political instrument to safeguard its legitimacy and effective governance, changes and reforms of the media, including television, the Internet and other forms of new media, will take place only gradually, as an integral part of political reform. As democracy and a free press are always the goals for modern China, reforms of television and the Internet will inevitably reflect the will of the 1,300 million Chinese people to achieve their goals. On the other hand, popular consumer culture has deeply penetrated China through the global mass media network, via television and the Internet. China's challenges and opportunities in the digital age of communication and globalization can be seen in the kaleidoscopic scene of consumer popular culture, shaping the young generation as they come of age to lead the country in the decades to come.

Notes

1. Information on the history of Chinese television is drawn from Li Xiaoping, 'The Chinese Television System and Television News', *China Quarterly*, 126, 1991, 340–55; Yu Huang and Xu Yu, 'Broadcasting and Politics: Chinese Television in the Mao Era, 1958–1976', *Historical Journal of Film, Radio, and Television*, 17, 1997, 563–75.
2. Guo Zhenzhi, *Zhongguo dianshi shi* [A History of Chinese Television], Beijing, Wenhua yishu chubanshe, 1997.
3. Wei Wenbin *et al.* (eds.), *Zhongguo dianshi shichang baogao 2004–2005* [Market Report on Chinese Television 2004–2005), Beijing, CCTV–CSM Research, 2005; State Administration of Radio, Film and Television (SARFT) (ed.), *Zhongguo guangbo dianshi*

nianjian 2004 [Annual book of Chinese radio and television 2004], Beijing, SARFT, 2004; *Annual Report of Chinese Television Industry*, Beijing, CCID Consulting, 2006.

4. Wei Wenbin *et al.* (eds.), Market Report, p. 73.

5. Chi Anyun, 'Zhonghua shizi dianshi chanye fazhan jingcheng tanxi' [Notes on the Growth of Chinese Digital Television], *Global Sources*, January 2006. www.ed-china.com/ART_8800012404_400002_500002_OT.HTM

6. J. D. White, *Global Media: The Television Revolution in Asia*, New York, Routledge, 2005, p. 142.

7. Li Xiaoping, 'The Chinese Television System', p. 349.

8. Yuezhi Zhao, *Media, Market, and Democracy in China*, Urbana, University of Illinois Press, 1998, pp. 111–12; Tsan-kuo Chan, *China's Window on the World: TV News, Social Knowledge and International Spectacles*, New Jersey, Hampton Press, 2002, pp. 22–3; H. de Burgh, *The Chinese Journalist*, London, RoutledgeCurzon, 2003, p. 41.

9. Zhao Yuezhi, *Media, Market, and Democracy in China*, p. 117.

10. *Ibid.,* p. 119.

11. Chen Xin, 'Nanjing ling juli shoushi lu jingren' [Surprising Ratings for Nanjing Zero Distance], *Nanfang zhoumo* [Southern Weekend], 29 August 2003, p. 4.

12. CCTV–CSM Research, Shanghai Media Group, *China TV Drama Report 2005–2006*, Beijing, CCTV–CSM Research, p. 43.

13. SARFT, *2004 Zhongguo dianying shichang baogao* [2004 Report on Chinese Film Industry], Beijing, Guangbo dianshi chubanshe, pp. 12–13.

14. *Ibid.,* p. 795.

15. China Internet Network Information Center (CNNIC) website home page. www. cnnic.net.cn/en/index/0O/index.htm

16. www.internetworldstats.com/top20.htm

17. China Internet Network Information Center (CNNIC) Survey Reports. www.cnnic.net.cn/en/index/0O/index.htm

18. www.pewinternet.org/trends/Internet_Activities_7.19.06.htm

19. Lin Wenxin, 'Sun Zhigang shijian zhangxiang wangluo yulun liliang' [Sun Zhigang Incident Shows the Power of the Internet Media], 14 January 2004, www.sina.com.cn

20. Liu Kang, *Globalization and Cultural Trends in China,* University of Hawai'i Press, 2004, p. 154.

21. Xinhua News Agency, 'China's Mobile Phone Subscribers hit 443 Million', *China Daily*, 25 October 2006.

22. Xinhua News Agency, 'China Mobile Users send 700 Million SMS Per Day', *China Daily*, 6 January 2006.

23. C. Thompson, 'Google's China Problem (and China's Google Problem)', *New York Times,* 23 April 2006.

Guide to further reading

Chan, Tsan-kuo, *China's Window on the World: TV News, Social Knowledge and International Spectacles*, New Jersey, Hampton Press, 2002.

China Internet Network Information Center (CNNIC) Survey Reports. www.cnnic.net.cn/en/index/0O/index.htm

    website home page, www.cnnic.net.cn/en/index/0O/index.htm

de Burgh, Hugo, *The Chinese Journalist*, London, RoutledgeCurzon, 2003.

Donald, Stephanie, Michael Keane and Hong Yin (eds.), *Media in China: Consumption, Content and Crisis*, London: RoutledgeCurzon, 2002.

Lee, Chin-chuan, (ed.), *Chinese Media, Global Contexts*, London, Routledge, 2003.

Li Xiaoping, 'The Chinese Television System and Television News', *China Quarterly* 126 (1991), 340–55.

Liu Kang, *Globalization and Cultural Trends in China*, Honolulu: University of Hawai'i Press, 2004.

Yu Huang and Xu Yu, 'Broadcasting and Politics: Chinese Television in the Mao Era, 1958–1976', *Historical Journal of Film, Radio, and Television* 17, 1997, 563–75.

Zhao, Yuezhi, *Media, Market, and Democracy in China*, Urbana, University of Illinois Press, 1998.

17

Physical culture, sports and the Olympics

The Chinese people's desire to host the Olympic Games is nearly as old as the modern Games (established in 1896) themselves. As early as 1907, patriots in the Chinese YMCA promoted a campaign that linked physical education to national strength, posing three questions:

1. When will China be able to send a winning athlete to the Olympic contests?
2. When will China be able to send a winning team to the Olympic contests?
3. When will China be able to invite all the world to come to Peking for an International Olympic contest ...?[1]

The first two questions would be answered at the 1984 Los Angeles Olympic Games, and the third will be answered at the 2008 Beijing Olympics.

The first member of the International Olympic Committee (IOC) from the Republic of China, C. T. Wang (Wang Zhengting) was coopted in 1922. China sent its first team to the 1932 Olympic Games in Los Angeles. Up to three IOC members were allowed from the one country, so in order to maximize China's influence on the IOC, Wang recommended two more members; H. H. Kung (Kong Xianxi) was coopted in 1939 and Shou-yi Tung (Dong Shouyi) was the third member coopted in 1947. It shows the relative strength of China's regional position in international sport that, on the eve of the establishment of the PRC, there were only eight IOC members from Asia, and three of these were Chinese (three were from Japan and two from India). In 1946, the Chinese National Amateur Athletic Federation decided to bid for the 1952 Games, but the outbreak of the civil war prevented this.[2]

In 1993 Beijing mounted a hotly contested bid for the 2000 Olympics, and lost by only two votes to Sydney, Australia. Beijing's second bid, in 2001, was successful. Why has hosting the Olympic Games been so important to China over the last century? The answer can be found in the importance of the body and physical culture in China's encounter with the West over the last century.

The nineteenth-century Orientalist stereotype: competitive spirit vs Oriental despotism

In Europe from the French Revolution onward, sport had played a role in the neoclassical, civil religion associated with freedom and incipient forms of democracy, which were often conceived in opposition to 'Oriental despotism'. The concept of 'Western civilization' was one important way in which the emerging nation-states of the Western hemisphere defined their identities, and athletics and the ancient Olympic Games thus became important symbols. The 'Orient' served as a contrasting Other against which this identity was formed. Western scholars considered athletics to be incompatible with Oriental despotism and the perceived spiritual decadence of the Orient. Leading classicists such as Ernst Curtius (1814–96) and Jacob Burckhardt (1818–97) argued that an essential trait of the Aryan people was their competitive or 'agonistic' spirit, a legacy of the ancient Greeks, which was in opposition to the rigid hierarchy of Oriental despotism and its pursuit of sensual pleasure and material possessions. This competitive spirit was identified as the spirit of modernity and an essential characteristic of Western civilization.

In the last decade of the nineteenth century, Western sports were introduced into the coastal areas of China by Prussian and Japanese military drill instructors, the North American YMCA and missionary schools.[3] The ancient Confucian tradition was criticized for its contempt for physical activity and respect for the intellect: 'Those who work with their brains rule; those who work with their brawn are ruled' (*laoxinze zhi ren, laolizhe zhiyu ren*), a saying from Mencius, has been used for a century to illustrate the traditional Confucian aversion to physical exercise, including sports. In late nineteenth- and early twentieth-century Western accounts of Chinese sports these Orientalist assumptions are evident: Western sports were considered to introduce to Chinese culture something new and beneficial to China's modernization. The sinologist Herbert A. Giles's 1906 article on 'Football and Polo in China' may be the first article ever written on ancient Chinese sports by either a Chinese or a Western scholar; he began it by wondering whether 'anyone would take an interest in, or even believe, the fact that football was played by the Chinese several centuries before Julius Caesar landed in Britain'.[4]

The received view was that, since the Song Dynasty (960–1279), written examinations had been the standard method for selecting government officials. The Imperial Examinations required memorization of the classics, which occupied many years of study. *Zhong wen qing wu* – 'esteem literacy and despise martiality' – became the elite ideal. The rise of intellectualism and the decline of Tang martiality in the Song are said to have led to the virtual disappearance of sport in Chinese society, including the football and polo played in the Tang imperial courts that had been described by Giles. This view is still the prevailing one among Chinese and Western scholars writing about sports in China. In sinology, the Imperial Examinations occupied a position similar to that occupied by the ancient Olympic Games in nineteenth-century classicism: both embodied the essence of their respective civilizations, and both were used as emblems for the way of life and worldview of a people. These views were also gendered. The West was personified as a manly athlete and China as an effeminate intellectual. In 1911 Giles concluded a discussion of ancient sports by noting, 'The age of manly sport, as above described, has long passed away; and the only hope is for a revival under the changing conditions of modern China.'[5]

The Western Orientalist view was internalized by Chinese reformers and revolutionaries. In his first published essay, 'A Study of Physical Culture' (1917), Mao Zedong complained that '[e]xercise is important for physical education, but today most scholars are not interested in sports'.[6] Throughout his political career, Mao held to the concept that *yundong*, which means 'activity' or 'movement', was the remedy for the passivity and weakness that ailed China. *Yundong* is also one of the words that can be used for sport, as well as the word used to label the endless political 'campaigns' of the Maoist period. These debates reveal the Orientalist stereotype of the quiet, still (*jing*) East, which could only become a strong nation by getting into motion like the active (*dong*) West.

At the time when Western sports were introduced into China, the most influential theory in shaping Chinese nationalism and sports was Social Darwinism. In Social Darwinism, nations were seen as biological organisms struggling for survival among other like organisms. The word *tiyu* (physical education, physical culture, sports) was a neologism created in Japan (Japanese *taiiku*) to translate the Social Darwinist Herbert Spencer's concept of physical education. He argued that moral, intellectual and physical education shaped strong citizens for a strong nation; this division of humans into three parts, each requiring a specialized kind of education, remained the linchpin of Chinese educational theory through the 1980s. The absence of a competitive spirit in China was seen as a cause of national weakness. The Buddhist ideal of 'no contest with the world' (*yu shi wu zheng*) was identified as a traditional mindset that must be changed. Reformist intellectual Liang Qichao proposed that China needed to learn from Japan, and to recover the *bushido* ('way of the warrior') spirit it had once had.[7]

All of this crystallized in the Chinese imagination as the image of the 'sick man of East Asia' (*dongya bingfu*), an insulting label that the Chinese believed was applied to China by Japan and the West. For a century, the goal of erasing the label of the 'sick man of East Asia' has been the justification for the quest for international sports success.

Orientalist assumptions blinded both Western observers and Chinese nationalists to the world that actually lay around them. They ignored the textual and archaeological evidence for ancient Chinese sports traditions; they overlooked contemporary activities such as dragon boat racing (which was called a 'religious festival, not a sport'), acrobatics, Qing imperial court wrestling, and the martial arts. The Orientalist stereotype of the effeminate, intellectual Chinese was strongly contradicted by the martial arts tradition. Kam Louie has argued that over the centuries, Chinese masculinity was constructed around the two poles of *wen* (literary arts) and *wu* (military arts). Both poles offered a model for a masculine ideal, whether that of the refined, genteel scholar whose weapon was the calligraphy brush, or of the chivalrous hero possessed of military prowess.[8] While there were always popular male heroes who exemplified martial masculinity, the educational system, which was oriented toward the Imperial Examinations, emphasized literary ideals. Compounding the effect of the Imperial Exams was the fact that the Qing dynasty (1644–1911) was a Manchu minority with cultural roots in the northern equestrian nomadic way of life. The Manchu prided themselves on a martial masculinity derived from their nomadic military techniques, while the Han majority, who constituted the scholar–official class, distinguished themselves from the 'Qing barbarians' by their scholarly refinement.

Furthermore, the Imperial Examinations revolved around a notion of excellence through competition, and the Chinese were every bit as concerned with ensuring the fairness of the examinations as the Greeks were with ensuring the fairness of their sporting events. In short, there was ample observable evidence that could have contradicted the notion of the intellectualized, effeminized, non-competitive Chinese with no sports of their own, but their pre-existing views did not predispose Westerners to see them, and, seeing themselves through Western eyes, reform-minded Chinese people echoed these views. Self-Orientalism – application of Orientalist views to their own culture by native intellectuals – led reform-minded Chinese to criticize their own culture for its lack of a sporting tradition. Thus, sports became a key symbol in China's quest for modernity.

The Chinese vs the Western culture of the body: *Yang sheng* vs *tiyu*

Chinese forms of sport and exercise were anchored in a culture of the body that was fundamentally different from Western body culture. It was based on the traditions of Chinese medicine, Buddhist and Taoist meditation and longevity techniques, and popular martial arts. By the second century AD, in the writings of the Greek physician Galen, what was to become a fundamental split in Western culture had already started to appear: the schism between voluntary action and natural processes, and ultimately between mind and body.[9] In the sixteenth century this would lead to Cartesian dualism in philosophy, and in the twenty-first century it would manifest itself in a Western medicine that relies on instruments and machines to treat a body that is in many ways viewed as separate from the person who inhabits it.

Mind–body dualism was never as clearly articulated in Chinese culture. There are at least three different root words for 'body' in Chinese: *shen*, animate body; *ti*, inanimate body; and *shi*, dead body or corpse. In thinking about themselves and their relationships with other people, Chinese people use the word *shen*, which can be translated into English phrases such as 'person', 'self', or 'lifetime', rather than concepts such as 'personality' or 'individual'.[10] The root characters can be combined in multiple ways, as in *shenti*, (body/health) and *shiti* (corpse). Both *shen* and *ti* have a subjective, experiential component; neither word has the disembodied Western connotation in which a person is somehow inside a body that is separate from the experiencing subject. *Ti* is the character that is used in the words for 'physique' (*tizhi, xingti, tixing, tipo*) and 'physical exercise' (*ticao*). The primary sense of *ti* is of an individual unit or a closed system; that it is inanimate is indicated by its frequent use in combinations that translate abstract Western scientific phrases such as 'system', 'particle', and so on.

The traditional view of the human body assumed that it was intimately connected with the world around it: the body and the environment mutually influenced one another, each being permeated by essences that circulated throughout the cosmos. The most important influence on both the cosmos and the body was the balance of *yin* and *yang*, which were the source of the universe, of life and death, and of health and illness in the individual parts and organs of the body. The traditional view also emphasized the importance of body fluids that circulate throughout the body. The four most important substances were *jing* (seminal essence), *qi* (vital energy), *shen* (spirit), and *xue* (blood). The mouth and digestive system mediated between the internal fluids and the outside world. Food was the main means of incorporating outside substances into the body, and diet was an important way of regulating the body's internal balance. The line between food and medicine was unclear.[11]

This view of the body was very different from that encapsulated in the Mandarin neologism *tiyu*. In 1952 Chairman Mao penned the sports slogan that was painted on almost every gymnasium wall and displayed in the placard section of almost every opening ceremony: 'Develop physical culture and sports, strengthen the people's physiques' (*fazhan tiyu yundong, zengqiang renmin tizhi*). It dominated popular body culture until the late 1980s and established *ti* as the dominant concept in Maoist body culture. Thus, Western science and physical education introduced into China a detached, objective and instrumental view of the body that was utilized and carried to extremes under Maoism. It was different from the view expressed by *yang sheng* (to cultivate life), which had roots in the Daoist physical exercises that were supposed to make the body immortal. Today it is used to refer to a whole range of health-preserving practices.[12] Thus, in the course of the twentieth century, and particularly during the heights of Maoist ideology, China moved away from the Daoist 'way of life-cultivation' (*yang sheng zhi dao*) and towards 'physical culture' (*tiyu*).

However, this shift was ultimately a rather superficial movement across a more stable substratum that reasserted itself after the end of the Maoist period. In the 1980s, *qigong*, exercises centred on breathing control and often associated with mystical powers, became extremely popular. Some *qigong* masters became celebrities whose performances in lecture halls and gymnasiums attracted audiences of thousands. They became so threatening to the state that some were arrested and jailed.[13] The furore seemed to die down a bit in the 1990s, but in fact this was just the quiet before the storm of Falungong emerged.

Falungong was a form of *qigong* developed by Li Hongzhi in China in the early 1990s, which quickly attracted followers all over China and, after Li's emigration to the US in 1997, in major cities around the world. In 1999 the Chinese government began to crack down on Falungong practitioners, and this began to emerge as a point of contention in criticisms of China's record on human rights and religious freedom by Western governments. It occupied a prominent place during Beijing's bid for the Olympic Games in 2001, when the fax machines and email in-boxes of IOC members were flooded with messages opposing the bid on the basis of China's human rights record. At the 2004 Athens Olympic Games, there were almost daily Falungong demonstrations in Syntagma square. These were wordless demonstrations expressing the Falungong position that their goals are not political, an assertion that revealed differences between Western and Chinese interpretations of 'political'. From the Western perspective, it was hard to understand why the Chinese government would feel threatened by these practices. From the Chinese perspective, however, the chaos created by 'heterodox sects' in the previous century, discussed below, made the government's wariness understandable. There was not only this historical experience, but also an associated mythology that waves of popular heterodoxy are an omen of dynastic fall.

The martial arts tradition

Western sports were called 'new', 'foreign', or 'Western' sports, and were conceived in opposition to the Chinese martial arts. Because they were viewed as the indigenous Chinese equivalent of Western sports, Chinese martial arts have occupied an important position in China's encounter with the West, often serving as the focus of traditionalist backlashes. In the Boxer Rebellion of 1900–1, martial arts and meditation techniques formed the core practices of a popular uprising that swept across China and resulted in a siege of the foreign legation quarters in Beijing. It was finally put down by the Western Eight Powers, who extracted a large indemnity from the Qing government. However, martial arts continued to occupy an important place in the popular imagination. In the second decade of the twentieth century, martial arts novels became very popular, and developed side-by-side with Chinese nationalism because the novels portrayed heroes who were able to defeat modern weapons with skills that were perceived as quintessentially Chinese. In opposition to reformers such as Mao Zedong and the New Culture Movement who criticized these traditions, the National Essence School spearheaded an effort to develop physical education programmes based on the martial arts rather than on Western sports and exercises. In the 1920s, the martial arts began to be sportified according to the Western model of sports, a National Martial Arts Hall was founded, and a national competition was held in 1923. Over time *wushu* was developed as a judged sport like gymnastics. A group of Chinese kung fu artists toured Germany in association with the 1936 Berlin Olympics, giving many Westerners their first live exposure to Chinese martial arts.

After the beginning of the era of reform, the Chinese State Sports Commission began an attempt to promote *wushu* worldwide, with the eventual goal of seeing it included in the Olympic Games. The International Wushu Federation was established in 1990 with its headquarters in Beijing. There are only two sports of clearly non-Western origin on the Olympic programme: *judo* was added for the 1964 Olympic Games in Tokyo, and *taekwondo* for the 1988 Olympics in Seoul. Of these three martial arts, *wushu* is the one that deviates most from the Western model of sport. However, the IOC decided not to include *wushu* in the official programme, in part due to its attempt to limit the number of official sports in the events, but also because there were some IOC members who did not feel *wushu* was a suitable 'sport'. This decision was received with a great deal of regret and anger in China. It will be contested under the auspices of the Beijing Organizing Committee for the Olympic Games (BOCOG) in 2008 but will not be an official sport. The future of *wushu* is a hotly debated topic in Chinese sports circles. Traditionalists feel that its cultural background is richer and more complicated than those of the other Olympic sports, and that its continued internationalization and inclusion in the Olympic Games would lead to a loss of its cultural depth and Chinese character. They complain that proper *wushu* training requires years of cultivation of *qi*, which cannot be scored by judges, and international *wushu* has become too similar to gymnastics. Some radical thinkers consider the Olympic Games themselves to be a form of

Western cultural domination, and for them *wushu* is a symbol of an alternative non-Western sports tradition that must be preserved against the onslaught of the West.

Thanks to the popularity of Chinese martial arts from the 1960s, and film heroes from Bruce Lee to Jackie Chan to Jet Li, the stereotype of the sickly and effeminate Chinese is probably no longer the dominant one among Western youth. Kam Louie even argues that Chinese martial masculinity is now influencing global images of masculinity.[14] However, because Chinese children are still taught a history that emphasizes national humiliation, most Chinese believe that the 'sick man of East Asia' is still a widely held image in Japan and the West.

This excursion into the traditional Chinese culture of the body and *wushu* returns us to the forces of globalization that China has faced over the last century. Sports have played a central role in China's emergence as a world power since the establishment of the PRC in 1949.

Sports and Cold War politics

At the time of the founding of the People's Republic of China (PRC) in 1949, over 50 per cent of the IOC membership came from Western Europe, North America or Oceania (Australia and New Zealand). They regarded the new socialist nation with a great deal of distrust. At the first Olympic Games after the founding of the PRC – the 1952 Helsinki Olympics – China's IOC member Dong Shouyi encountered hostility and suspicion. The Chinese government allowed him to attend IOC meetings despite his past association with the Nationalist regime, at the urging of Premier Zhou Enlai, whom he had taught basketball while working for the YMCA in Tianjin. Although he arrived too late to attend the Session, he was in time to attend an Executive Board meeting. When he entered the meeting hall, President Sigfrid Edström asked, 'Have we met?', and Dong had to recount their past meetings in order to prove who he was. Edström demanded that Dong's interpreter leave, and Dong stood up and left with him. It was not until later that Dong learned that based on assertions by Taiwan, IOC members feared that Dong had been sent to a labour camp or killed and an impostor sent in his place. They also believed that the interpreter had been sent by the Communist Party to control him. Edström's behaviour had been a ploy to get rid of the interpreter so that they could speak with Dong alone. Today, it is amusing to look back and realize that Dong's interpreter at the 1955 and 1956 IOC

Sessions was He Zhenliang, who would later be the first IOC member coopted from the PRC (1981), and would become widely respected in the IOC and a key figure in Beijing's successful Olympic bid.

In accordance with the 'one China principle', the PRC sought recognition from the IOC as the sole legitimate government of China. In 1954 the IOC Session recognized the 'Olympic Committee of Democratic China'; but Taiwan relinquished its claim to sole representation, so the IOC was left with two National Olympic Committees in what was claimed to be one national territory – a point that was used by the Mainland Chinese and their supporters for the next twenty-five years to argue that the IOC had violated its own Olympic Charter, which stated that only one Olympic Committee could be recognized in a country.

This state of affairs was unacceptable to the PRC because of the 'one China principle', and because the policy was to demand the expulsion of 'the Chiang Clique' before joining international organizations. At IOC meetings in 1955 and 1956 the Chinese felt that their legitimate request for recognition and the expulsion of Taiwan was not heard, and that other socialist nations were not standing up for what was right because they were more concerned with their own agendas. This was the time when the Chinese were beginning to feel that the Soviets were too conciliatory to the West, but before 1960 when the Sino-Soviet split flared publicly. When China's advance group arrived at the Melbourne Olympic Games in 1956, it discovered that the Taiwan side had already entered the Olympic Village, registered under the name 'Formosa, China', and the 'illegitimate national flag' of the Republic of China had been raised. The Mainland Chinese declared that they were pulling out of the Games.

At its 52nd Session in Melbourne in November, the IOC decided that a letter should be sent to the Peking Chinese Committee expressing 'displeasure [at its] repeatedly raising political questions which have no place in IOC discussions'. Dong Shouyi expressed his opposition in a letter written to Avery Brundage, the American President of the IOC from 1952 to 1972, in December of 1957 contesting the minutes of the Session. This was the beginning of the end of China's relationship with the IOC. As it happened, Brundage was one of the world's foremost collectors of East Asian art. Today his collection in the Asian Art Museum in San Francisco is valued at more than US$60 million. But rather than helping the situation, this created difficulties, because Brundage felt he understood Chinese history and disliked the fact that the Communists only 'talked politics'. His frequent collecting trips to Taiwan no doubt made him feel that the Nationalists had a better appreciation of culture. In letters exchanged with Dong about the history of the China problem, he lectured Dong on his misinterpretation of his own nation's history, which enraged Dong. In August 1958 the Chinese Olympic Committee issued a press release stating that it was suspending all relations with the IOC. Dong also wrote to President Brundage and the IOC members expressing his resignation and accusing Brundage of being 'a faithful menial of the US imperialists bent on serving their plot of creating "two Chinas"'. And further, 'To uphold the Olympic spirit and tradition, I hereby declare that I will no longer cooperate with you or have any connections with the IOC while it is under your domination.'[15] Even in the most heated exchanges during the period of extreme leftist ideology, the Chinese never criticized the Olympic ideals, but rather claimed to uphold them. This seems to show that China always wanted to be a player on the world playing field, even if it meant supporting ideals that were identified with Western civilization. China thus began a period of twenty-one years of exclusion from the IOC, along with internal chaos. The anti-rightist campaign and the economically disastrous Great Leap Forward began in 1958.

The Western-dominated IOC was generally ignorant about East Asia. Despite the fact that the names used to designate the Olympic Committees of China and Taiwan were at the centre of the China question for thirty years, the IOC rarely managed to get the names right. In the minutes of the 1952 through 1955 Sessions, the PRC was called 'Democratic China', and in 1954, with no representatives from Taiwan or China present, the Athens Session recognized the 'Olympic Committee of Democratic China' by a vote of 23 to 21. In the 1956 Session minutes the PRC was named the 'Democratic People's Republic of China'. Dong Shouyi protested this misnaming at the 1956 Session, but the Session minutes did not reflect it, so he wrote a letter asking that the minutes be corrected to reflect the official name of his country. Although it was under Lord Killanin's leadership that the name question was resolved in 1979, in his 1983 book he misnames the PRC as the 'People's Democratic Republic of China'. Taiwan was often designated with the label Formosa, a Portuguese word first applied to the island by Portuguese sailors in the sixteenth century. This is not a Chinese word and is not used by Chinese speakers, but as late as 1979, Taiwan's IOC member Henry Hsu still had to explain this to the IOC Session that debated China's readmission. New Zealand's member Lance Cross said that he had once suggested to Taiwan that it call itself by the ancient name 'Cathay'. Personal names were also consistently misspelled. Dong Shouyi (Shou-yi Tung) was almost never spelled accurately in the minutes, and in his book, Killanin misspelled it as Shou Yi-Tung.

A better understanding of China could not be reached because productive conversation was impossible due to the unofficial policy against 'talking politics'. Western IOC leaders probably sincerely believed that this policy was the only way to maintain the existence of the IOC amidst the tensions of the Cold War. However, they could not see that the effect of this policy was to silence the voices of the new nations formed in the wake of World War II while allowing the West to talk, which was itself a political act.

Ping-pong diplomacy

Sports played an important role in the formation of a national identity in the early years of the PRC; television made this possible. The national network, China Central Television (CCTV), did not come into being until 1980; its predecessor was the Beijing Television Station, which made its first experimental broadcast in May 1958 and was received by thirty-odd television sets in Beijing. In 1959 the First National Sports Games of the PRC were televised.[16]

Table tennis played the major role in China's sporting interactions with the outside world because China, Japan and Korea held greater power in the International Table Tennis Federation (ITTF) than in the other major international sports federations – since table tennis was not then an Olympic sport, the Western powers had less interest in it. In addition, in the 1950s the president of the ITTF was a member of the British Communist Party sympathetic to the PRC. As a result, after the founding of the PRC, the ITTF was one of only three international sports federations in which the PRC had membership and Taiwan did not. Chinese table tennis players had entered the ranks of the world's best with a gold medal in men's singles in the 1959 World Championships. The 1961 World Championships in Beijing were the first world sports championship held in China, and China won three gold medals. Both events stimulated a great deal of patriotic fervour amidst the hardships of the times. They were broadcast live to the 10,000 television sets that were estimated to exist in Beijing at the time. Because these television sets were set up in public places for such events as the World Championships, the broadcast reached many more viewers than this. After the broadcast of the World Championships, the Beijing station received over 3,000 letters and telegrams from viewers, as well as several thousand phone calls.[17]

After China's withdrawal from the IOC in 1959 its diplomatic efforts turned towards Asia, Africa and Latin America. The 1962 Asian Games were held in Indonesia, with which the PRC had established diplomatic relations. The Indonesians privately assured the Mainland Chinese that Taiwan would not compete, but they were unwilling to take a public stance. In the end, the identity cards mailed by the Indonesian organizers to Taiwan mysteriously disappeared in the mail, and the team was unable to enter Indonesia. The IOC withdrew its patronage of the Asian Games and threatened sanctions, which angered Indonesia's President Sukarno. Inspired by the success of the 1955 Bandung Conference, which had led to the formation of the Non-Aligned Movement in 1961, Sukarno led the establishment of the Games of the New Emerging Forces (GANEFO). Ultimately the First GANEFO in Djakarta in 1963 attracted 48 nations. It also marked China's first full-scale participation in a major international, multi-sport event. The Games were planned as a quadrennial event, but a coup d'état in Indonesia and the Cultural Revolution in China put an end to them. However, this attempt to set up an alternative Olympic Movement served notice to the Western-dominated world of international sports that the newly independent and non-Western states were becoming a force to be reckoned with.

The cadres of the State Sports Commission suffered a great deal during the Cultural Revolution because Mao's wife Jiang Qing had a special vendetta against the Commission. It was dismantled and placed under the control of the military from 1968–71, and most of the leading cadres were sent to May Fourth cadre schools in the countryside to 'labour with the peasants'. The popular first chairman of the commission, Marshal He Long, was harassed to his death, as were outstanding sports figures throughout the nation. China stopped taking part in international sporting events until a personal plea from the head of the Japanese Table Tennis Federation persuaded Chairman Mao to send a team to the 31st World Cup in Table Tennis in Japan in March 1971, where they had friendly contacts with the US team. In April, Mao decided to accept the US request to send a table tennis delegation to China. 'Ping-pong diplomacy' paved the way for China's admission to the UN in October 1971. With the restoration of its functions in 1971, the Sports Commission planned to expand its diplomacy through ping pong. The phrase 'friendship first, competition second' became the guiding slogan of sports.

In 1971 the Asia–Africa Table Tennis Invitational was held in Beijing, followed by the 1972 Asian Table Tennis Cup. In 1973 over 80 nations and territories, many of which did not have diplomatic relations with China, participated in the First Asia–Africa–Latin America Table Tennis Friendship Invitational in Beijing, which became a launching pad for the establishment of diplomatic relations. This tournament was also notable for the fact that a contingent of Taiwanese living in the USA and Japan took part under the name 'Table Tennis Team of Overseas Compatriots, China, Taiwan Province'.[18] Because of its importance in international relations, table tennis is known in China as 'the little globe that moved the big globe'.

The struggle for readmission to the IOC

Lord Killanin followed Avery Brundage as IOC president in 1972. He had spent time in Shanghai as a reporter in 1937 and had seen at first-hand the Japanese occupation, which had left him sympathetic to China. In contrast to Brundage, from the very start he expressed his friendship and support to the Chinese, while he was considered antagonistic by the Taiwanese.[19]

The China problem heated up before the 1976 Montreal Olympics. Canada had recently established diplomatic relations with the PRC, and Prime Minister Pierre Trudeau declared that Taiwan could only compete under the name 'Taiwan'. Taiwan did not accept Trudeau's conditions and withdrew at the last minute.

The Cultural Revolution officially ended in 1976, Chairman Mao died, Deng Xiaoping rose to power, and in 1978 the Era of Reform and Opening-up began. On 1 January 1979, the USA and China announced the establishment of diplomatic relations. Although the 'one China principle' was still in effect, China changed its Taiwan policy so that it could accept Taiwan's membership in international organizations if Taiwan was represented as a local organization under the Chinese national organization. At the 81st Session of the IOC in Montevideo in April 1979, the Mainland Chinese conceded that after their 'rightful place' was restored, they could allow Taiwan to remain in the IOC as a local Chinese organization. The prerequisite would be that Taiwan could not use the written words 'Republic of China' or the word 'Taiwan' alone; nor could it use the flag, anthem or any other symbol representing the 'Republic of China'. This was the first time in an IOC meeting that the Chinese

Olympic Committee had made such a concession. Despite Killanin's opposition, the Montevideo Session produced a resolution requiring both sides to change their names.[20] The Mainland Chinese issued a statement that they could not accept this resolution but were willing to engage in further discussions with the IOC.

The Executive Board returned to the table and developed a resolution at its October meeting in Nagoya, which requested only Taiwan to change its name, flag and anthem.[21] Since there was not enough time to take the resolution to the IOC Session before the 1980 Lake Placid Winter Games, the IOC membership approved the resolution through a postal vote by 62 votes to 17, with one abstention.[22] After this, the 'Olympic formula' was used to settle the question of the use of national symbols in other organizations and international settings, and in this sense Olympic sports provided a blueprint for China–Taiwan diplomatic relations. China is known as the 'Olympic Committee of the People's Republic of China' and competes under the national anthem and flag of the PRC. Taiwan is known as the 'Olympic Committee of Chinese Taipei' and competes under the anthem and flag of its Olympic committee.

Following the admission of the Chinese Olympic Committee, in 1981, He Zhenliang was coopted into the IOC as its first member from the PRC.

Reform and opening up (1978–2001)

China thus re-entered the Olympic Games at the same time that the era of reform began, and with China's first-ever gold medal in the 1984 Los Angeles Olympic Games, sports were a realm in which Chinese people could feel some national pride two decades before China started to become a world power in the realms of economics and politics. The establishment of a national television network and the rapid improvements in television transmission technology contributed to the centrality of sports in the shaping of national identity. Only the national Spring Festival programme had a larger television audience than major sports events. China Central Television was formed in 1980, just in time for a watershed year. In 1981, after a series of televised international sports victories that inspired patriotic reactions, a particularly momentous event occurred in November, when the Chinese women's team defeated Japan to win the Volleyball World Cup. Broadcast from Tokyo, this was the first simultaneous satellite broadcast in China. The win was China's first world championship in an Olympic sport, and the victory had special significance because China defeated Japan in the final match. The Japanese women had reigned over the volleyball world for many years, and the match was played in Japan. The championship became much more than a volleyball match: it was a victory over China's long-time Asian rival. When the live broadcast of the Chinese victory came to an end, spontaneous demonstrations erupted across China. People flooded into the streets, setting off firecrackers and weeping openly. Approximately 30,000 letters were sent to the women on the team, along with money, gifts and proposals of marriage. Many of the letters were written in blood, a customary way of expressing deep sentiment. Many people mark the victory as the beginning of the revival of Chinese patriotism after the devastation of the Cultural Revolution. It was possibly the most significant event in the realm of public culture in the period after the death of Mao. It aroused more optimism than the event that was officially meant to have done so: the Party Congress in 1978 during which the Cultural Revolution was declared at an end and the era of reform underway.

As the market reforms progressed, 'competition' (*jingzheng*) became a key buzzword in China's move toward a competitive market economy and job market and away from rigid state planning and guaranteed life-long jobs. Echoing the Social Darwinist critiques of the early twentieth century, articles in the press portrayed an outdated, 'traditional' Chinese mentality of 'contending with one's lot' that must be changed. Sport was cited as a model for how a competitive economy should work. The State Sports Commission was at the forefront of China's shift toward a more competitive economy. In 1981, it became one of the first ministries to 'break the big pot' by instituting a new incentive system. Other ministries cited it as a model. Elite athletes in all sports had been state-supported at sports boarding schools since the establishment of a Soviet-style sports system in 1955. Corporate and private sponsorship of sports was first officially called for in 1984, the year in which the PRC took part in its first Olympic summer games after readmission to the IOC. The timing makes it likely that the goal of the document was to promote Olympic sports, but it also paved the way for corporate sponsorship of non-Olympic sports, especially bodybuilding. By the late 1980s, corporate and private sponsorship of sports clubs was proliferating, and newspapers reported many examples of wealthy individuals, mostly peasants and private entrepreneurs, who spent tens of thousands of yuan to fund sports clubs. Families, villages, occupational groups and strangers could form the basis for these clubs. In the mid-1990s the first professional sports leagues were formed in men's soccer and men's basketball, with the teams sponsored by corporations. However, leading up to the 2008 Olympics, the vast majority of top athletes were still trained in state-supported teams.

Sports were also at the forefront of the development of a new consumer culture of the body that began to replace the militaristic Communist body culture. Most emblematic of this change was the rapid growth of the sport of bodybuilding and the media furore over it – the sport had been banned because of its bourgeois vanity in 1953. The State Sports Commission gave it official approval in 1983, when the first formal competitions were held, but women were not permitted to wear bikinis in competitions. In 1985, China joined the International Bodybuilding Federation, the rules of which required women to wear two-piece bathing suits. Top state leaders, the National People's Congress, and the Ministry of Culture opposed the bikini, while most of the leaders of the State Sports Commission supported it. Its opponents felt that the baring of the body, especially the female body, was 'bourgeois' and might incite social disorder. The first officially approved bikinis were worn in October 1986, at a national competition held in Shenzhen. Since Shenzhen was a special economic zone more open to the outside world than any other area in China, it was considered the proper place for this 'experiment'.

Bodybuilding and other sports provided a channel for a degree of relaxation in state controls. Regulations against 'spiritual pollution' in the media prohibited body-revealing photos, including bikini calendars. Magazine editors apparently took the national bodybuilding contest as a go-ahead signal. Sporting photos of scantily-clad female bodies, especially Western bodies, proliferated in magazines, and on calendars and postcards. Pictures of Western women bodybuilders were popular items for the front and back covers and the central colour photo sections of sports magazines and many magazines that had little to do with sports. Calendars featuring Western sportswomen or Chinese gymnasts in various athletic poses were popular fixtures on household walls. Sports were perhaps the major medium for transmitting the 'modern' concepts of the body that were supposed to accompany modernity and consumer culture.

The commercialization of physical fitness caused a shift away from the collective, militarized notion of *tiyu* toward an individual, recreational notion of *jianshen* (fitness) pursued for personal health and enjoyment. The change in language was officially reflected in the 1995 Sports Law, which dropped the old 'mass physical culture' (*qunzhong tiyu*) for the new 'fitness for all' (*quanmin jianshen*). This seemingly small change in vocabulary marked a revolution in body culture. The objectified body, *ti*, which had been reduced to a tool in the service of the revolution and nation-building for forty-six years, was replaced by the subjective body, *shen*, and with it Chinese people began to take control of their experiences and lives.

The significance of the Beijing Olympic Games (2001–2008)

In 2008, the Olympic Games will be hosted by the least Westernized nation in the world to host them to date. It will only be the third time the Olympic Summer Games have been held outside the West – after Tokyo 1964 and Seoul 1988 – and it will be the greatest-ever meeting of East and West in peacetime. It is a good moment to reflect upon what globalization has meant for China over the last century. Leaders such as China's IOC member He Zhenliang envisioned that Chinese culture would take its place as an equal on the world stage. But it is not so easy for a non-Western nation, even one as large and powerful as China, to write itself into world history. The Olympic Museum at the IOC headquarters in Lausanne, Switzerland, largely features exhibits from the modern Olympic Games, along with a modest collection of ancient Greek sports art. In 1999, leading up to Beijing's second bid for the Olympics, He Zhenliang organized an exhibition there on '5,000 Years of Sport in China: Art and Tradition'. But first he had to overcome the opposition of members of the IOC's Executive Board, who felt that Chinese sports art was not 'Olympic'. He argued that 'Times have changed … Can we only transmit Greek sports culture to the nations of the world and should we not at the same time introduce the sport cultures from different sources?'[23] This points to larger questions about the future place of Chinese culture in global culture. Because of its link with the ancient Greek Olympic Games, most of the history and symbolism of the modern Olympics is linked to Western civilization. Nearly a hundred years after Herbert Giles wrote his article on ancient Chinese polo and football, very little information on Chinese sports culture is available in the West. For 200 years Western scholars have been fascinated with studying ancient sports as part of their 'own' history, but they have shown almost no interest in the sports of non-Western 'civilizations'. As a result, the basic material for museum exhibits, textbooks, documentaries and other cultural products hardly exists.

BOCOG established *renwen aoyun* as one of three themes for the Olympic Games. *Renwen* is difficult to translate. It is formed from the characters for 人 *ren* (human) and 文 *wen* (writing, literary pursuits, culture). Normally it is the translation for the 'humanities'. It has two senses for BOCOG, which are reflected in the two translations, the 'People's Olympics' and the 'Humanistic Olympics'. The People's Olympics means that the Games will provide an opportunity to train Chinese people for a globalizing world. The Humanistic Olympics means they will promote a blending of Chinese and Western culture, enriching both Chinese and global culture.

One of the main ways in which the 'people's' Games will be realized is through 'Olympic education' on a scale never seen before. There are academic and professional conferences, textbooks and courses for public schools and universities, educational television and radio shows, magazine and newspaper essays, Internet training, and more. BOCOG and Olympic scholars see the enthusism of volunteers as an opportunity to improve the public educational level and morality with education in Olympic history and values, traditional Chinese culture, Beijing history, public etiquette, international customs, foreign languages and lifesaving first-aid skills. Five hundred thousand volunteers are slated to receive training. Because of the need for English language skills and the desire to train the next generation, a large proportion of the volunteers will be college students.

The Chinese organizers see the Olympic Games as an opportunity for China to gain knowledge from the West that will benefit China's development. Although they state that the result of the Games will be a 'combination of East and West', if the Olympic Games are only a one-way process in which China learns from the West, the cultural exchange will not be truly mutual.

The goal of the humanistic Olympics is to contribute Chinese culture to global culture, propelling the Olympic Movement to become a truly multi-cultural, global cultural system. But there are practical obstacles, and China faces the challenge of presenting symbols of its cultural heritage to a global audience that will be unprepared to interpret them. One example is the opening ceremony, which BOCOG considers to be the most important opportunity to express Chinese culture to the world.

There was widespread discontent with the segment that the famous film director Zhang Yimou choreographed for the closing ceremony of the Athens Olympic Games, because it was not 'Chinese' enough and catered to Western stereotypes. At the same time, some critics also recognize that perhaps a Westernized Chinese culture will be better appreciated by non-Chinese.

Stimulated by the 2008 Olympic Games, the intense public debate about what it means to be 'Chinese' will contribute to the formation of a new Chinese national identity in the coming decades.

Notes

1. C. H. Robertson, 'A Plan for Promoting Missionary Activity among Association Boys', *Annual Reports of the Foreign Secretaries of the International Committee, October 1, 1909 to September 30, 1910*, New York, International Committee, YMCA, 1910, p. 192; see also Andrew Morris, *Marrow of the Nation: A History of Sport and Physical Culture in Republican China*, Berkeley, University of California Press, 2004, pp. 1–2.

2. Tan Hua and Dong Erzhi, *Suyuan – Dong Shouyi Zhuan* [Long-cherished Wish – the Story of Dong Shouyi], Beijing, People's Sports Publishing House, 1993, p. 93.

3. F. Hong, *Footbinding, Feminism and Freedom: The Liberation of Women's Bodies in China*, London and Portland, Frank Cass, 1997; Morris, *Marrow of the Nation*.

4. Herbert A. Giles, 'Football and Polo in China', *The Nineteenth Century* 59, 1906, p. 508.

5. Herbert A. Giles, *The Civilization of China,* London, Williams and Norgate, 1911, p. 159.

6. Mao Zedong, '*Tiyu zhi yanjiu*' [A Study of Physical Culture], *Xin qingnian* [New Youth] III, no. 2, April 1917, 7. Excerpts in English translation are found in F. Hong, *Footbinding, Feminism and Freedom*, pp. 313–17.

7. Liang Qichao, *Zhongguo zhi wushidao* [China's Bushido], Yinbing shi quanji [Collected Writings from the Ice-drinker's Studio], vol. 44, Taipei, Wenguang tushu gongsi, 1959 [1916], pp. 43–9.

8. Kam Louie, *Theorising Chinese Masculinity: Society and Gender in China*, Cambridge, Cambridge University Press, 2002.

9. Shigehisa Kuriyama, *The Expressiveness of the Body and the Divergence of Greek and Chinese Medicine*, New York, Zone Books, 1999.

10. Sun Lungkee, *Zhongguo wenhuade 'shenceng jiegou'* [The 'deep structure' of Chinese Culture], Hong Kong, Jixianshe, 1983, p. 20; Mark Elvin, 'Tales of *shen* and *xin*: Body–Person and Heart–Mind in China during the Last 150 Years', Michel Feher (ed.), *Fragments for a History of the Human Body*, Part 2, New York, Zone Books, 1989, p. 275.

11. Judith Farquhar, *Knowing Practice: The Clinical Encounter of Chinese Medicine*, Boulder, CO, Westview Press, 1994; Farquhar, *Appetites: Food and Sex in Postsocialist China*, Durham, NC, Duke University Press, 2002.

12. Judith Farquhar and Qicheng Zhang, 'Biopolitical Beijing: Pleasure, Sovereignty, and Self-cultivation in China's Capital', *Cultural Anthropology* 20, no. 3, August 2005, 303–27.

13. Nancy Chen, *Breathing Spaces: Qigong, Psychiatry, and Healing in China*, New York, Columbia University Press, 2003.

14. Louie, *Theorising Chinese Masculinity*, pp. 140–65.

15. Letter from Dong Shouyi to Avery Brundage, 19 August 1958 (IOC Archives).

16. Guo Zhenzhi, *Zhongguo dianshishi* [History of Chinese Television], Beijing, Chinese People's University Publishing House, 1991, pp. 3, 29.

17. *Ibid.*, p. 43.

18. Liang Lijuan, *He Zhenliang and China's Olympic Dream*, Beijing, Foreign Languages Press, 2007, pp. 95–6.

19. Susan Brownell, '"Sport and Politics don't Mix": China's Relationship with the IOC during the Cold War', in Stephen Wagg and David Andrews (eds.), *East Plays West: Essays on Sport and the Cold War*, New York, Routledge, 2007, p. 273; Liang, *He Zhenliang*, pp. 128–9; Hsu Heng [Henry Hsu], *Xu Heng Xiansheng fangtanlu* [Conversations with Henry Hsu], Taipei, National Historical Archives, 1998, p. 67.

20. 'Decisions', p. 39 of the minutes of the 81st Session of the IOC, Montevideo, 7 April 1979 (IOC Archives).

21. Liang, *He Zhenliang*, pp. 183–4.

22. Minutes of the Executive Board meeting, Nagoya, Japan, 23–25 October 1979, p. 103 (IOC Archives).

23. Liang, *He Zhenliang*, p. 383.

Guide to further reading

Brownell, S. *Training the Body for China: Sports in the Moral Order of the People's Republic*, Chicago, The University of Chicago Press, 1995.

　　'China and Olympism', in J. Bale and M. K Christenson (eds.), *Post-Olympism? Questioning Sport in the Twenty-first Century*, Oxford, Berg Press, 2004, pp. 51–64.

　　'"Sport and Politics don't Mix": China's Relationship with the IOC during the Cold War', in S. Wagg and D. Andrews (eds.), *East Plays West: Essays on Sport and the Cold War*, New York, Routledge, 2007, pp. 262–79.

　　Beijing's Games: What the Olympics Mean to China, Lanham, MD, Rowman and Littlefield, 2008.

Chen, N. *Breathing Spaces: Qigong, Psychiatry, and Healing in China*, New York, Columbia University Press, 2003.

Jinxia Dong, *Women, Sport and Society in Modern China: Holding Up More than Half the Sky*, London and Portland, Frank Cass, 2003.

Elvin, M. 'Tales of *Shen* and *Xin*: Body-Person and Heart-Mind in China during the Last 150 Years', in Michel Feher (ed.), *Fragments for a History of the Human Body*, Part 2, New York, Zone Books, 1989.

Fan Hong, *Footbinding, Feminism and Freedom: The Liberation of Women's Bodies in China*, London and Portland, Frank Cass, 1997.

Farquhar, J. *Knowing Practice: The Clinical Encounter of Chinese Medicine*, Boulder, CO, Westview Press, 1994.

　　Appetites: Food and Sex in Postsocialist China, Durham, NC, Duke University Press, 2002.

Farquhar, J. and Qicheng Zhang, 'Biopolitical Beijing: Pleasure, Sovereignty, and Self-cultivation in China's Capital', *Cultural Anthropology* 20, no. 3 (August 2005), 303–27.

Giles, H. A. 'Football and Polo in China', *The Nineteenth Century* 59 (1906), 508–13.

Kuriyama, S. *The Expressiveness of the Body and the Divergence of Greek and Chinese Medicine*, New York, Zone Books, 1999.

Louie, K. *Theorising Chinese Masculinity: Society and Gender in China*, Cambridge, Cambridge University Press, 2002.

Liang Lijuan, *He Zhenliang and China's Olympic Dream* (trans. Susan Brownell), Beijing, Liang Foreign Languages Press, 2007.

Morris, A. *Marrow of the Nation: A History of Sport and Physical Culture in Republican China*, Berkeley, University of California Press, 2004.

Olympic Museum (ed.), *5000 Years of Sport in China: Art and Tradition*, Lausanne, Musée Olympique, 1999.

Riordan, J. and R. Jones (eds.), *Sport and Physical Education in China*, London, E & FN, 1999.

Appendix

List of Chinese phrases in pinyin and characters

The entries are listed as they appear in the text, with pinyin added for Anglicized items.

A brighter summer's day (Guling jie shaonian sharen shijian)	牯岭街少年杀人事件
A spring river flows east (Yi jiang chunshui xiang dong liu)	一江春水向东流
A time to live and a time to die (Tongnian wangshi)	童年往事
A veggie cake (Yikou cai bingzi)	一口菜饼子
Adrienne Poy Clarkson (Wu Bingzhi)	伍冰枝
Ah Long	阿龙
Amy Tan (Tan Enmei)	谭恩美
Ang Lee (Li An)	李安
Aomen	澳门
Army nurse (Nü'er lou)	女儿楼
Atayal (Taiya)	泰雅
Ba Jin	巴金
Bai Liusu	白流苏
baihua	白话
baihuawen	白话文
Baiyun guan	白云观
Bali (Baizu)	白族
baogao wenxue	报告文学
Baoshen gong	包身工
Beautiful duckling (Yangya renjia)	养鸭人家
Bei Dao	北岛
Beidaihe	北戴河
Beijing bastards (Beijing zazhong)	北京杂种
Beiping shi sili Zhongguo gaoji xiqu zhiye xuexiao	北平市私立中国高级戏曲职业学校
Benbao neibu xiaoxi	本报内部消息

Big shot's funeral (Da wan)   大腕
Bingdian   冰点
Bishang Liangshan   逼上梁山
Blue kite (Lan fengzheng)   蓝风筝
Blush (Hong fen)   红粉
boke   博客
Bridge (Qiao)   桥
Bruce Lee (Li Xiaolong)   李小龙

Cai Yuanpei   蔡元培
Can Wu   残雾
Can Xue   残雪
Cao Bai   曹白
Cao Yu   曹禺
caoshu   草书
Cell phone (Shouji)   手机
Centre Stage (Ruan Lingyu)   阮玲玉
Chaguan   茶馆
Chao Yuan Ren (Zhao Yuanren)   赵元任
Chen Duxiu   陈独秀
Chen Kaige   陈凯歌
Chen Lai   陈来
Cheng Chung-ying (Cheng Zhongying)   成中英
Chezhan   车站
Chiang Kai-shek (Jiang Jieshi)   蒋介石
Chilin (Zhilian)   志莲
Chongqing   重庆
Chow Yun-Fat (Zhou Yunfa)   周潤发
Chu   楚
Chuangzao she   创造社
Chuanju   川剧
Chun Qiu   春秋
Chungking express (Chongqing senlin)   重庆森林
Chunliu   春柳
Cijigongdehui   慈济功德会
City of sadness (Beiqing chengshi)   悲情城市
Cixi   慈禧
Crazy stone (Fengkuang de shitou)   疯狂的石头
Crouching Tiger Hidden Dragon (Wohu
      canglong)   卧虎藏龙
Cui Jian   崔健
Cuicui   翠翠

Dai (Daizu)   傣族
Dai Jitao   戴季陶
daibiao   代表
dan   旦
danghua   党化

danwei	单位
daotong	道统
Daoxue	道学
Dashanzi	大山子
datong	大同
Datong shu	大同书
Daur (Dawoerzu)	达斡尔族
David D. Ho (He Dayi)	何大一
David Henry Huang (Huang Zhelun)	黄哲伦
Demuchukedonglupu	德穆楚克栋鲁普
Deng Xiaoping	邓小平
Deng Yingchao	邓颖超
DeWang	德王
dianshi ju	电视剧
Ding Ling	丁玲
Dingjun Mountain (Dingjun shan)	定军山
Dong (Dongzu)	侗族
dong	动
Dong Shouyi (Shou-yi Tung)	董守义
Dong Xiwen	董希文
dongfang shikong	东方时空
Dongxiang	东乡族
dongya bingfu	东亚病夫
Dongyao	动摇
dongyuan	动员
doufugan ti	豆腐干体
Dragon gate inn (Longmen kezhan)	龙门客栈
Dragon's eight tribes (Tianlong babu)	天龙八部
Dream of the red chamber (Honglou meng)	红楼梦
duanzi	段子
dun	顿
Dunhuang	敦煌
Dust in the wind (Lianlian fengchen)	恋恋风尘
Edward Yang (Yang Dechang)	杨德昌
Election (Hei shehui)	黑社会
Er-er-ba	二二八
Evening bell (Wanzhong)	晚钟
Ewenki (Ewenkezu)	鄂温克族
Fagushan	法鼓山
Falungong	法轮功
Fan Liuyuan	范柳原
Fan Wenlan	范文澜
Fan Zhongyan	范仲淹
Fang Dongmei	方东美
Fang Lijun	方力均
Farewell, my concubine (Bawang bieji)	霸王别姬

fazhan tiyu yundong, zengqiang renmin tizhi	发展体育运动，增强人民体质
Fei Mu	费穆
Feng Xiaogang	冯小刚
Feng Youlan	冯友兰
fengshui	风水
Foguangshan	佛光山
Fu Baoshi	傅抱石
Fugui	福贵
Fung Yu-lan (Feng Youlan)	冯友兰
funü wenti	妇女问题
funü,	妇女
funüzhuyizhe	妇女主义者
Gadameiran	嘎大梅染
gaige kaifang	改革开放
Gao Jianfu	高剑父
Gao Xingjian	高行健
Gao Yihan	高一涵
Gaoshan (Gaoshanzu)	高山族
geju	歌剧
geming yangbanxi	革命样板戏
gong	工
Gongyang	公羊
Great Han Emperor Wudi (Han wu dadi)	汉武大帝
Gu Cheng	顾城
Gu Hongming (Ku Hung-ming)	辜鸿铭
Gu Jiegang	顾颉刚
Gu Mu	谷牧
Gu Wenda	谷文达
Guan Shanyue	关山月
guangda	广大
Guangxu	光绪
Guangzhou	广州
Guangzhou sannianzhan	广州三年展
guanhua	官话
guazhong lanyin	瓜种兰因
Gugong	故宫
Guo Moruo	郭沫若
guohua	国画
guojia zhi shang	国家至上
guomin	国民
Guomindang	国民党
guoxue re	国学热
guoyu	国语
guoyu de wenxue, wenxue de guoyu	国语的文学，文学的国语
guoyu luomazi	国语罗马字
guqin	古琴

hai pai	海派
Hakka (Kejia)	客家
Han (Hanzu)	汉族
Han Shaogong	韩少功
Han Zhixun	韩志勋
Hanfei	韩非
hanyu	汉语
hanyu pinyin	汉语拼音
Hao Ran	浩然
He Jianjun	何建军
He Lin	贺麟
He Long	贺龙
He never gives up (Haiyang zhong de yitiao chuan)	汪洋中的一条船
He Zhen	何震
He Zhenliang	何振梁
Heilongjiang Ribao	黑龙江日报
Heinu yutian lu	黑奴吁天录
Heshang	河殇
Hohhot (Huhehaote)	呼和浩特
Honglou meng	红楼梦
Hong Shen	洪深
Hongdeng ji	红灯记
Hongse niangzi jun	红色娘子军
Hou Bo	侯波
Hou Hsiao-hsien (Hou Xiaoxian)	侯孝贤
Hsiao Kung-ch'uan (Xiao Gongquan)	萧公权
Hsu, Henry (Xu Heng)	徐亨
Hu Feng	胡风
Hu Hanmin	胡汉民
Hu Mei	胡玫
Hu Sheng	胡绳
Hu Shi	胡适
Hu Yepin	胡也频
huaju	话剧
huang pi shu	黄皮书
Huangdan chuanju	荒诞川剧
Huanmie	幻灭
huaqiao	华侨
Huaqiao huaren baike quanshu	华侨华人百科全书
huaren	华人
huayi	华裔
huayu	华语
huayu dianying	华语电影
Hui	回族
huida	回答
hunhe	混合

Huojudaoshi	火居道士
hexie shehui	和谐社会
Ili (Yili)	伊犁
In the face of demolition (Weilou chunxiao)	危楼春晓
Inner Mongolia (Nei Menggu)	内蒙古
Iron-toothed Ji Xiaolan (Tiechi tongya Ji Xiaolan)	铁齿铜牙纪晓岚
Jet Li (Li Lianjie)	李连杰
Jia	家
Jia Zhangke	贾樟柯
Jiang Kanghu	江亢虎
Jiang Qing	江青
jianghu	江湖
Jiangsu	江苏
jianshen	健身
jiao (belief)	教
Jiao (Daoist ritual)	醮
jiaodian fangdan	焦点访谈
Jidujiaohui	基督教会
Jin Ping Mei	金瓶梅
jing (essence)	精
jing (silence)	静
jingji jianshe	经济建设
Jingju	京剧
Jingpo (Jingpozu)	景颇族
Jinguang dadao	金光大道
jingzheng	竞争
jiusi yisheng	九死一生
John Woo (Wu Yusen)	吴宇森
Johnnie To (Du Qifeng)	杜琪峰
Journey to the West (Xiyou ji)	西游记
Juedui xinhao	绝对信号
junzi	君子
Kang Youwei	康有为
Kangxi Dynasty (Kangxi wangchao)	康熙王朝
Kashgar (Kashen)	喀什
Kawakami Hajime (He Shang Zhao)	河上肇
Kazak (Hasakezu)	哈萨克族
kexue fazhan guan	科学发展观
Khaw Soo Cheang (Xu Shuzhang)	许泗漳
King Hu (Hu Jin)	胡金
Kong Xiangxi (H. H. Kung)	孔祥熙
Korean (Chaoxianzu)	朝鲜族
Kotoko Shusui (Xingde Qiushui)	幸德秋水
Kucong (Kucong ren)	苦聪人
kungfu (gongfu)	功夫

Kyrgyz (Keerkezizu)	柯尔克孜族
Lao Can	老残
lao guoyin	老国音
Lao She	老舍
laoxinze zhi ren, laolizhe zhiyu ren	劳心者治人，劳力者治于人
laoye taitai shaoye xiaojiemen	老爷太太少爷小姐们
Lee Guan Kin (Li Yuanjin)	李元瑾
Lee Kuan Yew (Li Guangyau)	李光耀
Lee Xing (Li Xing)	李行
Leiyu	雷雨
li	理
Li Ang	李安
Li Dazhao	李大钊
Li Feigan (Ba Jin)	李芾甘 （巴金）
Li Hongzhang	李鸿章
Li Hongzhi	李洪志
Li Keran	李可染
Li Lianjie	李連杰
Li sao	离骚
Li Shaohong	李少红
Li Shizeng	李石曾
Li Shuangshuang	李双双
Li Tie	李铁
Li Xiaojiang	李小江
Li Yinhe	李银河
Li Youcai banhua	李有才板话
Li Zhensheng	李振盛
Liang Qichao	梁启超
Liang Shuming	梁漱溟
Liang Sicheng	梁思成
liangxing douzheng	两性斗争
Lim Boon Keng (Lin Wenqing)	林文庆
Lin Chong	林冲
Lin Fengmian	林风眠
Lin Zexu	林则徐
Lin Zhaohua	林兆华
ling	灵
Liu Baiyu	刘白羽
Liu Binyan	刘宾雁
Liu Chunhua	刘春华
Liu E	刘鹗
Liu Guosong	刘国松
Liu Haisu	刘海粟
Liu Kaiqu	刘开渠
Liu Shifu	刘师傅
Liu Shipei	刘师培
Liu Shuxian (Liu Shu-hsien)	刘述先

liyi	利益
liyi fenshu	理一分殊
liyun	礼运
Lo Hui-min (Luo Huimin)	骆惠敏
Lu Dongbin	吕洞宾
Lu Ling	陆翎
Lu Shoukun	吕寿琨
Lu Xun	鲁迅
Lu Zhuangzhang	卢戆章
luntan	论坛
Luotuo xiangzi	骆驼祥子
Ma Yifu	马一浮
Ma Yoyo (Ma Youyou)	马友友
Ma Yuan	马原
Makesi zhuyide zhongguo hua	马克思主义的中国化
Mama	妈妈
Manchu (Manzu)	满族
Mang Ke	芒克
Mao Dun	茅盾
Mao Shi	毛诗
Mao Zedong	毛泽东
Mao Zedong jiniantang	毛泽东纪念堂
Maxine Hong Kingston (Tang Tingting)	汤婷婷
Mei Guangdi	梅光迪
Mei Lanfang	梅兰芳
meinü zuojia	美女作家
menglong	朦胧
mianzi wenti	面子问题
Miao	苗
Ming	明
min'ge	民歌
Minglang de tian	明朗的天
minjian shiren	民间诗人
minsheng	民生
minsheng xinwen	民生新闻
minzu	民族
minzu xingshi	民族形式
Mo Yan	莫言
Mongols (Mengguzu)	蒙古族
Mou Zongsan	牟宗三
Mozi	墨子
My hero (Hao nan'er)	好男儿
My show (Wo xing wo xiu)	我型我秀
Nahm-mouh-lao (Nanmlao)	喃呒佬
Nanjing	南京
Nanjing lingjuli	南京零距离

nannü pingdeng	男女平等
Network news (Xinwen lianbo)	新闻联播
Ni Huanzhi	倪焕之
Ni Tuosheng	倪柝声
nong	农
nü qiangren	女强人
nüquanzhuyi	女权主义
nüren	女人
nüxing	女性
nüzi jiefang	女子解放
Oei Tiong Ham (Huang Zhonghan)	黄仲涵
Oroqen (Elunchunzu)	鄂伦春族
Osugi Sakae	大杉栄
Ouyang Yuqian	欧阳予倩
Oyster girl (Kenü)	蚵女
pai	派
Pan Jiajun	潘嘉峻
Pan Jinlian	潘金莲
People's Daily (Renmin ribao)	人民日报
pinyin	拼音
Popora (Babula)	巴布拉
Prime Minister Hunchback Liu (Zaixiang Liu luoguo)	宰相刘罗锅
Princess Pearl returned (Huanzhu gege)	还珠格格
putonghua	普通话
qi	气
Qi Rushan	齐如山
Qian Mu	钱穆
Qian Xuantong	钱玄同
qiancheng	虔诚
Qiangguo luntan	强国论坛
qigong	气功
Qing	清
qingguan	清官
Qinghai	青海
qiye danwei	企业单位
Qiyue	七月
qiyue	器乐
qu	取
Qu Yuan	屈原
quanmin jianshen	全民健身
quanzhen	全真
qunzhong tiyu	群众体育
quyi	曲艺
re'nao	热闹

Red beads (Xuanlian)	悬恋
Red sorghum (Hong gaoliang)	红高粱
Remorse at death (Shengsi hen)	生死恨
ren (benevolence)	仁
ren (people)	人
Ren Bonian	任伯年
Renmin dahuitang	人民大会堂
Renmin juchang	人民剧场
Renmin yingxiong jinianbei	人民英雄纪念碑
renquan	人权
renwen	人文
renwen aoyun	人文奥运
Richu	日出
Right a wrong with earthenware dish (Wapan shen'en)	瓦盆申冤
Ruan Lingyu	阮玲玉
sangang	三纲
sanmin zhuyi	三民主义
Serfs (Nongnu)	农奴
Shafei nüshi de riji	莎菲女士的日记
shang	商
Shanghai	上海
Shanghai baby (Shanghai baobei)	上海宝贝
Shanghai shuangnianzhan	上海双年展
shanshuihua	山水画
Shanxi	山西
Shaolin kids (Shaolin xiaozi)	少林小子
shaoshu minzu	少数民族
shehui fazhan	社会发展
shehui xingbie	社会性别
shen (spirit)	神
shen (body)	身
Shen Congwen	沈从文
sheng	生
shengping shi	升平世
shengyan	圣严
shenshi	绅士
shenti	身体
shenti xiezuo	身体写作
shi	士
Shi Chongming	石崇明
Shi Lu	石鲁
Shi Xiu	石秀
Shi Zhecun (Shi Zhicun)	施蛰存
shijie de da lianhe	世界的大联合
shiye danwei	事业单位
Shu Qingchun	舒庆春

Shu Ting	舒婷
shuailuan shi	衰乱世
Shui	水
Shuihu zhuan	水浒传
Shun	舜
shuochang	说唱
Sing-song girl red peony (Genü hongmudan)	歌女红牡丹
Six scholars of the western chamber (Liu caizi xixiangji)	六才子西厢记
Song	宋
Song Yuan xiqu kao	宋元戏曲考
souhu	搜狐
Spring festival gala (chunjie lianhuan wanhui)	春节联欢晚会
Spring in a small town (Xiaocheng zhi chun)	小城之春
Stanley Kwan (Guan Jinpeng)	关锦鹏
Stealing a roasted duck (Tou shaoya)	偷烧鸭
Su Tong	苏童
Subei	肃北
Summer at grandpa's (Dongdong de jiaqi)	冬冬的假期
Sun Chuanfang	孙传芳
Sun Yat-sen (Sun Zhongshan)	孙逸仙（孙中山）
Supergirl (Chaoji nüsheng)	超级女声
Suzhou	苏州
Tai	傣
Taibei	台北
taiji	太极
Taiping	太平
taiping shi	太平世
Taiwan	台湾
Taixu	太虚
Taiyang she	太阳社
Taiyang zhao zai Sanggan he shang	太阳照在桑干河上
Taizhou	泰洲
Tajik	塔吉克族
Tan Cheng Lock (Chen Zhenlu)	陈贞禄
Tan Dun	谭盾
Tan Sitong	谭嗣同
Tang Junyi	唐君毅
Taranchi (Talanqi)	塔兰其
The burning of the red lotus temple (Huoshao hongliansi)	火烧红莲寺
The days (Dongchun de rizi)	冬春的日子
The first intimate touch (Di yici qinmi jiechu)	第一次亲密接触
The goddess (Shennü)	神女
The killer (Diexue shuanghong)	喋血双雄
The shaolin temple (Shaolin si)	少林寺
The show must go on (Jianghu ernü)	江湖儿女

ti	体
Tian Han	田汉
Tian Heng	田横
Tian Zhuangzhuang	田壮壮
Tiananmen	天安门
Tiananmen guangchang	天安门广场
tianxia	天下
Tianya Community (Tianya shequ)	天涯社区
Tibetan (Zangzu)	藏族
ticao	体操
tipo	体魄
tixing	体形
tiyu	体育
tizhi	体质
Togtokh (Talanqi)	塔兰其
Tongmen hui	同盟會
tongyong pinyin	通用拼音
Tsai Ming-liang (Cai Mingliang)	蔡明亮
Tu Wei-ming (Du Weiming)	杜维明
tuanjie	团结
tuichen chuxin	推陈出新
Tujia	土家族
Turfan	吐鲁番
Ulanfu (Wulanfu)	伍兰夫
Urumqi (Wulumuqi)	乌鲁木齐
Uyghurs (Weiwuerzu)	维吾尔族
Uzbeks (Wuzibiekezu)	乌孜别克族
waiwang	外王
Wan Jiabao	万家宝
Wang Bin	王滨
Wang Gen	王艮
Wang Guangyi	王广义
Wang Guowei	王国维
Wang Wuxie	王无邪
Wang Xiaobo	王小波
Wang Xiaonong	汪笑侬
Wang Xiaoshuai	王小帅
Wang Yangming	王阳明
Wang Zhengting (C.T. Wang)	王正廷
wangluo wenxue	网络文学
wangyi	网易
Wei Hui	卫慧
Wei Minglun	魏明伦
wei rensheng er yishu	为人生而艺术
weihu	维护
wen	文

Wen Lou	文楼
Wen Yiduo	闻一多
wenhua	文化
wenhua dageming	文化大革命
wenhua re	文化热
wenren	文人
wentan	文坛
wenti	问题
wenxue	文学
wenxue yanjiu hui	文学研究会
wenyanwen	文言文
White gold dragon (Baijin long)	白金龙
Wong Kar-wai (Wang Jiawei)	王家卫
wu	武
Wu Changshuo	吴昌硕
Wu Jianren (Wu Woyao)	吴趼人（吴沃尧）
Wu Mi	吴宓
Wu zhihui	吴稚晖
Wu Ziniu	吴子牛
Wu Zuxiang	吴组缃
wuju	舞剧
wushu	武术
wusi yundong	五四运动
wuxia shenguai	武侠神怪
Xi Chuan	西川
Xia Yan	夏衍
Xia Zengyou	夏增佑
xiandai	现代
xianfeng pai	先锋派
Xianggang	香港
xianren	贤人
Xiao Erhei jiehun	小二黑结婚
Xiao Wu	小武
xiaokang	小康
xiaopin	小品
xiaopin wen	小品文
xiaoshuo	小说
xiaoshuo yuebao	小说月报
Xibo (Xibozu)	锡伯族
xibu dakaifa	西部大开发
xiesheng	写生
xieyi	写意
Ximen Qing	西门庆
xin	心
xin guoyin	新国音
xin Rujia	新儒家
xin Ruxue	新儒学

xin shiji	新世纪
xin wenhua yundong	新文化运动
xin wenxue	新文学
xin wutai	新舞台
xinbian lishi ju	新编历史剧
xingbie	性别
xingshu	行书
xingti	形体
Xingyun	星云
Xinjiang	新疆
xinlang	新浪
xinshixue	新史学
xinwen diaocha	新闻调查
xinwenhua yundong	新文化运动
xinxin renlei	新新人类
xinxing	心性
xinxing zhi xue	心性之学
Xiong Shili	熊十力
xiqu	戏曲
Xu Beihong	徐悲鸿
Xu Bing	徐冰
Xu Fuguan	徐复观
Xu Zhenya	徐枕亚
Xu Zhimo	徐志摩
xue	血
Xue Pinggui yu Wang Baochuan	薛平贵与王宝钏
Xueheng	学衡
xuetong	学统
xungen pai	寻根派
Y. M. Pei (Bei Yiming)	贝聿铭
Yan Fu	严复
Yan Haiping	阎海平
Yan'an	延安
Yan'an shenghuo	延安生活
Yang Chen Ning (Yang Zhenning)	扬振宁
Yang Lian	杨炼
yangsheng zhi dao	养生之道
Yang Xiong	杨雄
yangban xi	样板戏
yangsheng	养生
yanjingshe	眼镜蛇
Yao (medicine)	药
Yao (legendary sage-king)	尧
Yao (Yaozu)	瑶族
yaogun yinyue	摇滚音乐
Ye Shengtao	叶圣陶
Yearnings (Kewang)	渴望

Years of burning passions (Jiqing ranshao de shuiyue)	激情燃烧的岁月
Yellow earth (Huang tudi)	黄土地
Yeren	野人
Yi (Yizu)	彝族
yi feng	艺风
Yi li	仪礼
Yige nüren he yige nanren	一个女人和一个男人
Yiguan dao	一贯道
yin yang	阴阳
yinguang	印光
yiren	艺人
Yiwu suoyou	一无所有
yong	用
Yongzheng Dynasty (Yongzheng wangchao)	雍正王朝
you wenhua	有文化
Yu Guozhen	俞国桢
Yu Hua	余华
Yu Jian	于坚
yu shi wu zheng	与世无争
Yu Ying-shih (Yu Yingshi)	余英时
Yuan	元
Yuan Shikai	袁世凯
Yuan Weishi	袁伟时
Yuanmingyuan	圆明园
Yuanyc	原野
yueguo changcheng, zouxiang shijie	越过长城，走向世界
Yueju	越剧
yulun daoxiang	舆论导向
yundong	运动
Yunnan	云南
Zai qiaoliang gongdi shang	在桥梁工地上
zai yanan wenyi zuotanhui shang de jianghua	在延安文艺座谈会上的讲话
zawen	杂文
Zen Ze-kiun (Chen Rijun)	陈日君
Zeng Guofan	曾国藩
zhaijiao	斋教
Zhang Ailing (Eileen Chang)	张爱玲
Zhang Binglin	章炳麟
Zhang Dainian	张大年
Zhang Daqian	张大千
Zhang Hongtu	张宏图
Zhang Junmai (Carsun Chang)	张君劢
Zhang Shichuan	张石川
Zhang tianshi	张天师
Zhang Yimou	张艺谋
Zhang Yuan	张元

Zhang Zhidong	张之洞
Zhao Shuli	赵树理
Zhao Wuji	赵无极
Zheng Chenggong (Koxinga)	郑成功
Zheng He	郑和
zhengtong	政统
zhengyan	证严
zhengyi	正一
zhibo fenli	制播分离
zhibo qi	直播期
zhishi fenzi	知识分子
zhong wen qing wu	重文轻武
Zhongguo	中国
Zhongguo guojia jiaoxiang yuetuan	中国国家交响乐团
Zhongguo guomindang	中国国民党
Zhongguo lishi bowuguan	中国历史博物馆
Zhongguo shehui zhuyi dang	中国社会主义党
Zhongguo zuoyi zuojia lianmeng	中国左翼作家联盟
Zhonghua minguo	中华民国
Zhonghua quanguo wenyijie kangdi xiehui	中华全国文艺界抗敌协会
Zhonghua renmin gongheguo	中华人民共和国
zhongti xiyong	中体西用
zhongwen	中文
zhongxue wei ti, xixue wei yong	中学为体西学为用
Zhongyang renmin guangbo diantai	中央人民广播电台
Zhou Enlai	周恩来
Zhou li	周礼
Zhou Nanjing	周南京
Zhou Shuren	周树人
Zhou Zuoren	周作人
Zhu fu	祝福
Zhu Ming	朱铭
Zhu Shilin	朱石麟
Zhu Xi	朱熹
Zhuang	壮族
Zhuiqiu	追求
zhuyin fuhao	注音符号
zhuyin zimu	注音字母
ziji de xing	自己的性
ziyou shi	自由诗
zouxiang gonghe	走向共和
Zuo zhuan	左传
Zuo Zongtang	左宗棠

Index

Abbas, Ackbar, 310
abstract inheritance method, 11, 17
academic research & debates
  Chinese culture, 3
  Christianity, 193
  gender, 68, 71, 77, **80–2**, 83
  historiography, 58–61, 63–5
  literature, 246
  socialism, 193
  sociopolitical history, 38–9, 43
advertising, 322, 326–8
agriculture, 20–1, 40–1, 43, 57, 76, 159, 162,
  166–7, 283
Ah Long, 223
Air China, 323
Alitto, Guy, 143
All China Resistance Association of Writers
  and Artists, 227
All China Women's Federation, 71, 75, 77,
  80–3, 85
Altaic languages, 201
anarchism, 27, 39, **156–63**, 166
ancestor veneration, 173, 176–7, 182–3, 189
Anderson, Benedict, 54
Anhui, 199
Appadurai, Arjun, 314–15
Apter, David, 57–8
Arabic language, 198
Arabs, 106
architecture, 8–9, 282, 287–8, 293
art, 13–14, **272–96**
  diaspora cultures, 118
  gender, 70, 77
  Maoist China (1949–76), **283–8**
  post-Maoist China, **288–95**
  Republic (1912–49), 34, **276–82**
  sociopolitical history, 22, 37–9, 348
Asian Economic Miracle, 11

Asian Games (1962, Indonesia), 351
Asian values, 17, 151
Asiatic mode of production, 57–9
assimilation
  China's peoples, 92, 95, 102, 109, 111–12
  diaspora cultures, 116, 119–20, 122–3, 129,
    131
Australasia
  art, 272
  Chinatowns, 10
  diaspora culture, 116–17, 122–4, 127–31
  economic development, 108
  migrant society, 10, 16, 96
  sports, 347, 349
Austro-Asiatic languages, 95, 201
Austronesian languages, 201
autonomous areas, 92–7, 99–102, 108
avant-garde
  art, 291
  literature, **247–50**, 251–2

Ba Jin, 220–1
Baba culture. *see peranakan*
Bai people, 98–9
baihuawen. see vernacular language
Bajin. see Li Feigan
ballroom dancing, 18, 43
Bandung Conference (1955), 351
barbarism, 16, 49–50, 135, 284, 342
Barlow, Tani, **74**
BBS chat rooms, 251, 331–2, 334
Beckett, Samuel, 246, 263
Bei Dao, 246–7
Beijing
  architecture, 282
  art, 280, 287–8, 291, 293
  cinema, 297, 300, 310, 312, 315
  Confucianism, 152

gender, 72, 83
Internet, 330
languages, 199
literature, 221, 225–6, 241–2, 247
music & performing arts, 259–60, 262,
    264–6, 268 (*see also* Peking Opera (*jingju*))
Olympic Games (2008) (*see* Olympics)
religious traditions, 188, 192
socialism, 158
sociopolitical history, 25, 31, 345
sports & physical culture, 346, 352, 357–8
TV, 319, 323, 327, 350–1
University (*see* Peking University)
see also Forbidden City; White Cloud
    Temple (Baiyunguan); Yuanmingyuan
Beijing Opera. *see* Peking Opera
Beijing Organizing Committee for the
    Olympic Games (BOCOG), 346, 357–8
Beijing University. *see* Peking University
Beiping. *see* Beijing
Beiyang Navy, 62
Belgrade embassy bombing (1999), 97, 331–2
Berry, Chris, chapter by, 13, **297–317**
Bible, 191, 193–4, 208
Blang language, 201
Blogging China, 334
BOCOG. *see* Beijing Organizing Committee
    for the Olympic Games
body culture. *see* martial arts; physical
    culture
bodybuilding, 354–5
Bolshevism, 160–2, 164, 170
Bourgeois Revolution. *see* Revolution of 1911
bourgeoisie
    cinema, 306–7
    gender, 75–6, 84
    historiography, 56
    literature, 229
    music & performing arts, 258
    socialism, 163, 165
    sociopolitical history, 28, 30–2
    sports & physical culture, 355
Boxer Uprising (1900), 6, 25, 57, 61–2, 158,
    174, 189, 191–2, 345
British
    art, 288
    cinema, 299, 303
    Confucianism, 148
    culture, 15
    diaspora culture &, 117, 125
    ethnicity, 96
    historiography, 52
    housing developments, 8–9
    literacy, 22
    literature, 241, 243
    religious traditions, 189, 191, 194

socialism, 156
sociopolitical history, 3, 22, 26, 32, 310
sports, 350
see also Opium Wars
Brownell, Susan, chapter by, 18, **339–60**
Brundage, Avery, 348–9, 352
Buddha's Birthday, 188
Buddhism, 18, 173, 175–6, 179–80, **183–6**
    art, 282
    Confucianism &, 11, 53, 140, 143, 145–6
    diaspora culture, 119–20, 125
    ethnicity, 111
    Hong Kong, 187–8
    physical culture, 342–3
    socialism &, 161
    sociopolitical history, 22, 27
    Taiwan, 186–7
Bulag, Uradyn, 100, 108
Bum Cai (Pizi Cai), 333–4
bureaucracy
    Chinese language, 202–3, 207, 212–13
    Confucianism, 135–6, 151
    ethnicity &, 106–7, 110
    historiography, 46–7
    literature, 220, 231, 238
    media, 321–2, 327, 335
    religious traditions, 175–6, 181, 184, 192,
        194
    socialism, 162, 165, 167–8
    sociopolitical history, 21–2, 24–6, 33, 39, 42
    sports & physical culture, 341
    see also civil service examinations
business. *see* commerce

cadres. *see* Communist cadres
Cai Yuanpei, 280
Cai, Zong-qi, 14
calligraphy, 22, 215, 274, 289–90, 292, 342
Can Xue, 248
Canada, 115, 194, 352
    see also North America
Canton. *see* Guangzhou
Canton Peasant Movement Training
    Institute, 73
Cantonese dialect (Yue), 95, 198–9, 210, 213,
    293, 300, 303, 309
Cantonese opera, 300, 309
Cantonese people, 187
Cao Bai, 223
Cao Yu (Wan Jiabao), 257, 259
capitalism
    art, 293
    cinema, 305, 307, 309, 313
    gender, 69, 79, 83, 86–7
    historiography, 46, 56, 58, 62
    literature, 220, 230

religious traditions, 193
  socialism &, 155–8, 161, 163, 165–70
  sociopolitical history, 28, 32, 37, 39–40,
    42–3
Cartesian dualism, 343
Catholics. *see* Roman Catholic Christianity
CCP. *see* Communist Party
cellular phones, 318, 329, 334–5
censorship
  cinema, 301–3, 309, 313, 315
  historiography, 61
  literature, 225, 245–7, 250–2
  media, 318, 325, 332, **335–6**
  music & performing arts, 259, 263, 265
  sociopolitical history, 43
Central Asia, 21, 49, 174, 183, 308
  see also Xinjiang
Central People's Radio Station (*Zhongyang
  renmin guangbo diantai*), 323
Chan, Jackie, 347
Chang, Carson. *see* Zhang Junmai
Chang, Eileen. *see* Zhang Ailing
change
  Confucianism, 144–5, 147
  cultural, 2–3, 6–8, 12–15, 17–18, 121
  diaspora cultures, 121
  gender, 84
  literature, 218, 236–8, 247, 250
  music & performing arts, 253
  religious traditions, 195
  sociopolitical history, 21, 30
  see also social change
Chao Yuan Ren, 206
charitable activities, 183, 185, 187, 191, 194–5
Chekhov, Anton, 257
Chen Duxiu, 18, 30, 72, 235
Chen Kaige, 297, 312
Chen Lai, 153
Chen, Ping, chapter by, 15, **198–217**
Chen Xiaomei, 85, 261, 263–4
Cheng brothers, 141
Cheng Chung-ying, 141
Chengdu, 263, 265
Chiang Kai-shek, 32–3, 35–6, 52
China Academic Network (CANet), 330
China Blog, 334
'China Can Say "No"', 6
China Central Television (CCTV), 264, 266,
  319–21, 323–5, 328–9, 350, 353
China Mobile, 335
China National Symphony Orchestra, 260
China Petroleum Co., 323
China Philharmonic Orchestra, 266
China Telecom, 323, 330
China Trade Daily, 331
China Unicom, 335

Chinatowns, 9–10, 124
Chinese art. *see* art; *guohua* (national
  painting)
Chinese calligraphy. *see* calligraphy
Chinese Chamber of Commerce, 33
Chinese characters. *see* Chinese script
Chinese cinema. *see* cinema
Chinese civilization, 1–2, 5, 8
  diaspora cultures, 116, 118–19, 128
Chinese Communist Party. *see* Communist
  Party
Chinese culture
  Confucianism, 135, 140, **141–3**, 144–50
  definition, 1–3, 11–13, 17–18
  ethnicity, 92
  gender, 82, 87
  historiography, 59, 63
  sociopolitical history, 29–30, 44
  see also diaspora cultures
Chinese dialects
  cinema, 298, 302–3
  diaspora culture, 7
  ethnicity &, 97
  geographic distribution, 198–9
  imperial era, 202–3
  language reform, 205–6
  script, 204, 208, 210
  Taiwan, 194
  use, 212–16
Chinese diaspora. *see* diaspora cultures
Chinese language, 5, 14–15, 30, 191, 198, 216
  cinema, 298, 302, 309–10
  diaspora cultures, 119, 122, 125, 130, 198,
    303
  foreign students, 1
  gender, 81
  geographic distribution, 198–9, 214–15
  historiography, 53
  Internet, 332, 334
  literature, 14, 242, 247, 249
  music & performing arts, 255–6, 262, 266
  number of speakers, 198
  policy & planning, 213–16
  premodern times, 201–5
  present-day use, **212–15**, 216
  reform, 201–4, **205–12**, 213, 215–16
  religious traditions, 183, 188, 191
  sports & physical culture, 356
  translations into, 5, 191
  see also Chinese dialects; classical Chinese
    language; non-Chinese languages; Old
    Chinese; vernacular language
Chinese masculinity. *see* gender
Chinese medicine, 55, 343
Chinese New Year, 316, 328–9, 335
Chinese Olympic Committee, 348–9, 353

Chinese script, 14–16, 22, 95, 200, 202–6,
     207–11, 212–13, 215–16, 247, 291
see also calligraphy
Chinese Socialist Party (*Zhongguo shehui zhuyi
     dang*), 157–8
Chinese State Sports Commission, 346
Chineseness
     art, 289, 293
     cinema, **299–301**, 305
     definition, 3, 5–6, **7–14**, 17
     diaspora cultures, 115, 119, 122, 125, 131–2
     ethnicity, 7–9, 92
     gender, 69–70, 83
     historiography, 50, 63–4
     sociopolitical history, 27
     sports, 358
Chongqing, 227, 282, 302
Chow Yun-Fat, 297, 311
Christianity, 18, 173, 175–6, 183, 185, 187,
     188–95
     Confucianism &, 139, 142, 188
     diaspora cultures, 116, 125
     historiography, 54
     language, 216
     missionaries, 23, 25, 142, 175, **188–95**, 208,
        340
     sociopolitical history, 25, 62
     see also Protestant Christianity; Roman
        Catholic Christianity
Chu culture, 242, 249
Chuangzao she. see Creation Society
Ciji gongdehui, Compassionate Relief Merit
     Society, 186–7
cinema, **297–317**
     censorship, 43
     culture &, 1, 13, 16, 18
     gender, 70, 76–7
     historiography, 52, 264, 282
     Hong Kong, 297, 299–301, 303, 305, **309–14**
     language, 213
     late Qing period, **299–301**
     People's Republic of China (PRC), **306–9**,
        347
     Republic (1912–49), 34, 239
     revolutionary tradition, 34, 239
     Taiwan, 297–300, 306, 308–9, **311–14**, 315
     television &, 326–7
     transnational, 13, 130, 297, 299, **314–16**, 347
citizenship
     diaspora cultures, 128
     ethnicity, 93, 101, 105, 108–9, 112
     historiography, 47, 54, 62–4
     sociopolitical history, 20, 26, 29, 31, 44
civil service examinations, 4, 16–17, 22–3, 25,
     29, 235, 341–3
     see also bureaucracy

civil war (1946–49)
     art, 282
     cinema, 299
     diaspora cultures, 126
     literature, 230
     music & performing arts, 261
     religious traditions, 175, 185–6, 194
     socialism, 166
     sociopolitical history, 36
     sports & physical culture, 261
Cixi, Empress Dowager, 24–5, 60
clans & lineages, 22, 38, 43, 51, 102, 104, 173,
     176
     see also family
Clarke, David, chapter by, 13, **272–96**
Clarkson, Amy Poy, 132
class
     Chinese language, 202
     cinema, 307–8
     Confucianism, 120–1, 124
     culture &, 16
     diaspora cultures, 120–1, 124
     gender, 74, 76, 80
     historiography, 56–7, 60, 65
     literature, 220–2, 224–30, 237–9, 242, 244
     music & performing arts, 258, 260–1
     religious traditions, 177
     socialism, 163–5, 167–8
     sociopolitical history, 20, 27–8, 34, 37–9, 41
     see also bourgeoisie; elites; peasant
        culture; scholar-gentry; workers
classical Chinese language (*wenyanwen*), 203,
     205, 211–12, 216, 241
     historiography, 53
     literature, 237, 239–41, 251
     performing arts, 258
     sociopolitical history, 30–1
coastal China, 116, 118–19, 121–2, 264, 282,
     326, 340
Cock-Crow Society, 158
Cold War, 123, 126–8, 170, 307, 313, 347–50
collectivism, 37–8, 41, 57, 167, 242
colonialism
     art, 290
     cinema, 303, 309–1, 313
     diaspora cultures, 117, 123–4, 126, 131
     gender, 68–9
     religious traditions, 193
     socialism &, 165
     sociopolitical history, 15, 23, 32, 47, 51,
        57–8, 63
commerce
     art, 281
     Confucianism, 13, 136
     diaspora cultures, 116–17, 125
     gender, 78

socialism, 166
sociopolitical history, 20, 22–4, 31, 42, 68
Common Language and Script Law (2000), 212, 215
communes, 37–8, 41, 159, 167, 306–8
Communist cadres, 36–40, 57, 246, 351
Communist International (Comintern), 32, 34, 162–3, 225, 227, 285
Communist Party (CCP)
   art, 273, 283, 286–7
   cinema, 301–3, 305–8, 310, 312
   Confucianism, 136, 146–7, 153
   diaspora culture, 123, 126
   early twentieth century, **30–7**
   ethnicity, 93
   gender, 70, 72–9, 81–3, 86–7
   historiography, 54–7, 59, 62
   Internet, 336
   literature, 220–2, 225, 227–8, **228–9**, 231, 236, 251
   media, 318–24, 330
   modern culture, 2–6, 11–12
   music & performing arts, 253, 258–60, 263
   religious traditions, 18, 174–6, 179, 185, 189, 193–4
   socialism, 155–7, 160–70
   sociopolitical history, 29, 39–40, 42–3
   sports, 347–8, 354
   see also leftists
Communist Revolution (1949)
   art, 282
   cinema, 302
   literature, 220, 236–7, 243, 245
   socialism, 155, 157, 163
   sociopolitical history, 20, 35–7
community festivals. see festivals
concessions, foreign, 9, 23–4, 28, 31, 118, 225, 275, 281, 305
Confucianism, **135–54**
   Chineseness, 11–13
   cinema, 303–5
   culture, 16, 18
   diaspora cultures, 125, 132
   ethnicity, 8, 92
   gender, 72–3
   historiography, 46, 48, 50, 53, 55, 60, 63
   literature, 239, 242, 249
   modernizing in nineteenth century, 5, **135–41**
   music & performing arts, 257, 263
   physical culture, 340
   religious traditions, 139, 145, 149, 173, 188
   socialism &, 158
   sociopolitical history, 21–2, 24–31, 36, 39
   see also New Confucianism

Confucius, 2, 12–13, 24, 47, 136–40, 144–5, 147, 149, 151, 173, 202
Confucius Institutes, 2
conservatism, 11, 17, 25, 60, 82, 86, 136–7, 144, 223, 239
constitution, 24–5, 50, 138–9, 219
consumer culture
   art, 291–3
   gender, 69, 76, 78–9, 85–6
   media, 330, 333, 336
   socialism &, 155
   sociopolitical history, 41, 44
   sports & physical culture, 355
   see also marketization
cooking. *see* food
corruption, 24, 37, 109, 230–1, 238, 305, 324, 327–9, 335
countryside. *see* rural areas
Creation Society (*Chuangzao she*), 225
Critical Review (Xueheng), 240
Cross, Lance, 349–50
Cubism, 281
Cui Jian, 265
cultural diversity, **94–7**
   diaspora cultures, **128–32**
   ethnicity, 93, 95, 97, 101, **108–9**
   see also multi-culturalism
Cultural Revolution (1960s–1970s)
   art, 273, 283–4, 287
   cinema, 312
   Confucianism, 12, 147
   diaspora culture, 129
   ethnicity, 96, 99
   gender, 69, 71, 76–7, 84–5
   historiography, 56, 62
   language, 213
   literature, 231, 246–7, 249
   music & performing arts, 255, 260–6, 268
   nationalism, 6, 58, 61
   religious traditions, 174–6, 178, 181, 185
   socialism, 156, 167–8
   sociopolitical history, 38–40, 43
   sports, 351–2, 354
   TV, 319, 327
cultural studies, 16
culture (*wenhua*)
   definition, 3–13, **14–19**
   ethnicity &, 91
   historiography, 48–50
   sociopolitical history, 21–2, 27, 36
   see also diaspora cultures
Curtius, Ernst, 340
cyberculture. *see* Internet

Dadaism, 291
Dai Jitao, 162

Dai people, 111
Dalai Lama, 187
dance. *see* music & performing arts
danwei. *see* work units
Daoism, 18, 53, 140, 158, 161, 173, 175–6,
     179–83, 187, 263, 343–4
Daur language, 201
Davis, Darrell William, 313
de Bary, William Theodore, 136
Deang language, 201
Declaration (1958), 11–12
democracy
     cinema, 311
     Confucianism, 138–40, 143–5, 149–53
     culture, 5, 15–16
     historiography, 59
     Internet, 15
     literature, 219
     media, 336
     religious traditions, 195
     socialism, 161–2, 167
     sociopolitical history, 15, 23–4, 27, 30, 32, 43
     sports & physical culture, 340
demonstrations. *see* dissent; Tiananmen
     Square demonstrations (1989)
Deng Xiaoping, 4–5, 40–3, 156, 166, 169, 231,
     310, 320, 352
Deng Yingchao, 75
Dewey, John, 30, 53
diaspora cultures, 14, **115–34**
     art, 275–6, 289, 292–3
     Chinese language, 119, 122, 125, 130, 198,
          303
     Chineseness, 8–10
     cinema, 298, 309–10, 314
     cultural diversity, **128–32**
     historical background, **116–21**
     historiography, 63–4
     literature, 245
     modern choices, **125–8**
     modernity, **121–5**
     sports & physical culture, 345
     see also migrant societies
Ding Ling, 74–5, 220, 226, 228, 230
Dirlik, Arif, chapter by, 6, **155–72**
dissent, 41, 43, 94, 105, 174, 251, 318
     see also human rights; Tiananmen Square
          demonstrations (1989)
Document 19, 175–6
Dong Shouyi (Shou-yi Tung), 339, 347–50
Dong Xiwen, 283
Dongxiang language, 201
Dragon TV, 329
drama. *see* literature; music & performing
     arts; television
DTV (digital television), 321

Duara, Prasenjit, chapter by, 5–6, **46–67**
Dunhuang, 282
Durkheim, Emile, 178
Dutch. *see* Netherlands

Eastern culture
     art, 290, 293, 348
     Confucianism, 135, 140, 144, 151–2
     historiography, 49, 64–5
     religious traditions, 18
     socialism, 156, 158, 160–1
     sports & physical culture, 342, 347, 349,
          355, 357
     see also Orientalism
economic conditions & growth, 1–2
     art, 273, 282, 289–91
     Confucianism, 135, 140, 151–2
     diaspora cultures, 118, 120–1, 127, 129
     ethnicity &, 96, 98, 100–1, 103, 105–7, 110
     gender &, 70–1, 74–5, 78, 80, 83–5, 87
     historiography, 46, 48, 63–4
     language, 211, 214
     literature, 218, 237
     media, 318–24, 330–1, 333, 335
     religious traditions, 173, 177, 195–6
     socialism, 163, 165, 167–8
     sociopolitical history, 20, 22, 24, 29, 31,
          33–6, 38, 40, 42–4
     sports & physical culture, 1–2, 349, 353–6
Edstrøm, Sigfrid, 347
education
     art, 274, 279–80, 289
     Chinese language, 1–2, 203–4, 206–9,
          212–15
     cinema, 306
     Confucianism, 136–7, 147
     culture &, 1–2, 14, 16–17
     diaspora cultures, 116–17, 122–4, 129–31
     ethnicity &, 92, 103, 105, **106–8**, 109
     gender &, 69, 71, 73–4, 78, 80
     historiography, 52–3, 61, 63, 65
     literature, 222, 235
     media, 320, 333
     music & performing arts, 256, 266
     religious traditions, 191, 195
     socialism, 157, 159–60, 162
     sociopolitical history, 22–7, 29–31, 38, 40–1
     sports & physical culture, 342, 357
egalitarianism. *see* equality
elites
     Chinese language, 202
     cinema, 312
     diaspora cultures, 126
     ethnic, 92, 94
     historiography, 46, 54–5
     literature, 239

sociopolitical history, 22, 24, 30, 33, 36, 41, 43
sports, 354
emigration. *see* diaspora cultures; migrant societies
England. *see* British
English language, 198–9, 203–4, 208, 211
anglophone culture, 1, 15, 80
'China,' 7
cinema, 298
diaspora culture, 117, 125
ethnicity, 107
gender, 82
Internet, 334
literature, 250
music & performing arts, 255
sociopolitical history, 43
sports, 343, 357
Enlightenment, 48, 52, 57, 69, 81, 151–2, 161
entrepreneurs, 42, 46, 78, 104, 117, 122, 167, 196
environment, 41–2, 169–70
equality
cinema, 311
Confucianism, 135, 139–40
ethnicity, 92, 100
gender, 70–1, 80–1, 84–5, 138–9
historiography, 53, 57, 63
socialism, 158, 168–9
sociopolitical history, 21, 27, 29–30, 32, 37
Era of Reform and Opening-up. *see* post-Maoist China
Ererba, 2/28, 194, 313
ethics
Confucianism, 137, 144, 147–52
diaspora cultures, 121
ethnicity, 92
literature, 219, 231, 238–9
media, 325, 333, 335
music & performing arts, 254, 262
religious traditions, 173, 177, 180, 184
socialism, 159
sociopolitical history, 22, 26
sports & physical culture, 342
ethnic nationalism, 51, 64, 94, 108–10, 112, 174
ethnicity, **91–114**
Chineseness, 7–9, 92
cinema, 302, 308, 310
Confucianism, 139, 141
diaspora cultures, 12–13, 116, 118–19, 124, 127–8
historiography, 49–52, 63–4
history, culture & identity, 108–9
identification & assertion, 98–101
independence, 51, 64, 94, 108–10, 112, 174

languages & education, **106–8**, 199–201, 210, 212, 214
literature, 242, 249
minorities, **101–2** (*see also* Hui; Manchus; Mongols; Uyghurs)
music & performing arts, 259
racism, 31
religious traditions, 173–4
sociopolitical history, 26–8, 42
state politics and, 98–101
urban areas, 109–12
xenophobia, 6
Xinjiang, 102–6
see also Han Chinese
Euken, Rudolf, 145
European culture
art, 272–4, 279, 281, 293
cinema, 316
Confucianism, 152
diaspora cultures &, 116–17, 120–6, 129–30
ethnicity, 94, 100
gender, 68–9, 80–1
historiography, 15, 46–7, 49, 51–4, 56–7, 59, 61–2, 65
housing developments, 8–9
Internet, 333
languages, 201, 211, 302–3
literature, 224, 227, 239
modernity, 3
music & performing arts, 13, 260
physical culture, 340
religious traditions, 188, 191
socialism, 156, 158, 160–2, 170
sociopolitical history, 15, 26, 31
sports, 347
TV, 322
European powers. *see* foreign powers
Evans, Harriet, chapter by, 17, **68–90**
Ewenki language, 201
Expressionism, 279

Fagushan, Dharma Drum Mountain, 187
Falungong, 56, 179, 332, 345
family
art, 284
cinema, 304, 307, 309
Confucianism, 136–8, 140, 149, 151
culture, 17
diaspora cultures, 118–20
ethnicity, 102, 104, 107
gender, 72–3, 79–80, 84
religious traditions, 173, 177–8, 187, 195
socialism, 159
sociopolitical history, 20–2, 29–31, 38, 41, 43
see also clans & lineages

Fan Kuan, 293–4
Fan Wenlan, 56
Fang Dongmei (Thomé H. Fang), 141
Fang Lijun, 291–2
Fang, Thomé H. *see* Fang Dongmei
Fei Mu, 305
Felski, Rita, 68
femininity. *see* gender
feminism. *see* women's movement
Feng Xiaocai, 60
Feng Xiaogang, 316
Feng Youlan, 11, 17, 56, 141
fengshui, 177
festivals
    music & performing arts, 259, 264
    popular religious, 55, 60, 173, 175–8, 180,
        182–4, 188–9, 195–6
feudalism
    cinema, 303, 308
    Confucianism, 11, 153
    literature, 220, 222
    modernity &, 5, 46, 54–5, 57–8
    music & performing arts, 258–9, 267–8
    religious traditions, 175–6
    socialism &, 163, 165, 167
fiction. *see* literature
Field, Andrew, 304
Fifth Generation (cinema), 13, 297, 312, 314
film. *see* cinema
Flath, James, 61
Foguangsham, Buddha's Light Mountain,
    186–8
folk culture, 3, 55–6, 61, 100, 176, 253, 259,
    263–4, 328
food, 11, 96–7, 104–5, 174, 178, 185–6, 344
footbinding, 2, 29, 95, 259
Forbidden City, Beijing, 282, 287
foreign concessions, 9, 23–4, 28, 31, 118, 225,
    275, 281, 305
foreign cultures, 8, 86
    art, 273–4, 280, 284
    cinema, 297–300, 302, 316
    literature, 219, 241, 246, 250
    media, 321, 327, 332
    music & performing arts, 257, 260
    see also Japan; Western culture
foreign investment, 20, 42–3, 63, 163
foreign powers, 4, 22, 298, 345
    art, 275, 285
    cinema, 298
    Confucianism &, 141
    diaspora cultures, 121, 126–7
    gender, 74
    historiography, 46, 48–9, 51–4, 56–7, 59,
        61–2, 65
    literary response, 218–20, 222, 227, 230

military, 4, 23, 25–6, 135–6, 189, 191–2,
    218–19, 298
    music & performing arts, 256
    religious traditions, 174, 189–92
    socialism, 159, 163, 170
    sociopolitical history, 22–5, 28, 31–2
    sports, 349
foreign students, 1, 265
Formosa. *see* Taiwan
France
    art, 275–6, 279, 283, 288
    cinema, 315
    ethnicity, 92
    historiography, 3, 52, 55
    literature, 225
    music & performing arts, 262–3, 267
    religious traditions, 189
    socialism, 158, 160, 162
frontier societies. *see* migrant societies
Fu Baoshi, 276, 282, 286–8
Fu Manchu, 2
Fu Poshek, 305
Fujian, 7, 95, 119, 181–2, 186, 194, 199

Gan dialect, 198
Gang of Four, 12
Gansu, 101, 174, 199, 201
Gao Jianfu, 276–8, 285
Gao Xingjian, 249, 262–3
Gao Yihan, 30
Gaoshans language, 201
GDP, 40, 42–3
gender, 17, **68–90**
    academic debates, **80–2**
    diaspora cultures, 120
    equality & discrimination, 70–1, 80–1,
        84–5, 138–9
    ethnicity &, 107
    literature, 245
    market narratives, 77–9
    marketization, 70–1, **77–9**, 81, 83
    May Fourth Movement (1919), 72–3
    narrative interventions, 83–7
    neutrality (androgyny), 76–9, 84–5, 245,
        261, 329
    performing arts, 261, **266–8**
    socialism, **73–7**
    sociopolitical history, 27
    sports & physical culture, 341–3, 347, 353–5
'Generation X,' 250
gentry. *see* scholar-gentry *(wenren)*
Germany, 9, 31, 157, 225, 266, 285, 330, 340,
    346
Giles, Herbert A., 340–1, 355
Gladney, Dru, 97, 100, 173–4
globalization

art, 272–4, 293
capitalism & socialism, 155–6, 169
cinema, 13, 130, 297, 299, **314–16**, 347
Confucianism, 143–4, 146, 148–9, **150–3**
cultural influences, 1, 13, 16–19
diaspora cultures, 117–18, 124, 126, 131–2
gender, 69–70, 79, 81, 83, 85–7
historiography, 53
literature, 242, 250
media, 318, 330–3, 336
music & performing arts, 266, 269
religious traditions, 194
sociopolitical history, 44
sports & physical culture, 346–58
see also international politics;
    internationalism
GMD. *see* Nationalist Party
Google.com, 336
governance, 4–5, 13, 20, 30, 124, 138, 150–1
Great Commonwealth, 5
Great Leap Forward (1958–60), 36–7, 166,
    319, 349
Greece, classical, 15, 57, 145, 148, 241, 340,
    343, 355
Gu Cheng, 246
Gu Hongming, 125
Gu Jiegang, 51–2, 54
Gu Mu, 136
Gu Wenda, 292
Guan Shanyue, 285, 288
Guangdong, 7, 95, 119, 181–3, 199
    see also Guangzhou (Canton)
Guangxi, 199, 201, 214
Guangxu emperor, 4, 24
Guangzhou (Canton)
    art, 274, 280, 293
    historiography, 59, 61
    Internet, 332
    music & performing arts, 265
    religious traditions, 191
    socialism, 156, 163
    sociopolitical history, 28, 31, 33
Guanyin, 187
Guizhou, 199, 201
Gunn, Edward, 245
Guo Moruo, 257
Guo Yuhua, 83
guohua (national painting), 276
Guomindang. *see* Nationalist Party
guoyu. see Modern Standard Chinese

Hainan, 199, 332
Hainan spy plane encounter (2001), 97
Hakka dialect (Kejia), 198, 298, 308–9
Hakka people, 95, 182
Han Chinese

cinema, 308
Confucianism, 137
diaspora culture, 125
ethnicity, 8, 92–3, 95–102, 104–6, 108,
    111–12
gender, 69
historiography, 49–50, 52, 63–4
homogenization myth, **94–7**
languages, 199–200, 214
literature, 248
music & performing arts, 258
physical culture, 342
religious traditions, 173, 194
sociopolitical history, 24, 26–7, 30
Han dynasty (206 BC–AD 220), 47, 56, 181, 183,
    203, 277, 327
Han Shaogong, 249–51
Han Zhixun (Hon Chi-fun), 289–90
Hanfei, 12
Hangzhou, 280, 291
Hao Ran, 230
Harrison, Henrietta, 29
He Bingsong, 56
He Jianjun, 315
He Lin, 141
He Long, 351
He Zhen, 158
He Zhenliang, 348, 353, 355
Hebei, 199
Heilongjiang, 199, 201
Henan, 199
Hindi/Urdu language, 198
Hinduism, 119–20
historiography, **46–67**
    cultural sites, 3
    diaspora cultures, **116–21**
    ethnicity, **108–9**
    gender, 68, 70, 72, 87
    imperial era, 21
    Liang Qichao, **48–50**
    literature, 219
    Maoist China (1949–76), **55–8**
    periodization, 3–4, 47–50, 68, 72, 87, 273
    reform era & globalization, **58–65**
    religious traditions, **174–6**
    Republic (1912–49), **50–5**
    socialism, **155–72**
HIV/AIDS, 80
Hmong language, 95
Ho, David, 130
Hobsbawm, Eric, 60
Hockx, Michel, chapter by, 14, **235–52**
Hodgson, Dorothy L., 69, 78
Hohhot, 92, 105–6
Hokkien language. *see* Hakka dialect
Hollywood cinema, 307, 315–16

Hon Chi-fun. *see* Han Zhixun
Hong Kong
    art, 275, 288–90, 293
    Buddhism, 187–8
    Chineseness, 9, 11
    cinema, 297, 299–301, 303, 305, **309–14**
    Confucianism, 150, 152
    culture, 124, 129–30, 132
    Daoism, 181–3
    ethnicity, 95, 100, 118
    gender, 86
    historiography, 61, 63
    Internet, 331
    languages, 200, 208, 215
    literature, 244–5
    modernity, 7
    religious traditions, 176, 178, 190
    Special Administrative Region, 182, 311
    TV, 322
Hong Shen, 257
Hou Bo, 284
Hou Hsiao-hsien, 297, 313
Hsiao Kung-ch'uan, 139
Hsu, Henry, 349
Hu, King, 310
Hu Feng, 223
Hu Hanmin, 162
Hu Jintao, 169
Hu Mei, 312–13
Hu Sheng, 57
Hu Shi, 30, 53–4, 211, 257
Hu Yepin, 226
Huang, David Henry, 132
huaqiao. see diaspora cultures
huayu. see Modern Standard Chinese
Hubei, 199, 214
Hui dialect, 198
Hui people, 95, **102–6**, 111, 174, 201
human rights, 43, 73–4, 151, 332, 336, 345
    see also dissent
humanism, 11, 22, 73, 75, 151–2, 357
humanitarianism, 30
Hunan, 191, 199, 201, 214, 242, 266, 329
Hundred Flowers Campaign, 231

Ibsen, Henrik, 72, 257
ideology
    art, 280, 283, 286–7
    cinema, 307
    Confucianism, 147
    diaspora cultures, 123, 126–9
    gender, 69, 72, 75, 77, 81, 84, 87
    historiography, 55, 58, 63–4
    literature, 218, 221, 243, 246, 248
    media, 318–19, 324, 328, 330
    music & performing arts, 258–9, 265

socialism, 157, 161, 163–5, 167, 170
sociopolitical history, 31–3, 37, 40–1, 44
sports & physical culture, 344, 349
imperial China
    art, 274, 277, 280, 293
    Chinese language, **201–5**, 208
    Confucianism, **135–41**, 151
    culture, 6, 47
    diaspora cultures, 116, 118, 120–1, 128, 132
    ethnicity, 92, 95
    historiography, 47–53, 55–6, 58, 60, 62
    history, 7–8
    media portrayals, 309, 327–8
    music & performing arts, 262, 267
    sociopolitical history, **20–30**
    TV depictions, 327
    see also the names of dynasties
imperial examinations. *see* civil service
    examinations
imperialism, foreign. *see* foreign powers
Impressionism, 279
India, 144–5, 183, 330, 339
Indo-European languages, 201
Indonesia, 115, 119–20, 123, 125, 130–1, 351
industry
    art, 283
    Confucianism, 136, 143
    gender, 69, 78
    language reform, 215
    literature &, 219, 225–6
    socialism, 158–9, 162, 166–7
    sociopolitical history, 21, 28, 31–2, 35, 37,
        40–2, 121
Inner Mongolia, 96–7, 99, 101, 105, 108–9,
    201, 214
integration
    diaspora cultures, 119
    ethnic minorities, 93, 101, 308
intellectuals
    Chinese language, 201–2
    Confucianism, 151
    diaspora cultures, 129
    ethnicity, 102–3, 109–10
    gender, 72–3
    historiography, 56, 58
    literature, 219–20, 227, 229, 231, 235,
        237–9, 247, 249, 251
    modernity, 7
    music & performing arts, 262
    physical culture, 340–3
    religious traditions, 173–4
    socialism, 156–60, 165–6
    sociopolitical history, 27–8, 30, 32, 34–5,
        38–40, 42–3
International Olympics Committee (IOC),
    339, 345–51, **352–3**, 355

international politics
  contemporary, 1, 3, 100
  diaspora cultures, 132
  ethnicity, 106
  ping-pong diplomacy, 350–2
  religious traditions, 190–1, 195
  sports, 342, **347–55**
  see also Cold War; Communist
      International (Comintern)
International Settlement, Shanghai, 225
internationalism, 6, 164, 225
  see also globalization
Internet
  alternative media & public forum, **330–2**
  censorship, 43, **335–6**
  culture &, 18
  gender, 79
  literature, 250–1
  religious traditions, 179
  urban youth culture, 7, **332–5**
  written language, 15
  see also television
involutionary tradition (literature), 218, 220,
      232, **235–52**
IPTV (Internet television), 321, 330, 335
Islam
  diaspora culture, 119, 125, 131
  Mainland culture, 18, 50–1, 103–6, 111,
      173–5, 188
Italy, 188

Jankowiak, William, chapter by, 8, **91–114**
Japan
  art, 274–6, 282, 285
  cinema, 298–9, 305, 308, 313, 316
  Confucianism, 136, 151–2
  diaspora culture, 116, 119, 122–3, 126
  ethnicity, 94, 100, 109
  gender, 72, 86
  historiography, 48–9, 51–2, 54, 56–7, 60–2,
      64–5
  Internet, 330, 332–3
  language, 205, 209
  literature, 219, 223, 225–7, 239, 241–2, 245
  modernity, 3, 5
  music & performing arts, 254–8, 260–1,
      300
  Olympics, 339
  religious traditions, 175–6, 179, 185–6,
      190, 192–4
  socialism, 156, 158, 162, 165–6
  sociopolitical history, 22, 24–7, 30–2, 34–6
  sports, 340, 342, 347, 350–4
  Taiwan occupation (1895–1945), 176, 308
  TV, 322, 327
  war with China (1894–5), 24, 136

war with China (1937–55) (see Japanese
      occupation (1937–45))
  war with Russia (1904–6), 255
Japanese language, 204
Japanese occupation (1937–45)
  art, 282
  cinema, 305
  diaspora cultures, 122, 126
  literature, 223, 226–7, 237, 242, 244–5, 255
  religious traditions, 176
  sport, 352
  war atrocities, 64
Jesuits, 188, 208, 216
  See also Roman Catholic Christianity
Jesus Family, 192
Jet Li (Li Lianjie), 301, 347
Jews, 99, 117–18, 188
Jia Lusheng, 231
Jia Zhangke, 315
Jiang Kanghu, 157–8
Jiang Qing, 260, 266, 351
Jiangsu, 95–6, 199, 325–6
Jiangxi, 199
Jiangxi Soviet, 34–5
Jilin, 199, 201
Jin dialect, 198
Jin Yong, 327
Jing language, 201
jingju. see Peking Opera
journalism. *see* media
Ju Ming. *see* Zhu Ming
Judaism, 99, 117–18, 188

Kam-Tai languages, 95, 201
Kang Youwei, 4–5, 24, 26, 48, 60, 62, 137–41,
      146
Kant, Immanuel, 147–8
Katayama Sen, 162
Kawakami Hajime, 156, 162
Kazakh language, 95, 201
Kazakhs, 94–5, 174
Kejia. *see* Hakka dialect
Key, Ellen, 73
Khaw Soo Cheang, 131
Killanin, Lord, 349–50, 352–3
Kingston, Maxine Hong, 132
Kirgiz language, 201
Koguryo, 62, 65
Kong Xianxi. *see* Kung, H. H.
Korea
  Confucianism, 151–2
  diaspora culture, 52, 116, 119
  ethnicity, 100
  gender, 86
  historiography, 62, 64–5
  socialism, 156, 167

sociopolitical history, 24
sports, 350
TV, 327
Korean language, 95, 201, 204
Korean War, 167, 230, 259
Koreans (minority), 308
Koselleck, Reinhart, 48
Kotoku Shusui, 156
Koxinga. *see* Zheng Chenggong
Kropotkinites, 145, 158, 161–2, 166
Kucong people, 99
Kung, H. H. (Kong Xianxi), 339
kung fu, 16, 297, 302, 346
Kwan, Stanley, 304

Lai Chi Tim, 182
land reform, 34–6, 41, 158, 167, 185
languages, 7–8, **198–217**
    cinema, 298, 302
    Confucianism, 136
    culture &, 15
    diaspora cultures, 14, 118, 125
    ethnicity &, 95, 97–8, 104–5, **106–8**, 111
    media, 334
    religious traditions, 176, 194–5
    sociopolitical history, 22
    see also Chinese language
Lao She (Shu Qingchun), 221, 227, 259–60
Latin America, 116, 123–4, 283, 351
Latin script. *see* romanization
Laughlin, Charles, chapter by, 14, **218–34**
League of Left-wing Writers (*Zhongguo zuoyi
    zuojia lianmeng*), 225–6
Lee, Ang (Li Ang), 130, 297
Lee, Bruce, 297, 347
Lee, Haiyan, 62
Lee Kuan Yew, 130
Lee Xing, 309
leftists, 34, 218, 225–6, 303, 305, 309, 349
    see also Communist Party
Legalism, 12–13, 53
Leninism, 32–3, 156, 163–4, 168
Levenson, Joseph, 55, 136
Li Ang (Ang Lee), 130, 297
Li Da, 73
Li Dazhao, 73
Li Feigan (Bajin), 152
Li Hong-zhang, 60, 135
Li Hongzhi, 179, 345
Li, Jet (Li Lianjie), 301, 347
Li Keran, 285, 287
Li Lianjie (Jet Li), 301, 347
Li Shaohong, 302
Li Shizeng, 158
Li Tie, 309
Li Xiaojiang, 80–1

Li Yinhe, 80, 82
Li Yuchun, 329
Li Zhensheng, 284
Liang Qichao
    literature, 60, 219, 223, 235, 254
    New Historiography, 47, **48–50**, 53–4
    reformism, 4–5, 26, 342
    women's education, 29
Liang Shuming, 11, 18, 141, 143–6
Liang Sicheng, 288
Liaoning, 199, 201
liberalism
    art, 273, 293
    Confucianism, 151, 153
    diaspora cultures, 124, 127–8
    gender, 70, 72–3
    historiography, 54, 62
    literature, 219, 231
    sociopolitical history, 34
Liebold, James, 64
Lim Boon Keng (Lin Wenqing), 125
Lin Fengmian, 27, 276, 279–81, 283, 287
Lin Wenqing. *see* Lim Boon Keng
Lin Zexu, 135
Lin Zhaohua, 262
lineages. *see* clans & lineages
literacy, 22, 26, 202–4, 215, 219, 225, 341
Literary Association (*Wenxue yanjiu hui*),
    224, 226
Literary Revolution, 235
literati. *see* scholar-gentry (*wenren*)
literature
    Chinese language, 203, 211–12, 215
    Communist Party, **228–9**
    culture &, 1–2, 14–16
    diaspora cultures, 123
    gender, 70, 77, 82
    genres, **237–9**, 346
    historiography, 53–5
    involutionary tradition, 14, **235–52**
    media &, 328, 333–4
    recent developments, **250–1**
    revolutionary tradition, 14, 26, 54, **218–34**,
        235–42, 250, 252
    socialism, 162
    sociopolitical history, 22, 26–8, 30–1, 34,
        37–9, 43, 254–9
    see also New Literature
Liu Baiyu, 229
Liu Binyan, 230–1
Liu Chunhua, 283–4
Liu E, 237–8
Liu Guosong (Liu Kuo-song), 289–90, 293
Liu Haisu, 279
Liu Kaiqu, 288
Liu Kang, chapter by, 6–7, **318–38**

Liu Kuo-song. *see* Liu Guosong
Liu Shipei, 11, 158
Liu Shuxian, 141
Liu Sifu (Shifu), 158
London Missionary Society, 191
Long March, 35, 163
Louie, Kam, 235, 342, 347
   chapter by, **1–19**
Lu Dongbin, 182–3
Lu Ling, 223
Lu Shoukun (Lui Shou-kwan), 289–90
Lu Xun (Zhou Shuren), 31, 54, 220, **223**, 223,
   225, 241–2
Lu Zhuangzhang, 209
Lui Shou-kwan. *see* Lu Shoukun
Lutherans, 195

Ma Yifu, 141
Ma Yoyo, 132
Ma Yuan, 248
Macau, 7, 95, 118, 124, 129, 132, 188, 191, 274
McDougall, Bonnie S., 235
Mackay, George L., 194
Mackerras, Colin, 108
   chapter by, 13, **253–71**
Malaysia, 108, 117, 119, 123, 125, 127, 130–2
management. *see* governance
Manchu dynasty. *see* Qing (Manchu) dynasty
   (1644–1911)
Manchu-Tungus languages, 95, 201
Manchuria, 34, 51–2
Manchurians, 201
Manchus
   minority, 50, 99, 342
   music & performing arts, 259
   religious traditions, 174, 185
Mandarin Chinese, 198–200, 202–3, 205–7,
   212–13, 216
   cinema, 302–3, 308–9
   distribution, 198
   ethnicity, 95, 98, 105–7
   religious traditions, 194–5
   sports, 344
   see also Modern Standard Chinese
mandarins. *see* bureaucracy; scholar-gentry
   (*wenren*)
Mang Ke, 246
Manichaeism, 188
Manifesto (1958), 142–3
Mao Dun, 224–5, 228
Mao Zedong
   art, 283–6, 288
   cinema, 312
   historiography, 57–8, 65
   as 'Kang Liang,' 4
   literature, 227, 231

   music & performing arts, 258, 260–1, 265
   physical culture, 341, 344, 346, 351–2
   religious traditions, 194
   socialism, 156, 160, 163–6
   sociopolitical history, 34–6
   'Talks' (1942), 227–9, 282
   TV, 319–20
Maoist China (1949–1976)
   art, **283–8**, 292
   Confucianism, 147
   culture, 15
   diaspora culture, 129
   gender, 70–1, 75, 77, 83, 85, 87
   historical consciousness, **55–8**
   historiography, 54
   Internet, 333
   literature, 229, **245–7**
   music & performing arts, **258–61**,
     267–8
   physical culture, 344
   socialism, 168
   sociopolitical structures, 20, **37–44**
Marchetti, Gina, 307
marketization
   art, 295
   cinema, 312–16
   Confucianism, 152
   ethnicity &, 103, 106
   gender, 70–1, **77–9**, 81, 83
   historiography, 61
   literature, 236, 252
   media, 321–3, 330, 333–5
   music & performing arts, 269
   sociopolitical history, 40–2
   sports & physical culture, 354
   see also consumer culture
martial arts, 18, 297, 300–2, 309–10, 316,
   327–8, 341–3, **345–7**
Marxism
   Chinese revolution, 5, **161–7**
   Confucianism &, 147
   gender, 70, 73–5
   historiography, 56–7
   literature, 223, 229
   sinicization of (*Makesi zhuyide*
     Zhongguohua), 164
   socialism &, 156, 160, 162, 164–5, 168, 170
   sociopolitical history, 22, 32, 34
masculinity. *see* gender
mass culture
   art, 282
   historiography, 16, 55, 62
   literature, 228
   music & performing arts, 258–9
   socialism, 157, 165
   sociopolitical history, 34, 37–8

materialism, 56–7, 84, 142, 144–5, 147, 150, 168
May Fourth Movement (1919)
  art, 282
  culture, 3–5
  gender, 70, 72–3, 75, 82
  historiography, 53–6, 59–60
  literature, 232, 248
  music & performing arts, 254, 256–7
  socialism, 156, 160, 162
  sociopolitical history, 31, 33
  sports & physical culture, 326, 350–1, 353–5
May Thirtieth Movement, 33, 163
media
  art, 280, 287
  diaspora cultures, 122, 124
  gender, 72–3, 77–80, 83–4, 86
  historiography, 61
  language, 213
  literature, 219, 223, 229, 231, **236–7**, 240, 248, 250
  music & performing arts, 256, 264–6
  religious traditions, 179, 185, 193–5
  sociopolitical history, 24, 27–8, 31, 43
  sports & physical culture, 355
  see also Internet; television
medicine, Chinese, 55, 343
Mei Guangdi, 240
Mei Lanfang, 257, 268, 300
Meiji Restoration (Japan), 5, 49, 205, 219
Mencius, 140, 151, 340
merchants. *see* commerce
Miao people, 98, 242
Miao-Yao languages, 95, 201
middle class. *see* bourgeoisie
migrant societies, 10, 16, 117–18, 123–4, 128–9
  see also diaspora cultures
migration, internal, 41–2, 78, 80, 84, 96, 101–2, 106
military
  foreign powers, 4, 23, 25–6, 135–6, 189, 191–2, 218–19, 298
  historiography, 48, 60
  literature, 222, 226, 228–30
  music & performing arts, 258
  socialism &, 163–4
  sociopolitical history, 24, 29–30, 32–7, 39–40
  sports & physical culture, 340–2, 345–6, 351, 355–6
  Taiwan, 176, 194–5, 293, 313
  see also martial arts; Red Army
Min dialect, 194, 198–9, 209, 213
Ming dynasty (1368–1644), 21, 59, 120, 141–2, 181, 202–3, 310

Ming Taizu, 3
minorities. *see* ethnicity
minsheng. see people's livelihood
missionaries
  Buddhist, 183, 196
  Christian, 23, 25, 142, 175, **188–95**, 208, 340
Mo Yan, 250
mobile phones. *see* cellular phones
mode of production, Asiatic, 57–9
modern Chinese culture
  definition, **1–19**
  diaspora cultures, 132
Modern Chinese Dictionary (1998), 204, 207
Modern Chinese language, 206, 211
Modern Standard Chinese (*putonghua, guoyu, huayu*), 125, 199–200, 204, 206–7, 210, 212–14, 302–3
Modern Written Chinese, 205, 211–12
modernity
  artistic modernism, 273–9, 281–3, 287, 289–90, 293
  cinema, 298, 300, **301–3**, 304–5, 309, 311–24
  definition, **3–7**, 12–13, 18
  diaspora cultures, 115–19, **121–5**
  gender, 68–9, 71, 76, 78–9, 84–7
  historiography, 46–50, 53, 56, 58
  literary modernism, 218, 220, 232, 235, 238–9, 243–4, 247, 250–1
  music & performing arts, 262
  New Confucianism, **141–3**
  religious traditions, 193, 195
  socialism, 160–1, 169
modernization
  art, 276
  cinema, 298–9, 309, 314
  Confucianism, 135–41, 143–7, 150–3
  diaspora cultures, 118, 122, 124–5, 128
  gender, 83, 85
  historiography, 3, 5, 59, 61
  languages, **198–217**
  literature, 219, 239, 242
  music & performing arts, 254, 264
  religious traditions, 174, 195
  socialism &, 158
  sociopolitical history, 20–1, 23–4, 27–9, 43
  sports & physical culture, 158, 340–1, 343, 346, 355
Moism, 12–13, 53
Mongolia, 21, 52, 64
Mongolian languages, 95, 109, 201
Mongoloid peoples, 116
Mongols, 50–1, 92, 94, 97, 99, 101, 105–9, 111, 174
monks & nuns, 180, 183–8
mono-culturalism, 91–4, 102, 106, 108
Moore, Henry, 290

morality. *see* ethics
Morrison, Robert, 191
Mou Zongsan, 12, 141–3, **147–50**
movies. *see* cinema
Mozi, 12–13, 53
multi-culturalism, 91–5, 102, 106, 109–11, 153
Murphy, Henry K., 282
museums, 3, 61–2, 280, 356–7
music & performing arts, 13, **253–71**
    Chinese language, 203
    Confucianism, 148
    diaspora cultures, 130, 132
    gender, 72, 76, 78–9, **266–8**
    historiography, 55
    late Qing reform, **254–6**
    literary drama, 218, 220, 224, 226–8
    Maoist China (1949–76), 39, **258–61**
    post-Maoist China, 43, **261–6**
    Republic (1912–1949), **256–8**
    television, 328–9
    see also opera; television
Muslims. *see* Islam
mythology, 21–2, 52, 75, 108, 135, 242, 345

Nahm-mouh lao, 182
Nanjing, 33, 240, 280, 282, 325–6
Nanjing Decade (1928–37), 20, 33, 40
'National Culture.' *see* popular culture
National Day, 29
National Essence School, 11, 27, 346
national identity. *see* nationalism
national language. *see* Modern Standard
    Chinese
National Language Movement, 205
national minorities. *see* ethnicity
National People's Congress, 260, 355
National Salvation Movement, 166
nationalism
    art, 273, 276–7, 279–80, 283, 285, 288–9,
      293
    Chinese language, 201
    cinema, 297–9, 304–5, **306–9**, 310–16
    culture &, 6, 16
    diaspora cultures, 122–3, 126, 129
    ethnicity, 91–2, 94, 97, 101–1, **108–9**, 112
      (*see also* ethnic nationalism)
    gender, 79
    historiography, 47–56, 59–65
    media, 332
    music & performing arts, 255, 257, 259
    national identity, 5–6, **46–67**
    socialism &, 155, 162–4, 170
    sociopolitical history, 20–1, 26, 28–35,
      42, 44
    sports & physical culture, 339–42, 346–7,
      350, 353–4, 358

Nationalist Party (Guomindang, GMD)
    architecture, 282
    art, 288, 293
    cinema, 301–2, 305–6, 308, 312–13
    diaspora culture, 126
    early twentieth century, **30–7**
    historiography, 6, 52, 56–7, 59
    languages, 207
    literature, 225
    religious traditions, 175–6, 185–6, 190, 194
    socialism &, 157, 162–6
    sports, 347–8
nationalization, 37, 306
naturalism. *see* realism
Neilson ratings (TV), 322, 326
Neo-Confucians
    modern (*see* New Confucianism)
    Song & Ming dynasty, 141–2
Nestorian Christianity, 188
Netherlands, 115–16, 190, 194
Netherlands East Indies. *see* Indonesia
Network News (*Xinwen lianbo*), 323–5
New Confucianism (*xin ruxue*), 11–13, 17–18,
    140, **141–53**
    anarchism, 161
    global discourses, **150–3**
    Mou Zongsan, **147–50**
    response to iconoclastic modernizers,
      143–7
    Western modernity and, **141–3**
    see also Confucianism
New Culture Movement (*xin wenhua yundong*)
    art, 273, 282
    Confucianism &, 12, 143
    languages, 211, 216
    literature, 240, 242
    music & performing arts, 256–7
    physical culture, 346
    socialism, 158, 162
    sociopolitical history, 30–1, 40
New Democracy, 165–9
The New Era, 158
New Literature (*xin wenxue*), **239–41**
New National Pronunciation (*xin guoyin*),
    206
New Policy (Qing), 25
New Wave. *see* cinema
New World Society, 158
New Youth (journal), 53, 256
New Zealand. *see* Australasia
Newer New Humanity
    (*xinxin renlei*), 333
news, 318–20, 323–6, 331–2, 335
newspapers. *see* media
NGOs, 43, 80
Ni Tuoshen, 192

Ningxia, 199
Nobel Prize, 262
Non-Aligned Movement, 351
non-Chinese languages, 200–1, 210, 212,
    214–15, 239, 298, 357
    see also English language
North America
    art, 272, 283
    cinema, 316
    diaspora culture, 116–17, 122–4, 127–31
    socialism, 158
    sports, 347
    see also Canada; United States
northern China, 100, 178, 180, 191–3, 198,
    202–3, 206
Northern Expedition, 32–3, 225
novels. *see* literature

Oceania, 115, 123–4
    See also Australasia
Oei Tiong Ham, 131
officials. *see* bureaucracy
Old Chinese language, 202–3, 211–12
Old National Pronunciation (*lao guoyin*), 206
Old Summer Palace. *see* Yuanmingyuan
Olympic Charter, 348
Olympic Committee of the People's Republic
    of China, 353
Olympics, 18, **339–60**, 341, 350–1
    2008 Games (Beijing), 1, 18, 346, 348, 355,
    356–8
    post-Maoist period, 339–40, 345–6, **353–6**,
    358
    struggle for readmission to IOC, 352–3
    see also International Olympics
    Committee
one-child policy, 41
one China principle, 348, 352
opening up. *see* post-Maoist China
opera
    cinema, 300, 308
    European, 260, 263, 266
    gender, 69, 76–7
    historiography, 55
    religious traditions, 177–8, 182–3, 196
    revolutionary model, 230
    sociopolitical history, 22, 253, 258, 268
    see also Cantonese opera; Peking Opera
    (*jingju*)
opium, 189, 191
Opium Wars, 3–4, 22, 61–2, 174, 191
Orientalism, 2, 10, 85, 142, 340–3
Osugi Sakae, 156
Outer Mongolia, 51
Ouyang Yuqian, 257, 267
Ovechkin, Valentin, 230

Overmyer, Daniel L., chapter by, 17–18,
    173–97
overseas Chinese. *see* diaspora cultures

painting. *see* art
Pan Jiajun, 283–4
Pan, Lynn, 63
Pang Laikwan, 299
patriotism. *see* nationalism
peasant culture
    cinema, 306
    Confucianism, 151
    ethnicity, 92–3, 102–3
    gender, 76, 78
    literature, 222, 224, 226–9, 242
    music & performing arts, 258–9, 264
    rebellions, 22, 25, 54, 226
    socialism, 15, 164–5
    sociopolitical history, 27, 33–8, 40–2
Pei, Y. M., 130
Peking. *see* Beijing
Peking Opera (*jingju*), 230, 255, 260–1, 300
Peking University, 12, 30, 53, 241, 280
Pentecostalists, 192, 195
People's Daily (Renmin ribao), 323, 331
People's Liberation Army. *see* Red Army
People's Literary Press, 259
people's livelihood (*minsheng*), 32, 163
People's Republic of China (PRC)
    art, 273, 275–6, 282–8, 292
    Chineseness, 8
    cinema, 297, 299, 301–3, **306–9**, 310, 312,
    314
    Confucianism, 141, 146–7, 150, 153
    diaspora cultures &, 128
    ethnicity, 93–5, 103, 109
    gender, 74, 83
    historiography, 56–7, 63–5
    languages, 206, 208, 212–13, 215
    literature, 222, 229, 248
    modernity, 4, 6
    Olympics, 339
    religious traditions, 175, 178, 180, 185,
    187–9, 193
    socialism, 167, 169
    sports, 347–53
    TV, 319
    underground literature, **245–7**
    see also Maoist China (1949–76); post-
    Maoist China (1978–)
peranakan (Baba) culture, 119, 125, 131
performing arts. *see* music & performing arts
periodization. *see* historiography
Philippines, 116, 119, 125, 130–1, 190
philosophy
    body culture, 343

Confucianism, 135–6, 138–44, 147, 150, 153
culture, 1–2, 11–12, 15
  gender, 73
  historiography, 53
  literature, 218–19
  socialism, 159, 164
  sociopolitical history, 22, 27, 31
physical culture, 18, **339–60**
  Chinese vs Western body culture, **343–5**
  sociopolitical history, 29
  see also martial arts
pilgrimages
  Buddhist, 183, 186
  Muslim, 173
ping-pong diplomacy, **350–2**
pinyin *(hanyu pinyin)*, 15, 209–11, 213
Pizi Cai. *see* Bum Cai
plays. *see* music & performing arts
poetry. *see* literature
politics
  art, 273, 277, 282–9, 291, 293
  Chinese language, 201–2, 205, 208, 213
  cinema, 302, 306, 310, 312
  Confucianism, 135, 138–40, 147–52
  culture &, 15–16
  diaspora cultures, 9, 117–21, 123–30
  early twentieth century, **24–30**, 32
  ethnicity, 94–7, **98–101**, 102–3, 110, 112
  gender, 71, 73–7, 82–3, 85–7
  historiography, 46, 48, 50, 52, 54, 56, 58–9,
    63–4
  history, 4, 6–7, 13, **20–45**, 68
  literature, 218–22, 225, 227–32, 235–6, 238,
    245, 247, 250–1
  media, 318–19, 322, 325, 327, 330–2, 335–6
  music & performing arts, 253–5, 261, 265
  religion &, 18, 187, 193–5
  socialism &, 156–7, 160–1, 164–5, 167–9
  sports & physical culture, 341, 345, 347–53
  see also international politics;
    sociopolitical structures; state
pollution. *see* environment
popular culture ('National Culture')
  art, 293
  Chineseness, 11
  diaspora cultures, 119
  literature, 218, 220, 254, 309
  Maoist, 15, 54–6
  media, 328–30, 333, 335
  music & performing arts, 254, 259, 335
pornography, 43, 80, 266
Portuguese, 188, 349
post-Chinese culture, 13–14
post-Maoist China (1978–)
  art, 273, 275, 284, **288–95**
  Chinese language & culture, 1–2

Chineseness, 11
cinema, 301, **311–16**
  ethnicity, 93
  gender, 71, **77–9**, 80, 83, 85
  government, 1–2
  historiography, **58–65**
  literature, 237, 244–52
  media, **318–38**
  modernity, 5
  music & performing arts, 254, **261–6**, 269
  Olympics, **353–6**
  religious traditions, 193
  socialism, 157, 166, 169
  sociopolitical history, 20–1, **37–44**
  sports & physical culture, 344–6, 352,
    353–8
Postal system, 209
postmodernism, 13, 275
postsocialist society, 169
poverty, 20, 43, 103, 120, 221
power
  culture &, 16
  diaspora cultures, 117
  gender, 75, 261
  literature, 219–20, 231, 235
  socialism &, 155, 168, 170
Presbyterian Church, 176, 191–2, 194–5
print culture. *see* media
privatization, 42
progress
  cinema, 299, 314
  Confucianism, 135, 138
  diaspora cultures, 117
  ethnicity &, 100, 103
  gender &, 87
  historiography, 47–8, 50, 55–7
  language &, 212
  sociopolitical history, 21, 26
proletarian literature, **225–6**
proletariat. *see* workers
Protestant Christianity, 173, 175–6, 189, **191–5**
publishing. *see* media
Pure Land School, 183, 186

Qi Rushan, 257
Qian Gang, 231
Qian Mu, 141
Qian Xuantong, 257
Qiangguo luntan. see Strong Power Forum
Qianlong era (1796), 49
qigong (energy cultivation), 1, 78, 179, 344–5
Qin dynasty (221–206 BC), 7, 49, 56, 199, 203
Qin Zhaoyang, 231
Qing (Manchu) dynasty (1644–1911)
  art, 282, 288, 290
  cinema, 298, **299–301**, 310

Confucianism, 135, **135–41**, 136, 139
diaspora culture, 120, 125
ethnicity, 94–5
historiography, 4–5, 46, 48, 50–1, 53, 57–8,
    60, 62
languages, 203
late reformers, 4–5
literature, 218–19, 236–8
music & performing arts, **254–6**, 255
physical culture, 342
reformists, 4–5, 23–6, 50, 60, 135–40, 158,
    174–5, 185, 254–6, 341–3
religious traditions, 174–5, 181, 185–6, 189
socialism, 156–8
sociopolitical history, 20, **21–4**, 25–30, 33,
    38, 43
sports, 340, 346
TV depictions, 327
Qinghai, 101, 214
Qinghua University, 143
Qu Yuan, 242
Quanzhen Complete Perfection School,
    180–3
quoyu. see Modern Standard Chinese

race. *see* ethnicity
Rack, Mary, 98
re-education, 38, 231
realism
    art, 276–7, 283, 285, 290
    cinema, 299, 303, 305–9, 312–13
    literature, 218–20, **223–5**, 236, 248
    performing arts, 257, 259
Reclus, Elisee, 158
rectification campaign (1942), 36–7, 75
Red Army (later, People's Liberation Army),
    34, 163, 166, 308, 312
Red Guards, 39, 43, 61, 76–7, 85
Reform Era. *see* post-Maoist China
reformists. *see* Qing (Manchu) dynasty
Religious Affairs Bureau, 175, 189
religious traditions, 17–18, **173–97**
    art &, 280, 284
    Confucianism &, 139, 145, 149, 173
    culture &, 15
    diaspora cultures, 117, 119, 121, 125
    ethnicity &, 103–5
    historical background, 52, **174–6**
    indigenous popular sects, 173, 176, **178–9**,
        180, 184–6, 189, 192, 249
    local community traditions, 17, 55, 60, 173,
        175, **176–8**
    media, 332
    music & performing arts, 254, 264
    sociopolitical history, 22, 38, 43
    sports & physical culture, 342, 345

see also Buddhism; Christianity; Daoism;
    festivals; monks & nuns; pilgrimages;
    temples
Ren Bonian, 282
Renan, Ernest, 55
Renmin ribao. see People's Daily
reportage literature *(baogao wenxue)*, 226,
    229–32
Republic (1912–1949)
    art, 273–5, **276–82**, 283, 285, 287–8
    cinema, 298, 300, **301–6**
    Confucianism, 139
    ethnicity, 94
    gender, 70
    historiography, 50, **50–5**, 64
    languages, 209
    literature, 220, 237, 241–5, 249
    modernity, 3, 6
    music & performing arts, **256–8**, 268
    Olympics, 339
    religious traditions, 174–5, 178, 185–6
    socialism, 156, 158
    sociopolitical history, 26–7, **30–7**
    TV, 319
Republic of China. *see* Taiwan
Republic of Five Nationalities, 51–2, 63
restaurants. *see* food
Revolution of 1911, 20, 23, 26–7, 29–30, 32, 51,
    57, 60, 159
Revolutionary Alliance *(tongmeng hui)*, 175
revolutionary tradition
    art, 273, 276, 285–6, 288
    cinema, 306–7
    diaspora cultures, 117
    gender, 69, 74, 82–5
    historiography, 4, 46, 54–5, 57–61
    literature, 14, 26, 54, **218–34**, 235–42, 250,
        252
    Marxism, 161–7
    media, 327–8, 333
    music & performing arts, 254, 258, 260–1,
        265
    socialism, 155–66, 168–9
    sociopolitical history, 20, 26–7, 35–7,
        39–40
    sports & physical culture, 341, 356
    see also Communist Revolution (1949);
        Revolution of 1911; social change
Ricci, Matteo, 188
rock music *(yaogun yinyue)*, 264–5, 269
Roman Catholic Christianity, 62, 116, 139,
    173, 175, **188–91**, 193, 208, 216
romanization, 15, 194, 208–10
romanticism
    cinema, 306
    gender, 77–8, 84

literature, 218, 238, 241, 244–5
media, 327, 333–4
sociopolitical history, 31
roots seeking literature (*xungen pai*), 243,
     247–50
Ruan Lingyu, 298, **304–6**
rural areas
art, 283
cinema, 307, 312
ethnicity, 93, 109
historiography, 59
language, 213, 215
literature, 226–30, 242–3, 249
music & performing arts, 253–4, 264, 269
religious traditions, 175–6
socialism, 156, 163, 166–7, 169
sociopolitical history, 21, 33–42
Russia, 51–2, 94, 161, 255, 267
See also Soviet Union
Russian language, 201

Saich, Tony, 57–8
Sanger, Margaret, 73
SARS (Severe Acute Respiratory Syndrome),
     332
scholar-gentry (*wenren*)
art, 285
Confucianism, 140
culture, 16–17
diaspora cultures, 121, 124–5
historiography, 46, 48, 53–4
literature, 219, 235, 237
media portrayal, 327
physical culture, 327
sociopolitical history, 20–5, 27, 29, 33, 36–7
science & technology
cinema, 299–301, 307, 330
Confucianism, 135, 142–5, 148–50, 152
diaspora cultures, 117, 120–1, 125, 129
ethnicity &, 103
historiography, 55, 58–9
literature &, 219
media, 322, 328, 330, 333, 335, 353
modernity, 5
religious traditions, 188
socialism, 161, 167, 169
sociopolitical history, 30
secret societies, 27
self-criticism, 37–8, 41, 74
self-strengthening movement (1860s), 60,
     135–6
Severe Acute Respiratory Syndrome (SARS),
     332
sexual relations, 11, 16, 73, 76–7, 80–2, 86
cinema, 304–5
ethnicity, 100

literature, 239, 244, 250–1
media, 333, 335
music & performing arts, 266–7
Shaanxi, 174, 199, 258, 286
see also Yan'an
Shandong, 31, 61–2, 173, 180, 192, 199
Shanghai
art, 275, 279–80, 287, 293
art & architecture, 281–2
cinema, 299–300, 302–3, 305, 310
diaspora culture &, 118
ethnicity, 96
foreign concessions, 9, 23
gender, 68–9
historiography, 60, 65
housing developments, 8–9
Internet, 333
Labour University, 162
languages, 199, 214
literature, 225, 237–9, 244–5, 250
music & performing arts, 255–6, 265
religious traditions, 180, 192
socialism, 156, 162–3
sociopolitical history, 28, 31–3, 352
TV, 319, 321, 329
see also International Settlement, Shanghai
Shanghai Incident (1932), 226
Shanxi, 96, 199
Shaoxing Opera (*yueju*), 268
Shen Congwen, **242–3**, 246, 249
Shengyan, 187
Shenzhen, 78, 355
Sherpa people, 99
Shi Chongming, 287
Shi Lu, 285–6
Shi Zhecun (Shi Zhicun), **243–4**, 246
Shifu. *see* Liu Sifu
Shifu'ism, 158
Shih, Chi-Yu, 98
Shu Qingchun. *see* Lao She
Shu Ting, 246
Shun (sage-king), 47, 138
Sichuan, 101, 199, 201, 214, 263, 267, 290, 302
silk route, 7
Sima Qian, 47
Singapore, 63, 117, 119, 125, 127, 130, 132, 152,
     200, 208
single-child policy. *see* one-child policy
Sino-Tibetan languages, 95, 201
Sinocentrism, 6–7, 123
sinology, 142, 340–1
Sixth Generation, 13, 315
social change, 4, **20–45**
art, 273
literature, 219–20, 222, 236, 239, 247, 250
media, 318

music & performing arts, 253, 256
sociopolitical history, 27
Social Darwinism, 5, 26, 30, 47, 51, 341–2, 354
social realism. *see* realism
social revolution. *see* social change
socialism
    art, 283, 285, 287–8
    cinema, 299, 305–8, 312
    Confucianism &, 146
    diaspora cultures, 123, 127
    gender, 71, **73–7**, 83–5
    historiography, 56–8, 62
    language, 212
    literature, 222, 228, **229–32**, 236, 248
    Marxism in Chinese revolution, **161–7**
    music & performing arts, 258–9, 263
    origins in China, **157–61**
    sociopolitical history, 6, 11, 27, 32, 40,
        155–72
    sports, 347–8
    state, **167–9**
Socialist Party. *see* Chinese Socialist Party
socialist realism. *see* realism
socialist revolution. *see* Communist
    Revolution (1949); revolutionary
    tradition
Society for the Study of Socialism, 158
sociopolitical structures
    art, 273
    Confucianism, 144
    early twentieth century, **24–30**
    gender, 69
    Maoist China, **37–44**
    post-Maoist China, **37–44**
    Qing (Manchu) dynasty (1644–1911), **21–4**
Sohu Blog, 334
soldiers. *see* military
Song dynasty (960–1276), 120, 141–2, 180, 183,
    203, 254–5, 293, 341
Soto sect, 186
South America. *see* Latin America
Southeast Asia, 115–16, 120, 122–5, 130–1, 178,
    183, 186
southeast China, 104, 199
southern China
    art, 274
    cinema, 316
    dialects, 198, 203, 205, 210
    diaspora cultures, 118, 121
    ethnicity, 99–100
    music & performing arts, 264
    socialism, 158, 163
Southern Min dialect, 194
southwest China, 98
Soviet Union
    art, 13, 284

cinema, 306–7
diaspora culture &, 126, 129
ethnicity, 94
historiography, 56–7
literature, 225, 230
music & performing arts, 13, 253, 300
socialism, 156, 161–8
sociopolitical history, 32, 35, 39
sports, 348, 354
Spanish, 9, 116, 190
Spencer, Herbert, 342
spirituality, 7, 13, 143, 145–6, 148–50, 219, 280,
    340, 355
sports, 18, **339–60**
    Cold War, **347–50**
    media, 326, 350–1, 353–5
    Orientalism, **340–3**
    see also martial arts
Sports Law (1955), 356
Spring Willow (Chunliu) Society, 255
Standard Chinese. *see* Modern Standard
    Chinese
Standard Modern Written Chinese, 216
state
    art, 283, 287, 295
    Chinese culture, 8
    Chinese language, 201, 207–10, 212–14
    cinema, 297–9, 301–3, 306–10, 312–15
    Confucianism, 135–40, 151
    diaspora cultures, 127
    ethnicity &, 91–7, **98–101**, 102, 104–8, 111–12
    gender &, 75, 84, 87
    historiography, 46, 49, 51, 56, 58, 60, 64
    literature, 229, 231, 237, 248, 250–2
    media, 318–21, 323–5, 331, 335–6
    music & performing arts, 265, 269
    religious traditions, 174–5, 177–9, 181,
        184–5, 188–91, 193–5
    socialism, 156–8, 161, **167–9**, 170
    sociopolitical history, **20–45**
    sports & physical culture, 340, 347, 355–6
    see also governance
Strong Power Forum (*Qiangguo luntan*), 331
students
    art, 284
    Confucianism, 136
    diaspora cultures, 124
    ethnicity, 105
    foreign, 1, 265
    historiography, 58–9
    literature, 240
    media, 331
    socialism, 157–8, 163
    sociopolitical history, 27–8, 30–2, 35–6,
        43, 68
    sports & physical culture, 357

Su Tong, 247
Su Xiaokang, 59, 231
subaltern culture, 16, 20
Sukarno, President, 351
Sun Chuanfang, 279
Sun Society (*Taiyang she*), 225
Sun Yat-sen
    art, 276–7
    ethnicity, 94
    historiography, 47, 51, 53
    socialism, 158, 162–3, 165
    sociopolitical history, 22, 27, 31–3
Sun Yusheng, 325
Sun Zhigang, 332
superstition, 50, 175–6, 301, 303, 307
surrealism, 248, 281

table tennis, 350–2
Tahiti, 115
Tai Chi, 290
Tainan, 194
Taipei. *see* Taiwan
Taiping Rebellion, 22, 54, 57, 174, 181, 183,
    189, 192
Taiwan
    art, 275, 283, 288–90, 293
    Buddhism, 186–7
    Chineseness, 8–9, 11
    cinema, 297–300, 306, 308–9, **311–14**, 315
    Confucianism, 150, 152
    Daoism, 181–3
    diaspora cultures &, 124, 128–30, 132
    Ererba, 2/28 (28 February 1947 incident),
        194, 313
    ethnicity, 97, 100, 104, 108, 118, 176, 190, 194
    gender, 86
    historiography, 51, 63–5
    Internet, 331, 333
    Japanese occupation (1895–1945), 176, 308
    languages, 199–201, 208–9, 215, 298, 300,
        308
    literature, 245
    martial law, 176, 194–5, 293, 313
    modernity, 7
    Protestant Christianity, **194–5**
    religious traditions, 173, 176, 178–9, 188
    Roman Catholic Christianity, **190–1**
    socialism, 156
    sociopolitical history, 24, 43
    sports, 347–53
    White Terror, 313
Taiwan Straits tension, 332
Taixu, 186
Taiyang she. see Sun Society
Taizhou school, 144
Tajik language, 201

Talimankan Desert, 102
Tan, Amy, 132
Tan Cheng Lock, 131
Tan Dun, 129–30, 266
Tan Shen, 80
Tan Sitong, 18
Tan, Sor-Hoon, chapter by, 11, **135–54**
Tang dynasty (618–907), 2, 52, 183, 188, 203,
    341
Tang Junyi, 12, 141–3
Tang Lian, 246
Tantric tradition, 185
Taoism. *see* Daoism
technology. *see* science & technology
television
    culture &, 16
    drama & entertainment, 60, **326–30**
    history & structures, 7, 58–9, 264–6, 313,
        319–23, 335–6
    language, 213
    news programmes, 323–6
    ratings, 322, 326–9
    sports, 326, 350–1, 353–5
temples, 43, 55, 60, 173–8, 180–7, 189, 192
Teo, Stephen, 310
terrorism, 94
Thailand, 119, 123, 125, 130–1, 188
Thatcher, Margaret, 310
theatre. *see* music & performing arts
Third Force, 166
Three People's Principles, 32, 34, 163, 165
Three Selfs policy, 193
Tian Han, 227, 257
Tian Zhuangzhuang, 312
Tiananmen Square, 287–8
Tiananmen Square demonstrations (1989)
    art, 275, 291
    cinema, 312–13
    ethnicity, 93, 312–13, 315
    Internet, 332
    music & performing arts, 265
    socialism, 156, 169
    sociopolitical history, 42–3, 58–9
Tianjin, 28, 319, 347
Tianyu Community, 332
Tibet
    cinema, 308
    ethnicity, 97, 100–1
    historiography, 52, 64
    Internet, 332
    languages, 201, 214
    literature, 248
    religious traditions, 185
    sociopolitical history, 21
    TV, 320
Tibetan Buddhism, 185, 187

Tibetan-Burman languages, 98, 201, 214
Tibetan language, 95, 201
Tibetans, 26, 51, 94, 97, 101, 107–8, 111, 174,
   185, 308
To, Johnnie, 311
Tocqueville, Alexis de, 93
Tolstoy, Leo, 158
tongmeng hui. see Revolutionary Alliance
trade
   art, 274–5
   diaspora cultures, 116, 118, 120–1, 124
   ethnicity, 102–3
   media, 328
   religious traditions, 173, 178, 189, 191, 196
   sociopolitical history, 4, 7, 20, 27, 41–2
transnationalization. *see* globalization
travel, 2, 78, 191, 274, 280, 282, 284–5
   see also diaspora cultures; migration,
      internal
treaty ports. *see* concessions, foreign
Trudeau, Pierre, 352
True Jesus Church, 192
Tsai Ming-liang, 315
Tu Wei-ming, 12, 63, 129, 141, 150–3
Tujia language, 214–15
Tujia people, 98–9, 215
Tung, Shou-yi. *see* Dong Shouyi
Turkic-Altaic languages, 95
Turkic languages, 201
Turkic peoples, 103–4, 111

underground literature (PRC), 245–7
united front
   first, 32
   second (anti-Japanese war), 35, 56, 165
United Nations, 80, 210, 351
United States
   architecture, 8–9, 282
   art, 289–90, 292, 348
   Chineseness, 12
   cinema, 307
   Confucianism, 136, 141, 148, 150, 152
   ethnicity, 92, 100
   gender, 80
   historiography, 55, 63
   Internet, 330–3, 336
   literature, 53, 225, 240, 245
   music & performing arts, 256, 259, 266,
      300
   religious traditions, 179, 191, 195
   socialism, 156, 158, 162, 167, 170
   sports, 340, 345, 348–9, 351–2
   TV, 322–3, 327, 329
   see also Hollywood cinema; North America
urban areas
   art, 275, 282, 292–3

cinema, 299–300, 306, 316
diaspora cultures, 117, 125
ethnicity, 92–3, 97, 101–7, **109–12**
gender, 69, 77–9, 84–6
historiography, 58–9
language, 213
literature, 225–8, 238–9, 243–5
media, 7, 318, 328, 330, **332–5**
music & performing arts, 253–4, 264, 269
religious traditions, 175
socialism, 156, 163, 166–7, 169
sociopolitical history, 21, 23, 28–9, 31,
   33–41
utopian socialism, 155–6, 168–9
   see also anarchism
Uyghur language, 95, 201
Uyghurs, 26, 94, 97, **102–3**, 102–6, 105, 107,
   111, 174, 308

Va language, 201
Van Gogh, Vincent, 293–4
Van Lau. *see* Wen Lou
Vatican, 189–91
vernacular language *(baihuawen)*, 30–1, 53–4,
   203, 205–7, 211–12, 216, 218–19, 237–41,
   251
Vietnam, 119, 156
Vietnamese language, 95
visual arts. *see* art
Volleyball World Cup, 353–4

Wade-Giles system, 209–10
Wan Jiabao. *see* Cao Yu
Wan-Li-Ma-Wang (rock band), 264
Wang Bin, 307
Wang, C. T. (Wang Zhengting), 339
Wang, David Der-wei, 236
Wang Gen, 144
Wang Guangyi, 291–2
Wang Gungwu, chapter by, 9, **115–34**
Wang Guowei, 254
Wang Wuxie (Wucius Wong), 289–90, 293
Wang Xiaobo, 82
Wang Xiaonong, 255
Wang Xiaoshuai, 315
Wang Yangming, 144, 151
Wang Zhe, 180
Wang Zhengting (C. T. Wang), 339
warlords, 6, 28–33, 35, 41, 185, 279, 301
Way of Pervading Unity *(Yiguan dao)*, 176
Wei Hui, 250–1, 333
Wei Minglun, 263, 267–8
Wen, King, 138
Wen Lou (Van Lau), 290
Wen Yiduo, 240
wenhua. see culture

wenren. see scholar-gentry *(wenren)*
Wenxue yanjiu hui. see Literary Association
wenyanwen. *see* classical Chinese language
Western culture
    art, 272–3, 275–7, 279–85, 290, 292–3
    cinema, 299, 303
    Confucianism &, 135–7, 140–6, 149–52
    diaspora culture &, 116–17, 122, 124, 126,
       128, 130–1
    ethnicity, 103, 108, 110, 112
    gender, 69, 72–3, 79, 81, 83, 85–7
    historiography, 59–60
    interaction with, 3, 5–6, 9, 13, 15, 18
    Internet, 333, 336
    languages, 208, 211, 216
    literature, 219, 230, 238–40, 243, 246
    music & performing arts, 253, 255–8,
       260–6, 268
    physical culture, 340–2, **343–5**, 346–8
    religious traditions, 175, 192
    socialism, 170
    sociopolitical history, 22, 28, 30
    sports, 349–51, 355–6, 358
    thinking on China, 2
    TV & Internet, 318
Western imperialism. *see* foreign powers
Westernization, 6, 22, 143, 146, 148–9, 152,
    239–40, 356, 358
White Cloud Temple (Baiyunguan), Beijing,
    180
women
    cinema, 304–5, 307
    ethnicity, 95
    historiography, 55, 60
    literature, 235, 245
    media, 327, 329
    music & performing arts, 259, 261, 265–8
    religious traditions, 191
    socialism, 157, 159
    sociopolitical history, 28–30, 42–3
    sports & physical culture, 341–3, 347, 353–5
    see also gender
women's movement, 29, 70–7, 80–3, 85, 159,
    239, 266–7
Wong, Wucius. *see* Wang Wuxie
Wong Kar-wai, 311
Woo, John, 297, 310–11
work camps, 38
work ethic, 17, 120, 151, 308
work units *(danwei)*, 38–9
workers
    diaspora cultures, 124
    gender, 76, 83
    proletarian literature, 221–2, 224, **225–6**,
       227–30
    proletarian performing arts, 258

socialism, 163, 165
    sociopolitical history, 27–34, 37–43
World Trade Organization, 269
World Wars, 15, 31, 123, 126–7, 143, 167, 176,
    289, 305, 350
    see also Japanese occupation (1937–45)
World Wide Web. *see* Internet
writing systems
    non-Chinese languages, 201, 210, 214
    see also Chinese script
Wu Changshuo, 282
Wu dialect, 198, 213–14
Wu Jianren (Wu Woyao), 237–8
Wu Mi, 240
Wu Woyao. *see* Wu Jianren
Wu Zetian (emperor), 267
Wu Ziniu, 312
Wu Zuxiang, 227
Wuhan, 28, 227
wushu. see martial arts

Xi Chuan, 247
Xia Yan, 226
Xia Zengyou, 219
Xiamen dialect, 209
Xiang dialect, 198
Xiang Ding, 79
Xiao Chu'nü, 73
Xiao Zhiwei, 302
Xibe language, 201
xin wenhua yundong. see New Culture
    Movement
xin wenxue. see New Literature
Xingyun, 186
Xinjiang, 64, 96–7, 101, **102–6**, 107, 111, 174,
    201, 214, 320
    See also Central Asia
Xinlang Blog, 334
Xinwen lianbo. see Network News
xinxin renlei. see Newer New Humanity
Xiong Shili, 11, 141
Xu Beihong, 276–7, 279–80, 283
Xu Bing, 291–3
Xu Fuguan, 12, 141–2
Xu Zhenya, 239
Xu Zhimo, 241
Xueheng. see Critical Review
Xunzi, 12, 151

Yamazaki Ansai, 151
Yan Fu, 5, 219
Yan Haiping, 262
Yan'an, 35, 74–6
Yan'an period, 57, 166, 222, 227–9, 258
Yang Chen Ning, 129
Yang, Edward, 297, 313

Yang Liwei, 328
Yang, Rae, 76, 85
Yangtze River, 7, 33, 35, 198
Yao (sage-king), 47, 138
Ye Shengtao, 224–5
Yeh, Emilie Yueh-yu, 313
Yellow Emperor, 51, 63
Yellow River, 7, 59, 198
Yellow River Piano Concerto, 260
Yi Feng (art magazine), 281
Yi people, 107
Yi T'oegye, 151
Yi Zhongtian, 82
Yinguang, 186
YMCA, 339–40, 347
youth culture
    cinema, 306
    Cultural Revolution (1960s–70s), 96
    historiography, 61
    language, 214
    literature, 229, 239, 246, 249
    media, 7, 318, 327–31, **332–5**, 336
    music & performing arts, 265, 269
    socialism, 159
    sociopolitical history, 28–9
    see also students
Yu Dan, 13
Yu Guozhen, 192
Yu Hua, 247, 250
Yu Jian, 251
Yu Long, 266
Yu Ying-shih, 129, 141
Yuan dynasty (1276–1368), 120, 203, 254–5
Yuan Shikai, 30, 60, 259
Yuan Weishi, 61
Yuanmingyuan (Old Summer Palace, Beijing), 3, 62
Yue. *see* Cantonese dialect
yueju. see Shaoxing Opera
Yunan, 199
Yunnan, 98, 101, 201

Zao Wou-ki. *see* Zhao Wuji
Zarrow, Peter, chapter by, 4, **20–45**

Zen Ze-kiun Joseph, 190
Zeng Guofan, 60, 135, 141
Zhang Ailing (Eileen Chang), **244–5,** 246
Zhang Binglin, 11, 27, 51, 53
Zhang Dainian, 152
Zhang Daq, 282
Zhang Daqian, 283
Zhang Hongtu, 292–4
Zhang Junmai (Carson Chang), 12, 141–3
Zhang lineage, 181
Zhang Shichuan, 300
Zhang Tianshi, 181
Zhang Yimou, 297, 312, 358
Zhang Yuan, 315
Zhang Zhen, 299, 301
Zhang Zhidong, 136–7, 141
Zhao An, 328
Zhao Shiyu, 60
Zhao Shuli, 227–9
Zhao Wuji (Zao Wou-ki), 283
Zhejiang, 199, 214, 268
Zheng Chenggong (Koxinga), 190
Zheng He, 120
Zhengyan, 187
Zhengyi (Correct and Unified) Order, 181–2
Zhongguo shehui zhuyi dang. see Chinese Socialist Party
Zhongsan suit, 69
Zhongyang renmin guangbo diantai. see Central People's Radio Station
Zhou Bichang, 329
Zhou Enlai, 147, 268, 347
Zhou Shuren. *see* Lu Xun
Zhou Zuoren, **241–2,** 244, 246
Zhu Ming (Ju Ming), 290
Zhu Rongji, 325
Zhu Shilin, 309–10
Zhu Xi, 141, 148, 151
Zhuang people, 98
Zou Rong, 51
Zuo Zongtang, 135